GENESIS
AND EXODUS

GENESIS AND EXODUS

A New English Rendition

TRANSLATED WITH
COMMENTARY AND NOTES BY

EVERETT FOX

SCHOCKEN BOOKS NEW YORK

Library of Congress Cataloging-in-Publication Data

Bible. O.T. Genesis. English. Fox. 1991.
Genesis and Exodus : a new English rendition with commentary and
notes / Everett Fox
p.   cm.
A combined edition of the author's two previous works, In the
beginning and Now these are the names.
Includes bibliographical references.
ISBN 0-8052-0994-8
1. Bible. O.T. Genesis—Commentaries. 2. Bible. O.T. Exodus—
Commentaries. I. Fox, Everett. II. Bible. O.T. Exodus.
English. Fox. 1991. III. Title.
BS1233.F68 1991
222'.11077—dc20   90-52942

To the Memory of Arthur A. Cohen

צלח רכב....

CONTENTS

PREFACE TO THE PAPERBACK EDITION   XIII

ACKNOWLEDGMENTS   XXXI

TO AID THE READER   XXXIII

ON THE NAME OF GOD AND ITS TRANSLATION   XXXV

GUIDE TO THE PRONUNCIATION OF HEBREW

     NAMES   XXXVII

Genesis: In the Beginning

ON THE BOOK OF GENESIS AND ITS STRUCTURE   3

PART   I. The Primeval History (1–11)   9

    God as Creator (1:1–2:4a)   10
    Garden and Expulsion (2:4b–3:24)   16
    The First Brothers (4:1–16)   24
    The Line of Kayin (4:17–26)   26
    From Adam to Noah (5)   28
    Antiquity and the Preparation for the Flood (6:1–8)   31
    The Deluge (6:9–8:19)   32
    Aftermath (8:20–9:19)   40
    Drunkenness and Nakedness (9:20–29)   43
    The Table of the Nations (10)   44
    The Unfinished Citadel (11:1–9)   46
    Noah to Avram (11:10–32)   48

THE PATRIARCHAL NARRATIVES   51

PART   II. Avraham (12–25:18)   53

    The Call and the Journey (12:1–9)   54
    The Wife—I (12:10–20)   55
    Lot; The Land (13)   56
    War and Rescue (14)   58
    The Covenant between the Pieces (15)   62

The Firstborn Son (16)   64
The Covenant of Circumcision (17)   67
Visit and Promise (18:1–15)   70
The Great Intercession (18:16–33)   72
The End of Sedom and Amora (19)   75
The Wife—II (20)   80
Yitzhak Born (21:1–8)   82
Yishmael Banished (21:9–21)   83
Treaty (21:22–34)   85
The Great Test (22)   86
Purchase and Burial (23)   90
The Betrothal Journey (24)   93
Avraham's Descendants and Death (25:1–18)   100

PART   III. Yaakov (25:19–36:43)   103

Rivka's Children (25:19–34)   104
In the Land (26:1–6)   106
The Wife—III (26:7–11)   108
Blessing (26:12–33)   108
Deceit and Blessing (26:34–28:9)   111
Yaakov Sets Out (28:10–22)   118
Arrival in Aram (29:1–14)   120
Deception Repaid (29:15–30)   122
Love, Jealousy, and Children (29:31–30:24)   124
Yaakov in Exile: Stealth and Prosperity
   (30:25– 32:1))   128
Preparations for Esav (32:2–24)   136
The Mysterious Stranger: Struggle at the Yabbok
   (32:25–33)   139
Resolution (33:1–17)   140
Home: Peace and Violence (33:18–34:31)   143
Home: Blessing and Death (35)   147
Re'uven (35:21–22)   150
Esav's Descendants (36)   151

PART   IV. Yosef (37–50)   155

Young Yosef: Love and Hate (37)   156
Yehuda and Tamar (38)   162

Yosef: Rise and Fall (39)   166
The Rise to Power: Dreams (40:1–41:52)   170
Famine: The Brothers Come (41:53–42:38)   178
The Test (43–44)   184
Reconciliation (45)   192
Migration to Egypt (45:16–47:12)   194
Yosef the Life-Giver (47:13–26)   200
Yosef's Sons Blessed (48)   203
Yaakov's Testament and Death (49)   206
Yaakov's Burial (50:1–14)   210
The End of the Matter (50:15–26)   212

SUGGESTIONS FOR FURTHER READING   216

Exodus: Now These Are the Names

ON THE BOOK OF EXODUS AND ITS STRUCTURE   223

PART   I. The Deliverance Narrative (1–15:21)   233

The Early Life of Moshe and Religious Biography   234
On the Journey Motif   236
Moshe Before Pharaoh: The Plague Narrative
    (5–11)   238
    Prologue in Egypt (1)   241
    Moshe's Birth and Early Life (2:1–22)   245
    God Takes Notice (2:23–25)   251
    At the Bush: The Call (3:1–4:17)   252
    The Journey Back (4:18–31)   261
    Before Pharaoh (5:1–6:1)   265
    The Promise Renewed (6:2–13)   269
    The Genealogy of Moshe and Aharon (6:14–27)   271
    The Mission Renewed (6:28–7:13)   273
    First Blow (7:14–25)   275
    Second Blow (7:26–8:11)   277
    Third Blow (8:12–15)   279
    Fourth Blow (8:16–28)   279

Fifth Blow (9:1–7)   281
Sixth Blow (9:8–12)   283
Seventh Blow (9:13–35)   283
Eighth Blow (10:1–20)   287
Ninth Blow (10:21–29)   289
The Final Warning (11:1–10)   291
The Tenth Blow in Its Context   293
The Passover Ritual (12:1–28)   295
Tenth Blow and Exodus (12:29–42)   297
Who May Make Passover (12:43–50)   301
Passover and the Firstborn (12:51–13:16)   301
The Route and the Escort (13:17–22)   304
At the Sea of Reeds (14)   305
The Song of God as Triumphant King (15:1–21)   311

PART   II. In the Wilderness (15:22–18:27)   317

Grumbling I (15:22–27)   319
Grumbling II (16)   321
Grumbling III (17:1–7)   325
War with Amalek (17:8–16)   327
The New Society: Yitro's Visit (18)   329

PART   III. The Meeting and Covenant at Sinai
        (19–24)   333

On Covenant   334
On Biblical Law   335
The Meeting and the Covenant (19)   339
The Ten Words (The Decalogue) (20:1–14)   343
Aftermath (20:15–23)   345
On the Laws   347
Laws Regarding Israelite Serfdom (21:1–11)   347
Capital Crimes of Violence (21:12–17)   349
Injuries (21:18–32)   351
Property (21:33–22:14)   353
Laws Concerning Social Relations and Religious
    Matters (22:15–23:19)   355
Epilogue: The Future Conquest (23:20–33)   361

Sealing the Covenant (24:1–11)   363
Moshe Ascends Alone (24:12–18)   365

PART   IV. The Instructions for the Dwelling and
               the Cult (25–31)   367

The "Contribution" (25:1–9)   371
The Coffer (25:10–16)   372
The Purgation-Cover (25:17–22)   373
The Table (25:23–30)   375
The Lampstand (25:31–40)   377
The Dwelling Proper (26:1–14)   377
The Framework (26:15–30)   379
The Curtain and the Screen (26:31–37)   381
The Altar (27:1–8)   381
The Courtyard (27:9–19)   383
The Oil (27:20–21)   385
The Priestly Garments (28:1–5)   385
The *Efod* (28:6–12, 13–14)   385
The Breastpiece (28:15–30)   387
The Tunic (28:31–35)   389
The Head-Plate (28:36–38)   391
Other Priestly Garments (28:39–43)   391
The Investiture Ceremony (29:1–45)   391
The Incense Altar (30:1–10)   399
Census and Ransom (30:11–16)   399
The Basin (30:17–21)   401
The Anointing Oil (30:22–33)   401
The Incense (30:34–38)   403
Craftsmen (31:1–11)   403
The Sabbath (31:12–17); The Tablets (31:18)   405

PART   V. The Covenant Broken and Restored
               (32–34)   407

The Sin of the Molten Calf (32:1–6)   409
Response: God's Anger (32:7–14)   411
Response: Moshe's Anger (32:15–29)   413
After the Purge (32:30–33:6)   415
Moshe at the Tent (33:7–11)   417

Moshe's Plea and God's Answer (33:12–34:3)   419
God Reveals Himself (34:4–9)   421
The New Covenant (34:10–28)   423
Moshe Radiant (34:29–35)   425

PART   VI. The Building of the Dwelling (35–40)   427

The Sabbath Restated (35:1–3)   429
The Contribution Restated (35:4–19)   429
Preparations for the Construction (35:20–36:7)   429
Dwelling II (36:8–19)   433
Boards II (36:20–34)   435
Curtain and Screen II (36:35–38)   435
Coffer and Purgation-Cover II (37:1–9)   435
Table II (37:10–16)   437
Lampstand II (37:17–24)   437
Incense Altar II (37:25–28)   437
Anointing Oil and Incense II (37:29)   439
Altar II (38:1–7)   439
Basin and Pedestal II (38:8)   439
Courtyard II (38:9–20)   439
Accountings (38:21–31)   441
Garments II (39:1)   443
Efod and Breastpiece II (39:2–21)   443
Tunic II (39:22–26)   445
Other Priestly Garments II (39:27–29)   445
Head-Plate II (39:30–31)   445
The Completion of the Parts; Bringing Them to
    Moshe (39:32–43)   445
Final Instructions: Setting Up (40:1–16)   447
The Implementation (40:17–33)   449
The End: God's Glory (40:34–38)   450

APPENDIX: SCHEMATIC FLOOR PLAN OF THE

DWELLING   451

SUGGESTIONS FOR FURTHER READING   452

WEEKLY PORTIONS IN JEWISH TRADITION   458

PREFACE TO THE PAPERBACK EDITION

> . . . read the Bible as though it were something entirely unfamiliar, as though it had not been set before you ready-made. . . . Face the book with a new attitude as something new. . . . Let whatever may happen occur between yourself and it. You do not know which of its sayings and images will overwhelm and mold you. . . . But hold yourself open. Do not believe anything a priori; do not disbelieve anything a priori. Read aloud the words written in the book in front of you; hear the word you utter and let it reach you.
>
> *—adapted from a lecture of Martin Buber, 1926*

1

THIS BOOK originally appeared as two volumes, *In the Beginning* (1983) and *Now These Are the Names* (1986). It is here offered to the reader with revised Preface but substantially the same text and accompanying material. The final form of the project will be the Five Books of Moses, which will contain a revised version of Genesis and Exodus, as well as the three books that follow.

The present translation is guided by the principle that the Hebrew Bible, like much of the literature of antiquity, was meant to be read aloud, and that consequently, it must be translated with careful attention to rhythm and sound. This work, which therefore differs markedly from conventional translations, tries to reflect the particular rhetoric of the Hebrew wherever possible, preserving such devices as repetition, allusion, alliteration, and wordplay. It is intended to echo the Hebrew, and to lead the reader back to the sound structure and form of the original.

Such an approach was first espoused by Martin Buber and Franz Rosenzweig in their monumental German translation of the Bible (1925–

1962) and in subsequent interpretive essays. *Genesis and Exodus* is in many respects an offshoot of the Buber-Rosenzweig translation (hereafter abbreviated as B-R), and traces its basic principles, its general layout of the text, and many specific readings of the text to its influence. At the same time I have made numerous departures from B-R for reasons that will be explained later in this Preface.

Buber and Rosenzweig based their approach on the Romantic nineteenth-century notion that the Bible was essentially oral literature written down. In the present century there have been Bible scholars who have found this view attractive; on the other hand, there has been little agreement on how oral roots manifest themselves in the text. One cannot suggest that the Bible is a classic work of oral literature in the same sense as the *Iliad* or *Beowulf.* It does not employ regular meter or rhyme, even in sections that are clearly formal poetry. The text of the Bible that we possess is most likely a mixture of oral and written materials from a variety of periods and sources, and recovering anything resembling original oral forms would seem to be impossible. This is particularly true given the considerable chronological and cultural distance at which we stand from the text, which does not permit us to know how it was performed in ancient times.

A more fruitful approach, less dependent upon theories whose historical accuracy is unprovable, might be to focus on the way in which the biblical text, *once completed,* was copied and read. Recent research reveals that virtually all literature in Greek and Roman times—the period when the Hebrew Bible was put into more or less the form in which it has come down to us (but not the period of its composition)—was read aloud. This holds for the process of copying or writing, and also, surprisingly, for solitary reading. As late as the last decade of the fourth century, Saint Augustine expressed surprise at finding a sage who read silently. Such practices and attitudes seem strange to us, for whom the very definition of a library, for instance, is a place where people have to keep quiet. But it was a routine in the world of antiquity, as many sources attest.

So the Bible would have been read aloud as a matter of course. But the implications of this for understanding the text are considerable. The rhetoric of the text is such that many passages and sections are understandable in depth only when they are analyzed *as they are heard.* Using echoes, allusions, and powerful inner structures of sound, the text is often able to convey ideas in a manner that vocabulary alone cannot do.

A few illustrations may suffice to introduce this phenomenon to the reader; it will be encountered constantly throughout this volume.

Sound plays a crucial role in one of the climactic sequences in Genesis, Chapters 32–33. Jacob, the protagonist, has not seen his brother Esau for twenty years. Now a rich and successful adult, he is on his way back to Canaan after a long exile. He sends messengers to forestall Esau's vengeance—for twenty years earlier, Jacob had stolen the birthright and the blessing which Esau felt were rightly his own. When Jacob finds out that his brother "is already coming . . . and four hundred men are with him" (32:7), he goes even further, preparing an elaborate gift for Esau in the hopes of appeasing his anger. The text in vv.21–22 presents Jacob's thoughts and actions (the translation is taken from the New English Bible):

> for he thought, "I will appease him with the present that I have sent on ahead, and afterwards, when I come into his presence, he will perhaps reccive me kindly." So Jacob's present went on ahead of him. . . .

This is an accurate and highly idiomatic translation of the Hebrew, and the reader will notice nothing unusual about the passage as it reads in English. The sound of the Hebrew text, on the other hand, gives one pause. It is built on variations of the word *panim*, whose basic meaning is "face," although the Hebrew uses it idiomatically to cncompass various ideas. (Note: in Hebrew, the sound *p* is pronounced as *ph* under certain circumstances.) If the text is translated with attention to sound, its oral character, and something quite striking, emerge (italics mine):

> For he said to himself:
> I will wipe (the anger from) his *face (phanav)*
> with the gift that goes ahead of my *face; (le-phanai)*
> afterward, when I see his *face, (phanav)*
> perhaps he will lift up my *face! (phanai)*
> The gift crossed over ahead of his *face*. . . . *(al panav)*

Comparison of these two English versions is instructive. In the New English Bible, as in most other contemporary versions, the translators are apparently concerned with presenting the text in clear, modern, idiomatic English. For example, they render the Hebrew *yissa phanai* as "receive me kindly." The N.E.B. translates the *idea* of the text; at the same time it translates *out* the sound by not picking up on the repetition of *panim* words.

What does the reader gain by hearing the literalness of the Hebrew?

And what is lost by the use of its idiomatic meaning? As mirrored in the second translation, it is clear that our text is signaling something of significance. The motif of "face" (which might be interpreted as "facing" or "confrontation") occurs at crucial points in the story. The night before his fateful meeting with Esau, as he is left to ponder the next day's events, Jacob wrestles with a mysterious stranger—a divine being. After Jacob's victory, the text reports (32:31):

> Yaakov called the name of the place: Peniel/*Face of God,*
> for: I have seen God,
> *face to face,*
> and my life has been saved.

The repetition suggests a thematic link with what has gone before. One could interpret that once the hero has met and actually bested this divine being, his coming human confrontation is assured of success. Thus upon meeting Esau at last, Jacob says to him (33:10):

> For I have, after all, seen your *face,* as one sees the *face* of
> God,
> and you have been gracious to me.

It could be said that in a psychological sense the meetings with divine and human adversaries are a unity, the representation of one human process in two narrative episodes. This is accomplished by the repetition of the word *panim* in the text.

The above interpretation depends entirely on sound. Once that focus is dropped, either through the silent reading of the text or a standard translation, the inner connections are simply lost and the reader is robbed of the opportunity to make these connections for himself. Clearly there is a difference between translating what the text means and translating what it says.

While the Jacob passages use the sound of a specific word to indicate an important motif in the narrative, there are other cases where sound brings out structure, and the structure itself conveys the principal idea of the passage. A striking example of this is found at the beginning of Genesis. God's first acts of creation in 1:3–5 are portrayed in a highly ordered fashion, suggesting that creation itself is orderly, and this idea is the thematic backbone of the whole chapter. We are meant to experience the orderliness of God's activity through the sensuality of the

language and through the particular way in which the text speaks. A
translation keyed to the sound of the Hebrew reads:

> God said: Let there be light! And there was light.
> God saw the light: that it was good.
> God separated the light from the darkness.
> God called the light: Day! and the darkness he called: Night!

The four occurrences of "God" plus verb accomplish the narrator's
goal, and give a tone to the creation account that makes it akin to poetry.
In contrast, virtually all modern translations treat the passage as prose,
rendering it into clear written English but simultaneously removing its
inner structure. What remains is a statement of what is taking place in
the narrative, but without its underlying thrust. Again the New English
Bible:

> God said, "Let there be light," and there was
> light; and God saw that the light was good, and
> he separated light from darkness. He called the
> light day, and the darkness night.

This translation is cast in good English style. For just that reason two
occurrences of "God" have been omitted, and the passage consequently
reads smoothly—so smoothly that one glides past it as if creation were
the same as any other narrated action. But what has been lost is the
characteristic oral ring of the text, and simultaneously its intent to say
something beyond the content of words alone.

Another example of translating with an ear to the sound and structure
of the original, this time from the book of Exodus, comes from the
dramatic story of the Sea of Reeds (14:11–12). The newly freed Israelites
find themselves pursued by their former masters, the Pharaoh and his
army; with their backs to the Sea, they panic, and bitterly harangue their
would-be deliverer, Moses. The present translation, attempting to reflect the repetition and structure of the original, yields the following:

> they said to Moshe:
> Is it because there are no graves in Egypt
> that you have taken us out to die in the wilderness?
> What is this that you have done to us, bringing us out of
>   Egypt?
> Is this not the very word that we spoke to you in Egypt,
> saying: Let us alone, that we may serve Egypt!
> Indeed, better for us serving Egypt
> than our dying in the wilderness!

This passage demonstrates several aspects of a rhetorical translation method, if we may so term it: the laying out of the text in "cola" or lines meant to facilitate reading aloud (more on this below); the repetition of words—"Egypt" five times and "wilderness" twice—to stress the irony of the Israelites' predicament (as they see it, Egypt means life, and the wilderness, certain death); and the double use of "serve", the very word that Moses constantly drummed into Pharaoh's ears in the early part of the book to denote the Israelites' desire to go and worship their God ("Send free my people, that they may serve me"). If we juxtapose the above translation with that found in, say, the New International Version, the importance of this approach to the text becomes clear:

> They said to Moses, "Was it because there were no graves in Egypt that you brought us to the desert to die? What have you done to us by bringing us out of Egypt? Didn't we say to you in Egypt, 'Leave us alone; let us serve the Egyptians'? It would have been better for us to serve the Egyptians than to die in the desert!"

Here the rhetorical force of the Hebrew has been ignored. The Hebrew text does not transpose "desert to die" to "die in the desert" at the end of the passage (the word order repeats in the original, for emphasis); it does not distinguish in sound between "Egypt" and "Egyptians"; and it certainly does not read like standard colloquial prose. Indeed, all of Chapter 14 of Exodus demonstrates the Bible's use of an intermediate form between poetry and prose, a form designed to instruct as well as to inspire.

But it is not only in narrative that the rhetoric of biblical language makes itself felt. Fully half of the book of Exodus is law or instruction, and one can find there further examples of the importance of sound structure in the Bible. Take, for instance, the law concerning the protection of widows and orphans (22:23–24). This time I shall present the text first through the eyes of the Jerusalem Bible:

> You must not be harsh with the widow, or with the orphan; if you are harsh with them, they will surely cry out to me, and be sure that I shall hear their cry; my anger will flare and I shall kill you with the sword, your own wives will be widows, your own children orphans.

This is powerful language, especially in a law code. But the Hebrew text goes much farther, utilizing as it does a double form of the verb rarely found in multiple sequence:

> Any widow or orphan you are not to afflict.
> Oh, if you afflict, afflict them . . . !
> For (then) they will cry, cry out to me,
> and I will hearken, hearken to their cry,
> my anger will rage
> and I will kill you with the sword,
> so that your wives become widows, and your children,
>   orphans!

Here the text is in effect slowed down by the division into lines, and the verb forms are isolated to underscore their unique rhetoric. The effect of the whole is to focus attention on this particular law among a host of others.

2

ONCE THE SPOKENNESS of the Bible is understood as a critical factor in the translation process, a number of practical steps become necessary which constitute radical changes from past translation practices. Buber and Rosenzweig introduced three such major innovations into their work: the form in which the text is laid out, the reproduction of biblical names and their meanings, and the "leading-word" technique by means of which important repetitions in the Hebrew are retained in translation.

First, as is obvious from the excerpts quoted above, the text is printed in lines resembling blank verse. These cola are based on spoken phrasing, with each unit representing a unit of breathing. Each similarly represents a unit of meaning and therefore illustrates the deep connection between form and content in the Bible. Division of the text into cola facilitates its being read aloud and makes it possible for the listener to feel its inner rhythm. Only at that point can the text begin to deliver its message with full force.

Cola do not correspond to the traditional verse divisions found in printed Bibles. Those divisions are of late origin (perhaps from the ninth century, in written form), and were adopted for the sake of reference. Jews and Christians have used them in roughly the same form since the middle ages. Cola, on the other hand, arise from the experience of reading the Hebrew text aloud and of feeling its spoken rhythms. The specific divisions are somewhat arbitrary in that each reader will hear the text differently. What is important, however, is that this practice, in general, points away from the apprehension of the Bible as a written book and restores the sense of it as spoken performance.

Second, personal and place names generally appear in Hebrew forms throughout this translation. Thus, for example, the Hebrew *Moshe* is retained instead of Moses, *Kayin* instead of Cain, and *Rivka* instead of Rebecca. This practice stems from the central role that names play in biblical stories (as often in literature). In biblical Israel as throughout the ancient world, names are often meant to give clues about their bearer's personality or fate. The meaning of a name is often explained outright in the text itself. In *Genesis and Exodus,* this is represented by a slash in the text, as in the following example (Gen. 30:23–24):

> She said:
> God has removed/*asaf*
> my reproach.
> And she called his name: Yosef,
> saying:
> May YHWH add/*yosef*
> another son to me.

The name here is a play on words, hinting at Joseph's eventual fate (he will be a son "removed" and "added," that is, lost and found by his family). By retaining the Hebrew sounds in translation, a meaningful portion of the narrative is thus moved from footnotes, where it appears in most modern translations, back to the body of the text. That this is important is demonstrated by the fact that virtually every major (usually male) character in Genesis has his name explained in this manner.

It should be noted that such interpretations of names in the Bible are not based on philological derivations, that is, on scientific etymology. The name Jacob/Yaakov, for instance, which is understood in Gen. 25 as "Heel-Holder" and in Chapter 27 as "Heel-Sneak," probably held the original meaning of "may (God) protect." But the biblical writers were not so much concerned with what a name originally meant as they were with its sound, and with the associations inherent in that sound. Therefore what is important in our example is that "Yaakov" recalls *'ekev,* "heel." This kind of interpretation is known as "folk etymology" or "popular etymology." A similar phenomenon appears in the naming of Moses (Ex. 2:10).

A third important technique with which biblical literature often conveys its message, and which must influence the translation of the text, is what Buber called the "leading-word" *(Leitwort)* principle. Key ("leading") words are repeated within a text to signify major themes and concerns, like recurring themes in a piece of music (hence the similarity of Buber's term to composer Richard Wagner's word *Leitmotif*). A leading-word operates on the basis of sound: the repetition of a word or word root encourages the listener to make connections between diverse parts of a story (or even of a book), and to trace a particular theme throughout. This is not to be seen, however, as a static process. A leading-word may appear in different forms and contexts, with changed meaning, thus lending a sense of movement and development to the text and its characters. One example may be cited here; others appear throughout this book.

Buber's essay, "Abraham the Seer," traces the biblical tradition's portrayal of Abraham through the use of key words and phrases in the text. Chief among these is the verb "to see" (Hebrew *ra'o*), which appears constantly in the Abraham narratives and which tells us something significant about both the man himself and how he is meant to be remembered. At the outset of Abraham's journey to Canaan, which signals his entry into biblical tradition as an independent personality, God sends him off to a land that he will "let him see" (12:1). Arriving in the land, Abraham is granted a communication from God, expressed by the phrase "YHWH was seen by Avram . . ." (12:7). God subsequently promises the land to him and his descendants ("see from the place that you are . . . for all the land that you see, to you I give it and to your seed, for the ages" [13:15]). "Seeing" comes to the fore in the story of Abraham's concubine Hagar; her encounter with God's messenger ends with her addressing a "God of Seeing" (16:13). Further meetings between Abraham and God (17:1, 18:1) likewise express themselves visually, with the latter scene, where God announces Isaac's impending birth at Abraham's tent, almost unique in the Bible for its bold picture of God appearing directly to human beings. Finally, with the great test of Abraham in Chapter 22, the "Binding of Isaac," the theme of seeing is brought to a climax. Buber describes the use of the leading-word in that passage, summarizing how it rounds out the entire Abraham cycle:

> It appears here more often than in any previous passage. Abraham *sees* the place where the act must be accomplished, at a distance. To the question of his son, he replies that God will provide ("see to") the lamb for the burnt offering. In the saving moment he lifts up his eyes and *sees* the ram. And now he proclaims over the altar the name that makes known the imperishable essence of this place, Mount Moriah: YHWH Will

> See. . . . God sees man, and man sees God. God sees Abraham, and tests
> him by seeing him as the righteous and "whole" man who walks before
> his God (17:1), and now, at the end of his road, he conquers even this final
> place, the holy temple mountain, by acting on God's behalf. Abraham sees
> God with the eye of his action and so recognizes Him, just as Moses,
> seeing God's glory "from behind," will recognize Him as Gracious and
> Merciful.*

Buber goes one step further in his analysis of the leading-word *see:* he
views it as a clue to the biblical concept of Abraham's role in history.
Taking the hint from I Sam. 9:9 ("the prophet of our day was formerly
called a seer"), he posits that the Bible wants us to understand Abraham
as the spiritual father of the later prophets. Abraham, then, is preemi-
nent as the first man in the Bible of whom it is reported that God "was
seen by him."

Such an understanding of the role of leading-words as crucial to
biblical style rarely makes itself felt in translation. Bible translators are
reluctant to reproduce repetitions of Hebrew words in the text because
they are generally fearful of creating a tedious English style. However,
once one abandons the idea of the Bible as primarily a written work, the
repetitiveness of leading-words becomes a signal rather than a stumbling
block, freeing the reader to experience the dynamic manner in which
the Bible expresses itself. That this sometimes entails a loss of nuance
in the translation (where "see" in Hebrew may signify "perceive" or
"understand" in a particular passage, for instance) is a price that must
be paid; yet such a translation may in fact retain more of the breadth
of the Hebrew than is immediately apparent.

A final word needs to be said about the leading-word technique. It
may serve a purpose in the text beyond conveying meaning: it may play
a structural role, unifying sections that have been culled from different
sources within biblical Israel to form a composite account. The ancient
redactors of the Bible apparently crafted the material they received into
an organic whole. Using such means as leading-word repetition, they in
effect created a new literature in which deep relationships exist between
the parts of the whole.

The above three translation techniques—setting out the text in cola,
transliterating and explaining Hebrew names, and reproducing leading-
words—form the crux of an approach to the Bible's spokenness, but

*Martin Buber, *On the Bible: Eighteen Studies,* edited by Nahum N. Glatzer (New York:
Schocken Books, 1982), p. 42.

there are other methods used by the text to the same end. Three are particularly worthy of mention: word-play, allusion, and what I have termed small-scale repetition.

The Bible uses word-play to make a point forcefully, especially in prophetic passages or those with a prophetic flavor. In Gen. 40:13 and 19, for instance, Joseph predicts that the king of Egypt will end the imprisonment of two of his courtiers. When the cupbearer is to be restored to his former position, Joseph says,

> in another three days
> Pharaoh will lift up your head. . . .

In contrast, when Joseph predicts that the chief baker will be executed, the text reads:

> in another three days Pharaoh will lift up your head
> from off you. . . .

By beginning both statements with the same phrasing, the narrator is able to heighten the impact of "from off you" on both audience and victim.

A powerful example of the second device, allusion, occurs near the beginning of Exodus. Baby Moses, floating precariously yet fetus-like on the Nile, is one of the enduring images in the book, as children have long attested. Modern English readers, however, are seldom aware that the Hebrew word for Moses's floating cradle—rendered by virtually all standard translations as "basket"—is the same as the one used in Gen. 6:14ff. to describe Noah's famous vessel *(teva)*. Preserving the connection between the two, as I have tried to do in the Exodus passage with "little-ark" (and which, incidentally, the authors of the King James Version did with "ark"), is to keep open the play of profound meaning that exists between the two stories.

Finally, we may give an example of small-scale repetition. Unlike the leading-word technique, this is limited to a brief report and is used to express one specific idea. In Gen. 6:11–13, for instance, it illustrates an important biblical concept: just punishment. Three times in the passage we hear the word "ruin," indicating what human evil has done to the world; the fourth time (v.13) it appears in a causative form, to show that God retaliates in exactly the same terms, measure for measure.

> Now the earth had gone to *ruin* before God; the earth
> was filled with wrongdoing.

God saw the earth, and here: it had gone to *ruin,*
for all flesh had *ruined* its way upon the earth.

God said to Noah:
An end of all flesh has come before me,
for the earth is filled with wrongdoing through them;
here, I will bring *ruin* upon them, along with the earth.

The Bible is fond of this technique, which it uses in a number of narratives that deal with human misbehavior (e.g., the Tower of Babel story in Gen. II). It is another example of how the form in which the text is cast goes a long way toward expressing its intent.

From the above examples it may appear that it is not difficult to carry out the Buber-Rosenzweig principles in a translation. In practice, however, the translator who wishes to bring the language spoken by his audience into consonance with the style of the Hebrew text runs the risk of doing violence to that language, forced as he or she is into "hebraizing" the language. There will of necessity be a certain strangeness and some awkward moments in such a translation. Buber and Rosenzweig themselves came under fire for creating a strange new kind of German in their work; one critic in 1933 accused them of "unusual affectations." My renditions of Genesis and Exodus, while limited in what they wreak with the English language both by my cautiousness and by the less pliable nature of English (than German), have been liable to similar characterization.

This problem, however, is inherent in this kind of undertaking, and I have accepted its risks willingly. In the last generation there have been any number of clear, smooth-reading translations of the Bible, all aimed at making the text readily accessible to the reader. I have taken a different road, arguing (along with Buber and Rosenzweig) that the reader must be prepared to meet the Bible at least halfway and must become an active participant in the process of the text, rather than a passive listener. To this end, there is no alternative but to force the language of the translation to become the instrument through which the Hebraic voice of the text speaks.

I have taken pains to illustrate some of the rhetorical devices that emerge from an oral reading of the text in order to indicate the direction taken in *Genesis and Exodus.* A concluding observation must be made. Every critic knows, or should know, that art defies categorization and exact description. We try to understand what makes a masterpiece tick, whether it be a painting, a piece of music, or a work of literature, yet in the end our analyses fall silent before the greatness and subtlety of the work itself. The techniques that I have described above must remain suggestive rather than definitive; they point out a direction rather than speak directly. Biblical narratives do not end with the phrase "The moral of the story is . . . ," any more than biblical laws overtly spell out their assumptions. Translating with attention to sound therefore may help to preserve not only the message of the text but also its ambiguity and open-endedness. In that persona the Bible has been familiar to Jewish and Christian interpreters, who for centuries have sought to fill in the gaps and resolve the difficulties in the text by means of their own ingenuity. This volume is aimed at helping present-day readers to share in that experience.

3

READING THE BIBLE in the literary, rhetorical manner I have just explicated is grounded in certain assumptions about the text. *Genesis and Exodus* stays close to the basic "masoretic" text-type of the Torah, that is, the vocalized text that has been with us for certain for about a millenium. Deviations from that form, in the interest of solving textual problems, are duly mentioned in the Notes. In following the traditional Hebrew text, I am presenting to the English reader an unreconstructed book, but one whose form is at least verifiable in a long-standing tradition. This translation, therefore, is not a translation of some imagined "original" text, or of the Genesis and Exodus of Moses' or Solomon's or even Jeremiah's time. These documents, could they be shown to have existed for certain or in recognizable form, have not been found, and give little promise of ever being found. *Genesis and Exodus* is, rather, a translation of the biblical text as it might have been known in the formative, postbiblical period of Judaism and early Christianity (the Roman era). As far as the prehistory of the text is concerned, readers who have some familiarity with biblical criticism will note that in my Commentary I have made scant reference to the by-now classic dissection of the Torah into clear-cut prior "sources" (designated J, E, P, and D by the Bible scholars of the past century); this is a theoretical construct, and the exact process by which the Bible came into being remains difficult to recover (for a recent attempt, see Friedman 1987).

Given the text that I am using, what has interested me here is chiefly the final form of Genesis and Exodus, how they fit together as artistic entities, and how they have combined traditions to present a coherent religious message. This was surely the goal of the final "redactor(s)," but it was not until recently a major goal of biblical scholars. While, therefore, I am not committed to refuting the tenets of source criticism in the strident manner of Benno Jacob and Umberto Cassuto, I have concentrated in this volume on the "wholeness" of biblical texts, rather than on their growth out of fragments. My Commentary is aimed at helping the reader to search for unities and thematic development.

At the same time, I must say that since the original publication of these books, I have found it increasingly fascinating to encounter the text's complex layering. It appears that every time a biblical story or law was put in a new setting or redaction, its meaning, and the meaning of the whole, must have been somewhat altered. A chorus of different periods and concerns is often discernible, however faintly. Sometimes these function to "deconstruct" each other, and sometimes they actually create a new text. In offering a rendition that does not try to gloss over stylistic differences, I hope that this book will make it possible for an inquisitive reader to sense that process at work. As far as analysis of the text in this manner is concerned, I would recommend to the reader the brilliant work of Greenstein (1985) and Damrosch (1987).

4

SOME READERS MAY wonder whether *Genesis and Exodus* is merely an English translation of B-R. It is not. Although B-R served as the theoretical basis for my work, I have found it necessary to modify their approach in the present setting. There are a number of reasons for this.

For one, Bible scholarship has made notable advances since Buber's heyday (Rosenzweig had already died in 1929). Although he completed the German translation in 1961, and kept abreast of work in the field, it must be said that Buber did not greatly modify the text of the Pentateuch translation, philologically speaking, between 1930 when the second edition appeared and the revised printings of the mid-1950s. It seemed imperative to me to bring the work of postwar biblical philology to bear on the English translation, rather than relying solely on Buber's etymologies. Some of the changes in this area have been cited in the Notes to the text (as "B-R uses . . .").

Second, in the attempt to make the German translation mirror the Hebrew original Rosenzweig did not hesitate to either create new German words or reach back into the German literature of past ages to find forms suitable for rendering certain Hebrew expressions. To perform a corresponding feat in English would simply not work; the language is not flexible, and usages change so quickly that an artful appeal to the past seems futile except for the benefit of linguistic historians. While I have endeavored to produce an English text that reflects the style of biblical Hebrew, I have in the main shied away from pushing the language beyond reasonable and comprehensible limits.

There are other significant deviations from B-R here. I have used a different rendering of the name of God, which had been a distinctive B-R trademark (for an explanation, see "On the Name of God and Its Translation"). I have sometimes opted for different line divisions, based on my own hearing of the Hebrew; indented purely poetic passages, a practice not followed by B-R in narrative texts; read a large number of clauses differently from a grammatical or syntactical point of view; and loosened the practice, sometimes overdone in B-R, of reproducing a Hebrew root by a single English one wherever it occurs.

Finally, I have included here one element that many readers felt was sorely lacking in B-R: notes and commentary. Every translation of the Bible implies a commentary, but few have included one with the text. *Genesis and Exodus* especially requires such an apparatus, both to explain its translation technique and to show how it may be used fruitfully in interpreting the Bible. Read in conjunction with the text, the explanatory material presents a methodology for studying and teaching the Bible.

This having been said, *Genesis and Exodus* is still very much in the B-R tradition. It retains the general approach of its predecessor, exclusive of those principles that are dependent on the form and character of the German language. It is therefore the child of B-R, with all the links and independent features that a parent-child relationship implies. It may also be seen as an attempt to bring the work of B-R into a new era of Bible scholarship, and as an artistic endeavor in its own right.

5

Genesis and Exodus is heavily indebted to B-R, but one may also view it in a more contemporary context. Over the past two decades, there has been an explosion of "literary" study of the Bible. Numerous scholars have turned their attention to the form and rhetoric of the biblical text, concentrating on its finished form rather than on trying to reconstruct history or the development of the text. Such an approach is hardly new. Already in late antiquity, Jewish interpretation of the Bible often centered around the style and precise wording of the text, especially as heard when read aloud. Similarly, the medieval Jewish commentators of Spain and France showed great sensitivity to the linguistic aspects of the Bible. In both cases, however, no systematic approach was developed; literary interpretation remained interwoven with very different concerns such as homiletics, mysticism, and philosophy.

It has remained for twentieth-century scholars, reacting partly against what they perceived to be the excessive historicizing of German Bible scholarship, to press for a literary reading of the Bible. Early pioneers in this regard include Umberto Cassuto, Buber and (later) Meir Weiss in Israel, and Benno Jacob (who was consulted frequently during the writing of B-R) in Germany. More recently we might mention James Muilenberg (who labeled his holistic approach "Rhetorical Criticism"), Edwin Good, James Ackerman, and Robert Alter in the U.S.; and J. P. Fokkelman in Holland. These names are now the tip of the iceberg, and one can speak of a whole school of interpreters in a literary or rhetorical vein. The reader will find a number of stimulating studies listed in "Suggestions for Further Reading," at the end of the book.

Genesis and Exodus is akin to many of these efforts, and especially in the case of Exodus, has benefited directly from them. Although I began my work independently of the literary movement, I have come to feel a kinship with it, and regard my text as one that may be used to study the Bible in a manner consistent with its findings. At the same time, I am not committed to throwing out historical scholarship wholesale. It would be a mistake to set up the two disciplines in an adversarial relationship, as has often been done. The Hebrew Bible is by nature a complex and multi-faceted literature, in both its origins and the history of its use and interpretation. No one "school" can hope to illuminate more than part of the whole picture, and even then, one's efforts are bound to be fragmentary. Probably, only a synthesis of all fruitful approaches available into a fully interdisciplinary methodology will provide a satisfactory overview of the biblical text (see Greenstein, 1989). In this respect, approaching the Bible is analogous to dealing with the arts in general, where a multitude of disciplines from aesthetics to the social and natural sciences is needed to flesh out the whole. It is to be hoped that *Genesis and Exodus* will make a contribution toward the process, by providing an English text, and an underlying reading of the Hebrew, that balances what has appeared previously.

There is another movement in biblical studies which, although its fruits have not been extensively applied in this volume, deserves both mention and study. As of this writing, feminist Bible criticism has come into its own. A substantial number of thoughtful and thought-provoking studies have appeared in recent years that examine the portrayal and position of women in biblical texts. One of the glaring gaps in previous Bible scholarship—and one of the difficult issues for contemporary readers of the Bible—lies in coming to terms with the social/sexual milieu assumed by the text. Wrestling with this issue is an appropriate complement to the other types of text-wrestling that have taken place throughout the ages. In order to at least present some of the findings of feminist criticism at the reader's disposal, I have listed some appropriate recent works in "Suggestions for Further Reading." Many of them bear directly on the stories and laws found in Genesis and Exodus.

6

TO WHAT EXTENT can any translation of the Bible be said to be more "authentic" than another? Because of lack of information about the various original audiences of our text, the translator can only try to be as faithful as the information will allow. This is particularly true where a work as universally known as the Bible is concerned. Even if the precise circumstances surrounding its writing and editing were known, the text would still be affected by the interpretations of the centuries. It is as if a Beethoven symphony were to be performed on period instruments, using nineteenth-century performance techniques: would it still sound as fresh and radical to us as it did in Beethoven's own day? Thus I would suggest that it is almost impossible to reproduce the Bible's impact on its contemporaries; all that the translator can do is to perform the task with as much honesty as possible, with a belief in his artistic intuition and a consciousness of his limitations.

Yet how is one to distinguish the point where explication ends and personal interpretation begins? From the very moment of the Bible's editing and promulgation, there began the historical process of interpretation, a process which has at times led to violent disagreement between individuals and even nations. Everyone who has ever taken the Bible seriously has staked so much on a particular interpretation of the text that altering it has become close to a matter of life and death. Nothing can be done about this situation, unfortunately, and once again the translator must do the best he can. Art, by its very nature, gives rise to interpretation—else it is not great art. The complexity and ambiguity of great literature invites interpretation, just as the complexities and ambiguities of its interpreters encourage a wide range of perspectives. The Hebrew Bible, in which very diverse material has been juxtaposed in a far-ranging collection spanning centuries, rightly or wrongly pushes the commentator and reader to make inner connections and draw over-arching conclusions. My interpretations in this book stem from this state of affairs. I have tried to do my work as carefully and as conscientiously as I can, recognizing the problems inherent in this kind of enterprise. I hope the result is not too far from what the biblical editors had intended.

My ultimate goal in this volume has been to show that reading the Hebrew Bible is a process, in the same sense that performing a piece of music is a process. Rather than carrying across ("translating") the con-tent of the text from one linguistic realm to another, I have tried to involve the reader in the experience of giving it back ("rendering"), of returning to the source and recreating some of its richness. My task has been to present the raw material of the text as best I can in English, and to point out some of the methods that may be fruitfully employed in wrestling with it.

Translators, said Goethe, should "arouse an irresistible desire for the original." They should also be able to communicate that the greatness of a work of art is not always something immediately accessible, but rather to be acquired through strenuous and loving effort. If *Genesis and Exodus* helps to provide a medium for that kind of encounter to take place, then my own strenuous and loving efforts will have been more than amply rewarded.

EVERETT FOX

Clark University
Worcester, MA
June 1990
Tammuz 5750

ACKNOWLEDGMENTS

ACKNOWLEDGMENTS for the original printings of these books (1983, 1986) are still, of course, valid. I should like here only to reiterate some important names, and to express my thanks for more recent support.

My gratitude goes to several people who have been supportive of this project from its inception, and whose encouragement has enabled me to continue: William Novak, Arthur Waskow, Cliff Anderson, and Prof. James Ackerman. Prof. Edward L. Greenstein, who served as special editor for *Now These Are the Names,* has been a long-time critical reader and a crucial advocate; his scholarship and energy have contributed immeasureably to the birth and growth of this project. Bonny Fetterman, Senior Editor of Schocken Books, has been my support and facilitator in the "real world" of publishing. Most importantly, my wife, Cherie Koller-Fox, has been my chief backer in many forums, and has enabled me to see the effectiveness of the translation for young students.

I should like to thank colleagues at Boston University and Clark University for their kind encouragement, and students at these two institutions and others at which I have given guest lectures on this work. Special thanks go to Profs. Herbert Mason, Theodor Gaster (who gave invaluable advice on *In the Beginning*), Jeremiah Unterman, and Lawrence Rosenwald. The Conference on Alternatives in Jewish Education, now entering its fifteenth year, has also provided me with an excellent sounding board for various ideas and texts.

It has meant a great deal to me to have heard from a variety of readers over the years: students, colleagues, clergy, and others, who have kept me from the full isolation that this kind of work often spawns. I am also particularly grateful to those colleagues, both known and unknown to me, whose use of this material in the classroom and whose support in other ways has validated what I set out to do.

The two original dedications to these books should be mentioned again. *In the Beginning* was dedicated to Nahum N. Glatzer, teacher and mentor. His connection with the Buber–Rosenzweig translation was profound: he served as bibliographer for Rosenzweig, reader (aloud) of the Hebrew text to help the translators stay true to their goals, and critical reader of the German translation.

Glatzer died in February of 1990. He leaves a legacy of deep respect for the voice of Jewish sources and of profound engagement with texts, both biblical and post-biblical. His own unique voice, his humility, and his kindness are irreplaceable. May the blessing of his memory be perceived in these pages.

Now These Are the Names was dedicated to the memory of attorney Paul Lichterman, who died in a tragic accident in December of 1983. Time has not dimmed the pain of his loss for family, friends, and co-workers. He would have gotten much pleasure from this work; he was a remarkable teacher of Jewish texts, and his unique presence continues to be deeply missed.

For this edition of the two books, I have chosen to remember Arthur A. Cohen, with respect and gratitude. His moral support for the original version of *In the Beginning* was deeply meaningful to me. A thinker of profundity, a critical mind of great acumen, and a formidable aesthete, he was by adoption a continuer of the legacy of Buber and Rosenzweig in America. His work will continue to stimulate thinking on the religious dilemmas of our century.

TO AID THE READER

GIVEN THE ILLUSTRIOUS predecessors that any translator of Genesis and Exodus follows, I have not tried to provide here either a comprehensive commentary or an all-encompassing system of notes. Rather, I have sought to suggest some fruitful avenues for thought and discussion in the Commentary, and to provide such information in the Notes as will be helpful to the non-specialist. Naturally, the selection of material for these purposes is entirely mine; others might single out different details and different aspects of the text. A future edition of the entire Pentateuch will include revised notes.

Since I have espoused a "rhetorical" approach to biblical texts in my work, I have decided to limit myself largely to literary remarks in the Commentary: indicating themes and motifs as they appear and are developed in these books and elsewhere in the Bible; pointing out structural aspects of the text; and treating issues of character development in the narrative. I have by and large eschewed historical issues, and those pertaining to the origins and textual history of Genesis and Exodus. These matters, which are highly theoretical and subject to detailed and often heated scholarly discussion, are treated comprehensively in standard works such as Speiser (1964) for Genesis and Childs (1974) for Exodus (see also the volumes of the Jewish Publication Society's *The Torah Commentary*, currently appearing). More detailed information on the ancient Near Eastern background and parallels to Genesis and Exodus can be found in Cassuto (1967, 1972/1974) and Sarna (1966, 1986). Readers whose interest is primarily archaeological will seek works such as Mazar (1990).

ON THE NAME OF GOD
AND ITS TRANSLATION

THE PERSONAL NAME of the biblical God, which has been transcribed here by the letters YHWH, has undergone numerous changes in both its writing and translation throughout the history of the Bible. At an early period the correct pronunciation of the name was either lost or deliberately avoided out of a sense of religious awe. Jewish tradition came to vocalize and pronounce the name as "Adonai," that is, "the/my Lord," a usage that has remained in practice since late antiquity. Another euphemism, regularly used among Orthodox Jews today, is "Ha-Shem," literally, "The Name."

Historically, Jewish and Christian translations of the Bible into English have tended to use "Lord," with some exceptions (notably, Moffatt's "The Eternal"). Both old and new attempts to recover the "correct" pronunciation of the Hebrew name have not succeeded; neither the sometimes-heard "Jehovah" nor the standard scholarly "Yahweh" can be conclusively proven.

For their part, Buber and Rosenzweig sought to restore some of what they felt was the name's ancient power; early drafts of their Genesis translation reveal a good deal of experimentation in this regard. They finally settled on a radical solution: representing the name by means of capitalized personal pronouns. The use of YOU, HE, HIM, etc., stemmed from their conviction that God's name is not a proper name in the conventional sense, but rather one which evokes his immediate presence. Buber and Rosenzweig—both of whom wrote a great deal about their interpretation (see Buber 1958)—based it on their reading of Exodus 3:14, a text in which another verbal form of YHWH appears, and which they translated as "I will be-there howsoever I will be-there" (i.e., my name is not a magical handle through which I can be conjured up; I am ever-present). For more on this passage, and the name, see the Commentary and Notes in the text below.

The B-R rendering has its attractiveness in reading aloud, but it is on doubtful ground etymologically. It also introduces an overly male emphasis through its constant use of "HE," an emphasis which is not quite so pronounced in the Hebrew. I have therefore decided to follow the practice of printed Hebrew Bibles, which leave the name YHWH unvocalized. As the translation is read aloud, the reader should pronounce the name according to his or her custom, or use one of the standard options found above, such as "the Lord." While the effect of this is jarring at first, it has the merit of approximating the situation of the text as we now have it, and of leaving open the unsolved question of the pronunciation and meaning of God's name.

Readers who are uncomfortable with the maleness of God in these texts may wish to substitute "God" for "he" in appropriate passages. While, as a translator, I am committed to reproducing the text as faithfully as I can, it is also true that the ancient Hebrews viewed God as a divinity beyond sexuality, and modern readers as well may see fit to acknowledge this.

GUIDE TO THE PRONUNCIATION OF HEBREW NAMES

THE PRECISE pronunciation of biblical Hebrew cannot be determined with certainty. The following guide uses a standard of pronunciation which is close to that of modern Hebrew, and which will serve for the purpose of reading the text aloud.

> *a* (e.g., Adam, Avraham, Aharon) as in fa ther
> *e* (e.g., Lea, Levi, Rahel, Elim) as the *a* in ca pe
> *o* (e.g., Edom, Lot, Moshe) as in ho rn
> *u* (e.g., Luz, Zevulun, Shur) as in Bu ber

When *e* occurs in both syllables of a name (e.g., Hevel, Lemekh), it is generally pronounced as the *e* in te n. In such cases the first syllable is the accented one; generally speaking, Hebrew accents the last syllable.

When *e* is the second letter of a name (e.g., Devora, Yehuda, Betzalel), it is often pronounced as the *a* in a go.

kh (e.g., Hanokh, Yissakhar) is to be sounded like the *ch* in Johann Sebastian Ba*ch*.

h (e.g., Havva, Het, Hur) most often indicates Hebrew *het,* pronounced less heavily than *kh* but not as English *h.*

The system for transcribing Hebrew words used in this volume follows the above model, rather than standard scholarly practice (e.g., *karev* instead of *qrb, sharatz* instead of *šrṣ*), in the interests of the general reader. For this reason, I also do not distinguish here between the Hebrew letters *alef* and *ayin* in transcription, even though technically their pronunciation differs.

Some very well-known names in the text have been transcribed in their traditional English spelling. These include Canaan (Hebrew *Kena'an*), Egypt *(Mitzrayim),* Israel *(Yisrael),* Jordan *(Yarden),* Pharaoh *(Par'o),* and Sinai *(Seenai).* Otherwise, I have indicated the familiar English forms of the names in the Notes, under the rubric "Trad. English. . . ."

GENESIS:
In the Beginning

ON THE BOOK OF GENESIS AND ITS STRUCTURE

THE TEXT of Genesis seems to speak with many voices. For a book whose basic arrangement is chronological, tracing the history of a single family, it exhibits a good deal of discontinuity on the surface. Here time flows uniformly, there takes startling jumps; fragments are followed by more or less full-blown tales; genres alternate, from mythic to genealogical to folkloristic. In addition, scholars often portray Genesis as a collection of historically diverse materials that were compiled by scribes for whom deviating from received tradition was anathema. Hence the repetitions, the inconsistencies, and the irregular pacing.

Is Genesis then, at best, a collection of stories related to the origins of Israel, with most of its seams still showing? Such an assessment does not do justice to what must have been a complex process of addition and growth or to the final product. An overview of the book does produce a certain scheme; at some point in the text's history a coherent picture must have begun to emerge from the disparate materials handed down. For the modern reader, utilizing the Buber-Rosenzweig method of focusing on repeating words and key themes as the text presents them, may make it possible to generalize about the organization of the book and also to speculate on its overall intent in the form in which it has come down to us.

On its most obvious level Genesis is a book about origins. It seeks to link the origin of the people of Israel with that of the world, relating in the process how various human characteristics and institutions arose.

On the surface this parallels much of ancient literature and folklore. All peoples are interested in their own beginnings, picturing them in a way which validates their present existence. Genesis, however, is different in that, like the rest of the Torah, it downplays the heroic element of the people's origins and in its place stresses God's role in them. Moreover the one great omission—the origin of God—establishes from the beginning a unique basis for a tribal chronicle. From Genesis and subsequent books we learn primarily about God's relationship to the people and what he expects of them; almost everything else is subordinated to this purpose.

Preliminarily one can speak of at least seven major themes whose recurrence establishes their importance in the book:

1. *Origins:* Of the world, of humanity, and of the people of Israel.
2. *Order/Meaning in History:* By means of stylized or patterned chronology—reliance on certain round numbers such as 3,7, and 40—it is suggested that human events are not random but somehow planned.
3. *Blessing:* From creation onward God bestows blessings on his creatures in general and on the fathers and mothers of Israel in particular.
4. *Covenant:* God concludes agreements with human beings.
5. *God Punishes Evildoing:* God is provoked to anger not by his capriciousness but by human failure to uphold justice and morality.
6. *Sibling Conflict, with the Younger Usually Emerging the Victor:* The order of nature (primacy of the firstborn) is overturned, demonstrating that God, not nature, is the ruling principle in human affairs.
7. *Testing:* God tests those who are to carry forth his mission; the result is the development of moral character.

Superseding these important themes, which occur throughout the Bible in various forms, is the dominant one of *continuity*, represented by the unifying word in Genesis *toledot* ("begettings"). The word appears eleven times, often accompanied by long genealogical lists. The names may deflect attention from what is central to Genesis. The major thrust of the book would seem to be toward human fecundity, following the early divine command to "bear fruit and be many" (1:28), and pointing toward the eventual fecundity of the people of Israel (which will only be realized in the book of Exodus). Such an emphasis seems appropriate in a book about origins.

Ironically, however, the undercurrent in Genesis points not to life and its continuation, but rather to its threatened extinction. In story after story the protagonist, his people, and occasionally the entire world are threatened. In at least one case (Avraham) a perfectly legal and natural solution is found—the birth of Yishmael as his heir—only to be rejected by God in favor of a more difficult one: a son born to an elderly woman.

It is clear that the stress on continuity and discontinuity has one purpose: to make clear that God is in control of history. Human fertility and continuity in history come not from magical rites or from the arbitrary decisions of the gods, but from a God who bases his rule on justice.

Nature disappears as a ruling factor in human affairs, replaced by a principle of morality which is unshakable precisely because it comes from a God who is beyond the rules of nature.

But the result is a book which abounds in tension. From the beginnings of human history (Chapter 4) we encounter contradictions and opposites, whether on a small scale (fertility and barrenness) or a large one (promise and delayed fulfillment). Nowhere is this so clear as in the dramatic high point of the book, Genesis 22. As Avraham stands with knife upraised, the entire enterprise of Genesis hangs in the balance. But the entire book is replete with such tensions and continuity-threatening situations. There are barren wives, brothers vowing to kill brothers, cities and even a world being destroyed by an angry God. The main characters of Genesis thus emerge as survivors, above all else. Noah sets the pattern, but he is merely the first, and too passive an example. The Patriarchs must brave hostile foreigners, bitter intrafamily struggles, and long wanderings before they can find peace.

While by the end of the book many of the tensions have been resolved, one conspicuously has not: God's promise of the land of Canaan. As the book ends, "in Egypt," we are left to ponder how this God, who keeps his promises to "those who love him" (Ex. 20:6), will bring the people back to their land—a land inhabited by someone else and in which the Children of Israel own only a burial site. Yet despite the tension, we may assume from the experiences of the Patriarchs that God will indeed "take account of" the Israelites (50:24), that he will take whatever ill has been planned against them and "plan-it-over for good" (50:20).

A word should also be said here about hero traditions. In the great epics of the ancient world the hero often stands as a lonely figure. He must overcome obstacles, fight monsters, acquire helpers (whether women, "sidekicks," or magic objects); and his triumph in the end signals man's triumph over his archenemy, Death. Every battle won, every obstacle hurdled, is psychologically a victory for us, the audience, a cathartic release from our own frustrating battle against death.

The Bible sees things rather differently. Death is also overcome, but not only by the individual's struggle. It is rather through the covenant community, bound together by God's laws and his promises, that the heroic vision is lived out. Despite the triumphs of the characters in Genesis, it is really in the book of Exodus that the great battle scenes (the plagues in Egypt, the Red Sea) and meetings with the divine (Mount Sinai) take place. And it is therefore God himself who is most properly the "hero" of these stories. No major character in Genesis achieves success without depending fully on God, and the standards that are held up to them are ultimately seen as God's own, to be imitated by imperfect humankind.

The book of Genesis falls naturally into four large sections. The first, usually termed the "Primeval History" (Chapters 1–11), begins with creation and progresses through the early generations of humanity, ending in Mesopotamia. The second (Chapters 12 through 25:18) is the cycle of stories concerning Avraham, the father of the people of Israel. Part III (Gen. 25:19 through Chapter 36) deals in the main with stories about his grandson Yaakov. The final section (Chapters 37–50) is the tale of Yosef and of how the Children of Israel came to live in Egypt (thus paving the way for the book of Exodus).

The following skeletal outline will lay out some of the interesting structural features of the book. There is an elemental symmetry that emerges from the four sections; further comments, especially about how the sections cohere, will be found in the explanatory material accompanying the text in this volume.

I. Chosen Figure (Noah)
    Sibling Hatred (Kayin–Hevel), with sympathy for youngest
    Family Continuity Threatened (Hevel murdered)
    Ends with Death (Haran, Terah; Sarai barren)
        Humanity Threatened (Flood)
        Ends Away from Land of Israel ("In Harran")

II. Chosen Figure (Avraham)
    Sibling Hatred (Yishmael–Yitzhak) Implied, with sympathy for
            youngest
    Family Continuity Threatened (Sarai barren, Yitzhak almost sacri-
            ficed)
    Ends with Death (Sara, Avraham)
        Rivalry Between Wives (Hagar–Sarai)
        Barren Wife (Sarai)
        Wife–Sister Story (Chaps. 12 and 20)
        Ends with Genealogy of Non-Covenant Line (Yishmael)

III. Chosen Figure (Yaakov)
    Sibling Hatred (Esav–Yaakov), with sympathy for youngest
    Family Continuity Threatened (Yaakov almost killed)
    Ends with Death (Devora, Rahel, Yitzhak)

  Rivalry Between Wives (Lea–Rahel)
  Barren Wife (Rahel)
  Wife–Sister Story (Chap. 26)
  Ends with Genealogy of Non-Covenant Line (Esav)

IV. Chosen Figure (Yosef)
  Sibling Hatred (Brothers–Yosef), with sympathy for youngest
  Family Continuity Threatened (Yehuda's sons die; Yosef almost
    killed; family almost dies in famine)
  Ends with Death (Yaakov, Yosef)
  Humanity Threatened (Famine)
  Ends Away from Land of Israel ("In Egypt")

There is of course great variety within this bare structure; each version of a motif has its own special characteristics and emphases. Yet the patterning observed above gives the book a general coherence, above and beyond differences. It also demonstrates a conscious hand at work, one concerned about the texture of the book as a whole and able, despite the possible rigidity of what had been handed down, to shape the received material into a plastic and breathing unity.

Two general observations about Genesis will round out the picture here. First, as the book progresses there is a tendency for the style of the literature to become smoother. The abrupt changes and sometimes fragmentary nature of the material in Part I, and the vignettes built around Avraham's life in Part II, give way to a greater coherence and concentration in Part III, and finally to a relatively flowing and psychologically complete narrative in Part IV. Along with this, the characters in the latter half of the book seem to be more changeable and human, in contrast to Noah and Avraham, who often appear almost perfect models of piety.

Second, contact with God becomes less and less direct as Genesis moves on. Avraham's dreams and visions seem a far cry from Adam's conversations with God in the garden (although see Chapter 18); Yaakov's encounters with God are less frequent than Avraham's; and finally, Yosef never has a conversation with God, although he receives dream interpretations from him. This process of distancing may reflect an often-observed tendency in religions to think of primeval times as a "golden age" of closeness between gods and men, as contrasted to today (whenever one is writing), when humankind finds itself tragically distant from the divine and in need of communication.

PART I The Primeval History
(1–11)

THE COLLECTION of stories which forms Part I of Genesis has been assembled for a number of purposes:

1. History is traced from the creation of the world, in a direct line, down to Avraham, father of the People of Israel. Through use of the leading-word *toledot*, "begettings," we are meant to view him as the logical end point in God's preliminary plan in history.

2. The nature of God, as he will appear throughout the Hebrew Bible, is firmly established. He is seen as a Creator who is beyond fate, nature, and sexuality; as an all-powerful orderer and giver of meaning to history; as a bestower of blessing to living creatures; as a giver of choice to human beings; as a just punisher of evil and, simultaneously, a merciful ruler; and as a maker of covenants. The one quality of God which does not unfold until the Patriarchal stories (Parts II–IV) is his shaping of human destiny through focusing on the People of Israel. It is portrayed as the logical outcome of the characteristics just mentioned.

3. It appears that the Mesopotamian origins of Israel are reflected in such narratives as the Creation, the Flood, and the Tower of Babel, and are transformed or repudiated in the biblical versions. What in the older culture appears arbitrary and chaotic has been changed in the Bible into stories that stress morality and order. Further, human beings in Genesis Chapters 1–11, despite their failure to live up to God's expectations, are nevertheless considered capable of doing so, in contrast to the Mesopotamian view that humankind was created merely to be slaves to the gods.

4. Like virtually all other creation stories, Part I is concerned with the origin of the world and its institutions. Chapter 1 expounds on the origins of earth, sky, vegetation, animals, and human beings (as well as the Sabbath); Chapter 2, of sexuality, death, pain in childbirth, and work; Chapter 4, of sin, hatred, and murder, as well as of cities and

crafts; Chapter 6, of giants; and Chapter 10, of nations (including the
low status of the Canaanites) and languages.

In sum, Part I serves as a fitting Prologue, not only to Genesis but to
the entire Bible. The reader's chief task in interpreting it is to be able to
determine the reason for the inclusion of any one section into the whole.

1:1 In the beginning God created the heavens and the earth.

2 —Now the earth had been wild and waste,
   darkness over the face of Ocean,
   breath of God hovering over the face of the waters—

3 God said: Let there be light! And there was light.
4 God saw the light: that it was good.
   God separated the light from the darkness.
5 God called the light: Day! and the darkness he called:
      Night!
   There was evening, there was morning: one day.

6 God said:
   Let there be a dome amid the waters,
   and let it separate waters from waters!
7 God made the dome
   and separated the waters that were below the dome from the
      waters that were above the dome.
   It was so.
8 God called the dome: Heaven!
   There was evening, there was morning: second day.

9 God said:
   Let the waters under the heavens be gathered to one place,
   and let the dry land be seen!
   It was so.
10 God called the dry land: Earth! and the gathering of the
      waters he called: Seas!
   God saw that it was good.

11 God said:

Let the earth sprout forth with sprouting-growth,
plants that seed forth seeds, fruit trees that yield fruit, after
  their kind, (and) in which is their seed, upon the earth!
It was so.

God as Creator (1:1–2:4a): Three principal themes emerge from the great
creation account with which Genesis opens. The first is the total and
uncompromised power of God as creator; the second, the intrinsic order
and balance of the created world; and the third, humankind's key position in the scheme of creation. These themes are brought home as much

1:1 **In the beginning . . .** : This phrase, which has long been the focus of
debate among grammarians, can also be read: "At the beginning of God's
creating of the heavens and the earth,/ when the earth was. . . ." The
translation here, which is traditional in English, has been retained for stylistic reasons.   **God created:** Indicative of God's power and not used in
reference to humans, although later in the chapter such words as "make"
and "form" do appear.

2 **Now the earth . . .** : Genesis 1 describes God's bringing order out of
chaos, not creation from nothingness.   **wild and waste:** Heb. *tohu va-vohu*,
indicating "emptiness."   **Ocean:** The primeval waters, a common (and
usually divine) image in ancient Near Eastern mythology.   **breath of God:**
Others use "wind," "spirit"; the word (Heb. *ru'ah*) is open to both possibilities. See Ps. 33:6.   **hovering:** Or "flitting." The image suggested by the
word (see Deut. 32:11) is that of an eagle protecting its young.

3–5 **God said . . . God saw . . . God separated . . . God called:** Here, from
the outset of the story the principle of order is stressed, through the rhythmic structure of "God" plus four verbs.

4 **God saw . . . that it was good:** The syntax is emphatic here; others use
"God saw how good it was." The phrase is reminiscent of ancient Near
Eastern descriptions of a craftsman being pleased with his work.

4 **separated:** The verb occurs four more times early in the chapter (vv.6, 7,
14, 18), and further points to the concept of order.

6 **dome:** Heb. *raki'a,* literally a beaten sheet of metal.

8 **Heaven:** The sky.

11 **sprout forth with sprouting-growth . . . seed forth seeds . . . fruit
trees . . . fruit:** The three sound doublets create a poetic effect in God's
pronouncement. Note that they are not repeated by the narrator in verse
12. See also verse 20, ". . . swarm with a swarm. . . ."   **after their kind:**
Here as in a number of passages in the translation I have shifted some
words that occur in the singular (especially collectives) for the sake of
clarity. See, for example, 6:3, 5.

12 The earth brought forth sprouting-growth,
   plants that seed forth seeds, after their kind,
   trees that yield fruit, in which is their seed, after their kind.
   God saw that it was good.
13 There was evening, there was morning: third day.

14 God said:
   Let there be lights in the dome of the heavens, to separate
      the day from the night,
   that they may be for signs—for set-times, for days and
      years,
15 and let them be for lights in the dome of the heavens, to
      provide light upon the earth!
   It was so.
16 God made the two great lights,
   the greater light for ruling the day and the smaller light for
      ruling the night,
   and the stars.
17 God placed them in the dome of the heavens
18 to provide light upon the earth, to rule the day and the
      night, to separate the light from the darkness.
   God saw that it was good.
19 There was evening, there was morning: fourth day.

20 God said:
   Let the waters swarm with a swarm of living beings, and let
      fowl fly above the earth, across the dome of the heavens!
21 God created the great sea-serpents
   and all living beings that crawl about, with which the waters
      swarmed, after their kind,
   and all winged fowl after their kind.
   God saw that it was good.
22 And God blessed them, saying:
   Bear fruit and be many and fill the waters in the seas,
   and let the fowl be many on earth!
23 There was evening, there was morning: fifth day.

24 God said:
   Let the earth bring forth living beings after their kind,

by the form in which they are presented as by their actual mention.

God (Heb. *elohim*, a generic term) is introduced into the narrative without any description of origins, sex, or limitations of power. As the only functioning character of the chapter, he occupies center stage. There is no opposition, no resistance to his acts of creation, which occur in perfect harmony with his express word.

As a sign of both God's total control and his intent, the world unfolds in symmetrical order. The division of God's labor into six days, plus a seventh for rest, itself indicates a powerful meaningfulness at work, as well as providing the external structure for the narrative. Interpreters have tended to divide these into either three groups of two days or two groups of three, with always the same results: a balanced and harmonious whole. In addition, the number seven is significant (as it will be elsewhere in the Bible) as a symbol of perfection, not only in Israel but in the ancient world in general.

The narrative uses several repeating words and phrases to both unify the story and underscore the theme of order. These include "God said," "Let there be . . . ," "God saw that it was good," "It was so," and "There was evening, there was morning . . ."

The text is so formed as to highlight the creation of humankind. Although in each previous day "God said" is the keynote, suggesting forethought as well as action, here (v.26) God fully spells out his intentions, as it were thinking out loud. Humanity, created in the divine "image," is to hold sway over the rest of creation. Only with the addition of humankind is God able to survey his newly formed world and to pronounce it "exceedingly good" (v.31).

At least two motifs appear in this chapter which will become important later in Genesis. The three occurrences of "blessing" (1:22, 1:28, 2:3) point to a central idea in the Patriarchal stories. In addition the concept of order and its logical conclusion—that history makes sense—figures prominently in the familial histories of the book. This is accomplished largely by the meaningful use of numbers, as above.

14 **lights:** In the sense of "lamps." **for signs—for set-times . . . :** Hebrew difficult.

21 **great sea-serpents:** The rebellious primeval monster of Ps. 74:13 (and common in ancient Near Eastern myth) is here depicted as merely another one of God's many creations.

22 **And God blessed them:** The first occurrence in Genesis of the key motif of blessing, which recurs especially throughout the Patriarchal stories. **Bear fruit and be many and fill:** Heb. *peru u-revu u-mil'u.*

herd-animals, crawling things, and the wildlife of the earth
after their kind!
It was so.

25 God made the wildlife of the earth after their kind, and the
herd-animals after their kind, and all crawling things of
the soil after their kind.
God saw that it was good.

26 God said:
Let us make humankind, in our image, according to our
likeness!
Let them have dominion over the fish of the sea, the fowl of
the heavens, animals, all the earth, and all crawling things
that crawl upon the earth!

27   God created humankind in his image,
          in the image of God did he create it,
          male and female did he create them.

28 God blessed them,
God said to them:
Bear fruit and be many and fill the earth
and subdue it!
Have dominion over the fish of the sea, the fowl of the
heavens, and all living things that crawl about upon the
earth!

29 God said:
Here, I give you
all plants that bear seeds that are upon the face of all the
earth,
and all trees in which there is tree fruit that bears seeds,
for you shall they be, for eating;

30 and also for all the living things of the earth, for all the fowl
of the heavens, for all that crawls about upon the earth in
which there is living being—
all green plants for eating.
It was so.

31 Now God saw all that he had made,
and here: it was exceedingly good!
There was evening, there was morning: the sixth day.

2:1 Thus were finished the heavens and the earth, with all of
their array.

2 God had finished, on the seventh day, his work that he had
   made,
   and then he ceased, on the seventh day, from all his work
   that he had made.
3 God gave the seventh day his blessing, and he hallowed it,
   for on it he ceased from all his work, that by creating, God
   had made.

The entire account concludes (2:1–3) with a tightly structured poem.
"God," "the seventh day," "work," and "made" are mentioned three
times, "finished," "ceased," and "all" twice; and "created" returns,
echoing 1:1, to round out the whole creation narrative.

The postscript (2:4a; some scholars align it with what follows in
Chapter 2 instead) introduces the key structural phrase of Genesis,
"These are the begettings. . . ." It may also indicate the polemical intent
of the creation story. Rosenzweig understood the verse to contrast "be-
getting," i.e., sexual creation as it occurs in non-Israelite myths, with the
"true" creation.

In that vein, a final word needs to be said about extrabiblical evidence.
As has often been pointed out, Genesis 1 is unmistakably reacting against
prevailing Near Eastern cosmogonies of the time. Most of the cultures
surrounding ancient Israel had elaborate creation stories, highlighting the
birth, sexuality, and violent uprisings of the gods. As we indicated at the
outset, the concept of God presented here militates against such ideas,
arguing chiefly out of omission and silence. (It should also be noted that
in poetic books such as Isaiah, Job, and Psalms, a tradition about violent

26 **in our image:** The "our" is an old problem. Some take it to refer to the
   heavenly court (although, not surprisingly, no angels are mentioned here).
27 **God created humankind:** The narrative breaks into verse, stressing the
   importance of human beings. "Humankind" (Heb. *adam*) does not specify
   sex, as is clear from the last line of the poem.
29 **I give you:** "You" in the plural.
30 **all green plants for eating:** Human beings in their original state were not
   meat-eaters. For the change, see 9:3ff.
31 **exceedingly good. . . . the sixth day:** The two qualifiers "exceedingly"
   and "the" are deviations from the previous expressions in the story, and
   underscore the sixth day (when humankind was created) as the crowning
   achievement of creation (or else serve as a summary to the whole).
2:3 **gave . . . his blessing:** Or "blessed," here expanded in English for rhythmical reasons. **by creating, God had made:** Hebrew difficult. Buber's
   working papers show numerous attempts at a solution.

4 These are the begettings of the heavens and the earth: their
   being created.

  On the day that YHWH, God, made earth and heaven,
5 no bush of the field was yet on earth,
   no plant of the field had yet sprung up,
   for YHWH, God, had not made it rain upon earth,
   and there was no human/*adam* to till the soil/*adama*—
6 but a surge would well up from the ground and water all
     the face of the soil;
7 and YHWH, God, formed the human, of dust from the
     soil,
   he blew into his nostrils the rush of life
   and the human became a living being.

8 YHWH, God, planted a garden in Eden/Land-of-Pleasure,
     in the east,
   and there he placed the human whom he had formed.
9 YHWH, God, caused to spring up from the soil
   every type of tree, desirable to look at and good to eat,
   and the Tree of Life in the midst of the garden
   and the Tree of the Knowing of Good and Evil.

10 Now a river goes out from Eden, to water the garden,
   and from there it divides and becomes four stream-heads.
11 The name of the first one is Pishon/Spreader—that is the
     one that circles through all the land of Havila, where gold
     is;
12 the gold of that land is good, there too are bdellium and the
     precious-stone carnelian.
13 The name of the second river is Gihon/Gusher—that is the
     one that circles through all the land of Cush.
14 The name of the third river is Hiddekel/Tigris—that is the
     one that goes to the east of Assyria.
   And the fourth river—that is Perat/Euphrates.

15 YHWH, God, took the human and set him in the garden of
     Eden,
   to work it and to watch it.

16 YHWH, God, commanded concerning the human, saying:
From every other tree of the garden you may eat, yes, eat,

17 but from the Tree of the Knowing of Good and Evil—
you are not to eat from it,
for on the day that you eat from it, you must die, yes, die.

---

conflict at creation has been preserved.) The Genesis narrative has taken such old mythological motifs as battles with the primeval (female) waters or with sea monsters and eliminated or neutralized them. What remains is both utterly simple and radical in its time.

Garden and Expulsion (2:4b–3:24): From the perspective of God in Chapter 1, we now switch to that of humankind (note how the opening phrase in 2:4b, "earth and heaven," reverses the order found in 1:1). This most famous of all Genesis stories contains an assortment of mythic

4b **On the day:** At the time.   **YHWH:** For a discussion of the name of God and its translation and pronunciation, see p. xxix.

5 **human**/*adam* . . . **soil**/*adama:* The sound connection, the first folk etymology in the Bible, establishes the intimacy of mankind with the ground (note the curses in 3:17 and 4:11). Human beings are created from the soil, just as animals are (v.19).

6 **surge:** Or "flow."

7 **rush:** Or "breath."

8 **Eden/Land-of-Pleasure:** For another use of the Hebrew root, see 18:12. The usage here may be a folk etymology; Speiser translates it as "steppe."

9 **Tree of Life:** Conferring immortality on the eater of its fruit.   **Knowing of Good and Evil:** Interpreters disagree on the meaning of this phrase. It could be a merism (as in "knowledge from A to Z"—that is, of everything), or an expression of moral choice.

10 **stream-heads:** Branches or tributaries.

12 **bdellium . . . carnelian:** Identification uncertain; others suggest, for instance, "lapis" and "onyx."

15 **work:** A different Hebrew word (here, *avod*) from the one used in 2:2–3 (*melakha*).

16 **eat, yes, eat:** Heb. *akhol tokhel,* literally, "eating you may eat." Others use "you may freely eat"; I have followed B-R's practice of doubling the verb throughout, which retains the sound as well as the meaning. In this passage, as in many instances, I have inserted the word "yes" for rhythmical reasons.

17 **die, yes, die:** Others use "surely die."

18 Now YHWH, God, said:
It is not good for the human to be alone,
I will make him a helper corresponding to him.
19 So YHWH, God, formed from the soil every living-thing of
the field and every fowl of the heavens
and brought each to the human, to see what he would call
it;
and whatever the human called it as a living being, that
became its name.
20 The human called out names for every herd-animal and for
the fowl of the heavens and for every living-thing of the
field,
but for the human, there could be found no helper
corresponding to him.
21 So YHWH, God, caused a deep slumber to fall upon the
human, so that he slept,
he took one of his ribs and closed up the flesh in its place.
22 YHWH, God, built the rib that he had taken from the
human into a woman
and brought her to the human.
23 The human said:
This-time, she-is-it!
Bone from my bones,
flesh from my flesh!
She shall be called Woman/*Isha*,
for from Man/*Ish* she was taken!
24 Therefore a man leaves his father and his mother and clings
to his wife,
and they become one flesh.

25 Now the two of them, the human and his wife, were nude,
yet they were not ashamed.

3:1 Now the snake was more shrewd than all the living-things
of the field that YHWH, God, had made.
It said to the woman:
Even though God said: You are not to eat from any of the
trees in the garden . . . !
2 The woman said to the snake:

elements and images which are common to human views of prehistory: the lush garden, four central rivers located (at least partially) in fabled lands, the mysterious trees anchoring the garden (and the world?), a primeval man and woman living in unashamed nakedness, an animal that talks, and a God who converses regularly and intimately with his creatures. The narrative presents itself, at least on the surface, as a story of origins. We are to learn the roots of human sexual feelings, of pain in childbirth, and how the anomalous snake (a land creature with no legs) came to assume its present form. Most strikingly, of course, the story seeks to explain the origin of the event most central to human consciousness: death.

The narrative unfolds through a series of contrasts: good and evil, life and death, heaven and earth, give and take, knowledge and ignorance, mankind and animals, hiding and revealing. Some of these concepts appear literally as key words in the text. The characters also appear through contrasts: man as God's image and as dust, woman as helper and hinderer, the snake as shrewd and (after the curse) lowly.

A further focus is provided by the echoing of the word "eat," whose connotation changes from sustenance/bounty (2:9, 16) to prohibition (2:17) to misunderstanding (3:1–5) and disobedience (3:6, 11–13), and finally to curse (3:14, 17, 19). Such a flexible use of words sets up a rhythmic drama which, as much of Genesis, bears resemblance to poetry rather than to prose.

Part I of the story (Chapter 2) sets the stage in the garden, focusing on *Adam*, "Everyman" (see *Cambridge Bible Commentary*, Gen. 1–11). God is here regularly called "YHWH, God," a rare designation which may suggest a preexpulsion view of the wholeness of God as well as of mankind. Man continues his status as "God's image" (1:26–27), imitating

18 **It is not good:** In contrast to the refrain of Genesis 1, "God saw that it was good." **corresponding to:** Lit. "opposite." The whole phrase (Heb. *ezer kenegdo*) could be rendered "a helping counterpart." At any rate, the Hebrew does not suggest a subordinate position for women.

20 **called out:** Or "gave." **for the human:** Others use "for Adam" or "for a man."

21 **ribs:** Or possibly "sides," paralleling other ancient peoples' concept of an original being that was androgynous.

23 **She:** Lit. "this-one."

3:1 **Even though God said:** Others use "Did God really say . . . ?" **in the garden . . . !:** Such an uncompleted phrase, known as aposeopesis, leaves it to the reader to complete the speaker's thought, which in the Bible is usually an oath or a threat (see also, for instance, 14:23, 21:23, 26:29, 31:50).

From the fruit of the other trees in the garden we may eat,
3 but from the fruit of the tree that is in the midst of the
      garden, God has said:
   You are not to eat from it and you are not to touch it,
   lest you die.
4 The snake said to the woman:
   Die, you will not die!
5 Rather, God knows
   that on the day that you eat from it, your eyes will be
      opened
   and you will become like gods, knowing good and evil.
6 The woman saw
   that the tree was good for eating
   and that it was a delight to the eyes,
   and the tree was desirable to contemplate.
   She took from its fruit and ate
   and gave also to her husband beside her,
   and he ate.
7 The eyes of the two of them were opened
   and they knew then
   that they were nude.
   They sewed fig leaves together and made themselves
      loincloths.

8 Now they heard the sound of YHWH, God, who was
      walking about in the garden at the breezy-time of the day.
   And the human and his wife hid themselves from the face
      of YHWH, God, amid the trees of the garden.
9 YHWH, God, called to the human and said to him:
   Where are you?
10 He said:
   I heard the sound of you in the garden and I was afraid,
      because I am nude,
   so I hid myself.
11 He said:
   Who told you that you are nude?
   From the tree about which I command you not to eat,
   have you eaten?
12 The human said:

> The woman whom you gave to be beside me, she gave me
>   from the tree,
> and so I ate.
> 13 YHWH, God, said to the woman:
> What is this that you have done?
> The woman said:
> The snake enticed me,
> and so I ate.

---

the divine act of giving names (1:5, 8, 10). He is also nevertheless a creature of the dust, both at the beginning (2:7) and end (3:19) of the story.

The bridge to Part II (Chapter 3) is deftly accomplished by linking two identical-sounding words in the Hebrew, *arum* (here, "nude" and "shrewd"). The choice of the snake as the third character is typically ancient Near Eastern (it is so used in other stories about death and immortality, such as the *Gilgamesh Epic* from Mesopotamia). Some interpreters have seen sexual overtones in this choice as well. Yet a plain reading of the text need not overemphasize the snake, who disappears as a personality once the fatal fruit has been eaten.

The ending of the story has also raised questions of interpretation. Buber was among those who see in the act of expulsion from the garden a deed of mercy rather than one of fear or jealousy. Certainly a creature whose first act upon acquiring new "knowledge" is to cover himself up poses no threat to the Creator. The text, like its late successor, the book of Job, may be suggesting that in the human sphere, unlike the divine, knowledge and mortality are inextricably linked. This is a tragic realization, but it is also the world as human beings know it.

Although the specifics of this story are never again referred to in the Hebrew Bible, and are certainly not crucial for the rest of Genesis, one general theme *is* central to the Bible's world view. This is that rebellion

5 **you:** Plural. **like gods:** Or "like God."
8 **breezy-time:** Evening. **face of God:** The "face" or presence of God is a dominating theme in many biblical stories and in the book of Psalms. Man seeks God's face or hides from it; God reveals it to him or hides it from him.
12 **gave to be:** Put. "Give" has been retained here, despite its awkwardness, as a repeating word in the narrative.

14 YHWH, God, said to the snake:
    Because you have done this, *cattle*   *wild beasts*
    cursed be you from all the animals and from all the
        living-things of the field;
    upon your belly shall you walk and dust shall you eat, all
        the days of your life.
15 I put enmity between you and the woman, between your
        seed and her seed:
    they will bruise you on the head, you will bruise them in
        the heel.
16 To the woman he said:
    I will multiply, multiply your pain (from) your pregnancy,
    with pains shall you bear children.
    Toward your husband will be your lust, yet he will rule
        over you.
17 To Adam he said:
    Because you have hearkened to the voice of your wife
    and have eaten from the tree about which I commanded
        you, saying:
    You are not to eat from it!
    Cursed be the soil on your account,
    with painstaking labor shall you eat from it, all the days of
        your life.
18 Thorn and sting-shrub let it spring up for you,
    when you seek to eat the plants of the field!
19 By the sweat of your brow shall you eat bread,
    until you return to the soil,
    for from it you were taken.
    For you are dust, and to dust shall you return.

20 The human called his wife's name: Havva/Life-giver!
    For she became the mother of all the living.

21 Now YHWH, God, made Adam and his wife coats of skins
        and clothed them.

22 YHWH, God, said:
    Here, the human has become like one of us, in knowing
        good and evil.

So now, lest he send forth his hand
and take also from the Tree of Life
and eat
and live throughout the ages . . . !
23 So YHWH, God, sent him away from the garden of Eden,
    to work the soil from which he had been taken.
24 He drove the human out
    and caused to dwell, eastward of the garden of Eden,
    the winged-sphinxes and the flashing, ever-turning sword
    to watch over the way to the Tree of Life.

---

against or disobedience toward God and his laws results in banishment/
estrangement and, literally or figuratively, death. Thus from the beginning the element of *choice*, so much stressed by the Prophets later on, is
seen as the major element in human existence.

All this said, it should be recognized that the garden story, like many
biblical texts, has been the subject of endless interpretation. One line of
thought takes the psychological point of view. The story resembles a
vision of childhood and of the transition to the contradictions and pain of
adolescence and adulthood. In every way—moral, sexual, and intellectual—Adam and Havva are like children, and their actions after partaking of the fruit seem like the actions of those who are unable to cope with
newfound powers. The resolution of the story, banishment from the
garden, suggests the tragic realization that human beings must make
their way through the world with the knowledge of death and with great

15 **seed:** Offspring, descendants.
17 **painstaking labor:** Heb. *itzavon.* Man and woman receive equal curses (see
    verse 16, "pain . . . pains").
18 **sting-shrub:** Heb. *dardar;* thistle ("thorns and thistles" suggests an allitera-
    tion not found in the Hebrew).
20 **Havva:** Trad. English "Eve."
21 **God . . . clothed them:** Once punishment has been pronounced, God cares
    for the man and the woman. Both aspects of God comprise the biblical
    understanding of his nature, and they are not exclusive of each other.
22 **one of us:** See note on 1:26. **throughout the ages:** Or "for the eons";
    others use "forever."
24 **winged-sphinxes:** Mythical ancient creatures, also represented on the Ark
    of the Covenant (Ex. 25:18). "Cherubim," the traditional English render-
    ing, has come to denote chubby, red-cheeked baby angels in Western art,
    an image utterly foreign to the ancient Near East.

4:1 The human knew Havva his wife,
she became pregnant and bore Kayin.
She said:
Kaniti/I-have-gotten
a man, as has YHWH!

2 She continued bearing—his brother, Hevel.
Now Hevel became a shepherd of flocks, and Kayin became a
worker of the soil.

3 It was, after the passing of days
that Kayin brought, from the fruit of the soil, a gift to
YHWH,

4 and as for Hevel, he too brought—from the firstborn of his
flock, from their fat-parts.
YHWH had regard for Hevel and his gift,

5 for Kayin and his gift he had no regard.
Kayin became exceedingly enraged and his face fell.

6 YHWH said to Kayin:
Why are you so enraged? Why has your face fallen?

7 Is it not thus:
If you intend good, bear-it-aloft,
but if you do not intend good,
at the entrance is sin, a crouching-demon,
toward you his lust—
but you can rule over him.

8 Kayin said to Hevel his brother . . .
But then it was, when they were out in the field
that Kayin rose up against Hevel his brother
and he killed him.

9 YHWH said to Kayin:
Where is Hevel your brother?
He said:
I do not know. Am I the watcher of my brother?

10 Now he said:
What have you done!
A sound—your brother's blood cries out to me from the
soil!

physical difficulty. At the same time the archetypal man and woman do not make the journey alone. They are provided with protection (clothing), given to them by the same God who punished them for their disobedience. We thus symbolically enter adulthood with the realization that being turned out of Paradise does not mean eternal rejection or hopelessness.

The First Brothers (4:1–16): With the story of Kayin and Hevel the narrative points both forward and backward. For the first time the major Genesis themes of struggle and sibling hatred, and discontinuity between the generations, make their appearance. In addition the concept of *sin* is introduced (Rosenzweig), having not appeared by name previously.

One may observe significant links to the garden story. Once again human beings are given a choice; once again disregarding the warning leads to death and estrangement from God; and once again the primal bond between mankind and the soil is ruptured. Chapter 3 is directly recalled by the use of specific wording: God echoes the curse he had put on the woman (3:16) in his warning to Kayin (4:7), and "Where is Hevel your brother?" (4:9) brings to mind "Where are you?" (3:9), which had been addressed to Kayin's father.

The text is punctuated by the use of "brother," a meaningful seven times, as well as by changing connotations of the word "face" (Kayin, unable to bring about a "lifting" of his own face, becomes estranged from God's). Repetition also helps to convey the harshness of Kayin's punishment: he is exiled to the "land of Nod/Wandering" (v.16), for which we have been prepared by the "wavering and wandering" of verses 12 and 14.

4:1 **knew:** Intimately; a term for sexual intercourse. **Kayin:** Trad. English "Cain." The name means "smith" (see also v.22, below). **I-have-gotten:** Others use "I have created." **as has YHWH:** Hebrew difficult.

2 **Hevel:** The name suggests "something transitory" (see the opening of the book of Ecclesiastes: *havel havalim*).

3 **gift:** Heb. *minha*, usually referring to sacrifices.

4 **fat-parts:** I.e., the choicest.

5 **enraged:** Lit. "his (anger) was kindled."

7 **Is it not thus . . . :** Hebrew obscure. **bear-it-aloft:** Others use "there is forgiveness," "there is uplift." **toward you his lust—/ but you can rule over him:** Recalling God's words to Havva in 3:16.

8 **Kayin said . . . :** The verse appears incomplete. Ancient versions add "Come, let us go out into the field."

10 **A sound:** Or "Hark!"

11 And now,
   cursed be you from the soil,
   which opened up its mouth to receive your brother's blood
      from your hand.
12 When you wish to work the soil
   it will not henceforth give its strength to you;
   wavering and wandering must you be on earth!
13 Kayin said to YHWH:
   My punishment is too great to be borne!
14 Here, you drive me away today from the face of the soil,
   and from your face must I conceal myself,
   I must be wavering and wandering on earth—
   now it will be
   that whoever comes upon me will kill me!
15 YHWH said to him:
   No, therefore,
   whoever kills Kayin, sevenfold will it be avenged!
   So YHWH set a sign for Kayin,
   so that whoever came upon him would not strike him down.
16 Kayin went out from the face of YHWH
   and settled in the land of Nod/Wandering, east of Eden.

17 Kayin knew his wife;
   she became pregnant and bore Hanokh.
   Now he became the builder of a city
   and called the city's name according to his son's name,
      Hanokh.
18 To Hanokh was born Irad,
   Irad begot Mehuyael,
   Mehuyael begot Metushael,
   Metushael begot Lemekh.

19 Lemekh took himself two wives,
   the name of the first one was Ada, the name of the second
      was Tzilla.
20 Ada bore Yaval,
   he was the father of those who sit amidst tent and herd.
21 His brother's name was Yuval,
   he was the father of all those who play the lyre and the
      pipe.

22 And Tzilla bore as well—Tuval-Kayin,
   burnisher of every blade of bronze and iron.
   Tuval-Kayin's sister was Naama.

23 Lemekh said to his wives:
         Ada and Tzilla, hearken to my voice,
         wives of Lemekh, give ear to my saying:
         Aye—a man I kill for wounding me,
         a lad for only bruising me!
24   Aye—if sevenfold vengeance be for Kayin,
         then for Lemekh, seventy-sevenfold!
25 Adam knew his wife again, and she bore a son.
   She called his name: Shet/Granted-One!
   meaning: God has granted me another seed in place of
     Hevel,
   for Kayin killed him.

Although this story may well have originated as a tale of enmity between two ways of life (farmer and shepherd), or in another context, it
has obviously been transformed into something far more disturbing and
universal.

The Line of Kayin (4:17–26): From whole stories the text turns to several
brief accounts, some of which are clearly fragments. The first of these
deals with origins: of cities, of certain crafts, and of worship. The former
two are associated (perhaps negatively) with Kayin's line. The only personality in these texts about whom we learn anything is Lemekh—and
his "saying" (vv.23–24) seems hopelessly obscure. Some interpreters
have understood it as a challenge to God, and thus believe that it has
been included here as an example of the wickedness typical of the generations that preceded the Flood.

The names of Adam and Havva's son and grandson (vv.25–26) are sad
reminders of Hevel's death—a personal touch in an otherwise prosaic
section of narrative.

15 **a sign:** The exact appearance of the sign is not specified. It is a warning and
   a protection, not the punishment itself (which is exile).
17 **Now he:** "He" refers to Kayin.
18 **Mehuyael begot:** Heb. *Mehiyael.*
19 **Ada . . . Tzilla:** The names suggest "dawn" and "dusk" (Gaster).
20 **father:** Ancestor or founder.
22 **burnisher . . . :** Or "craftsman of every cutting-edge of copper and iron."

26 To Shet as well a son was born,
   he called his name: Enosh/Mortal.

At that time they first called out the name of YHWH.

5:1 This is the record of the begettings of Adam/Humankind.
       On the day of God's creating humankind,
       in the likeness of God did he then make it,
2   male and female he created them
       and gave blessing to them
       and called their name: Humankind!
       on the day of their being created.
3 When Adam had lived thirty and a hundred years,
   he begot one in his likeness, according to his image,
   and called his name Shet.
4 Adam's days after he begot Shet were eight hundred years,
   and he begot other sons and daughters.
5 And all the days that Adam lived were nine hundred years
   and thirty years,
   then he died.

6 When Shet had lived five years and a hundred years, he
   begot Enosh,
7 and Shet lived after he begot Enosh seven years and eight
   hundred years, and begot other sons and daughters.
8 And all the days of Shet were twelve years and nine
   hundred years,
   then he died.

9 When Enosh had lived ninety years, he begot Kenan,
10 and Enosh lived after he begot Kenan fifteen years and
   eight hundred years, and begot other sons and daughters.
11 And all the days of Enosh were five years and nine hundred
   years,
   then he died.

12 When Kenan had lived seventy years, he begot Mehalalel,
13 and Kenan lived after he begot Mehalalel forty years and
   eight hundred years, and begot other sons and daughters.

14 And all the days of Kenan were ten years and nine hundred
    years,
    then he died.

15 When Mehalalel had lived five years and sixty years, he
    begot Yered.
16 and Mehalalel lived after he begot Yered thirty years and
    eight hundred years, and begot other sons and daughters.
17 And all the days of Mehalalel were ninety-five years and
    eight hundred years,
    then he died.

18 When Yered had lived sixty-two years and a hundred years,
    he begot Hanokh,
19 and Yered lived after he begot Hanokh eight hundred years,
    and begot other sons and daughters.
20 And all the days of Yered were sixty-two years and nine
    hundred years,
    then he died.

From Adam to Noah (5): The extraordinary numbers in this section are
significant, not so much for their length as for their message. Cassuto has
tried to fit them into a defined scheme, showing that the purpose, and
achieved effect, of our text is to convey that human history follows a
meaningful pattern. Pride of place on the list is occupied by the seventh
member, Hanokh, who is portrayed as the first man of God. He serves as
a preparation for Noah, who also "walks in accord with God" (6:9).
Hanokh's life span, 365 years, exemplifies the number scheme of Genesis: as an expression of numerical perfection (the number of days in a
year), it symbolizes moral perfection.

26 **called out the name of YHWH:** I.e., worshipped God.
5:1 **On the day . . . :** The language is reminiscent of the earlier poem in 1:27.
    In this case, however, the Hebrew creates a rhyming effect. The cola of the
    poem here end thus: *bera'am / otam / shemam: Adam/ hibare'am.* Such a
    rhyming scheme is rare in biblical Hebrew, and usually endows a passage
    with particular significance (see also, for instance, II Sam. 12:11).
18 **Hanokh:** Trad. English "Enoch."

21 When Hanokh had lived sixty-five years, he begot
    Metushelah,
22 and Hanokh walked in accord with God after he begot
    Metushelah three hundred years, and begot other sons
    and daughters.
23 And all the days of Hanokh were sixty-five years and three
    hundred years.
24 Now Hanokh walked in accord with God,
    then he was no more,
    for God had taken him.

25 When Metushelah had lived eighty-seven years and a
    hundred years, he begot Lemekh,
26 and Metushelah lived after he begot Lemekh eighty-two
    years and seven hundred years, and begot other sons and
    daughters.
27 And all the days of Metushelah were sixty-nine years and
    nine hundred years,
    then he died.

28 When Lemekh had lived eighty-two years and a hundred
    years, he begot a son.
29 He called his name: Noah!
    saying:
    Zeh yenahamenu/May he comfort-our-sorrow
    from our toil, from the pains of our hands
    coming from the soil, which YHWH has cursed.

30 And Lemekh lived after he begot Noah ninety-five years
    and five hundred years, and begot other sons and
    daughters.
31 And all the days of Lemekh were seventy-seven years and
    seven hundred years,
    then he died.

32 When Noah was five hundred years old,
    Noah begot Shem, Ham, and Yefet.

6:1 Now it was when humans first became many on the face of
    the soil
    and women were born to them,
  2 that the divine beings saw how beautiful the human women
    were,
    so they took themselves wives, whomever they chose.

  3 YHWH said:
    My breath shall not remain in humankind for ages, for they
    too are flesh;
    let their days be then a hundred and twenty years!

Antiquity and the Preparation for the Flood (6:1–8): The final pre-Flood
section of the text includes a theme common to other ancient tales: the
biological mixing of gods and men in dim antiquity. Perhaps this fragment, which initially seems difficult to reconcile with biblical ideas about
God, has been retained here to round out a picture familiar to ancient
readers, and to recall the early closeness of the divine and the human
which, according to many cultures, later dissolved. It is also possible that
the episode serves as another example of a world that has become dis-
ordered, thus providing further justification for a divinely ordered
destruction.

The stage is set for the Flood by means of a powerful sound reference.

22 **and Hanokh walked in accord with God . . . three hundred years:** The
    variation from the rigid formulations of this chapter draws attention to this
    key figure, the first pious man (similarly with Noah, 5:29). "Walked in
    accord with God" means walked in God's ways, led a righteous life.
24 **then he was no more:** He died. Later interpreters found the phrase ambig-
    uous, and fantastic postbiblical legends arose concerning Hanokh (see Ginz-
    berg).
31 **seventy-seven years and seven hundred years:** As in 4:24, a man named
    Lemekh is linked to multiples of seven.
6:2 **divine beings:** Or "godlings."
  3 **for they too are flesh:** Hebrew difficult. The text uses the singular. **a**
    hundred and twenty years: Some early interpreters take this to specify a
    "grace period" for mankind before the Flood. The text seems to be setting
    the limits of the human life span.

4 The giants were on earth in those days,
and afterward as well,
when the divine beings came in to the human women
and they bore them (children)—
they were the heroes who were of former ages, the men of
    name.

5 Now YHWH saw
that great was humankind's evildoing on earth
and every form of their heart's planning was only evil all the
    day.
6 Then YHWH was sorry
that he had made humankind on earth,
and it pained his heart.
7 YHWH said:
I will blot out humankind, whom I have created, from the
    face of the soil,
from human to animal, to crawling thing and to the fowl of
    the heavens,
for I am sorry that I made them.
8 But Noah found favor in the eyes of YHWH.

9 These are the begettings of Noah.
Noah was a righteous, whole man in his generation,
in accord with God did Noah walk.
10 Noah begot three sons: Shem, Ham, and Yefet.

11 Now the earth had gone to ruin before God, the earth was
    filled with wrongdoing.
12 God saw the earth, and here: it had gone to ruin,
for all flesh had ruined its way upon the earth.

13 God said to Noah:
An end of all flesh has come before me,
for the earth is filled with wrongdoing through them;
here, I am about to bring ruin upon them, along with the
    earth.
14 Make yourself an Ark of *gofer* wood,
with reeds make the Ark,

In 5:29 Noah was named, ostensibly to comfort his elders' "sorrow" over human "pains" in tilling the soil. Here (6:6), however, the meaning of the name has been ironically reversed. The one who was supposed to bring comfort only heralds God's own being "sorry" and "pained" (vv. 6–7). A similar ironic word-play, where the audience knows what the name-bestower does not, occurs in Ex. 2:3; curiously, the hero of that passage, the baby Moses, is also connected with an "ark"—the term for the little basket in which he is set adrift.

The Deluge (6:9–8:19): The biblical account of the Flood is replete with echoes and allusions which point to three clear motifs: God's justice, the totality of punishment, and a new beginning patterned after Genesis 1.

The first of these is brought out in 6:11–13: the repetition of the word "ruin" indicates not only the sorry state of society but also the principle of just retaliation, for God is to "bring ruin" upon the earth (v.13).

The totality of the disaster is conveyed by the repeated use of the word "all" in 7:21–23, as well as by the completeness of the list of those destroyed (7:21–23). Humans, as befits their place in the order of creation, appear last, but actually it is they who drag virtually all of creation down with them. This reflects a deeply held biblical idea that human

4 **came in to:** The common biblical term for sexual intercourse. The concept, also expressed in Arabic, is of the man entering the woman's tent for the purposes of sex.

5 **now YHWH saw . . . evildoing:** In contrast to the refrain of Chapter 1, "God saw that it was good." **every form of their heart's planning:** This lengthy phrase indicates human imagination (Speiser: "every scheme that his mind devised"). "Heart" (Heb. *lev* or *levav*) often expresses the concept of "mind" in the Bible.

9 **righteous:** A term with legal connotations; "in the right" or "just." **righteous, whole:** Foreshadowing Avraham, of whom similar vocabulary will be used (17:1). **whole:** A term used of animals fit for sacrifice: "perfect" or "unblemished." In reference to human beings it may denote "wholehearted."

11–12 **Now the earth . . . :** A poetic summary of the situation.

11 **before God:** In his sight.

12 **God saw the earth, and here: it had gone to ruin:** A bitter echo of 1:31, "Now God saw all that he had made,/ and here: it was exceedingly good!"

13 **has come before me:** Has been determined by me.

14 **Ark:** English as well as Hebrew etymology points to a box or chest, not strictly a boat. God, not human engineering, is the source of survival in the story. ***gofer:*** Identification unknown. **reeds:** Reading Heb. *kanim* for traditional text's *kenim* ("compartments").

and cover it within and without with a covering-of-pitch.

15 And this is how you are to make it:
   Three hundred cubits the length of the Ark, fifty cubits its
      breadth, and thirty cubits its height.

16 A skylight you are to make for the Ark, finishing it to a
      cubit upward.
   The entrance of the Ark you are to set in its side;
   With a lower, a second, and a third deck you are to make
      it.

17 As for me,
   here, I am about to bring on the Deluge, water upon the
      earth,
   to bring ruin upon all flesh that has breath of life in it, from
      under the heavens,
   all that is on earth will perish.

18 But I will establish my covenant with you:
   you are to come into the Ark, you and your sons and your
      wife and your sons' wives with you,

19 and from all living-things, from all flesh, you are to bring
      two from all into the Ark, to remain alive with you.
   They are to be a male and a female each,

20 from fowl after their kind, from herd-animals after their
      kind, from all crawling things of the soil after their kind,
   two from all are to come to you, to remain alive.

21 As for you,
   take for yourself from all edible-things that are eaten and
      gather it to you,
   it shall be for you and for them, for eating.

22 Noah did it,
   according to all that God commanded him, so he did.

7:1 YHWH said to Noah:
   Come, you and all your household, into the Ark!
   For you I have seen as righteous before me in this
      generation.

2 From all ritually pure animals you are to take seven and
      seven each, a male and his mate,
   and from all the animals that are not pure, two each, a male
      and his mate,

3 and also from the fowl of the heavens, seven and seven
   each, male and female,
   to keep seed alive upon the face of all the earth.
4 For in yet seven days
   I will make it rain upon the earth for forty days and forty
   nights
   and will blot out all existing-things that I have made, from
   the face of the soil.
5 Noah did it, according to all that YHWH had commanded
   him.

6 Noah was six hundred years old when the Deluge occurred,
   water upon the earth;
7 and Noah came, his sons and his wife and his sons' wives
   with him, into the Ark before the waters of the Deluge.
8 From the pure animals and from the animals that are not
   pure and from the fowl and all that crawls about on the
   soil—
9 two and two each came to Noah, into the Ark, male and
   female,
   as God had commanded Noah.

---

action directly affects the orderly and otherwise neutral functioning of
nature.

There are striking parallels between the Flood narrative and the creation account of Chapter 1. Just as the animals were created, each "according to its kind," their rescue, both in boarding and leaving the Ark,

15 **cubits:** A cubit equaled a man's forearm in length, about 17½ inches.
16 **skylight:** Hebrew obscure, including the end of the phrase.
17 **Deluge:** Heb. *mabbul*. Others suggest the more conventional word
   "Flood," but the term may be an Assyrian loan-word.
18 **covenant:** An agreement or pact, most notably (in the Bible) one between
   God and individuals or between him and the people of Israel.
7:2 **ritually pure:** An anachronism, referring to later Israelite laws about sacrifice and eating. **seven and seven each:** The contradiction between this
   and 6:19 has led scholars to posit two different sources for the
   story. **male:** Lit. "a man."
4 **in yet seven days:** Seven days from now. **forty:** Used in the Bible to
   denote long periods of time; also a favorite patterned number.

10 After the seven days it was
   that the waters of the Deluge were upon the earth.
11 In the six hundredth year of Noah's life, in the second
   New-Moon, on the seventeenth day of the New-Moon,
   on that day:
        then burst all the well-springs of the great Ocean
        and the sluices of the heavens opened up.
12 The torrent was upon the earth for forty days and forty
   nights.

13 On that very day came Noah, and Shem, Ham, and Yefet,
   Noah's sons, and Noah's wife and his three sons' wives
   with them, into the Ark,
14 they and all wildlife after their kind, all herd-animals after
   their kind, all crawling things that crawl upon the earth
   after their kind, all fowl after their kind, all
   chirping-things, all winged-things;
15 they came to Noah, into the Ark, two and two each from all
   flesh in which there is breath of life.
16 And those that came, male and female from all flesh they
   came,
   as God had commanded him.
   YHWH closed (the door) upon him.

17 The Deluge was forty days upon the earth.
   The waters increased and lifted the Ark, so that it was
   raised above the earth;
18 the waters swelled and increased exceedingly upon the
   earth, so that the Ark floated upon the face of the waters.
19 When the waters had swelled exceedingly, yes, exceedingly
   over the earth, all high mountains that were under all the
   heavens were covered.
20 Fifteen cubits upward swelled the waters, thus the
   mountains were covered.

21 Then perished all flesh that crawls about upon the earth—
   fowl, herd-animals, wildlife, and all swarming things that
   swarm upon the earth,
   and all humans;

22 all that had rush or breath of life in their nostrils,
   all that were on firm ground, died.
23 He blotted out all existing-things that were on the face of
   the soil,
   from human to animal, to crawling thing and to fowl of the
   heavens,
   they were blotted out from the earth.
   Noah alone remained, and those who were with him in the
   Ark.

———

is similarly worded. "Ocean" and the great "breath" which existed at
creation (1:2) return here, the former to signify a lapse into chaos and the
latter, the restoration of order and peace (7:11, 8:1). Finally, after the
Flood (9:1–3) Noah is blessed in wording that recalls Adam's blessing in
1:28–30. The world thus begins anew, with the implication of some
hope for the future.

Repetition emphasizes other aspects of the story's message. In general
the word-stem "live" occurs constantly throughout the text, highlighting
the rescue and renewal of life as well as its destruction. Noah's obedience, another major theme, is indicated by variations on the phrase
"according to all that God commanded him, so he did" (6:22). Of rhythmical, almost ritual-sounding import is the phrase "you and your sons
and your wife and your sons' wives."

Our story has often been compared, with much justification, to the
several Mesopotamian Flood accounts (e.g., in the *Gilgamesh* and *Atraha-
sis* epics), with which it shares a great deal of detail. At one time scholars

11 **then burst . . . :** Cassuto suggests that the poetic verses here and elsewhere
   in the Flood story are fragments of an Israelite epic. See also 9:11,
   15. **well-springs . . . sluices:** The normal sources of rain function here
   without any restraint (Cassuto). **Ocean:** The world returns to the primeval chaos of 1:2.
16 **YHWH closed:** Another sign of God's control over the events (and of his
   protection of Noah).
17–20 **increased . . . swelled and increased exceedingly. . . . swelled exceedingly, yes, exceedingly. . . . swelled:** The structure here mirrors the action: the surging and growing of the waters.
18 **swelled:** Lit. "grew mighty." **floated:** Lit. "went."
22 **firm ground:** Heb. *harava*, lit. "dry-land." Hebrew has two words for
   "dry" (*harev* and *yavesh*), while English uses only one.
23 **blotted out:** Twice repeated, echoing God's promise in 6:7.

24 The waters swelled upon the earth for a hundred and fifty
   days.

8:1 But God paid mind to Noah and all living-things, all the
    animals that were with him in the Ark,
    and God brought a breath-of-wind across the earth, so that
    the waters abated.
  2 The well-springs of Ocean and the sluices of the heavens
    were dammed up,
    and the torrent from the heavens was held back.
  3 The waters returned from upon the earth, continually
    advancing and returning,
    and the waters diminished at the end of a hundred and fifty
    days.
  4 And the Ark came to rest in the seventh New-Moon, on the
    seventeenth day of the New-Moon, upon the mountains of
    Ararat.
  5 Now the waters continued to advance and diminish until the
    tenth New-Moon.
    On the tenth, on the first day of the New-Moon, the tops of
    the mountains could be seen.

  6 At the end of forty days it was: Noah opened the window of
  7   the Ark that he had made,/ and sent out a raven;
    it went off, going off and returning, until the waters were
    dried up from upon the earth.
  8 Then he sent out a dove from him, to see whether the
    waters had subsided from the face of the soil.
  9 But the dove found no resting-place for the sole of her foot,
    so she returned to him into the Ark,
    for there was water upon the face of all the earth.
    He sent forth his hand and took her, and brought her to
    him into the Ark.
 10 Then he waited yet another seven days
    and sent out the dove yet again from the Ark.
 11 The dove came back to him at eventime,
    and here—a freshly plucked olive leaf in her beak!
    So Noah knew
    that the waters had subsided from upon the earth.

12 Then he waited yet another seven days
   and sent out the dove,
   but she returned to him again no more.

13 And so it was in the six hundred and first year, in the
      beginning-month, on the first day of the New-Moon,
   that the waters left firm ground upon the earth.
   Noah removed the covering of the Ark and saw:
   here, the face of the soil was firm.
14 Now in the second New-Moon, on the twenty-seventh day
   of the New-Moon, the earth was completely dry.

15 God spoke to Noah, saying:
16 Go out of the Ark, you and your wife, your sons and your
   sons' wives with you.
17 All living-things that are with you, all flesh—fowl, animals,
   and all crawling things that crawl upon the earth,

---

were quick to concentrate on the parallels, but the differences are now recognized as being much more significant. In general one may say that in contrast to the earlier (Mesopotamian) versions the biblical one is unambiguous in both tone and intent. It has been placed in Genesis to exemplify a God who judges the world according to human behavior, punishes evil and rescues the righteous. This is a far cry from the earlier accounts, where the gods plan the destruction of the world for reasons that are unclear (or in one version, because mankind's noise is disturbing the sleep of the gods), and where the protagonist, Utnapishtim, is saved as the result of a god's favoritism without any moral judgments being passed.

8:1 **paid mind:** More than merely "remembered." **breath-of-wind:** Reminiscent of the "breath of God" at creation.
3,5 **advancing and returning. . . . advance and diminish:** Again, as in 7:17–20, the motion of the waters is suggested by means of sound.
  7 **sent out:** Or "released."
  8 **dove:** This bird is portrayed in the Bible as beautiful (even pure) and delicate. From this passage, of course, stems the popular use of the dove as the symbol of peace.
13 **left firm ground:** Or "were fully dried up" (see note to 7:22).

have them go out with you,
that they may swarm on earth, that they may bear fruit and
become many upon the earth.

18 So Noah went out, his sons, his wife, and his sons' wives
with him,
19 all living-things—all crawling things, and all fowl, all that
crawl about upon the earth,
according to their clans they went out of the Ark.

20 Noah built a slaughter-altar to YHWH.
He took from all pure animals and from all pure fowl
and offered up offerings upon the altar.
21 Now YHWH smelled the soothing smell
and YHWH said in his heart:
I will never doom the soil again on humankind's account,
since what the human heart forms is evil from its youth;
I will never again strike down all living-things, as I have
done;
22 (never) again, all the days of the earth, shall
sowing and harvest,
cold and heat,
summer and winter,
day and night
ever cease!

9:1 Now God blessed Noah and his sons and said to them:
Bear fruit and be many and fill the earth!
2 Your fear, your dread shall be upon all the wildlife of the
earth and upon all the fowl of the heavens,
all that crawls on the soil and all the fish of the sea—
into your hand they are given.
3 All things crawling about that live, for you shall they be, for
eating,
as with the green plants, I now give you all.
4 However: flesh with its life, its blood, you are not to eat!
5 However, too: for your blood, of your own lives, I will
demand satisfaction—
from all wild-animals I will demand it,

and from humankind, from every man regarding his
    brother,
demand satisfaction for human life.
6   Whoever now sheds human blood,
        for that human shall his blood be shed,
        for in God's image he made humankind.

Aftermath (8:20–9:19): The passages immediately following the Flood narrative speak of a God who is remarkably receptive to a human kind of change. From having been "sorry" that he created mankind (6:6), he now evinces a change of heart about the entire issue of human evil, conceding mankind's imperfections (8:21). In a wonderfully structured declaration, where "never again" moves in position from the middle to the beginning of the phrase (8:21–22), God as it were chooses to restrain his own ability to radically disturb the processes of nature. Where later on in Genesis the human characters exhibit the capacity to change, here it is God himself.

The blessing in 9:1–3 establishes Noah as a kind of second Adam (and it might be noted that chronologically Noah is the first man born after Adam dies). It repeats the basic formulation of the blessing in 1:28–30, with an important exception: meat-eating is now to be allowed, as part of God's concession to human nature. Previously only the plant world had been accessible to humankind for food. However—and this very word punctuates the text twice in 9:4–5—there is to be an accounting for willful bloodshed, as if to suggest that the eating of meat is being permitted only under strict conditions. To underscore the importance of this concept, the section about bloodshed uses the vocabulary of creation: human beings are made "in the image of God."

19 **clans:** Classifications.
20 **slaughter-altar:** Etymologically the word *mizbe'ah* hearkens back to a time when such sites were used mainly for animal sacrifice; the Bible cites other uses such as libations and cereal offerings. **offered up:** The Hebrew verb *('alo)* implies upward movement.
21 **smelled the soothing smell:** Conveyed by the sound in Hebrew, *va-yarah et re'ah ha-niho'ah.* **evil from its youth:** That is, evil already begins in what we might call adolescence. But Speiser renders it "from the start."
22 **sowing and harvest . . . :** The solemn promise is expressed in verse.
9:6 Whoever . . . : A poem which plays on the sounds of "humankind" (*adam*) and "blood" (*dam*): *Shofekh dam ha-adam/ ba-adam damo yishafekh.* For that human: Or "by humans."

7 As for you—bear fruit and be many, swarm on earth and
   become many on it!

8 God said to Noah and to his sons with him, saying:

9 As for me—here, I am about to establish my covenant with
   you and with your seed after you,

10 and with all living beings that are with you: fowl,
   herd-animals, and all the wildlife of the earth with you;
   all those going out of the Ark, of all the living-things of the
   earth.

11 I will establish my covenant with you:
   All flesh shall never be cut off again by waters of the
      Deluge,
      never again shall there be Deluge, to bring the earth
      to ruin!

12 And God said:
   This is the sign of the covenant which I set
   between me and you and all living beings that are with you,
      for ageless generations:

13 My bow I set in the clouds,
   so that it may serve as a sign of the covenant between me
      and the earth.

14 It shall be:
   when I becloud the earth with clouds
   and in the clouds the bow is seen,

15 I will call to mind my covenant
   that is between me and you and all living beings—all flesh:
      never again shall the waters become a Deluge, to bring
      all flesh to ruin!

16 When the bow is in the clouds,
   I will look at it,
   to call to mind the age-old covenant
   between God and all living beings—
   all flesh that is upon the earth.

17 God said to Noah:
   This is the sign of the covenant that I have established
      between me and all flesh that is upon the earth.

18 Noah's sons who went out of the Ark were Shem, Ham,
   and Yefet.

Now Ham is the father of Canaan.

19 These three were Noah's sons, and from these were
   scattered abroad all the earth-folk.

20 Now Noah was the first man of the soil; he planted a
   vineyard.
21 When he drank from the wine, he became drunk and
   exposed himself in the middle of his tent.
22 Ham, the father of Canaan, saw his father's nakedness
   and told his two brothers outside.
23 Then Shem and Yefet took a cloak, they put it on the
   shoulders of the two of them,
   and walked backward, to cover their father's nakedness.
   —Their faces were turned backward, their father's
   nakedness they did not see.

With verses 8 and 9 the key concept of "covenant" appears for the
first time in the Bible. It is accompanied, as is usual in the Bible, by a
symbol or "sign" (in this case, the rainbow). We are led back to the
creation story again, as other biblical texts speak of the Sabbath as a
"sign of the covenant" between God and Israel (e.g., Ex. 31:12–17).

The sixfold repetition of the phrase "never again" provides a thematic
unity in these passages.

Drunkenness and Nakedness (9:20–29): From the lofty poetry of God's
blessings and promises, we encounter an all-too-brief description of a
bizarre event. The soil, which evidently has not entirely shaken off its
primeval curse, proves once again to be a source of trouble. The nature
of the crime mentioned here ("seeing the father's nakedness") has been
variously interpreted; Buber and others see in it a reference to the sexual
"immorality" of the Canaanites, which the Israelites found particularly
abhorrent. This would explain the emphasis on the *son* of the culprit in
the story, rather than on the perpetrator.

A similar undistinguished ancestry is traced in Chapter 19, referring to
the incestuous origins of Israel's neighbors and frequent enemies, the
Moabites and Ammonites.

18 **Now Ham is the father of Canaan:** See repetition in the story to follow,
   verses 20–27.

24 Now when Noah awoke from his wine, it became known (to
him) what his littlest son had done to him.

25 He said:
Cursed be Canaan,
servant of servants may he be to his brothers!

26 And he said:
Blessed be YHWH, God of Shem,
but may Canaan be servant to them!

27 May God extend/*yaft*
Yefet,
let him dwell in the tents of Shem,
but may Canaan be servant to them!

28 And Noah lived after the Deluge three hundred years and
fifty years.

29 And all the days of Noah were nine hundred years and fifty
years,
then he died.

10:1 Now these are the begettings of the sons of Noah,
Shem, Ham, and Yefet.
Sons were born to them after the Deluge.

2 The Sons of Yefet are Gomer and Magog, Madai, Yavan
and Tuval, Meshekh and Tiras.

3 The Sons of Gomer are Ashkenaz, Rifat, and Togarma.

4 The Sons of Yavan are Elisha and Tarshish, Cittites and
Dodanites.

5 From these the seacoast nations were divided by their lands,
each one after its own tongue:
according to their clans, by their nations.

6 The Sons of Ham are Cush and Mitzrayim, Put and
Canaan.

7 The Sons of Cush are Seva and Havila, Savta, Ra'ma, and
Savtekha;
the Sons of Ra'ma—Sheva and Dedan.

8 Cush begot Nimrod; he was the first mighty man on earth.

9 He was a mighty hunter before YHWH,

therefore the saying is:
Like Nimrod, a mighty hunter before YHWH.
10 His kingdom, at the beginning, was Bavel, and Erekh,
   Accad and Calne, in the land of Shinar;
11/12 from this land Ashur went forth and built Nineveh—along
   with the city squares and Calah,/ and Resen between
   Nineveh and Calah—that is the great city.
13 Mitzrayim begot the Ludites, the Anamites, the Lehavites,
14   the Naftuhites,/ the Patrusites, and the Casluhites, from
   where the Philistines come, and the Caftorites.

The Table of the Nations (10): Genesis, with its typically ancient Near Eastern emphasis on "begettings," now traces the development of humanity from the sons of Noah. The key formula throughout is "their lands, their nations." Commentators have noted numerical unity in the list, citing a total of seventy nations (once repetitions are omitted) laid out in multiples of seven. That number, as we have indicated, represents the concept of totality and perfection in the Bible. Thus the stage is set for the Babel story of the next chapter, with its condemnation of man's attempt to forestall the divinely willed "scattering" into a well-ordered world.

Many of the names in this chapter have been identified (see Speiser), but some are still not known with certainty. Israel is conspicuous in its absence; despite the biblical narrative's ability to trace Israel's origins, those origins are meant to be seen not solely in biological terms but rather in God's choice. Similarly, Israel arises from women who begin as barren—thus pointing to divine intervention in history, rather than the perfectly normal account that we have here.

24 **littlest:** Or "youngest," difficult in the light of verse 18.
26 **to them:** Others use "to him."
10:2 **Sons:** Here, and later, it may mean "descendants."
4 **Dodanites:** Some read "Rodanites," following I Chron. 1:7.
6 **Mitzrayim:** The biblical name for Egypt (the modern Egyptian name is *Misr*).
8 **mighty man:** Three times here; clearly Nimrod was well known as an ancient hero.
10 **Calne:** Some read *culanna*, "all of them."
11 **city squares:** Some read this as a name, "Rehovot-Ir."
14 **Casluhites . . . Caftorites:** Some reverse the order; the Bible often speaks of the origins of the Philistines in Caftor (Crete).

15/16 Canaan begot Tzidon his firstborn and Het,/ along with the
   17   Yevusite, the Amorite and the Girgashite,/ the Hivvite,
   18   the Arkite and the Sinite,/ the Arvadite, the Tzemarite
         and the Hamatite.
         Afterward the Canaanite clans were scattered abroad.
   19   And the Canaanite territory went from Tzidon, then as you
         come toward Gerar, as far as Gaza, then as you come
         toward Sedom and Amora, Adma, and Tzevoyim, as far
         as Lasha.
   20   These are the Sons of Ham after their clans, after their
         tongues, by their lands, by their nations.

   21   (Children) were also born to Shem,
         the father of all the Sons of Ever (and) Yefet's older
             brother.
   22   The Sons of Shem are Elam and Ashur, Arpakhshad, Lud,
         and Aram.
   23   The Sons of Aram are Utz and Hul, Geter and Mash.
   24   Arpakhshad begot Shelah, Shelah begot Ever.
   25   Two sons were born to Ever:
         the name of the first one was Peleg/Splitting, for in his days
             the earth-folk were split up,
         and his brother's name was Yoktan.
26/27 Yoktan begot Almodad and Shelef, Hatzarmavet and Yera,/
28/29   Hadoram, Uzal and Dikla,/ Oval, Avimael and Sheva,/
         Ofir, Havila, and Yovav—all these are the Sons of
         Yoktan.
   30   Now their settlements went from Mesha, then as you come
         toward Sefar, to the mountain-country of the east.
   31   These are the Sons of Shem after their clans, after their
         tongues, by their lands, after their nations.

   32   These are the clan-groupings of the Sons of Noah, after
         their begettings, by their nations.
         From these the nations were divided on earth after the
         Deluge.

11:1 Now all the earth was of one language and one set-of-words.

2 And it was when they migrated to the east that they found a
  valley in the land of Shinar and settled there.
3 They said, each man to his fellow:
  Come-now! Let us bake bricks and let us burn them
    well-burnt!
  So for them brick-stone was like building-stone, and
    raw-bitumen was for them like red-mortar.
4 Now they said:
  Come-now! Let us build ourselves a city and a tower, its
    top in the heavens,
  and let us make ourselves a name,
  lest we be scattered over the face of all the earth!
5 But YHWH came down to look over the city and the tower
  that the humans were building.

The Unfinished Citadel (11:1–9): At its most obvious, in an isolated
context, this famous story is about the overweening pride of man, as
represented by his technology. God's actions here recall the ending of the
garden story, where humanity was also within reach of the divine.

Yet more is involved than a threat. Buber felt that this episode has
been inserted at this point to show that mankind has failed again, as at
the time of the Flood. It has not spread out and divided into nations, as
in Chapter 10. The failure paves the way for a new divine plan, which is
to be realized through one man (Avraham) and his descendants.

Structurally, the story is a tiny literary masterpiece. It utilizes numerous plays on sound which make meaningful and often ironic linkages
between sections and ideas in the text. Most significant is how the general message—that God's response occurs in exactly the same terms as
the human challenge (i.e., divine justice)—is transmitted by means of
form. Fokkelman has provided a detailed study; it will suffice here to
indicate only the outline. The divine "Come-now!" of verse 7 clearly
stands as an answer to mankind's identical cry in verses 3 and 4. In

15 **Yevusite,** etc.: Collective names.
11:1 **language;** Lit. "lip."
3 **so . . . brick-stone . . . :** An explanation of Mesopotamian building techniques for the Hebrew audience. The text plays on sound (*levena . . .
  le-aven, hemer . . . la-homer*).   **raw-bitumen:** Asphalt, used for making ce-
  ment.
4 **make . . . a name:** That is, make sure that we and our works will endure.

6 YHWH said:
Here, (they are) one people with one language for them all,
   and this is merely the first of their doings—
now there will be no barrier for them in all that they devise
   to do!
7 Come-now! Let us go down and there let us baffle their
   language,
so that no man will understand the language of his fellow.
8 So YHWH scattered them from there over the face of all
   the earth,
and they had to stop building the city.
9 Therefore its name was called Bavel/Babble,
for there YHWH baffled the language of all the earth-folk,
and from there, YHWH scattered them over the face of all
   the earth.

10 These are the begettings of Shem:
Shem was a hundred years old, then he begot Arpakhshad,
   two years after the Deluge,
11 and Shem lived after he begot Arpakhshad five hundred
   years, and begot other sons and daughters.
12 Arpakhshad lived thirty-five years, then he begot Shelah,
13 and Arpakhshad lived after he begot Shelah three years and
   four hundred years, and begot other sons and daughters.
14 Shelah lived thirty years, then he begot Ever,
15 and Shelah lived after he begot Ever three years and four
   hundred years, and begot other sons and daughters.
16 When Ever had lived thirty-four years, he begot Peleg,
17 and Ever lived after he begot Peleg thirty years and four
   hundred years, and begot other sons and daughters.
18 When Peleg had lived thirty years, he begot Re'u,
19 and Peleg lived after he begot Re'u nine years and two
   hundred years, and begot other sons and daughters.
20 When Re'u had lived thirty-two years, he begot Serug,
21 and Re'u lived after he begot Serug seven years and two
   hundred years, and begot other sons and daughers.
22 When Serug had lived thirty years, he begot Nahor,
23 and Serug lived after he begot Nahor two hundred years,
   and begot other sons and daughters.

24 When Nahor had lived twenty-nine years, he begot Terah,
25 and Nahor lived after he begot Terah nineteen years and a
    hundred years, and begot other sons and daughters.
26 When Terah had lived seventy years, he begot Avram,
    Nahor, and Haran.

27 Now these are the begettings of Terah:

---

addition man, who congregated in order to establish a "name" and to avoid being "scattered over the face of all the earth" (v.4), is contravened by the action of God, resulting in the ironic name "Babble" and a subsequent "scattering" of humanity (v.9). The text is thus another brilliant example of biblical justice, a statement about a world view in which the laws of justice and morality are as neatly balanced as we like to think the laws of nature are.

There is an important cultural background to the story. "Shinar" refers to Mesopotamia, and the "tower," undoubtedly, to the ubiquitous *ziggurratu* (now unearthed by archeologists) which served as man-made sacred mountains (i.e., temples). By portraying an unfinished tower, by dispersing the builders, and by in essence making fun of the mighty name of Babylon, the text functions effectively to repudiate the culture from which the people of Israel sprang (Avram's "Ur" of 11:28 was probably the great Mesopotamian metropolis). From Chapter 12 on, a new world view is created.

Noah to Avram (11:10–32): Here are enumerated another ten generations, making the orderly connection between the origins of the world (Noah was viewed as a second Adam) and the origins of the people of Israel. The life spans are considerably shorter than those of Chapter 5, yet some sort of careful number scheme seems evident here as well (see Cassuto).

Beginning with verse 26 we are introduced to Avram, with little hint of what is to come in his momentous life. For the moment he is only a son, a brother, and a husband, and a man whose early life is marked principally by the death of the old world (Haran and Terah), with little hope for the new (his wife is barren).

10 **two years after the Deluge:** Possibly a typical popular way of telling time
    (see Amos 1:1, "two years after the earthquake").
26 **Avram:** Trad. English "Abram."

Terah begot Avram, Nahor, and Haran;
and Haran begot Lot.

28 Haran died in the presence of Terah his father in the land
   of his kindred, in Ur of the Chaldeans.

29 Avram and Nahor took themselves wives;
   the name of Avram's wife was Sarai,
   the name of Nahor's wife was Milca—daughter of Haran,
   father of Milca and father of Yisca.

30 Now Sarai was barren, she had no child.

31 Terah took Avram his son and Lot son of Haran, his son's
   son, and Sarai his daughter-in-law, wife of Avram his son,
   they set out together from Ur of the Chaldeans, to go to the
   land of Canaan.
   But when they had come as far as Harran, they settled
   there.

32 And the days of Terah were five years and two hundred
   years,
   then Terah died,
   in Harran.

28 **in the presence of Terah his father:** During his father's lifetime. **Chalde-ans:** An anachronism; see Speiser.

30 **barren, she had no child:** This doubling is characteristic of biblical style (formal poetry in the Bible uses parallelism of lines).

31 **Harran:** An important city and center of moon worship, like Ur. The name means "crossroads."

THE PATRIARCHAL NARRATIVES

THE STORIES about the fathers and mothers of Israel, as a collection, are almost contrapuntal in their richness. Life experiences are repeated and common themes recur; yet at the same time there is a remarkable variety of personalities.

Two prominent themes throughout are God's promises (of land and descendants) and his blessing. The texts revolve around the question of whether and how God will fulfill his promises, and how man will effect the transfer of the blessing. Each generation portrayed in the narratives must deal with the inherent tensions raised by these questions, since their resolution does not occur easily.

The stories are also marked by each figure's struggle to develop a concept of the religious life, of "walking in accord with God." Each one carves out his own distinct path, to arrive at a mature understanding of what it means to be a father of the people of Israel. In order to bring about such an understanding, God apparently "tests" them in both obvious and more oblique ways, often against a backdrop of bitter sibling rivalry. One also observes a physical unsettledness about the Patriarchs' quest; only Yitzhak is spared the wanderings that occur so regularly in the stories.

Rather interestingly, although the texts purport to be about "fathers," it is God himself who most consistently fits that role for the characters. God acts *in loco parentis* for each of the Patriarchs, always, significantly, after the loss of the human father. He first appears to Avraham after the death of Terah; to Yitzhak after that of Avraham; to Yaakov after he leaves home (and a seemingly dying father); and he helps Yosef directly, after he has left his father's home.

Numbers play an important role in the Patriarchal stories, as they did in Part I. It has been pointed out (see Sarna) that the life spans of the Patriarchs fit into a highly ordered pattern. Avraham lives for 175 years, equaling 7×5^2; Yitzhak, for 180 years, equaling 5×6^2; and Yaakov, for 147 years, or 3×7^2. This is unmistakably a purposeful scheme, meant to convey that human history is orderly and meaningful. Similarly an examination of the stories reveals that Avraham lives for 75 years in the lifetime of his father and 75 years in the lifetime of his son, while Yaakov spends 20 years away from his father, with Yosef roughly following suit in the next generation.

Last, it should be noted that the Patriarchal stories in various details anticipate the later Exodus of the Israelites from Egypt. The specific references will be mentioned in the Notes.

PART II Avraham
(12–25:18)

ALTHOUGH Avraham is the biological father of Israel, the diverse traditions about him which have been collected and connected to form a cycle of stories give evidence of much more. The cycle portrays an active *Homo religiosus* who converses with God, sometimes with an air of doubt and questioning, who proclaims God's name at various sacred sites, who is concerned about justice and the treatment of the oppressed, and who makes dramatic life decisions without flinching. The stories thus reveal struggle, despite the fact that Avraham often appears to be the "perfect" man, always obeying God's bidding and prospering.

Buber, noting the unifying effect of the verb "see" throughout the cycle, understood Avraham as the father of the Prophets of Israel (formerly called "seers"). He also viewed the cycle as based around the series of tests that Avraham must undergo, tests quite different, we might add, from the labors of Hercules and other such ancient challenges.

Other than "see," a number of leading-words launch the major concerns of the Patriarchs: "bless," "seed," and "land." At the same time the cycle contains previously encountered motifs, albeit with interesting refinements: punishment for sin (this time, with man's questioning), intimacy with God (here through visions), and sibling rivalry (with more complex results than murder). Above all we note the singling out of one man to perform the will of God, a man very different from the rather passive Noah.

Avraham stands at the core of the entire book of Genesis, as his experiences will in many ways be reflected in those who follow him. At the core of both the book and the cycle looms the disturbing Chapter 22, which brings together and resolves, for the moment, the major themes encountered so far.

12:1 YHWH said to Avram:
Go-you-forth
from your land,
from your kindred,
from your father's house,
to the land that I will let you see.
2 I will make a great nation of you
and will give-you-blessing
and will make your name great.
Be a blessing!
3 I will bless those who bless you,
he who reviles you, I will curse.
All the clans of the soil will find blessing through you!

4 Avram went, as YHWH had spoken to him, and Lot went
with him.
And Avram was five years and seventy years old when he
went out of Harran.
5 Avram took Sarai his wife and Lot his brother's son, all
their property that they had gained, and the persons
whom they had made-their-own in Harran,
and they went out to go to the land of Canaan.
When they came to the land of Canaan,
6 Avram passed through the land, as far as the Place of
Shekhem, as far as the Oak of Moreh.
Now the Canaanite was then in the land.

7 YHWH was seen by Avram and said:
I give this land to your seed!
He built an altar there to YHWH who had been seen by
him.
8 He moved on from there to the mountain-country, east of
Bet-El,
and spread his tent, Bet-El toward the sea and Ai toward
the east.
There he built an altar to YHWH
and called out the name of YHWH.
9 Then Avram journeyed on, continually journeying to the
Negev/ the Southland.

10 Now there was a famine in the land,
   and Avram went down to Egypt, to sojourn there,
   for the famine was heavy in the land.
11 It was when he came near to Egypt that he said to Sarai his
   wife:
   Now here, I know well that you are a woman fair to look
   at.
12 It will be, when the Egyptians see you and say: She is his
   wife,
   that they will kill me, but you they will allow to live.

The Call and the Journey (12:1–9): The Avraham cycle begins decisively, with a command from God to leave the past behind and go to an unnamed land. Prominent in this speech, clearly, is the concept of blessing, which will be realized by the gifts of land (Canaan) and seed (Yitzhak, the son).

The classic mythological motif of the journey, where the hero meets such dangers as monsters and giants, has here been avoided. All that the text wishes us to know about is God's speech and Avram's immediate obedience; as in Chapter 22, all other details of the actual trip have been omitted.

The Wife—I (12:10–20): Almost immediately upon his arrival in the promised land Avram is forced to leave it. It will be his son Yitzhak's task to remain there on a more permanent basis.

This is the first of three such stories which are practically identical (see Chapters 20 and 26). All pose a challenge for the interpreter. An honored

12:1 **kindred:** Others use "birthplace."
   3 **find blessing:** Or "seek to be blessed (as you)."
   5 **property . . . gained:** Heb. *rekhusham . . . rakhashu.*
   6 **Place:** Possibly with the implication of "sacred place." **Oak:** Some read "valley." **Moreh:** Some, like Buber, interpret this as "sage." **the Canaanite:** The peoples inhabiting the land at the time of the Israelite conquest under Joshua; see also 13:7.
   7 **was seen:** Others use "appeared to," which is more comfortable in English. "See" has been kept here as a leading word in the Avraham cycle.
   8 **toward the sea:** West.
  10 **sojourn:** To reside temporarily, as an alien. **heavy:** Severe.

13 Pray say that you are my sister
so that it may go well with me on your account, that I
myself may live thanks to you.

14 It was when Avram came to Egypt, that the Egyptians saw
how exceedingly fair the woman was;

15 when Pharaoh's courtiers saw her, they praised her to
Pharaoh,
and the woman was taken away into Pharaoh's house.

16 It went well with Avram on her account,
sheep and oxen, he-asses, servants and maids, she-asses and
camels, became his.

17 But YHWH plagued Pharaoh with great plagues, and also
his house, because of Sarai, Avram's wife.

18 Pharaoh had Avram called, and said:
What is this that you have done to me!
Why did you not tell me that she is your wife?

19 Why did you say: She is my sister?
—So I took her for myself as a wife.
But now, here is your wife, take her and go!

20 So Pharaoh put men in charge of him, who escorted him
and his wife and all that was his.

13:1 Avram traveled up from Egypt, he and his wife and all that
was his, and Lot with him, to the Southland.

2 And Avram was exceedingly heavily laden with livestock,
with silver and with gold.

3 He went on his journeyings from the Southland as far as
Bet-El, as far as the place where his tent had been at the
first, between Bet-El and Ai,

4 to the place of the altar that he had made there at
the beginning.
There Avram called out the name of YHWH.

5 Now also Lot, who had gone with Avram, had sheep and
oxen and tents.

6 And the land could not support them, to settle together,
for their property was so great that they were not able to
settle together.

7 So there was a quarrel between the herdsmen of Avram's
   livestock and the herdsmen of Lot's livestock.
   Now the Canaanite and the Perizzite were then settled in
   the land.
8 Avram said to Lot:
   Pray let there be no quarreling between me and you,
      between my herdsmen and your herdsmen,
   for we are brother men!

---

man of God seeks to save his own skin by passing his wife off as his
sister; in each case the Patriarch emerges safely and with increased
wealth.

Speiser has tried to use the analogy of Hurrian (i.e., from Harran) law
in which a wife can be elevated to the status of "sister" as one element in
the expansion of her status. The legal background, however, is unclear
and may not be decisive here. Coming as it does after God's promise to
biologically found "a great nation" (v.2) through Avram, the story in its
first version is probably best understood as an example of God's protection not only of the key male figure, but of the Matriarch as well.
Harming Sarai, or even the threat of violating her sexuality, brings with
it divine punishment. In addition the story also enables Avram to expand
his wealth—itself a sign of God's favor and the Patriarch's importance or
"weightiness" (see Polzin).

Lot; The Land (13): We return to the theme of the land. Not for the last
time, Avram's nephew Lot is used as a foil. Their "parting" shows how
Lot makes a bad choice—the "wicked and sinful" area of Sedom and
Amora—while Avram settles "in the land of Canaan," which had been
promised to him. From here (vv.14ff.), Avram is given God's twofold
promise again, with that of descendants being spelled out more vividly
this time.

This section is linked to the previous one by the repetition of the
phrase "he and his wife and all that was his."

15 **Pharaoh:** Heb. *Par'o.* This is an Egyptian title, "(Lord of) the Great
   House," and not a name.
13:2 **heavily laden:** Rich.
   8 **brother men:** Relatives.

9 Is not all the land before you?
Pray part from me!
If to the left, then I to the right,
if to the right, then I to the left.

10 Lot lifted up his eyes and saw all the plain of the Jordan—
how well-watered was it all, before YHWH brought ruin
upon Sedom and Amora,
like YHWH's garden, like the land of Egypt, as you come
toward Tzo'ar.

11 So Lot chose for himself all the plain of the Jordan.
Lot journeyed eastward, and they parted, each man from
the other:

12 Avram settled in the land of Canaan, while Lot settled in
the cities of the plain, pitching-his-tent near Sedom.

13 Now the men of Sedom were exceedingly wicked and sinful
before YHWH.

14 YHWH said to Avram, after Lot had parted from him:
Pray lift up your eyes and see from the place where you are,
northward, southward, eastward, seaward:

15 indeed, all the land that you see, I give it to you
and to your seed, for the ages.

16 I will make your seed like the dust of the ground,
so that if a man were able to measure the dust of the
ground, so too could your seed be measured.

17 Up, walk about through the land in its length and in its
breadth,
for I give it to you.

18 Avram moved-his-tent and came and settled by the oaks of
Mamre, which are by Hevron.
There he built an altar to YHWH.

14:1 Now it was in the days of Amrafel king of Shinar, Aryokh
king of Ellasar, Kedorla'omer king of Elam, and Tidal
king of Goyim:

2 They prepared for battle against Bera king of Sedom, Birsha
king of Amora, Shinav king of Adma, Shemever king of
Tzevoyim, and the king of Bela—that is now Tzo'ar.

3 All these joined together in the valley of
Siddim/Limestone—that is now the Salt Sea.

4 For twelve years they had been subservient to
   Kedorla'omer,
   and in the thirteenth year they had revolted,
5 but then in the fourteenth year came Kedorla'omer and the
   kings who were with him,
   they struck the Refaites in Ashterot-Karnayim, the Zuzites
6 in Ham, the Emites in Shaveh-Kiryatayim, /and the
   Horites in their mountain-country of Se'ir near El Paran,
   which is by the wilderness.
7 As they returned, they came to En Mishpat/Judgment
   Spring —that is now Kadesh,
   and struck all the territory of the Amalekites and also the
   Amorites, who were settled in Hatzatzon-Tamar.

War and Rescue (14): Abruptly Avram is presented in a new light: that of
successful warrior (see Muffs). Consistent with his character as we will
come to know it, he stands by his kinsman, acts intrepidly, and refuses
the spoils of war. Equally important, he is respected by foreigners, a
theme will will return both in Genesis and later. Perhaps this very different story has been included here as part of the early sections of the cycle
in order to establish Avram's status and stature. He is no longer merely a
wanderer but well on the road to becoming a powerful local figure.

   Whether the events described in this chapter are historical or part of
an elaborate symbolic or mythical scheme has been the subject of debate
among biblical scholars. The issue, barring unexpected archeological
finds, is likely to remain unsolved.

   The story is constructed around a geographical framework, using the
formula "—that is now *x*—" to identify older sites for a contemporary
audience. The one place which is *not* identified, the "Shalem" of verse
18, may well be Jerusalem. If so, this would substantiate the city's claim
to holiness. Historically it was not conquered until King David's reign in
the tenth century B.C.E.

   9 **before you:** Possibly a legal term concerning boundaries.   **left . . . right:**
   North and south.
  10 **YHWH brought ruin:** See Chapter 19.   **Sedom and Amora:** Trad. English "Sodom and Gomorrah."
  14 **seaward:** Westward.
14:3 **the Salt Sea:** The Dead Sea.

8 Then out marched the king of Sedom, the king of Amora,
   the king of Adma, the king of Tzevoyim, and the king of
   Bela—that is now Tzo'ar;
   they set-their-ranks against them in battle in the valley of
   Siddim,
9 against Kedorla'omer king of Elam, Tidal king of Goyim,
   Amrafel king of Shinar, and Aryokh king of Ellasar—
   four kings against the five.
10 Now the valley of Siddim is pit after pit of bitumen,
   and when the kings of Sedom and Amora fled, they flung
   themselves therein,
   while those who remained fled to the mountain-country.
11 Now they took all the property of Sedom and Amora and all
   their food, and went away,
12 and they took Lot and all his property—the son of Avram's
   brother—and went away,
   for he had settled in Sedom.
13 One who escaped came and told Avram the Hebrew—
   he was dwelling by the Oaks of Mamre the Amorite,
   brother of Eshcol and brother of Aner,
   they were Avram's covenant-allies.
14 When Avram heard that his brother had been taken
   prisoner,
   he drew out his retainers, his house-born slaves, eighteen
   and three hundred, and went in pursuit as far as Dan.
15 He split up (his forces) against them in the night, he and
   his servants, and struck them and pursued them as far as
   Hova, which is to the north of Damascus.
16 But he returned all the property, and he also returned his
   brother Lot and his property, and also the women and the
   other people.
17 The king of Sedom went out to meet him upon his return
   from the strike against Kedorla'omer and against the
   kings that were with him, to the valley of Shaveh—that is
   now the King's Valley.

18 Now Malki-Tzedek, king of Shalem, brought out bread and
   wine,

—for he was priest of God Most-High,
19 and gave him blessing and said:
Blessed be Avram by God Most-High,
Founder of Heaven and Earth!
20 And blessed be God Most-High,
who has delivered your oppressors into your hand!
He gave him a tenth of everything.

21 The king of Sedom said to Avram:
Give me the persons, and the property take for yourself.
22 Avram said to the king of Sedom:
I raise my hand in the presence of YHWH, God
Most-High,
Founder of Heaven and Earth,
23 if from a thread to a sandal-strap—if I should take from
anything that is yours . . . !
So that you should not say: I made Avram rich.
24 Nothing for me!
Only what the lads have consumed,
and the share of the men who went with me—Aner, Eshcol,
and Mamre,
let them take their share.

---

10 **bitumen:** Asphalt. **flung themselves:** Others use "fell."
12 **—the son of Avram's brother—:** The Hebrew places the phrase after
"property," not after "Lot," as would be comfortable in English. **for he
had settled:** The story abounds in similar explanatory phrases, which could
almost be put in parentheses.
14 **brother:** Kinsman.
15 **North:** lit., "left."
18 **Malki-Tzedek:** Trad. English "Melchizedek." The name is a Hebrew one,
and the character appears as if from nowhere. **Shalem:** Identified with the
later Jerusalem. **God Most-High:** Heb. *El Elyon.*
20 **a tenth:** Like the tithe later given to Israelite priests.
22 **I raise my hand:** I swear.
23 **from a thread to a sandal-strap:** As in "from A to Z," or "anything at all."
24 **lads:** Servants.

15:1 After these events YHWH's word came to Avram in a
        vision,
     saying:
     Be not afraid, Avram,
     I am a delivering-shield to you,
     your reward is exceedingly great.
  2 Avram said:
     My Lord, YHWH,
     what would you give me—
     for I am going (to die) disgraced,
     and the Son Domestic of My House is Damascan Eliezer.
  3 And Avram said further:
     Here, to me you have not given seed,
     here, the Son of My House must be my heir.
  4 But here, YHWH's word (came) to him, saying:
     This one shall not be heir to you,
     rather, the one that goes out from your own body, he shall
        be heir to you.
  5 He brought him outside and said:
     Pray look toward the heavens and count the stars,
     can you count them?
     And he said to him:
     So shall your seed be.
  6 Now he trusted in YHWH,
     and he deemed it as righteousness on his part.

  7 Now he said to him:
     I am YHWH
     who brought you out of Ur of the Chaldeans
     to give you this land, to inherit it.
  8 But he said:
     My Lord, YHWH,
     by what shall I know that I will inherit it?
  9 He said to him:
     Fetch me a calf of three, a she-goat of three, a ram of three,
        a turtle-dove, and a fledgling.
 10 He fetched him all these.

He halved them down the middle, putting each one's half
   toward its fellow,
but the birds he did not halve.
11 Vultures descended upon the carcasses,
   but Avram drove them back.
12 Now it was, when the sun was setting,
   that deep slumber fell upon Avram—
   and here, fright and great darkness falling upon him!

The Covenant between the Pieces (15): Amid scenes of great drama and
almost mystery, a number of significant motifs are presented: (1) Avram's expressions of doubt that God will keep his promise about descendants (thus heightening the tension and final miracle of Yitzhak's birth);
(2) the linking of the Patriarch to the event of the Exodus centuries later;
and (3) the "cutting" of a covenant, in a manner well known in the
ancient world. This last motif, especially with its setting of "great darkness" and "night-blackness," takes Avram far beyond the earlier figure
of Noah into a special and fateful relationship with God.

15:1 **YHWH's word came:** A formula often used by the Prophets. Avram is
    portrayed as their spiritual ancestor (Buber).
  2 **disgraced:** Heb. *ariri;* B-R uses "bare-of-children." **Son Domestic . . .
    Damascan:** Hebrew difficult. The translation here reflects the play on
    sound (Heb. *"ben meshek . . . dammesek"*).
  3 **Son of My House:** The chief servant, who could inherit the estate in
    certain circumstances. Note the play on "son": the Hebrew here is *ben beti,*
    while *ben* alone means "son." **heir:** Three times here, indicating Avram's
    main concern.
  6 **he deemed it:** "He" refers to God.
  7 **who brought you out:** Like the later "I am YHWH your God, who
    brought you out of the land of Egypt" (Ex. 20:2). The language is undoubt-
    edly intentional.
  8 **But he said:** Avram, having just demonstrated trust in verse 6, now ex-
    presses deep doubt.
  9 **of three:** I.e., three years old, and presumably mature and ritually fit for
    sacrifice.
  12 **deep slumber:** Not the conventional sleep, it is almost always sent by God
    in the Bible (see 2:21, for example). The result here is "fright and great
    darkness."

13 And he said to Avram:
   You must know, yes, know
   that your seed will be sojourners in a land not theirs;
   they will put them in servitude and afflict them
   for four hundred years.
14 But the nation to which they are in servitude—I will bring
      judgment on them,
   and after that they will go out with great property.
15 As for you, you will go to your fathers in peace;
   you will be buried at a good ripe-age.
16 But in the fourth generation they will return here,
   for the punishment of the Amorite has not been paid-in-full
      heretofore.
17 Now it was, when the sun had set,
   that there was night-blackness,
   and here, a smoking oven, a fiery torch
   that crossed between those pieces.

18 On that day
   YHWH cut a covenant with Avram,
   saying: I give this land to your seed,
   from the River of Egypt to the Great River, the river
      Euphrates,
19 the Kenite and the Kenizzite and the Kadmonite,
20 and the Hittite and the Perizzite and the Refaites,
21 and the Amorite and the Canaanite and the Girgashite and
      the Yevusite.

16:1 Now Sarai, Avram's wife, had not borne him (children).
    She had an Egyptian maid—her name was Hagar.
  2 Sarai said to Avram:
    Now here, YHWH has obstructed me from bearing;
    pray come in to my maid,
    perhaps I may be built-up-with-sons through her!
    Avram hearkened to Sarai's voice:
  3 Sarai, Avram's wife, took Hagar the Egyptian-woman, her
      maid,
    at the end of ten years of Avram's being settled in the land
      of Canaan,

and gave her to her husband Avram as a wife for him.
4 He came in to Hagar, and she became pregnant.
But when she saw that she was pregnant, her mistress
    became of light worth in her eyes.
5 Sarai said to Avram:
The wrong done me is upon you!
I myself gave my maid into your bosom,
but now that she sees that she is pregnant, I have become of
    light worth in her eyes.
May YHWH see-justice-done between me and you!

The Firstborn Son (16): In the face of Sarai's inability to bear children,
Avram is given the legitimate option of producing an heir through her
maid, Hagar. Somewhat embarrassing to later interpreters, this practice
was nevertheless common in the ancient Near East (see also 30:3ff.,
30:9ff.). Hagar abuses her temporarily exalted position (as her son Yishmael apparently does in a parallel story, in Chapter 21), but is saved by
God's intervention. The motif of "affliction" is continued from Chapter
15 (here, in vv.6, 9, and 11); also mentioned three times is God's "hearkening" (hence the name Yishmael/God Hearkens). Buber understood this
vocabulary to allude to the Exodus story, which in its early chapters uses
the same terms.

Although Yishmael is not ultimately the chosen heir, he is nonetheless
protected by God (see 21:20) and is eventually made into "a great nation" (17:20), as befits a child of Avram.

13 **afflict:** Looking toward the "affliction" of the Israelites in Egypt (Ex. 1:11,
    12).
15 **ripe-age:** Lit. "grayness" or "hoariness."
16 **But in the fourth generation . . . :** God here speaks of the future conquest
    of Canaan by Avram's descendants. The natives (here termed "Amorites")
    are viewed as having forfeited their right to the land by their immorality
    (see Lev. 18:25–8).
18 **cut:** Concluded; the usage is influenced by the act of cutting animals by the
    parties involved, as in this story.
19 **the Kenite . . . :** Canaanite tribes, here presented as a round ten in num-
    ber.
16:2 **built-up-with-sons:** Heb. *ibbane,* a play on *bano* (build) and *ben* (son).
   3 **wife:** Or "concubine."
   4 **became of light worth in her eyes:** A Hebrew idiom. *New Jewish Version:*
    "was lowered in her esteem."

6 Avram said to Sarai:
Here, your maid is in your hand, deal with her however
seems good in your eyes.
Sarai afflicted her, so that she had to flee from her.
7 But YHWH's messenger found her by a spring of water in
the wilderness, by the spring on the way to Shur.
8 He said:
Hagar, Sarai's maid, whence do you come, whither are you
going?
She said:
I am fleeing from Sarai my mistress.
9 YHWH's messenger said to her:
Return to your mistress and let yourself be afflicted under
her hand!
10 And YHWH's messenger said to her:
I will make your seed many, yes, many, it will be too many
to count!
11 And YHWH's messenger said to her:
Here, you are pregnant,
you will bear a son;
call his name: Yishmael/God Hearkens,
for God has hearkened to your being afflicted.
12 He shall be a wild-ass of a man,
his hand against all, hand of all against him,
yet in the presence of all his brothers shall he dwell.
13 Now she called the name of YHWH, the one who was
speaking to her:
You God of Seeing!
For she said:
Have I actually gone on seeing here
after his seeing me?
14 Therefore the well was called:
Well of the Living-One Who-Sees-Me.
Here, it is between Kadesh and Bered.

15 Hagar bore Avram a son,
and Avram called the name of the son whom Hagar bore:
Yishmael.
16 Avram was eighty years and six years when Hagar bore
Yishmael to Avram.

17:1 Now when Avram was ninety years and nine years
       YHWH was seen by Avram and said to him:
       I am God Shaddai.
       Walk in my presence! And be whole!
    2 I set my covenant between me and you,
       I will make you exceedingly, exceedingly many.

The Covenant of Circumcision (17): As Plaut notes, up to this point the
covenant betwen God and Avram has been rather one-sided. In this
chapter Avram is given a command to perform—not only of circumcision, but to be moral and upright (v.1, expanded in 18:19). Circumcision
is but the symbol of the ongoing imperative to do "what is just."

In many societies circumcision has been connected directly to puberty
and marriage, usually taking place (as it does here to Yishmael) at around
the age of thirteen. Our passage's moving back of the rite essentially to
birth is a daring reinterpretation, at once defusing the act of exclusively
sexual content while at the same time suggesting that the covenant, a
lifelong commitment, is nevertheless passed down biologically through
the generations. The males of the tribe are not simply made holy for
marriage. They bear the mark upon their bodies as a sacred reminder of
their mission.

The chapter echoes with repetition: "exceedingly, exceedingly" (vv.6

6 **afflicted:** Or "abused," "maltreated."
7 **YHWH's messenger:** Traditionally "angel," but the English word stems
   from the Greek *angelos,* which also means "messenger." In Genesis God's
   messengers seem to be quite human in appearance, and are sometimes
   taken for God himself (see 18:2ff.).
10 **too many to count:** Apparently fulfilling God's blessing and promise to
   Avram in 15:5. Until 17:16, nothing indicates that Yishmael is not Avram's
   long-awaited heir.
11 **Yishmael:** Trad. English "Ishmael."
13 **Have I actually gone on seeing . . . :** Heb. obscure. Hagar possibly is
   expressing surprise that she survived her encounter with God.
17:1 **Ninety years and nine years:** Thirteen years have elapsed since the events
   of the previous chapter. Now that Yishmael is entering puberty, God can
   no longer conceal that he is not the promised heir. See verses 16, 18.
   Shaddai: Hebrew obscure. Traditionally translated "Almighty"; others use
   "of the mountains." In Genesis the name is most often tied to promises of
   human fertility, as in verse 2.   **Walk . . . be whole:** Contrasted to Noah
   (6:9), Avram is a genuine religious man who lives his faith actively.
    2 **set:** Heb. *va-ettena.* The root *ntn* is repeated throughout the chapter (as
   "make" in verses 5 and 6, and as "give" in verses 8 and 16).

3 Avram fell upon his face.
  God spoke with him,
  saying:
4 As for me,
  here, my covenant is with you,
  so that you will become the father of a throng of nations.
5   No longer shall your name be called Avram,
        rather shall your name be Avraham,
        for I will make you *Av Hamon Goyyim*/Father of a
        Throng of Nations!
6 I will cause you to bear fruit exceedingly, exceedingly,
  I will make nations of you,
  (yes,) kings will go out from you!
7 I establish my covenant between me and you and your seed
    after you, into their generations as a covenant for the
    ages,
  to be God to you and to your seed after you.
8 I will give to you and to your seed after you, the land of
    your sojournings, all the land of Canaan, as a holding for
    the ages,
  and I will be God to them.
9 God said to Avraham:
  As for you,
  you are to keep my covenant, you and your seed after you,
    into their generations.
10 This is my covenant which you are to keep, between me
    and you and your seed after you:
  every male among you shall be circumcised.
11 You shall circumcise the flesh of your foreskin,
  so that it may serve as a sign of the covenant between me
    and you.
12 At eight days old, every male among you shall be
    circumcised, into your generations,
  whether house-born or bought with money from any
    foreigner, who is not your seed.
13 Circumcised, yes, circumcised shall be your house-born and
    your money-bought (slaves),
  so that my covenant may be in your flesh as a covenant for
    the ages.

14 But a foreskinned male,
   who does not have the foreskin of his flesh circumcised,
   that person shall be cut off from his kinspeople—
   he has broken my covenant!
15 God said to Avraham:
   As for Sarai your wife—you shall not call her name Sarai,
   for Sara/Princess is her name!
16 I will bless her, and I will give you a son from her,
   I will bless her
   so that she becomes nations,
   kings of peoples shall come from her!
17 But Avraham fell on his face and laughed,
   he said in his heart:
                  To a hundred-year-old man shall there be (children)
                     born?
                  Or shall ninety-year-old Sara give birth?

---

and 20, referring to the fruitfulness of Avram's descendants), "you and
your seed after you" (vv.7, 10; see also v.19), "for the ages" (covenant
and land, vv.7, 8, 13, 19), and "into your generations" (vv.7, 9, 12).
   Preparatory to Avram's assumption of fatherhood—of an individual
and of a people—his name is changed (v.5), as is that of Sarai (v.15).
This act is of the utmost significance in the biblical world. Since a
person's name was indicative of personality and fate, the receiving of a
new one signified a new life or a new stage in life. Similarly, Yaakov (and
in a sort of coronation, Yosef) will undergo a change of name. Such a
practice still survives among kings and popes.

4 **throng:** The word suggests the sound of a crowd, rather than merely a large
   number.
5 **Avraham:** Trad. English "Abraham."
8 **I will be God to them:** Often reiterated as part of the biblical covenant
   (e.g., 28:21).
12 **house-born or bought with money:** I.e., slaves. The entire household, as
   an extension of the man's personality, is to be brought into the covenant.
15 **you shall not call her name Sarai:** Significantly, Sara is the only woman in
   the Bible to have her name changed by God.
16 **so that she becomes nations:** Sara in essence shares the blessing of God.
   She is not merely the biological means for its fulfillment.
17 **laughed:** Laughter becomes the key word of most of the stories about
   Yitzhak.

18 Avraham said to God:
   If only Yishmael might live in your presence!
19 God said:
   Nevertheless,
   Sara your wife is to bear you a son,
   you shall call his name: Yitzhak/He Laughs.
   I will establish my covenant with him as a covenant for the
      ages, for his seed after him.
20 And as for Yishmael, I hearken to you:
   Here, I will make him blessed, I will make him bear fruit, I
      will make him exceedingly, exceedingly many—
   he will beget twelve princes, and I will make a great nation
      of him.
21 But my covenant I will establish with Yitzhak, whom Sara
      will bear to you at this set-time, another year hence.
22 When he had finished speaking with Avraham,
   God went up, from beside Avraham.

23 Avraham took Yishmael his son and all those born in his
      house and all those bought with his money,
   all the males among Avraham's household people,
   and circumcised the flesh of their foreskins on that very
      day,
   as God had spoken to him.
24 Avraham was ninety-nine years old when he had the flesh of
      his foreskin circumcised,
25 and Yishmael his son was thirteen years old when he had
      the flesh of his foreskin circumcised.
26 On that very day
   were circumcised Avraham and Yishmael his son,
27 and all his household people, whether house-born or
      money-bought from a foreigner, were circumcised with
      him.

18:1 Now YHWH was seen by him by the oaks of Mamre
      as he was sitting at the entrance to his tent at the heat of
         the day.
   2 He lifted up his eyes and saw:
      here, three men standing over against him.

When he saw them, he ran to meet them from the en
    to his tent and bowed to the earth
3 and said:
My lords,
pray if I have found favor in your eyes,
pray do not pass by your servant!
4 Pray let a little water be fetched, then wash your feet and
    recline under the tree;
5 let me fetch (you) a bit of bread, that you may refresh your
    hearts,
then afterward you may pass on—
for you have, after all, passed your servant's way!
They said:
Do thus, as you have spoken.

Visit and Promise (18:1–15): The announcement of Sara's impending
child is set in the familiar ancient garb of a tale about divine travelers
who visit an old couple. Central, as is usual in folklore, is the idea of
hospitality, emphasized in the text by the threefold use of "pray"
(please) (vv.3–4), "pass on/by" (vv.3–5), and by Avraham's flurry of
activity (he himself "runs" twice, "hastens" three times, and "fetches"
four times in serving his guests).

19 **Yitzhak:** Trad. English "Isaac."
20 **make him blessed . . . make him bear fruit . . . make him . . . many:**
    Heb. *berakhti oto ve-hifreti oto ve-hirbeti oto.* **twelve princes:** Thus equal-
    ing the twelve sons/tribes of Israel?
21 **another year:** Not nine months (Sara does not immediately become preg-
    nant). Again the events seem to take place in a realistic framework, rather
    than in a strictly supernatural one.
22 **God went up, from beside Avraham:** Perhaps a formula used to signify the
    end of the conversation.
23 **on that very day:** Underlining Avraham's customary obedience. **as God
    had spoken to him:** Like Noah in 6:22, 7:5, and 7:9, Avraham scrupu-
    lously follows God's commands without question (so too in 21:4 and 22:3).
18:1 **entrance to his tent:** Also used in verses 2 and 10, it may hint at the
    important events being portrayed: the "entrance to the tent" is often a
    sacred spot in subsequent books of the Bible.
2 **three men:** See note on 16:7. **over against him:** Heb. *alav* could mean
    "over" or "next to" him.
3 **My lords:** Some use "My Lord."
4 **wash your feet:** Customary for weary travelers in the ancient world.

6 Avraham hastened into his tent to Sara and said:
Make haste! Three measures of choice flour! Knead it,
  make bread-cakes!
7 Avraham ran to the oxen,
he fetched a young ox, tender and fine, and gave it to a
  serving-lad, that he might hasten to make it ready;
8 then he fetched cream and milk and the young ox that he
  had made ready, and placed it before them.
Now he stood over against them under the tree while they
  ate.
9 They said to him:
Where is Sara your wife?
He said:
Here in the tent.
Now he said:
10 I will return, yes, return to you when time revives,
and Sara your wife will have a son!
Now Sara was listening at the entrance to the tent, which
  was behind him.
11 And Avraham and Sara were old, advanced in days,
the way of women had ceased for Sara.
12 Sara laughed within herself, saying:
After I have become worn, is there to be pleasure for me?
  And my lord is old!
13 But YHWH said to Avraham:
Now why does Sara laugh and say: Shall I really give birth,
  now that I am old?
14 Is anything beyond YHWH?
At that set-time I will return to you, when time revives,
and Sara will have a son.
15 Sara pretended otherwise, saying:
No, I did not laugh.
For she was afraid.
But he said:
No, indeed you laughed.

16 The men arose from there, and looked down upon the face
  of Sedom,
and Avraham went with them to escort them.

17 Now YHWH had said to himself:
Shall I cover up from Avraham what I am about to do?

18 For Avraham is to become, yes, become a great and
   numerous nation,
   and all the nations of the earth will find blessing through
   him.

19 Indeed, I have known him,
   in order that he may charge his sons and his household after
   him:
   they shall keep the way of YHWH,
   to do what is right and just,
   in order that YHWH may bring upon Avraham what he
   spoke concerning him.

The Great Intercession (18:16–33): With verse 17 the narrative is interrupted, and there begins a remarkable scene in which man confronts God. As if to emphasize the importance of this encounter, the text presents God as thinking out loud, and using the intimate term "know" (see 4:1) to describe his relationship to Avraham. And Avraham, the man through whom the nations "will find blessing" (v.18; see 12:3), the progenitor of "a great . . . nation" (v.18; see 12:2) that will see in justice its great goal, is now confronted with an urgent question of justice. While Avraham seems to be testing God in this story, it may in fact be precisely the reverse that is intended. Perhaps here more than anywhere else in the entire cycle (with the possible exception of Chapter 22), Avraham appears as the worthy father of his people, the one who will "charge his sons and his household . . . to do what is right and just" (v.19). Without this story Avraham would be a man of faith but not a man of compassion and moral outrage, a model consistent with Moses and the Prophets of Israel.

   The tightly structured, almost formal dialogue allows us to focus totally on the issue at hand. Predominating as refrains are the words "innocent" and "guilty," along with the expected versions of "just/justice" that pervade Avraham's remarks.

10 **when time revives:** An idiom for "next year." B-R uses "at the time of life-bestowing."
11 **the way of women:** The menstrual period.
12 **pleasure:** Sexual.

20 So YHWH said:
   The outcry in Sedom and Amora—how great it is!
   And their sin—how exceedingly heavily it weighs!
21 Now let me go down and see:
   if they have done according to its cry that has come to me—
   destruction!
   And if not—
   I wish to know.
22 The men turned from there and went toward Sedom,
   but Avraham still stood in the presence of YHWH.
23 Avraham came close and said:
   Will you really sweep away the innocent along with the
      guilty?
24 Perhaps there are fifty innocent within the city,
   will you really sweep it away?
   Will you not bear with the place because of the fifty
      innocent that are in its midst?
25 Heaven forbid for you to do a thing like this,
   to deal death to the innocent along with the guilty,
   that it should come about: like the innocent, like the guilty,
   Heaven forbid for you!
   The judge of all the earth—will he not do what is just?
26 YHWH said:
   If I find in Sedom fifty innocent within the city,
   I will bear with the whole place for their sake.
27 Avraham answered, and said:
   Now pray, I have ventured to speak to my Lord,
   and I am but earth and ashes:
28 Perhaps of the fifty innocent, five will be lacking—
   will you bring ruin upon the whole city because of the five?
   He said:
   I will not bring ruin, if I find there forty-five.
29 But he continued to speak to him, and said:
   Perhaps there will be found there only forty!
   He said:
   I will not do it, for the sake of the forty.
30 But he said:
   Pray let not my Lord be enraged that I speak further:
   Perhaps there will be found there only thirty!

He said:
I will not do it, if I find there thirty.
31 But he said:
Now pray, I have ventured to speak to my Lord:
Perhaps there will be found there only twenty!
He said:
I will not bring ruin, for the sake of the twenty.
32 But he said:
Pray let my Lord not be enraged that I speak further just
     this one time:
Perhaps there will be found there only ten!
He said:
I will not bring ruin, for the sake of the ten.
33 YHWH went, as soon as he had finished speaking to
     Avraham, and Avraham returned to his place.

19:1 The two messengers came to Sedom at evening,
as Lot was sitting at the gate of Sedom.
When Lot saw them, he arose to meet them and bowed
     low, brow to the ground
  2 and said:
Now pray, my lords,
pray turn aside to your servant's house,
spend the night, wash your feet;
early tomorrow you may continue on your journey.

---

21 **destruction:** Some read "altogether (according to its cry)."
22 **but Avraham still stood in the presence of YHWH:** Some manuscripts
   read "But YHWH still stood in the presence of Avraham." The subject of
   the sentence has been reversed by scribes who were uncomfortable with the
   passage's human portrayal of God.
25 **Heaven forbid:** Lit. "May you have a curse," an ironic turn of phrase in
   this situation. **like the innocent, like the guilty:** Or "innocent and guilty
   alike."
26 **bear with:** Or "bear the sin," "forgive."
27 **earth and ashes:** Heb. *afar va-efer*, traditionally "dust and ashes." The
   phrase, while common in English, is used in the Bible again only in Job
   (30:19, 42:6).
33 **YHWH went:** See note on 17:22.

They said:
No, rather we will spend the night in the square.
3 But he pressed them exceedingly hard,
so they turned in to him and came into his house.
He made them a meal-with-drink and baked flat-cakes, and
they ate.
4 They had not yet lain down, when the men of the city, the
men of Sedom, encircled the house,
from young lad to old man, all the people (even) from the
outskirts.
5 They called out to Lot and said to him:
Where are the men who came to you tonight?
Bring them out to us, we want to know them!
6 Lot went out to them, to the entrance, shutting the door
behind him
7 and said:
Pray, brothers, do not be so wicked!
8 Now pray, I have two daughters who have never known a
man,
pray let me bring them out to you, and you may deal with
them however seems good in your eyes;
only to these men do nothing,
for they have, after all, come under the shadow of my
roof-beam!
9 But they said:
Step aside!
and said:
This one came to sojourn, and here he would act-the-judge
and adjudicate?!
Now we will treat you more wickedly than them!
And they pressed exceedingly hard against the man, against
Lot, and stepped closer to break down the door.
10 But the men put out their hand and brought Lot in to
them, into the house, and shut the door.
11 And the men who were at the entrance to the house, they
struck with dazzling-light—(all men) great and small,
so that they were unable to find the entrance.
12 The men said to Lot:
Whom else have you here—a son-in-law, sons, daughters?

Bring anyone whom you have in the city out of the place!

13 For we are about to bring ruin on this place,
   for how great is their outcry before YHWH!
   And YHWH has sent us to bring it to ruin.

14 Lot went out to speak to his sons-in-law, those who had
      taken his daughters (in marriage), and said:
   Up, out of this place, for YHWH is about to bring ruin on
      the city!
   But in the eyes of his sons-in-law, he was like one who
      jests.

15 Now when the dawn rose,
   the messengers pushed Lot on, saying:
   Up, take your wife and your two daughters who are here,
   lest you be swept away in the punishment of the city!

16 When he lingered,
   the men seized his hand, his wife's hand, and the hand of
      his two daughters
   —because YHWH's pity was upon him—
   and, bringing him out, they left him outside the city.

———————

The End of Sedom and Amora (19): The detailed and colorful story of Lot
in Sedom and in flight from it adds a great deal to the Avraham cycle.
On the one hand there is the portrayal of Lot's continuing his uncle's
tradition of hospitality (vv.1–3), even to the extent of being willing to
sacrifice his own daughters' virginity. On the other hand Lot comes
across as timid (vv.7–8) and fearful (vv.18–20). In fact the word "pray"
(which we noted in Chapter 18 as a "hospitality term," and which serves
that function in verse 2 here as well) is used later in this chapter in a way
that almost suggests whining. He thus once again brings Avraham's
personality into sharper focus.

The crimes of Sedom and Amora are at last indicated more openly:
abuse of the sacred duty of hospitality, and sexual immorality (v.5). The

19:5 **we want to know them:** The meaning is unmistakably sexual.
   8 **pray let me bring them out to you . . . :** For a similar story, see Judges 19.
      There the offer of rape is accepted by the townspeople.
   9 **act-the-judge and adjudicate:** Heb. *shafot yishpot.*
   10 **the men:** The messengers.
   11 **(all men) great and small:** Lit. "from small to great."

17 It was, when they had brought him outside, that (one of
   them) said:
   Escape for your life, do not gaze behind you, do not stand
   still anywhere in the plain:
   to the mountain-country escape, lest you be swept away!
18 Lot said to them:
   No, pray, my lord!
19 Now pray, your servant has found favor in your eyes,
   you have shown great faithfulness in how you have dealt
   with me, keeping me alive—
   but I, I am not able to escape to the mountain-country,
   lest the wickedness cling to me, and I die!
20 Now pray, that town is near enough to flee to, and it is so
   tiny;
   pray let me escape there—is it not tiny?—and stay alive!
21 He said to him:
   Here then, I lift up your face in this matter as well,
   by not overturning this town of which you speak.
22 Make haste, escape there,
   for I am not able to do anything until you come there.
   Therefore the name of the town was called: Tzo'ar/Tiny.
23 (Now) the sun was going out over the earth as Lot came to
   Tzo'ar.
24 But YHWH rained down brimstone and fire upon Sedom
   and Amora, coming from YHWH, from the heavens,
25 he overturned those cities and all of the plain, all those
   settled in the cities and the vegetation of the soil.
26 Now his wife gazed behind him, and she became a pillar of
   salt.

27 Early in the morning Avraham (arose) to the place where he
   had stood in YHWH's presence,
28 he looked down upon the face of Sedom and Amora and
   upon the whole face of the plain-country
   and saw:
   here, the dense-smoke of the land ascended like the
   dense-smoke of a furnace!

29 Thus it was, when God brought ruin on the cities of the
   plain,

that God kept Avraham in mind and sent out Lot from the
   overturning,
when he overturned the cities where Lot had settled.

30 Lot went up from Tzo'ar and settled in the
      mountain-country, his two daughters with him,
   for he was afraid to settle in Tzo'ar.
   So he settled in a cave, he and his two daughters.

-----

latter theme returns at the end of the story, with the incestuous incident
that takes place at the instigation of Lot's daughters.

The story uses some stylized vocabulary. In verse 13, the messengers
talk of "bringing ruin," just as we encountered in the Flood narrative
(6:13). The narrative also gives negative twists to words which were
positive in the previous chapter: "know" and "just" are changed to
indicate illicit sex (v.5) and a condemnation of the alien Lot (v.9, "act-
the-judge and adjudicate"). Here too, "door/entrance" is transformed
from a place of contact with God to one of confrontation with men.

The account of the destruction itself is terse and mysterious, but it also
reveals the predicament of an all-too-human man, Lot.

The final section of the Sedom and Amora story recounts the origins of
two of Israel's neighbors, the Moabites and Ammonites. As traditional
enemies, they are not treated very kindly, any more than was the ancestor of the Canaanites in 9:20–27.

17 **Escape:** Heb. *himmalet,* used five times here. Perhaps it is a pun on Lot's
    name; he is "the escaper" in a number of situations.
19 **lest the wickedness cling to me:** The expression of an idea common to
    many cultures: that evil is like a disease, a physical rather than purely moral
    entity.
20 **tiny:** Or "a trifle."
21 **lift up your face:** A similar Assyrian phrase means "save" or "cheer."
    overturning: Overthrowing. The word is used later in the Bible to describe
    the fate of the two cities again (e.g., Lam. 4:6).
22 **I am not able . . . until you come there:** In deference to Avraham (see
    verse 29).
26 **she became a pillar of salt:** An old folklore motif of what happens when
    humans see God (or his actions), made popular by the many mineral pillars
    in the region around the Dead Sea.
27 **Early in the morning Avraham (arose):** Or "In the morning Avraham
    hurried" (Speiser).

31 Now the firstborn said to the younger:
Our father is old,
and there is no man in the land to come in to us as befits
the way of all the earth!

32 Come, let us have our father drink wine and lie with him
so that we may keep seed alive by our father.

33 So they had their father drink wine that night,
then the firstborn went in and lay with her father—
but he knew nothing of her lying down or her rising up.

34 It was on the morrow that the firstborn said to the younger:
Here, yesternight I lay with father.
Let us have him drink wine tonight as well,
then you go in and lie with him,
so that we may keep seed alive by our father.

35 They had their father drink wine that night as well,
then the younger arose and lay with him,
but he knew nothing of her lying down or her rising up.

36 And Lot's two daughters became pregnant by their father.

37 The firstborn bore a son and called his name: Mo'av/By
Father,
he is the tribal-father of Mo'av of today.

38 The younger also bore a son, and called his name:
Ben-Ammi/Son of My Kinspeople,
he is the tribal-father of the Sons of Ammon of today.

20:1 Avraham traveled from there to the Southland, and settled
between Kadesh and Shur, sojourning in Gerar.

2 Avraham said of Sara his wife: She is my sister.
So Avimelekh king of Gerar sent and had Sara taken.

3 But God came to Avimelekh in a dream of the night and
said to him:
Here, you must die because of the woman whom you have
taken,
for she is a wedded wife!

4 Avimelekh had not come near her. He said:
My Lord,
Would you kill a nation, though it be innocent?

5 Did he not say to me: She is my sister,
and also she, she said: He is my brother!

With a whole heart and with clean hands have I done this.

6 God said to him in the dream:
I also know that it was with a whole heart that you did this,
and so I also held you back from being at fault against me,
therefore I did not let you touch her.

7 But now, return the man's wife
—indeed, he is a prophet, he can intercede for you—
and live!
But if you do not return her:
know that you must die, yes, die, you and all that is yours!

8 Avimelekh (arose) early in the morning and called all his
    servants,
he spoke all these words in their ears, and the men became
    exceedingly afraid.

9 Then Avimelekh had Avraham called and said to him:
What have you done to us?
In what did I fail you,
that you have brought me and my kingdom into such great
    fault?
Deeds which are not to be done, you have done to me!

10 And Avimelekh said to Avraham:
What did you foresee, that you did this thing?

The Wife—II (Chap. 20): The second occurrence of "The Matriarch
Protected" comes immediately before the story of Yitzhak's birth, as if to
emphasize God's hand in the process one more time. In this long variation on the theme, God is most active and Avraham most revealing of his
past. He emerges from danger as a man who clearly enjoys God's full
protection and bounty.

The story almost draws a web of magic around Sara. Avimelekh is
nearly killed by God, and Sara's childlessness is inflicted upon all the
women in the king's household—even though there is not the slightest
doubt of his innocence (he "had not come near her").

35 **but he knew nothing . . . :** The repetition of the phrase from verse 33 is
   meant either to absolve Lot or to ridicule him.
37 **Mo'av:** Trad. English "Moab."
20:3 **wedded wife:** Heb. *be'ulat ba'al.*
   5 **With a whole heart:** Lit. "In the wholeness of my heart."
   6 **being at fault:** Or "sinning," which is perhaps too theological a translation.

11 Avraham said:
  Indeed, I said to myself:
  Surely there is no fear of God in this place,
  they will kill me on account of my wife!
12 Then, too, she is truly my sister, my father's daughter,
  however not my mother's daughter—so she became my
    wife.
13 Now it was, when the power-of-God caused me to roam
    from my father's house,
  that I said to her:
  Let this be the faithfulness that you do me:
  in every place that we come, say of me: He is my brother.
14 Avimelekh took sheep and oxen, servants and maids, and
    gave them to Avraham,
  and returned Sara his wife to him.
15 Avimelekh said:
  Here, my land is before you,
  settle wherever seems good in your eyes.
16 And to Sara he said:
  Here, I have given a thousand pieces of silver to your
    brother,
  here, it shall serve you as a covering for the eyes for all who
    are with you
  and with everyone, that you have been decided for.
17 Avraham interceded with God
  and God healed Avimelekh: his wife and his slave-women,
    so that they gave birth.
18 For YHWH had obstructed, obstructed every womb in
    Avimelekh's household
  on account of Sara, the wife of Avraham.

21:1 Now YHWH took account of Sara as he had said,
        YHWH dealt with Sara as he had spoken.
  2 Sara became pregnant and bore Avraham a son in his old
      age,
    at the set-time of which God had spoken to him.
  3 And Avraham called the name of his son, who was born to
      him, whom Sara bore to him:
    Yitzhak/He Laughs.

4 And Avraham circumcised Yitzhak his son at eight ⟨
old, as God had commanded him.

5 Avraham was a hundred years old when Yitzhak his ⟨
born to him.

6 Now Sara said:
God has made laughter for me,
all who hear of it will laugh for me.

7 And she said:
Who would have declared to Avraham:
Sara will nurse sons?
Well, I have borne him a son in his old age!

8 The child grew and was weaned,
and Avraham made a great drinking-feast on the day that
Yitzhak was weaned.

9 Once Sara saw the son of Hagar the Egyptian-woman,
whom she had borne to Avraham, laughing. . . .

Yitzhak Born (21:1–8): Two principal ideas punctuate this climax for which we have waited since Chapter 12: God keeps his promises (hence the poem in verse 1), and the key word in the stories about Yitzhak: "laughter" (here the result of the actual birth).

Yishmael Banished (21:9–21): Once Yitzhak has been born, separation must be made between heir and firstborn. Despite Avraham's obvious love for him, Yishmael must leave; his mother must repeat her ordeal of

11 **fear:** Awe; often used of God in the Bible.
13 **roam:** A word which in Genesis suggests a wandering that is nevertheless directed by God. See 21:14 and 37:15 for other examples. This passage gives us a fascinating glimpse of Avraham's own perception of the events in Chapter 12. It is not unusual for the biblical storyteller to give out information in this manner (in a later speech of the protagonist). **faithfulness:** Or "favor."
16 **a covering for the eyes:** Hebrew obscure; apparently it has legal connotations (see also "decided for" at the end of the verse).
18 **YHWH had obstructed:** On account of Sara, the "obstructed" one of 16:2.
21:6 **laugh for me:** Out of joy or disbelief. Some suggest "laugh at."
9 **laughing:** Perhaps mockingly. The theme of Yitzhak's life continues.

10 She said to Avraham:
   Drive out this slave-woman and her son,
   for the son of this slave-woman shall not share inheritance
      with my son, with Yitzhak!

11 The matter was exceedingly bad in Avraham's eyes because
      of his son.

12 But God said to Avraham:
   Do not let it be bad in your eyes concerning the lad and
      concerning your slave-woman;
   in all that Sara says to you, hearken to her voice,
   for it is through Yitzhak that seed will be called by your
      (name).

13 But also the son of the slave-woman—a nation will I make
      of him,
   for he too is your seed.

14 Avraham (arose) early in the morning,
   he took some bread and a skin of water
   and gave them to Hagar—placing them upon her shoulder—
      together with the child and sent her away.
   She went off and roamed in the wilderness of Be'er-Sheva.

15 Now when the water in the skin was at an end, she cast the
      child under one of the bushes,

16 and went and sat by herself, opposite, as far away as a
      bowshot,
   for she said to herself:
   Let me not see the child die!
   So she sat opposite, and lifted up her voice and wept.

17 But God heard the voice of the lad,
   God's messenger called to Hagar from heaven and said to
      her:
   What ails you, Hagar? Do not be afraid,
   for God has heard the voice of the lad there where he is.

18 Arise, lift up the lad and grasp him with your hand,
   for a great nation will I make of him!

19 God opened her eyes, and she saw a well of water;
   she went, filled the skin with water, and gave the lad to
      drink.

20 And God was with the lad as he grew up,
   he settled in the wilderness, and became an archer, a
      bowman.

21 He settled in the wilderness of Paran, and his mother took
    him a wife from the land of Egypt.

22 It was at about that time that Avimelekh, together with
        Pikhol the commander of his army, said to Avraham:
    God is with you in all that you do.
23 So now, swear to me here by God:
    If you should ever deal falsely with me, with my progeny
        and my posterity . . . !
    Rather, faithfully, as I have dealt with you, deal with me,
    and with the land in which you have sojourned.
24 Avraham said:
    I so swear.
25 But Avraham rebuked Avimelekh
    because of a well of water that Avimelekh's servants had
        seized.
26 Avimelekh said:
    I do not know who did this thing,
    nor have you ever told me, nor have I heard of it apart from
        today.

Chapter 16 as well. Nonetheless the text emphasizes that God is there
"with the lad" (v.20); twice the Yishamel motif of "God hearkening"
resounds (v.17); and God promises that the boy will eventually attain the
same exalted status as his brother (vv.13, 18).

Structurally, this brief tale foreshadows the next chapter, the ordeal of
Yitzhak. It speaks of a journey into the unknown, a child at the point of
death, the intervention of God's "messenger," the parent's sighting of
the way out, and the promise of future blessing. Of course the differences between the two stories are equally important.

Treaty (21:22–34): This interlude, which usefully separates the life
threats to Avraham's two sons (for a similar example, see I Samuel 25), is
one of many scenes demonstrating Avraham's relationship with local
princes.

11 **bad in Avraham's eyes:** Displeasing or upsetting to him.
12 **seed will be called:** I.e., your line will be continued.
14 **Be'er-Sheva:** Trad. English "Beersheba."
23 **with my progeny and my posterity:** Heb. *u-le-nini u-le-nekhdi.*

27 So Avraham took sheep and oxen and gave them to
    Avimelekh,
    and the two of them cut a covenant.
28 Then Avraham set seven ewe-lambs of the flock aside.
29 Avimelekh said to Avraham:
    What mean these seven ewe-lambs that you have set aside?
30 He said:
    Indeed, these seven ewe-lambs you should take from my
    hand,
    so that they may be a witness for me that I dug this well.
31 Therefore that place was called Be'er-Sheva/Well of the
    Seven-Swearing,
    for there the two of them swore (an oath).
32 Thus they cut a covenant in Be'er-Sheva.
    Then Avimelekh and Pikhol the commander of his army
    arose
    and returned to the land of the Philistines.
33 Now he planted a tamarisk in Be'er-Sheva
    and there he called out the name: YHWH God of the Ages.
34 And Avraham sojourned in the land of the Philistines for
    many days.

22:1 Now after these events it was
      that God tested Avraham
      and said to him:
      Avraham!
      He said:
      Here I am.
  2 He said:
      Pray take your son,
      your only-one,
      whom you love,
      Yitzhak,
      and go-you-forth to the land of Moriyya/Seeing,
      and offer him up there as an offering-up
      upon one of the mountains
      that I will tell you of.
  3 Avraham (arose) early in the morning,
      he saddled his ass,

he took his two serving-lads with him and Yitzhak his son,
he split wood for the offering-up
and arose and went to the place that God had told him of.
4 On the third day Avraham lifted up his eyes
and saw the place from afar.
5 Avraham said to his lads:
You stay here with the ass,
and I and the lad will go yonder,
we will bow down and then return to you.

The Great Test (22): This story is certainly one of the masterpieces of
biblical literature. In a famous article by Erich Auerbach it is remarked
how biblical style as exemplified here, in contradistinction to that of
Homer and other epic bards, eschews physical and psychological details
in favor of one central preoccupation: a man's decision in relation to
God. The result of this style is a terrible intensity, a story which is so
stark as to be almost unbearable.

Chapter 22 is a tale of God's seeming retraction of his promise (of
"seed") to Avraham. The fact that other issues may be involved here
(i.e., Israel's rejection of local and widely practiced ideas of child sacrifice) may be quite beside the point. Coming just one chapter after the
birth of the long-awaited son, the story completely turns around the
tension of the whole cycle and creates a new, frightening tension of its
own. The real horror of the story lies in this threatened contradiction to
what has gone before.

Most noticeable in the narrative is Avraham's silence, his mute acceptance of, and acting on, God's command. We are told of no sleepless

30 **take:** Accept.
33 **tamarisk:** A tree rarely mentioned in the Bible, it may indicate a holy place,
similar to the oaks where Avraham dwells earlier. **God of the Ages:** A
name unique to this passage.
34 **Philistines:** Another anachronism. The Philistines appear first in the days
of the Conquest (Joshua and Judges).
22:1 **after these events:** Others use "Some time afterward." **Here I am:** A
term frequently used to convey readiness, usually in relation to God's command or address.
2 **Yitzhak:** The name is left until the end of the phrase, to heighten tension.
Similarly, see 27:32. **Moriyya:** Trad. English "Moriah." The mountain
here is later identified with the site of Solomon's Temple.
5 **bow down:** Worship.

6 Avraham took the wood for the offering-up,
   he placed them upon Yitzhak his son,
   in his hand he took the fire and the knife.
   Thus the two of them went together.
7 Yitzhak said to Avraham his father, he said:
   Father!
   He said:
   Here I am, my son.
   He said:
   Here are the fire and the wood,
   but where is the lamb for the offering-up?
8 Avraham said:
   God will see-for-himself to the lamb for the offering-up,
   my son.
   Thus the two of them went together.
9 They came to the place that God had told him of;
   there Avraham built the altar
   and arranged the wood
   and bound Yitzhak his son
   and placed him on the altar atop the wood.
10 Avraham stretched out his hand,
   he took the knife to slay his son.
11 But YHWH's messenger called to him from heaven
   and said:
   Avraham! Avraham!
   He said:
   Here I am.
12 He said:
   Do not stretch out your hand against the lad,
   do not do anything to him!
   For now I know
   that you are God-fearing—
   you have not withheld your son, your only-one, from me.
13 Avraham lifted up his eyes and saw:
   there, a ram caught behind in the thicket by its horns!
   Avraham went,
   he took the ram
   and offered it up as an offering-up in place of his son.
14 Avraham called the name of that place: YHWH Sees.
   As the saying is today: On YHWH's mountain (it) is seen.

15 Now YHWH's messenger called to Avraham a second time
   from heaven
16 and said:
   By myself I swear
   —YHWH's utterance—
   indeed, because you have done this thing, have not withheld
   your son, your only-one,

---

night, nor does he ever say a word to God. Instead he is described with a
series of verbs: arising, saddling, taking, splitting, arising, going (v.3;
similarly in vv.6 and 9–10). Avraham the bargainer, so willing to enter
into negotiations with relations (Chapter 13), allies (Chapter 14), local
princes (Chapter 20), and even God himself (Chapter 18), here falls
completely silent.

The chapter serves an important structural function in the Avraham
cycle, framing it in conjunction with Chapter 12. The triplet in verse 2
("Pray take your son,/ your only-one,/ whom you love") recalls "from
your land/ from your kindred/ from your father's house" in 12:1; "go-
you-forth" and "the land that I will tell you of" (v.2; the latter, three
times in the story) similarly point back to Avraham's call (12:1, "Go-you
forth . . . to the land that I will let you see"). There he had been asked
to give up the past (his father); here, the future (his son). Between the
two events lies Avraham's active life as man of God, ancestor, and inter-
cessor. After this God will never speak with him again.

In many ways this story is the midpoint of Genesis. It brings the
central theme of continuity and discontinuity to a head in the strongest
possible way. After Moriyya, we can breathe easier, knowing that God
will come to the rescue of his chosen ones in the direst of circumstances.
At the same time we are left to ponder the difficulties of being a chosen
one, subject to such an incredible test.

The story is also the paradigmatic narrative of the entire book. The

6, 8 **Thus the two of them went together:** Between these two statements is
   Avraham's successful deflection of Yitzhak's question, and perhaps the hint
   of a happy ending.
   7 **fire:** I.e., a torch or brand.
   8 **see-for-himself:** Or "select." See the name of the mountain in verse 14,
   "YHWH Sees." **offering-up,/ my son:** One might read it with a dash
   instead of a comma, to preserve what may be an ironic answer.
   13 **a ram caught behind:** Some read "one ram caught."
   16 **YHWH's utterance:** A phrase often found in the Prophetic books. See note
   on 15:1.

indeed, I will bless you, bless you,
I will make your seed many, yes, many,
like the stars of the heavens and like the sand that is on the
    shore of the sea;
your seed shall inherit the gate of their enemies,
18 all the nations of the earth shall enjoy blessing through your
    seed,
in consequence of your hearkening to my voice.
19 Avraham returned to his lads,
they arose and went together to Be'er-Sheva.
And Avraham stayed in Be'er-Sheva.

20 Now after these events it was, that it was told to Avraham,
    saying:
Here, Milca too has borne, sons to Nahor your brother:
21 Utz his firstborn and Buz his brother, Kemuel father of
22   Aram, /and Cesed, Hazo, Pildash, Yidlaf, and Betuel.
23 Now Betuel begot Rivka.—
These eight Milca bore to Nahor, Avraham's brother.
24 And his concubine—her name was Re'uma—bore too:
    Tevah, Gaham, Tahash and Maakha.

23:1 Now Sara's life was one hundred years and twenty years
    and seven years, (thus) the years of Sara's life.
2 Sara died in Arba-Town, that is now Hevron, in the land of
    Canaan.
Avraham set about to lament for Sara and to weep over her;
3 then Avraham arose from the presence of his dead
and spoke to the Sons of Het, saying:
4 I am a sojourner settled among you;
give me title to a burial holding among you,
so that I may bury my dead from my presence.
5 The Sons of Het answered Avraham, saying to him:
6 Hear us, my lord!
You are one exalted by God in our midst—
in the choicest of our burial-sites you may bury your dead,
no man among us will deny you his burial-site
for burying your dead!
7 Avraham arose,

he bowed low to the People of the Land, to the Sons of
  Het,
8 and spoke with them, saying:
  If it be then according to your wish
  that I bury my dead from my presence,
  hear me and interpose for me to Efron son of Tzohar,
9 that he may give me title to the cave of Makhpela, that is
  his, that is at the edge of his field,
  for the full silver-worth let him give me title in your midst
  for a burial holding.

Patriarch passes the test, and we know that the fulfillment of the divine
promise is assured. Yet there is an ominous note: love, which occurs here
by name for the first time, leads almost to heartbreak. So it will be for
the rest of Genesis.

Purchase and Burial (23): Even though he is now secure in God's covenant, Avraham must still live and function in the human world. His
purchase of a burial plot for Sara shows us once more his dealings with
his neighbors, here as their equal, and also establishes at last his legal

17 **indeed, I will bless you:** Avraham has received such blessings before, but
    never before "because you have hearkened to my voice" (v.18). **inherit
    the gate:** I.e., possess or take the city.
18 **all the nations . . . :** See 12:3.
19 **Avraham returned:** The fact that Yitzhak is not mentioned here has given
    rise to speculation for centuries (see Shalom Spiegel, *The Last Trial*). The
    omission may simply arise from the fact that Yitzhak as a personality is not
    important to the story, which is first and foremost a test of Avraham.
23 **Rivka:** Trad. English "Rebecca."
23:1 **(thus) the years of Sara's life:** She is the only biblical woman whose life
    span is given, again as a sign of importance.
  3 **Sons of Het:** Or "Hittites," not to be confused with the great Hittite
    empire in Asia Minor. Here the name describes a Canaanite group.
  4 **a sojourner:** Even after many years, Avraham is still acutely aware of his
    nonnative status in the land.
5–6 **saying to him:/ Hear us:** Others use "saying:/ No, hear us."
  6 **one exalted:** Others use "a prince."
  7 **People of the Land:** Possibly a title indicating notables, not, as in later
    usage, the "common folk."

10 Now Efron had a seat amidst the Sons of Het,
and Efron the Hittite answered Avraham in the ears of the
  Sons of Het,
of all who had entry to the council-gate of his city,
saying:

11 Not so, my lord, hear me!
The field I give to you,
and the cave that is therein, to you I give it;
before the eyes of the Sons of My People I give it to you—
bury your dead!

12 Avraham bowed before the People of the Land

13 and spoke to Efron in the ears of the People of the Land,
saying:
But if you yourself would only hear me out!
I will give the silver-payment for the field,
accept it from me,
so that I may bury my dead there.

14 Efron answered Avraham, saying to him:

15 My lord—hear me!
A piece of land worth four hundred silver weight,
what is that between me and you!
You may bury your dead!

16 Avraham hearkened to Efron:
Avraham weighed out to Efron the silver-worth
of which he had spoken in the ears of the Sons of Het—
four hundred silver weight at the going merchants' rate.

17 Thus was established the field of Efron, that is in
  Makhpela, that faces Mamre,
the field as well as the cave that is in it, and the trees that
  were in all the field, that were in all their territory round
  about,

18 for Avraham as an acquisition,
before the eyes of the Sons of Het, of all who had entry to
  the council-gate of his city.

19 Afterward Avraham buried Sara his wife
in the cave of the field of Makhpela, facing Mamre, that is
  now Hevron, in the land of Canaan.

20 Thus was established the field as well as the cave that is in
  it for Avraham as a burial holding, from the Sons of Het.

24:1 Now Avraham was old, advanced in days,
     and YHWH had blessed Avraham in everything.
   2 Avraham said to his servant, the elder of his household,
     who ruled over all that was his:
     Pray put your hand under my thigh!
   3 I want you to swear by YHWH, the God of Heaven and the
     God of Earth,
     that you will not take a wife for my son from the women of
     the Canaanites, among whom I am settled;

---

foothold in Canaan, albeit with a small piece of land. The long conversations and considerable formality of the chapter, which are not unusual in an ancient Near Eastern context, contrast with the extreme brevity of the previous chapter.

The narrative strikes a curious balance between the emotional reality of the situation (e.g., the repetition of "dead," "presence," and "bury") and the requirements of legal procedure ("Hear me," "give title," and "holding").

The Betrothal Journey (24): The last full episode of the Avraham cycle is the longest in the book. Its leisurely pace, attention to detail, and concentration on speeches as well as action belie the importance of what is being recounted: the finding of a wife for Yitzhak, who is biologically to continue the line. Yet after all that has happened in the previous chapters, we know that this will be taken care of by God. That is implied in Avraham's assured "he himself [God] will send his messenger on before you" (v.7).

Many meeting/betrothal scenes in the Bible take place at a well (e.g., Jacob, Moses); this was probably a literary convention (see Culley and Alter for a discussion of the significance of such a phenomenon). Like other crucial moments in Avraham's life the chapter involves a journey, albeit one made by his emissary. It is therefore natural that the key words of the chapter are "go," "journey," and "grant success." "Take" also appears frequently, as the biblical term often used for "marry."

   10 **of all who had entry:** Similar to "People of the Land"—the aristocrats.
   20 **established:** Others use "made over."
24:1 **put your hand under my thigh:** A symbol used in taking of an oath (see also 47:29). The use of "thigh" might allude to a curse of childlessness as the punishment for not keeping the oath.

4 rather, you are to go to my land and to my kindred, and
   take a wife for my son, for Yitzhak.
5 The servant said to him:
   Perhaps the woman will not be willing to go after me to this
      land;
   may I then bring your son back there,
   back to the land from which you once went out?
6 Avraham said to him:
   Watch out that you do not ever bring my son back there!
7 YHWH, the God of Heaven,
   who took me from my father's house and from my kindred,
   who spoke to me,
   who swore to me, saying:
   I give this land to your seed—
   he himself will send his messenger on before you,
   so that you take a wife for my son from there.
8 Now if the woman is not willing to go after you,
   you will be clear from this sworn-oath of mine,
   only: You are not to bring my son back there!
9 The servant put his hand under the thigh of Avraham his
      lord,
   and swore to him (an oath) about this matter.

10 The servant took ten camels from his lord's camels and
      went, all kinds of good-things from his lord in his hand.
   He arose and went to Aram Of-Two-Rivers, to Nahor's
      town.
11 He had the camels kneel outside the town at the water well
   at eventime, at the time when the water-drawers go out,
12 and said:
   YHWH, God of my lord Avraham,
   pray let it happen today for me, and deal faithfully with my
      lord Avraham!
13 Here, I have stationed myself by the water spring as the
      women of the town go out to draw water.
14 May it be
   that the maiden to whom I say: Pray lower your pitcher that
      I may drink,
   and she says: Drink, and I will also give your camels to
      drink—

let her be the one that you have decided on for your
   servant, for Yitzhak,
by means of her may I know that you have dealt faithfully
   with my lord.

15 And it was: Not yet had he finished speaking,
when here, Rivka came out,
—she had been born to Betuel, son of Milca, wife of Nahor,
   brother of Avraham—
her pitcher on her shoulder.

16 The maiden was exceedingly beautiful to look at,
a virgin—no man had known her.
Going down to the spring, she filled her pitcher and came
   up again.

17 The servant ran to meet her and said:
Pray let me sip a little water from your pitcher!

18 She said:
Drink, my lord!
And in haste she let down her pitcher on her arm and gave
   him to drink.

19 When she had finished giving him to drink, she said:
I will also draw for your camels, until they have finished
   drinking.

20 In haste she emptied her pitcher into the drinking-trough,
then she ran to the well again to draw,
and drew for all his camels.

21 The man kept staring at her,
(waiting) silently to find out whether YHWH had granted
   success to his journey or not.

22 It was, when the camels had finished drinking,

---

5 **back there:** The Hebrew text has "there" in the next line; it has been
moved up in the English text for reasons of style. The word occurs four
times in verses 5–8, as a signal of what is most important to Avraham: that
his son must stay in the land of Canaan.

7 **I give this land to your seed:** Quoting 12:7.

10 **Aram Of-Two-Rivers:** Others leave untranslated, "Aram-Naharayim."

11 **water-drawers:** Female.

12 **let it happen:** Or "let it go well."

that the man took a gold nose-ring, a half-coin in weight,
   and two bracelets for her wrists, ten gold pieces in weight,
23 and said:
Whose daughter are you? Pray tell me!
And is there perhaps in your father's house a place for us to
   spend the night?
24 She said to him:
I am the daughter of Betuel, son of Milca, whom she bore
   to Nahor.
25 And she said to him:
Yes, there is straw, yes, plenty of fodder with us, (and) yes,
   a place to spend the night.
26 In homage the man bowed low before YHWH
27 and said:
Blessed be YHWH, God of my lord Avraham,
who has not relinquished his faithfulness and his
   trustworthiness from my lord!
While as for me, YHWH has led me on the journey to the
   house of my lord's brothers!
28 The maiden ran and told her mother's household according
   to these words.
29 Now Rivka had a brother, his name was Lavan.
Lavan ran to the man, outside, to the spring:
30 and it was,
   as soon as he saw the nose-ring, and the bracelets on his
      sister's wrists,
   and as soon as he heard Rivka his sister's words, saying:
      Thus the man spoke to me,
   that he came out to the man—there, he was still standing by
      the camels, by the spring—
31 and said:
Come, you who are blessed by YHWH, why are you
   standing outside?
I myself have cleared out the house and a place for the
   camels!
32 The man came into the house and unbridled the camels,
they gave straw and fodder to the camels
and water for washing his feet and the feet of the men that
   were with him.

33 (Food) was put before him to eat, but he said:
I will not eat until I have spoken my words.
He said: Speak!
34 He said:
I am Avraham's servant.
35 YHWH has blessed my lord exceedingly, so that he has
become great,
he has given him sheep and oxen, silver and gold, servants
and maids, camels and asses.
36 Sara, my lord's wife, bore my lord a son after she had
grown old,
and he has given him all that is his.
37 Now my lord had me swear, saying:
You are not to take a wife for my son from the women of
the Canaanites, in whose land I am settled!
38 No! To my father's house you are to go, to my clan,
and take a wife for my son.
39 I said to my lord:
Perhaps the woman will not go after me!
40 He said to me:
YHWH, in whose presence I have walked, will send his
messenger with you,
he will grant sucess to your journey,
so that you take a wife for my son from my clan and from
my father's house.

---

25 **Yes, there is straw:** Not until Rivka has extended the offer of hospitality (and enthusiastically, with the triple "yes") is the servant sure that "YHWH has granted success to my journey." Hospitality, once again, is the determinant, over and above beauty or virginity.

27 **his faithfulness and his trustworthiness:** Others combine and translate as "steadfast kindness." The phrase is often found in the Psalms, describing God. **brothers:** Relatives.

29 **Lavan:** Trad. English "Laban." He will be a key figure in the story of Rivka's son Yaakov.

34 **He said . . . :** The servant's speech diplomatically omits certain emotional details of Avraham's speech, most notably his warning against Yitzhak himself's going back "there."

40 **will send his messenger:** Speaking figuratively.

41 Only then will you be clear from my binding-oath:
When you come to my clan,
if they do not give her to you, you will be clear from my
binding-oath.

42 Now I came to the well today and said:
YHWH, God of my lord Avraham,
pray, if you wish to grant success to the journey on which I
am going,

43 here: I have stationed myself by the water spring;
may it be
that the girl who comes out to draw,
to whom I say: Pray give me a little water from your pitcher
to drink,

44 and she says to me: You drink, and I will also draw for
your camels—
let her be the woman whom YHWH has decided on for the
son of my lord.

45 (And) I, even before I had finished speaking in my heart,
here, Rivka came out, her pitcher on her shoulder,
she went down to the spring and drew.
I said to her: Pray give me to drink!

46 In haste she let down her pitcher from herself and said:
Drink, and I will also give your camels to drink.
I drank, and she also gave the camels to drink.

47 Then I asked her, I said: Whose daughter are you?
She said: The daughter of Betuel, son of Nahor, whom
Milca bore to him.
I put the ring on her nose and the bracelets on her wrists,

48 and in homage I bowed low before YHWH, and blessed
YHWH, God of my lord Avraham,
who led me on the true journey to take the daughter of my
lord's brother for his son.

49 So now, if you wish to deal faithfully and truly with my
lord, tell me,
and if not, tell me,
that I may (know to) turn right or left.

50 Lavan and Betuel answered, they said:
The matter has come from YHWH;
we cannot speak anything to you evil or good.

51 Here is Rivka before you,

take her and go, that she may be a wife for the son of ¸
lord,
as YHWH has spoken.
52 It was
when Avraham's servant heard their words, that he bowed
to the ground before YHWH.
53 And the servant brought out objects of silver and objects of
gold and garments, and gave them to Rivka,
and he gave presents to her brother and to her mother.
54 They ate and drank, he and the men that were with him,
and spent the night.
When they arose in the morning, he said:
Send me off to my lord.
55 But her brother and her mother said:
Let the maiden stay with us a few days, perhaps ten— after
that she may go.
56 He said to them:
Do not delay me, for YHWH has granted success to my
journey;
send me off, that I may go back to my lord.
57 They said:
Let us call the maiden and ask (for an answer from) her
own mouth.
58 They called Rivka and said to her:
Will you go with this man?
She said:
I will go.
59 They sent off Rivka their sister with her nurse, and
Avraham's servant with his men,

---

41 **binding-oath:** Changed from Avraham's simple "sworn-oath," perhaps because it is reported from the servant's point of view.
50 **YHWH:** The family apparently worships the God of Avraham, in addition
to others (see 31:19, 30).
53 **objects of silver . . . and gold and garments:** A stock biblical phrase (see,
similarly, Ex. 3:22) for wealth or presents.
55 **a few days, perhaps ten:** Some interpret as "a year or ten months."
59 **with her nurse:** Yitzhak's life as the father of his people begins with the
marriage arranged in this chapter; curiously, when he dies in Chapter 35,
the nurse dies as well, perhaps to hint that Rivka dies too.

60 and they gave Rivka farewell-blessing and said to her:
    Our sister, may you become thousandfold myriads!
    May your seed inherit the gate of those who hate him!
61 Rivka and her maids arose, they mounted the camels and
    went after the man.
    The servant took Rivka and went away.

62 Now Yitzhak had come from where you come to the Well
    of the Living-One Who-Sees-Me—for he had settled in
    the Southland.
63 And Yitzhak went out to stroll in the field around eventide.
    He lifted up his eyes and saw: here, camels coming!
64 Rivka lifted up her eyes and saw Yitzhak;
65 she got down from the camel and said to the servant:
    Who is the man over there that is walking in the field to
      meet us?
    The servant said:
    That is my lord.
    She took a veil and covered herself.
66 Now the servant recounted to Yitzhak all the things that he
    had done.
67 Yitzhak brought her into the tent of Sara his mother,
    he took Rivka and she became his wife, and he loved her.
    Thus was Yitzhak comforted after his mother.

25:1 Now Avraham had taken another wife, her name was
    Ketura.
  2 She bore him Zimran and Yokshan, Medan and Midyan,
    Yishbak and Shuah.
  3 Yokshan begot Sheva and Dedan,
    Dedan's sons were the Ashurites, the Letushites, and the
    Leummites.
  4 Midyan's sons (were) Efa, Efer, Hanokh, Avida, and Eldaa.
    All these (were) Ketura's sons.
  5 But Avraham gave over all that was his to Yitzhak.
  6 And to the sons of the concubines that Avraham had,
    Avraham gave gifts, and he sent them away from Yitzhak
    his son while he was still alive, eastward, to the Eastland.

  7 Now these are the days and years of the life of Avraham,
    which he lived:

8 A hundred years and seventy years and five years, then he
   breathed-his-last.
   Avraham died at a good ripe-age, old and abundant (in
      days),
   and was gathered to his kinspeople.
9 Yitzhak and Yishmael his sons buried him, in the cave of
      Makhpela, in the field of Efron son of Tzohar the Hittite,
      that faces Mamre,
10 the field that Avraham had acquired from the Sons of
      Het.
   There were buried Avraham and Sara his wife.

11 Now it was after Avraham's death, that God blessed
      Yitzhak his son.
   And Yitzhak settled by the Well of the Living-One
      Who-Sees-Me.

12 Now these are the begettings of Yishmael son of Avraham,
      whom Hagar the Egyptian-woman, Sara's maid, bore to
      Avraham.
13 And these are the names of the sons of Yishmael, by their
      names after (the order of) their begettings:

Avraham's Descendants and Death (25:1–18): Avraham's death is bracketed by two passages dealing with his offspring: first, through Ketura (a
concubine), and then through Hagar (Yishmael's line). God's promise is
on the way to fulfillment, although Yitzhak is as yet childless and only a
small portion of the land has been permanently acquired.

60 **May your seed inherit the gate:** See Avraham's blessing in 22:17. Again,
   the matriarch shares in the blessing.
62 **Well of the Living-One:** Already a site of God's activity (16:14).
63 **stroll:** Hebrew obscure; some use "ponder."
67 **Sara:** As the story opened with Yitzhak's father in his last active moments,
   it closes with the memory of his mother. Yitzhak is on his own.
25:7 **days and years:** Lit. "days of the years."
   8 **A hundred years . . . :** See "The Patriarchal Narratives," pp. 45–6.
   breathed-his-last: Lit. "expired." It is translated as "perished" in
   7:21.   **abundant:** Or "full." For the complete expression, see 35:29.
11 **God blessed Yitzhak:** This is the first detail reported about Yitzhak after
   his father's death—lest there be any doubt about the continuation of God's
   care.

14 Yishmael's firstborn, Nevayot; and Kedar, Adbe'el,
    Mivsam, Mishma, Duma, Massa,
15 Hadad and Tema, Yetur, Nafish and Kedma.
16 These are the sons of Yishmael, these their names, in their
    villages and in their corrals,
    twelve princes for their tribes.
17 And these are the years of the life of Yishmael: a hundred
    years and thirty years and seven years, then he
    breathed-his-last.
    He died and was gathered to his kinspeople.
18 Now they dwelt from Havila to Shur, which faces Egypt,
    back to where you come toward Assyria;
    in the presence of all his brothers did (his inheritance) fall.

16 **corrals:** Others (including Buber) use "circled encampments." **twelve
   princes:** See 17:20.
18 **did (his inheritance) fall:** Hebrew difficult. Others interpret negatively,
   "made raids against" or "fell upon" (his kinsmen).

PART III Yaakov
(25:19–36: 43) see also 37–50

B EFORE COMMENTING on the Yaakov cycle, it is appropriate to consider why his father Yitzhak, the second of the Patriarchs, receives no true separate group of stories on his own.

Yitzhak functions in Genesis as a classic second generation—that is, as a transmitter and stabilizing force, rather than as an active participant in the process of building the people. There hardly exists a story about him in which he is anything but a son and heir, a husband, or a father. His main task in life seems to be to take roots in the land of Canaan, an admittedly important task in the larger context of God's promises in Genesis. What this means, unfortunately, is that he has almost no personality of his own. By Chapter 27, a scant two chapters after his father dies, he appears as (prematurely?) old, blind in both a literal and figurative sense, and as we will see, he fades out of the text entirely, only to die several chapters, and many years, later.

The true dynamic figure of the second generation here is Rivka. It is she to whom God reveals his plan, and she who puts into motion the mechanism for seeing that it is properly carried out. She is ultimately the one responsible for bridging the gap between the dream, as typified by Avraham, and the hard-won reality, as realized by Yaakov.

Avraham is a towering figure, almost unapproachable as a model in his intimacy with God and his ability to hurdle nearly every obstacle. Adding to this the fact that Yitzhak is practically a noncharacter, and that Yosef, once his rise begins, also lacks dimension as a personality, it becomes increasingly clear that it is Yaakov who emerges as the most dynamic and most human personality in the book. The stories about him cover fully half of Genesis, and reveal a man who is both troubled and triumphant. Most interestingly, he, and not Avraham, gives his name to the people of Israel.

Distinctive themes of the cycle include physical struggle, deception, and confrontation. These are expressed through the key words of Yaakov's name ("Heel-Holder" and "Heel-Sneak," then Yisrael, "God-Fighter"), "deceive" and similar words, and "face." Also recurring are the terms "love," "bless," "firstborn-right," and "wages/hire" (one word in Hebrew). The cycle is structured partly around etiologies (folk explanations of place-names and personal names) and also around Yaakov's use of stones in several of the stories.

Continuing from the Avraham cycle are such earlier themes as wandering, sibling rivalry, the barren wife, wives in conflict, the renaming of the protagonist, God perceived in dreams and visions; and particular geographical locations such as Bet-El, Shekhem, and the Negev (Cassuto).

Finally, it should be mentioned that the Yaakov stories are notable in the manner in which they portray the two levels of biblical reality: divine and human. Throughout the stories human beings act according to normal (though often strong) emotions, which God then uses to carry out his master plan. In this cycle one comes to feel the interpretive force of the biblical mind at work, understanding human events in the context of what God wills. It is a fascinating play between the ideas of fate and free will, destiny and choice—a paradox which nevertheless lies at the heart of the biblical conception of God and humankind.

19 Now these are the begettings of Yitzhak, son of Avraham.
   Avraham begot Yitzhak.
20 Yitzhak was forty years old when he took Rivka daughter of
   Betuel the Aramean, from the country of Aram, sister of
   Lavan the Aramean, for himself as a wife.
21 Yitzhak entreated YHWH on behalf of his wife, for she was
   barren,
   and YHWH granted-his-entreaty:
   Rivka his wife became pregnant.
22 But the children almost crushed one another inside her,
   so she said:
   If this be so,
   why do I exist?
   And she went to inquire of YHWH.

23 YHWH said to her:
   Two nations are in your body,
   two tribes from your belly shall be divided;
   tribe shall be mightier than tribe,
   elder shall be servant to younger!
24 When her days were fulfilled for bearing, here: twins were
   in her body!
25 The first one came out ruddy, like a hairy mantle all over,
   so they called his name: Esav/Rough-One.
26 After that his brother came out, his hand grasping Esav's
      heel,
   so they called his name: Yaakov/Heel-Holder.
   Yitzhak was sixty years old when she bore them.

Rivka's Children (25:19–34): Two stories of sibling confrontation begin
the Yaakov cycle. From the first, verses 19–28, all the necessary conditions are introduced for what is to come: struggle in the womb (foreshadowing Yaakov's wrestling match in Chapter 32, the structural resolution
of this earlier one), God's plan for the younger son to outdo the older
one, the importance of names as clues to personalities, and parental
preference. This last point seals the fate of the two boys.

   The second story (vv.29–34) is Yaakov's first act of stealth, and sets
the pattern for his whole life. Note at the same time the text's emphasis
on Esav's role (v.34), "Thus did Esav despise the firstborn-right."

   20 **forty years old:** Another schematic number. Twenty years later (see verse
      26), his wife will bear him children.   **Aramean:** Three times in this verse
      the root "Aram" confirms what we learned in the previous chapter—the
      importance of family and lineage here.   **country of Aram:** Others leave
      this untranslated, as "Padan-Aram."
   22 **almost crushed:** Others use "struggled."   **inquire:** Consult an oracle.
      Note that there is no indication that Yitzhak is aware of what God wants.
   23 **tribes:** Heb. *le'ummim*, a poetic term for "peoples."
   24 **here:** The text speaks from the point of view of the onlookers, not of
      Rivka, who is perfectly aware that she has twins.
   25 **Esav:** Trad. English "Esau."   **Rough-One:** A conjectural interpretation
      from Arabic *'athaya*.
   26 **Yaakov:** Trad. English "Jacob."   **Heel-Holder:** A popular reinterpreta-
      tion of the name Yaakov, which may have meant originally "May (God)
      protect."

27 The lads grew up:
Esav became a man who knew the hunt, a man of the field,
but Yaakov was a plain man, staying among the tents.
28 Yitzhak grew to love Esav, for (he brought) hunted-game
for his mouth,
but Rivka loved Yaakov.

29 Once Yaakov was boiling boiled-stew,
when Esav came in from the field, and he was weary.
30 Esav said to Yaakov:
Pray give me a gulp of the red-stuff, that red-stuff,
for I am so weary!
Therefore they called his name: Edom/Red-One.
31 Yaakov said:
Sell me your firstborn-right here-and-now.
32 Esav said:
Here, I am on my way to dying, so what good to me is a
firstborn-right?
33 Yaakov said:
Swear to me here-and-now.
He swore to him and sold his firstborn-right to Yaakov.
34 Yaakov gave Esav bread and boiled lentils;
he ate and drank and arose and went off.
Thus did Esav despise the firstborn-right.

26:1 Now there was a famine in the land, aside from the former
famine which there had been in the days of Avraham,
so Yitzhak went to Avimelekh, king of the Philistines, to
Gerar.
2 And YHWII was seen by him and said:
Do not go down to Egypt;
continue to dwell in the land that I tell you of,
3 sojourn in this land, and I will be with you and will give
you blessing—
for to you and to your seed I give all these lands
and will fulfill the sworn-oath that I swore to Avraham your
father:
4 I will make your seed many, like the stars of the heavens,
and to your seed I will give all these lands;

all the nations of the earth shall enjoy blessing through your
    seed—
5 in consequence of Avraham's hearkening to my voice
   and keeping what I would have him keep: my
      commandments, my laws, and my instructions.
6 So Yitzhak stayed in Gerar.

As before, these episodes point in two temporal directions. Esav resembles Yishmael, the man of the bow; and parental preference will
launch the initially tragic action in the Yosef story (Chapter 37).

In the Land (26:1–6): As we have suggested, there is no true collection of
stories about Yitzhak. That is, virtually nowhere does Yitzhak appear in
a tale where, as a distinct individual, he is a central character. And
unlike Yaakov and Yosef, Yitzhak never directly receives his father's
blessing. This is bestowed by God, and one gets the impression that even
Avraham does not deal with his son as an individual. This is not surprising, given Yitzhak's function in his father's life.

For the narrative, his main purpose, as we have stressed above, is
simply to remain in the land (note the repetition of the word "land" in
this section). It is almost as if Avraham, the man who lives in the shadow
of sacred trees, plants one in the person of his son. In this chapter
Yitzhak is forbidden to go beyond the borders of Canaan. Even his
death, so seemingly out of place in Chapter 35, occurs after Yaakov has
returned home from his wanderings: only when it is assured that there
will be continuity in the land is he allowed to die—despite the fact that as
a result the text must leave him blind and dying for twenty years.

27 **plain:** Hebrew unclear. Others use "simple."
28 **(he brought) hunted-game:** Hebrew difficult.
29 **boiling boiled-stew:** This phrase may connote plotting, as in our English
   "cook up," "brew," "concoct," or "stir up" trouble. Other forms of the
   Hebrew verb denote "insolence."
31 **here-and-now:** Others use "at once"; apparently a legal term.
34 **he ate . . . :** Esav's impulsive personality is brilliantly portrayed by the use
   of four rapid-fire verbs.   **despise:** Others use "belittle."
26:1 **a famine . . . Yitzhak went to Avimelekh:** Parallel to the story in Chapter
   20.
5 **in consequence of Avraham's hearkening . . . :** The blessing mirrors
   22:17ff.   **my commandments . . . :** These are not specified; this is probably a poetic phrase describing a general idea.

7 Now when the men of the place asked about his wife, he
   said: She is my sister,
   for he was afraid to say: my wife—
   (thinking): Otherwise the people of the place will kill me on
   account of Rivka, for she is beautiful to look at.
8 But it was, when he had been there a long time,
   that Avimelekh, king of the Philistines, looked out through
   a window
   and saw: there was Yitzhak laughing-and-loving with Rivka
   his wife!
9 Avimelekh had Yitzhak called and said:
   But here, she must be your wife!
   Now how could you say: She is my sister?
   Yitzhak said to him:
   Indeed, I said to myself: Otherwise I will die on account of
   her!
10 Avimelekh said:
   What is this that you have done to us!
   One of the people might well have lain with your wife,
   and then you would have brought guilt upon us!
11 Avimelekh charged the entire people, saying:
   Whoever touches this man or his wife must be put to death,
   yes, death!

12 Yitzhak sowed in that land, and reaped in that year a
   hundred measures;
   thus did YHWH bless him.
13 The man became great, and went on, went on becoming
   greater, until he was exceedingly great:
14 he had herds of sheep and herds of oxen and a large retinue
   of servants,
   and the Philistines envied him.
15 And all the wells which his father's servants had dug in the
   days of Avraham his father, the Philistines stopped up
   and filled with earth.
16 Avimelekh said to Yitzhak:
   Go away from us, for you have become exceedingly more
   numerous than we!

17 So Yitzhak went from there, he encamped in the wadi of
      Gerar and settled there.
18 Yitzhak again dug up the wells of water which had been
      dug in the days of Avraham his father, the Philistines
      having stopped them up after Avraham's death,
   and he called them by the names, the same names, by
      which his father had called them.
19 Yitzhak's servants also dug in the wadi, and found there a
      well of living water.
20 Now the shepherds of Gerar quarreled with the shepherds
      of Yitzhak, saying: The water is ours!
   So he called the name of the well: Esek/Bickering, because
      they had bickered with him.
21 They dug another well, and quarreled also over it,
   so he called its name: Sitna/Animosity.

The Wife—III (26:7–11): Here is the final "Yitzhak version" of the tale,
constructed around the same king whom Avraham had encountered in
Chapter 20. Its individual coloring is supplied by the "laughing-and-loving" of verse 8, playing on Yitzhak's name. Otherwise, just as in the
following episode, he is merely repeating his father's experience.

Blessing (26:12–33): Confirmation of Yitzhak's status as heir comes in
verses 12–14, in the form of material blessings (already referred to immediately after Avraham's death, 25:11). It will be Yaakov's task to reclaim
and continue the spiritual side of the tradition.
   The first episode is centered around not Yitzhak but Avraham. The
phrase "his father" reverberates; again Avimelekh returns. In the second
episode, Avraham's treaty with that king (Chapter 21) is replayed, with
the same result as before: an explanation of the name Be'er-Sheva.

   8 **laughing-and-loving:** Heb. *metzahek*, which can mean laughter or sexual
      activity. Trad. English "sporting."
   11 **touches:** Or "harms."
   12 **reaped:** Lit. "attained."
   17 **there:** The word occurs seven times through verse 25. It may be a counter-
      point to Chapter 24's usage, or stress that Yitzhak stays in the land.

22 He moved on from there and dug another well, but they did
    not quarrel over it,
    so he called its name: Rehovot/Space,
    and said: Indeed, now YHWH has made space for us, so
    that we may bear fruit in the land!
23 He went up from there to Be'er-Sheva.

24 Now YHWH was seen by him on that night and said:
    I am the God of Avraham your father.
    Do not be afraid, for I am with you,
    I will bless you and will make your seed many, for the sake
    of Avraham my servant.
25 He built an altar there
    and called out the name of YHWH.
    He spread his tent there, and Yitzhak's servants
    excavated a well there.
26 Now Avimelekh went to him from Gerar, along with
    Ahuzzat his aide and Pikhol the commander of his army.
27 Yitzhak said to them:
    Why have you come to me?
    For you hate me and have sent me away from you!
28 They said:
    We have seen, yes, seen that YHWH has been with you,
    so we say: Pray let there be a binding-oath between us,
    between us and you,
    we want to cut a covenant with you:
29 If ever you should deal badly with us . . . !
    Just as we have not harmed you and just as we have only
    dealt well with you and have sent you away in peace—
    you are now blessed by YHWH!
30 He made them a drinking-feast, and they ate and drank.
31 They (arose) early in the morning and swore to one another;
    then Yitzhak sent them off, and they went from him in
    peace.
32 Now it was on that same day
    that Yitzhak's servants came and told him about the well
    that they had been digging,
    they said to him: We have found water!

33 So he called it: Shiv'a/Swearing-Seven;
therefore the name of the city is Be'er-Sheva until this day.

34 When Esav was forty years old, he took to wife Yehudit
daughter of B'eri the Hittite and Ba'semat daughter of
Elon the Hittite.

35 And they were a bitterness of spirit to Yitzhak and Rivka.

27:1 Now when Yitzhak was old and his eyes had become too
dim for seeing,
he called Esav, his elder son, and said to him:
My son!
He said to him:
Here I am.

2 He said:
Now here, I have grown old, and do not know the day of
my death.

3 So now, pray pick up your weapons—your hanging-quiver
and your bow,
go out into the field and hunt me down some hunted-game,

Deceit and Blessing (26:34 to 28:9): Of all the stories of Genesis, this is perhaps the most brilliantly staged. Nowhere is the narrative so vivid as here, and nowhere, even including Chapter 22, is the tension so masterfully drawn out.

Despite the fact that the story line is a simple one, involving deception and the "taking" of the blessing, the text is imbued with great subtlety. Most striking is the sensuality it invokes: seven times we hear of "game," six of the "delicacy" (or "tasty-dish"), and three times Yitzhak "feels" Yaakov (who "comes close" four times). In fact the story makes use of all five of the senses. One sense—that of sight— is defective, and

26 **aide:** Lit. "friend."
30 **they ate and drank:** The cutting of a covenant is often accompanied by a
meal in biblical and other societies.
34 **forty years old:** The same age that his father was at the time of his marriage.

4 and make me a delicacy, such as I love;
bring it to me, and I will eat it,
that I may give you my own blessing before I die.

5 Now Rivka was listening as Yitzhak spoke to Esav his son,
and so when Esav went off into the fields to hunt down
hunted-game to bring (to him),

6 Rivka said to Yaakov her son, saying:
Here, I was listening as your father spoke to Esav your
brother, saying:

7 Bring me some hunted-game and make me a delicacy, I will
eat it
and give you blessing before YHWH, before my death.

8 So now, my son, listen to my voice, to what I command
you:

9 Pray go to the flock and take me two fine goat kids from
there,
I will make them into a delicacy for your father, such as he
loves;

10 you bring it to your father, and he will eat,
so that he may give you blessing before his death.

11 Yaakov said to Rivka his mother:
Here, Esav my brother is a hairy man, and I am a smooth
man,

12 perhaps my father will feel me—then I will be like a
trickster in his eyes,
and I will bring a curse and not a blessing on myself!

13 His mother said to him:
Let your curse be on me, my son!
Only: listen to my voice and go, take them for me.

14 He went and took and brought them to his mother,
and his mother made a delicacy, such as his father loved.

15 Rivka then took the garments of Esav, her elder son, the
choicest ones that were with her in the house,

16 and clothed Yaakov, her younger son;
and with the skins of the goat kids, she clothed his hands
and the smooth-parts of his neck.

17 Then she placed the delicacy and the bread that she had
made in the hand of Yaakov her son.

18 He came to his father and said:
Father!
He said:
Here I am. Which one are you, my son?
19 Yaakov said to his father:
I am Esav, your firstborn.
I have done as you spoke to me:
Pray arise, sit and eat from my hunted-game,
that you may give me your own blessing.

---

on that deficiency will turn the action of the story. Yet another level of meaning is apparent: "to see" in ancient Israel, as in many cultures, was a term connected to prophetic powers, as we observed regarding Avraham. So here, ironically, Yitzhak's blindness leads to both deception and to the proper transferral of the blessing.

Structurally the story is framed by two references to Esav and his wives: 26:34–35 prepares the way for his loss of the blessing, by showing that he has alienated himself from his parents (and broken Avraham's charge to Yitzhak in 24:3), and 28:6–9 finds Esav obeying his father and making a rather pathetic attempt to reassure himself of his love.

Some of the story's motifs will return later. The threefold "as he loves" looks to the crucial role that the theme of "love" will play later on in Genesis (as well as being a key to the story itself). The general theme of nonrecognition will return with an interesting twist in the Yosef novella (especially in Chapters 42–44).

27:4 **delicacy:** See 25:28. Yitzhak is tied to the senses, a trait that he prizes in Esav. **my own blessing:** Or "my special blessing." Heb. *nefesh* frequently means "self" or "personality."

7 **before YHWH:** Note that Rivka adds these words to her husband's.

9 **take:** Fetch (see also verses 13, 14, 45).

13 **Let your curse be on me:** Ominously, Rivka disappears from the narrative after verse 46.

18 **Which one are you:** Three times—here, in verse 21, and in verse 24—the father asks for assurances about the son's identity. **my son:** This phrase reverberates throughout the story, underlining the confusion over the identity of the sons.

19 **Esav, your firstborn:** From the first word the lie is blatant; contrast Esav's tension-filled reply to the same question in verse 32.

20 Yitzhak said to his son:
How did you find it so hastily, my son?
He said: Indeed, YHWH your God made it happen for me.

21 Yitzhak said to Yaakov:
Pray come closer, that I may feel you, my son,
whether you are really my son Esav or not.

22 Yaakov moved closer to Yitzhak his father.
He felt him and said:
The voice is Yaakov's voice, the hands are Esav's hands—

23 but he did not recognize him, for his hands were like the
hands of Esav his brother, hairy.
Now he was about to bless him,

24 when he said:
Are you he, my son Esav?
He said:
I am.

25 So he said: Bring it close to me, and I will eat from the
hunted-game of my son,
in order that I may give you my own blessing.
He put it close to him and he ate,
he brought him wine and he drank.

26 Then Yitzhak his father said to him:
Pray come close and kiss me, my son.

27 He came close and kissed him.
Now he smelled the smell of his garments
and blessed him and said:
See, the smell of my son
is like the smell of a field
that YHWH has blessed.

28   So may God give you
          from the dew of the heavens,
          from the fat of the earth,
          (along with) much grain and new-wine!

29   May peoples serve you,
          may tribes bow down to you;
          be master to your brothers,
          may your mother's sons bow down to you!
          Those who curse you, cursed!
          Those who bless you, blessed!

30 Now it was, when Yitzhak had finished blessing Yaakov,
   yes it was—Yaakov had just gone out, out from the
      presence of Yitzhak his father—
   that Esav his brother came back from his hunting.
31 He too made a delicacy and brought it to his father.
   He said to his father:
   Let my father arise and eat from the hunted-game of his
      son,
   that you may give me your own blessing.
32 Yitzhak his father said to him:
   Which one are you?
   He said:
   I am your son, your firstborn, Esav.
33 Yitzhak trembled with very great trembling
   and said:
   Who then was he
   that hunted down hunted-game and brought it to me—I ate
      it all before you came
   and I gave him my blessing!
   Now blessed he must remain!
34 When Esav heard the words of his father,
   he cried out with a very great and bitter cry,
   and said to his father:
   Bless me, me also, father!

---

20 **made it happen:** An appropriate expression to use with Yitzhak; see 24:12.
23 **hairy:** In the end Yitzhak relies more on the sense of touch than on his
   hearing. Yet the latter is usually regarded as the source of truth in the Bible
   (see Deut. 4:12, for example).
27 **a field:** Fitting for Esav, the "man of the field" (25:27).
29 **Those who bless you, blessed!:** Perhaps hearkening back to God's speech
   to Avraham in 12:3. Note that this blessing, at least in this particular
   wording, is never spoken to Yitzhak.
32 **Esav:** The exact identification is put off until the end of the sequence,
   heightening the drama. Similarly, see 22:2.
33,34 **very great:** Movingly, the father's terror and the son's anguish mirror one
   another via use of the same phrase (Heb. *ad me'od,* which is rare).
33 **blessed he must remain:** Once uttered, the words of blessing cannot be
   rescinded.

35 He said:
Your brother came with deceit and took away your blessing.
36 He said:
Is that why his name was called Yaakov/Heel-Sneak? For he
     has now sneaked against me twice:
My firstborn-right he took, and now he has taken my
     blessing!
And he said:
Haven't you reserved a blessing for me?
37 Yitzhak answered, saying to Esav:
Here, I have made him master to you,
and all his brothers I have given him as servants,
with grain and new-wine I have invested him—
so for you, what then can I do, my son?
38 Esav said to his father:
Have you only a single blessing, father?
Bless me, me also, father!
And Esav lifted up his voice and wept.
39 Then Yitzhak his father answered, saying to him:
          Behold, from the fat of the earth
          must be your dwelling-place,
          from the dew of the heavens above.
40   You will live by your sword,
          you will serve your brother.
          But it will be
          that when you brandish it,
          you will tear his yoke from your neck.
41 Now Esav held a grudge against Yaakov because of the
     blessing with which his father had blessed him.
Esav said in his heart:
Let the days of mourning for my father draw near
and then I will kill Yaakov my brother!
42 Rivka was told of the words of Esav, her elder son.
She sent and called for Yaakov, her younger son,
and said to him:
Here, Esav your brother is consoling himself about you,
     with (the thought of) killing you.
43 So now, my son, listen to my voice:
Arise and flee to Lavan my brother in Harran,

44 and stay with him for a few days, until your brother's fury
    has turned away,

45 until his anger turns away from you and he forgets what
    you did to him.
    Then I will send and have you taken from there—
    for should I be bereaved of you both in a single day?

46 So Rivka said to Yitzhak:
    I loathe my life because of those Hittite women;
    if Yaakov should take a wife from the Hittite women—like
    these, from the women of the land,
    why should I have life?

28:1 So Yitzhak called for Yaakov,
    he blessed him and charged him, saying to him:
    You are not to take a wife from the women of Canaan;

2 arise, go to the country of Aram, to the house of Betuel,
    your mother's father,
    and take yourself a wife from there, from the daughters of
    Lavan, your mother's brother.

3 May God Shaddai bless you,
    may he make you bear fruit and make you many,
    so that you become a host of peoples.

4 And may he give you the blessing of Avraham,
    to you and to your seed with you,
    for you to inherit the land of your sojournings,
    which God gave to Avraham.

---

36 **Heel-Sneak:** In effect, Esav puts a curse on his brother's name, which will
    be removed only in 32:29, twenty years later. **he has now sneaked
    against me:** Or "cheated me."

37 **invested:** Or "sustained."

39 **Behold, from the fat of the earth:** Some interpret this negatively as "Be-
    hold, *away* from the fat of the earth. . . ."

40 **brandish:** I.e., a sword; Hebrew obscure.

41 **let the days . . . :** That is, wait until my father dies!

44 **days:** May be an idiomatic usage meaning "years."

45 **Then I will send:** This never occurs in the later course of the story.

28:2 **arise, go to the country of Aram:** It is curious that Yitzhak sends his son
    on a journey that he himself had been forbidden to undertake.

4 **seed . . . land:** Again the two elements of the blessing given to Avraham.

5 So Yitzhak sent Yaakov off;
   he went to the country of Aram, to Lavan son of Betuel the
      Aramean,
   the brother of Rivka, the mother of Yaakov and Esav.

6 Now Esav saw
   that Yitzhak had given Yaakov farewell-blessing and had
      sent him to the country of Aram, to take himself a wife
      from there,
   (and that) when he had given him blessing, he had charged
      him, saying: You are not to take a wife from the women
      of Canaan!
7 And Yaakov had listened to his father and his mother and
      had gone to the country of Aram.
8 And Esav saw
   that the women of Canaan were bad in the eyes of Yitzhak
      his father,
9 so Esav went to Yishmael and took Mahalat daughter of
      Yishmael son of Avraham, sister of Nevayot, in addition
      to his wives as a wife.

10 Yaakov went out from Be'er-Sheva and went toward
      Harran,
11 and encountered a certain place.
   He had to spend the night there, for the sun had set.
   Now he took one of the stones of the place
   and set it at his head
   and lay down in that place.
12 And he dreamt:
   Here, a ladder was set up on the earth,
   its top reaching the heavens,
   and here: messengers of God were going up and down on it.
13 And here:
   YHWH was standing over against him.
   He said:
   I am YHWH,
   the God of Avraham your father and the God of Yitzhak.
   The land on which you lie
   I give to you and to your seed.

14 Your seed will be like the dust of the earth;
  you will burst forth, seaward, eastward, northward,
    southward.
  All the clans of the soil will find blessing through you and
    through your seed!
15 Here, I am with you,
  I will watch over you wherever you go
  and will bring you back to this soil;
  indeed, I will not leave you
  until I have done what I have spoken to you.

Yaakov Sets Out (28:10–22): Yaakov's journey takes him not only to a foreign land, but to the portals of adulthood. It begins fittingly with a dream vision, so that we will know from the start that God is with him. In fact Yaakov always encounters God at crucial life junctures, at the point of journeys (31:3—leaving Aram; 32:25ff.—meeting Esav; 35:1—returning to Bet-El; 35:9ff.—the homecoming; and 46:2ff.—on the way to Egypt).

The setting for this particular encounter is highly unusual, especially when compared to the generally nongeographical nature of the revelations to Avraham. The idea of a sacred site ("place," a biblical word with these connotations, occurs three times) is strongly suggested. The notion of a ladder or ramp (or "gateway," v.17) between the divine and human worlds is well known in ancient stories. A variation of the theme occurs in 32:2–3, where Yaakov sees "messengers" again in an "encounter"; these two stories frame the middle of the entire cycle.

As Yaakov enters his adult life, he resembles both his grandfather Avraham, the visionary, and his son Yosef, the dreamer.

5 **Yaakov and Esav:** In the end, the oracle to Rivka is confirmed, with younger son superseding elder.
6 **charged:** Or "commanded."
12 **Here:** The word (three times) emphasizes the immediacy of the report; it is the vocabulary of dreams, as in 37:7 (Andersen). **ladder:** Others use "ramp" or "stairway."
13 **over against:** See note to 18:2.
13ff. **the land,** etc.: Once again Yaakov receives the blessing of Avraham "his father" (!). See 13:14–16.

16 Yaakov awoke from his sleep
   and said:
   Why,
   YHWH is in this place,
   and I, I did not know it!
17 He was awestruck and said:
   How awesome is this place!
   This is none other than a house of God,
   and that is the gate of heaven!
18 Yaakov (arose) early in the morning,
   he took the stone that he had set at his head
   and set it up as a standing-pillar
   and poured oil on top of it.
19 And he called the name of the place: Bet-El/House of
      God—
   however, Luz was the name of the city in former times.
20 And Yaakov vowed a vow, saying:
   If God will be with me
   and will watch over me on this way that I go
   and will give me food to eat and a garment to wear,
21 and if I come back in peace to my father's house—
   YHWH shall be God to me,
22 and this stone that I have set up as a standing-pillar shall
      become a house of God,
   and everything that you give me
   I shall tithe, tithe it to you.

29:1 Yaakov lifted his feet and went to the land of the
        Easterners.
   2 He looked around him, and there: a well in the field, and
        there were three herds of sheep crouching near it,
     for from that well they used to give the herds to drink.
     Now the stone on the mouth of the well was large,
   3 so when all the herds were gathered there,
     they used to roll the stone from the mouth of the well, give
        the sheep to drink, and put the stone back on the mouth
        of the well in its place.

4 Now Yaakov said to them:
Brothers, where are you from?
They said:
We are from Harran.
5 He said to them:
Do you know Lavan, son of Nahor?
They said:
We know him.
6 He said to them:
Is all well with him?
They said:
It is well—
and here comes Rahel his daughter with the sheep!
7 He said:
Indeed, it is still broad daylight,
it is not time to gather in the livestock,
so give the sheep to drink and go back, tend them.

———

Arrival in Aram (29:1–14): As one might expect from the usual biblical pattern, Yaakov meets his bride-to-be at a well. As in other ancient stories (see also Ex. 2:15–17) the hero performs a feat of physical strength, this time with a large stone—continuing the use of stones as a motif in the Yaakov stories.

Lavan is once again the chief representative of the family, as he was in the betrothal account of Chapter 24.

18 **standing-pillar:** A stone marker, common to the culture of the region. **Bet-El:** Trad. English "Beth El."
21 **in peace:** Or "safely." This functions as a key word in the Yaakov cycle, extending into the Yosef story as well. Yaakov, the "sneak" and wanderer, seeks peace and safety; he does not find it until the end of his life, albeit in a foreign land.
22 **tithe:** See note to 14:20.
29:1 **lifted his feet:** Colloquially, "picked up and went."
5 **We know him:** Biblical Hebrew expresses the idea "yes" by repeating the words of the question. See also verse 6 and 24:58.
6 **Rahel:** Trad. English "Rachel." The name means "ewe."
7 **to gather in:** For the night.

8 But they said:
  We cannot, until all the herds have been gathered;
  only then do they roll the stone from the mouth of the well,
    and then we give the sheep to drink.
9 While he was still speaking with them,
  Rahel came with the sheep that were her father's
  —for she was a shepherdess.
10 Now it was when Yaakov saw Rahel, the daughter of Lavan
   and the sheep of Lavan his mother's brother,
   that Yaakov came close,
   he rolled the stone from the mouth of the well
   and gave drink to the sheep of Lavan his mother's brother.
11 Then Yaakov kissed Rahel, and lifted up his voice and
     wept.
12 And Yaakov told Rahel
   that he was her father's brother
   and that he was Rivka's son.
   She ran and told her father.
13 Now it was, as soon as Lavan heard the tidings concerning
     Yaakov, his sister's son,
   that he ran to meet him, embraced him and kissed him, and
     brought him into his house.
   And he recounted all these events to Lavan.
14 Lavan said to him:
   Without doubt you are my bone, my flesh!
   And he stayed with him the days of a
     Renewing-of-the-Moon.

15 Lavan said to Yaakov:
   Just because you are my brother, should you serve me for
     nothing?
   Tell me, what shall your wages be?
16 Now Lavan had two daughters: the name of the elder was
     Lea, the name of the younger was Rahel.
17 Lea's eyes were delicate, but Rahel was fair of form and fair
     to look at.
18 And Yaakov fell in love with Rahel.
   He said:
   I will serve you seven years for Rahel, your younger
     daughter.

19 Lavan said:
    My giving her to you is better than my giving her to
        another man;
    stay with me.
20 So Yaakov served seven years for Rahel,
    yet they were in his eyes as but a few days, because of his
        love for her.
21 Then Yaakov said to Lavan:
    Come-now, (give me) my wife, for my days-of-labor have
        been fulfilled,
    so that I may come in to her.
22 Lavan gathered all the people of the place together and
        made a drinking-feast.
23 Now in the evening
    he took Lea his daughter and brought her to him,
    and he came in to her.
24 Lavan also gave her Zilpa his maid,
    for Lea his daughter as a maid.
25 Now in the morning:
    here, she was Lea!
    He said to Lavan:
    What is this that you have done to me!

Deception Repaid (29:15–30): The language of the text here, as well as
the tenor of the situation, suggest that the Bible has set up Yaakov's
punishment for having stolen Yitzhak's blessing from his brother. "Deceived" (v.25) and "younger . . . firstborn" (v.26) echo the Chapter 27
narrative, and provide another example of biblical justice.

10 **his mother's brother:** Three times here, to accentuate the familial ties.
12 **brother:** Relative (so also verse 15).
14 **Renewing-of-the-Moon:** Heb. *hodesh*, a month.
16 **Lea:** Trad. English "Leah." The name means "wild cow."
17 **delicate:** Others use "weak." Either the term is meant negatively or else
    Lea is being praised for one attribute but Rahel for total beauty.
18 **seven:** Aside from forty, this is the other schematic number found often in
    Genesis and elsewhere (for instance, as the basic number of the biblical
    calendar, in days, months, and years).
19 **with me:** Or "in my service," "under me."
21 **fulfilled:** I.e., over, completed.

Was it not for Rahel that I served you?
Why have you deceived me?
26 Lavan said:
Such is not done in our place, giving away the younger
    before the firstborn;
27 just fill out the bridal-week for this one, then we shall give
      you that one also,
for the service which you will serve me for yet another
    seven years.
28 Yaakov did so—he fulfilled the bridal-week for this one,
and then he gave him Rahel his daughter as a wife.
29 Lavan also gave Rahel his daughter Bilha his maid,
for her as a maid.
30 So he came in to Rahel also,
and he loved Rahel also,
more than Lea.
Then he served him for yet another seven years.

31 Now when YHWH saw that Lea was hated,
he opened her womb,
while Rahel was barren.
32 So Lea became pregnant and bore a son;
she called his name: Re'uven/See, a Son!
for she said:
Indeed, YHWH has seen my being afflicted,
indeed, now my husband will love me!
33 She became pregnant again and bore a son,
and said:
Indeed, YHWH has heard that I am hated,
so he has given me this one as well!
And she called his name: Shim'on/Hearing.
34 She became pregnant again and bore a son,
and said:
Now this time my husband will be joined to me,
for I have borne him three sons!
Therefore they called his name: Levi/Joining.
35 She became pregnant again and bore a son,
and said:
This time I will give thanks to YHWH!

Therefore she called his name: Yehuda/Giving-Thanks.
Then she stopped giving birth.

30:1 Now when Rahel saw that she could not bear (children) to
    Yaakov,
Rahel envied her sister.
She said to Yaakov:
Come-now, (give) me children!
If not, I will die!
2 Yaakov's anger raged against Rahel,
he said:
Am I in place of God,
who has denied you fruit of the body?
3 She said:
Here is my slave-girl Bilha;
come in to her,
so that she may give birth upon my knees, so that I too may
    be built-up-with-sons through her.
4 She gave him Bilha her maid as a wife,
and Yaakov came in to her.
5 Bilha became pregnant and bore Yaakov a son.

Love, Jealousy, and Children (29:31–30:24): The narrative now demonstrates (1) how Yaakov prospers in exile, increasing both in wealth and in progeny, and thus (2) how God fulfills his promise to the Patriarchs to "make them many." Characteristically for the Bible, this takes place as a result of human emotions: the jealousy of two sisters who are married to the same man. The emotions, interestingly, are portrayed largely through the names given to Yaakov's sons. In the end Lea seems to be the victor, at least in the terms of a culture that prizes the production of male children; she becomes the mother of fully half of the sons of Israel (Redak).

31 **hated:** Others use "rejected," "unloved."
32 **Re'uven:** Trad. English "Reuben."
33 **Shim'on:** Trad. English "Simeon."
35 **Yehuda:** Trad. English "Judah."
30:3 **give birth upon my knees:** An idiom for legal adoption (here, by Rahel).

6 Rahel said:
    God has done-me-justice; yes, he has heard my voice!
    He has given me a son!
    Therefore she called his name: Dan/He-Has-Done-Justice.
7 And Bilha, Rahel's maid, became pregnant again and bore a
    second son to Yaakov.
8 Rahel said:
    A struggle of God have I struggled with my sister; yes, I
    have prevailed!
    So she called his name: Naftali/My Struggle.

9 Now when Lea saw that she had stopped giving birth,
    she took Zilpa her maid and gave her to Yaakov as a wife.
10 Zilpa, Lea's maid, bore Yaakov a son.
11 Lea said:
    What fortune!
    So she called his name: Gad/Fortune.
12 And Zilpa, Lea's maid, bore a second son to Yaakov.
13 Lea said:
    What happiness!
    For women will deem me happy.
    So she called his name: Asher/Happiness.

14 Now Re'uven went in the days of the wheat-harvest and
    found some love-apples in the field,
    and brought them to Lea his mother.
    Rahel said to Lea:
    Pray give me (some) of your son's love-apples!
15 She said to her:
    Is your taking away my husband such a small thing
    that you would now take away my son's love-apples?
    Rahel said:
    Very well, he may lie with you tonight in exchange for your
    son's love-apples.
16 So when Yaakov came home from the fields in the evening,
    Lea went out to meet him and said:
    You must come in to me,
    for I have hired, yes, hired you for my son's love-apples.
    So he lay with her that night.
17 And God hearkened to Lea,

so that she became pregnant and bore Yaakov a fifth son.

18 Lea said:
God has given me my hired-wages,
because I gave my maid to my husband!
So she called his name: Yissakhar/There-Is-Hire.

19 Once again Lea became pregnant, and she bore a sixth son
    to Yaakov.

20 Lea said:
God has presented me with a good present,
this time my husband will prize me—
for I have borne him six sons!
So she called his name: Zevulun/Prince.

21 Afterward she bore a daughter, and called her name Dina.

22 But God kept Rahel in mind,
God hearkened to her and opened her womb,

23 so that she became pregnant and bore a son.
She said:
God has removed/*asaf*
my reproach!

24 So she called his name: Yosef,
saying:
May YHWH add/*yosef*
another son to me!

---

13 **What happiness:** Others use "Happy am I!"

14 **love-apples:** Heb. *duda'im;* a plant believed to have aphrodisiac powers. Others use "mandrakes."

15 **taking away:** The theme of "taking," so prominent in Chapter 27, returns, in the context of sibling rivalry again.

18 **hired-wages:** "Wages" recurs as a theme throughout this part of the Yaakov cycle (Fokkelman). It is perhaps a veiled portrayal of the events of Yaakov's adulthood as "payment" for what he did to his brother. **Yissakhar:** Trad. English "Issachar."

20 **this time my husband will prize me:** Lea's six pregnancies and birthings are bracketed by this verse and 29:32, "Now my husband will love me." **Zevulun:** Trad. English "Zebulun."

23–24 **removed. . . . add:** Yosef's naming prefigures his destiny as a son lost and found.

24 **Yosef:** Trad. English "Joseph."

25 Now it was, once Rahel had borne Yosef, that Yaakov said
     to Lavan:
   Send me free, that I may go back to my place, to my land,
26 give over my wives and my children,
   for whom I have served you,
   and I will go.
   Indeed, you yourself know my service that I have served
     you!
27 Lavan said to him:
   Pray, if I have found favor in your eyes . . .
   I have become wealthy,
   and YHWH has blessed me on account of you.
28 And he said: Specify the wages due you from me, and I will
     give you payment.
29 He said to him:
   You yourself know
   how I have served you,
   and how it has gone with your livestock in my charge.
30 For you had but few before me,
   and they have since burst out into a multitude.
   Thus has YHWH blessed you at my every step!
   But now, when may I too do something for my household?
31 He said:
   What shall I give you?
   Yaakov said:
   You are not to give me anything—
   only do this thing for me,
   then I will return, I will tend your flock, I will keep watch:
32 Let me go over your whole flock today
   removing from there every speckled and dappled head;
   and every dark head among the lambs, and each dappled
     and speckled-one among the goats—they shall be my
     wages.
33 And may my honesty plead for me on a future day:
   when you come-to-check my wages (that are) before you,
   whatever is not speckled or dappled among the goats, or
     dark among the lambs,
   it will be as though stolen by me.
34 Lavan said:

Good, let it be according to your words.
35 And on the same day he removed the streaked and dappled
     he-goats
   and every speckled and dappled she-goat, every one that
     had any white on it,
   and every dark-one among the lambs,
   and handed them over to his sons.
36 Then he put a three-days' journey between himself and
     Yaakov.
   Now Yaakov was tending Lavan's remaining flock.
37 Yaakov took himself rods from moist poplar, almond, and
     plane trees
   and peeled white peelings in them, exposing the white that
     was on the rods,
38 then he presented the rods that he had peeled in the
     gutters, in the water troughs where the flock would come
     to drink, in front of the flock.

Yaakov in Exile: Stealth and Prosperity (30:25-32:1): The long account of
how Yaakov outwits Lavan rounds out the portrait of his personality: he
is a man at once clever, successful, and harassed. The text goes to great
lengths to describe both men in behavior and thought, and we are given
enough dialogue to be able to understand their motivations. The repeating words point to major themes: "serve," "wages," "face" (which will
become central to the whole cycle by Chapter 32), and a whole vocabulary of trickery: "steal" (with the variations "be stealthy" and "steal the
wits"), "take away" (see Chapter 27!), "snatch," and "rob."

26 **give over my wives and my children:** In the law of the region, slaves did
   not retain control of their families. Does this suggest something about
   Yaakov's treatment by Lavan? (Speiser)
27 **Pray, if I have found:** Or "May I now find." **I have become wealthy,/
   and YHWH . . . :** Some interpret this as "I have divined that
   YHWH . . ."
32 **Let me go:** Some read "Go." **every speckled . . . :** This would appeal to
   Lavan, since such animals would be in the minority.
35 **white:** Heb. *lavan.* Also the word "poplar" in verse 37 is a play on Lavan
   (*livne*). The conniving father-in-law is tricked with words resembling his
   own name.

Now they would be in heat as they came to drink;

39 thus the flock came to be in heat by the rods,
and the flock bore streaked, speckled, and dappled (young).

40 But the sheep, Yaakov set apart,
and gave position among the flock to each streaked-one and
every dark-one among Lavan's flocks;
thus he made special herds for himself, but did not make
them for Lavan's flock.

41 So it was that whenever the robust flock-animals were in
heat,
Yaakov would put the rods in sight of the flock-animals, in
the gutters, to make them be in heat next to the rods.

42 But when the flock-animals were feeble, he would not put
them there.
And so it was that the feeble-ones became Lavan's, and the
robust-ones, Yaakov's.

43 The man burst-forth-with-wealth exceedingly, yes,
exceedingly, he came to have many flock-animals and
maids and servants, and camels and he-asses.

31:1 Now he heard the words of Lavan's sons, (that they) said:
Yaakov has taken away all that was our father's,
and from what was our father's he has made all this
weighty-wealth!

2 And Yaakov saw by Lavan's face:
here, he was no longer with him as yesterday and the
day-before.

3 And YHWH said to Yaakov:
Return to the land of your fathers, to your kindred!
I will be with you!

4 So Yaakov sent and had Rahel and Lea called to the field,
to his animals,

5 and said to them:
I see by your father's face:
indeed, he is no longer toward me as yesterday and the
day-before.
But the God of my father has been with me!

6 You yourselves know that I have served your father with all
my might,

7 but your father has cheated me and changed my wages ten
   times over,
   yet God has not allowed him to do me ill.
8 If he said thus: The speckled-ones shall be your wages,
   all the animals would bear speckled-ones,
   and if he said thus: The streaked-ones shall be your wages,
   all the animals would bear streaked-ones.
9 So God has snatched away your father's livestock and given
   them to me.
10 Now it was at the time of the animals' being in heat
   that I lifted up my eyes and saw in a dream:
   here, the he-goats that mount the animals—streaked,
     speckled, and spotted!
11 And God's messenger said to me in the dream: Yaakov!
   I said: Here I am.
12 He said:
   Pray lift up your eyes and see:
   All the he-goats that mount the animals—streaked,
     speckled, and spotted!
   For I have seen all that Lavan is doing to you.

---

39 **by the rods:** Folk belief holds that what the animals see as they mate will influence the color of their offspring.

40 **gave position:** Following the interpretation of Fokkelman.

43 **he came to have many flock-animals:** Like his father (26:14) and grandfather (12:16).

31:2 **he was no longer with him:** Others use "Lavan's manner toward him was no longer . . ."

3 **land of your fathers . . . your kindred:** Here, unlike 12:1, the land is Canaan, not Harran! **I will be with you:** Heb. *ehye immakh*, interpreted here and throughout by B-R as "I will be-there with you," stressing that it is God's presence that is indicated by the verb *hyh*, "to be." See especially Ex. 3:14.

4 **to the field:** As a place where such conversations would be certain to be private.

7 **ten times:** Many times.

10 **Now it was . . . in a dream:** Several times in this chapter we hear of important events secondhand, in speech rather than in action. See note to 20:13. **streaked, speckled, and spotted:** Heb. *akuddim, nekuddim, u-ve-ruddim*. The rhyme (rare in biblical Hebrew) suggests a vision or a dream.

13 I am the God of Bet-El,
   where you anointed the pillar,
   where you vowed a vow to me.
   So now, arise,
   get out of this land,
   return to the land of your kindred!
14 Rahel and Lea answered him, they said to him:
   Do we still have a share, an inheritance in our father's
      house?
15 Is it not as strangers that we are thought of by him?
   For he has sold us and eaten up, yes, eaten up our
      purchase-price!
16 Indeed, all the riches that God has snatched away from our
      father—
   they belong to us and to our children.
   So now, whatever God has said to you, do!
17 So Yaakov arose, he lifted his children and his wives onto
      the camels
18 and led away all his livestock, all his property that he had
      gained,
   the acquired-livestock of his own acquiring which he had
      gained in the country of Aram,
   to come home to Yitzhak his father in the land of Canaan.
19 Now Lavan had gone to shear his flock;
   Rahel, meanwhile, stole the *terafim* that belonged to her
      father.
20 Now Yaakov stole the wits of Lavan the Aramean,
   by not telling him that he was about to flee.
21 And flee he did, he and all that was his;
   he arose and crossed the River, setting his face toward the
      mountain-country of Gil'ad.
22 Lavan was told on the third day that Yaakov had fled;
23 he took his tribal-brothers with him and pursued him, a
      seven-days' journey,
   and caught up with him in the mountain-country of Gil'ad.
24 But God came to Lavan the Aramean in a dream of the
      night
   and said to him:

Be on your watch
lest you speak to Yaakov, be it good or ill!

25 When Lavan caught up with Yaakov,
   —Yaakov had pegged his tent in the mountains, and Lavan
   along with his brothers had pegged (his tent) in the
   mountain-country of Gil'ad—

26 Lavan said to Yaakov:
   What did you mean to do
   by stealing my wits and leading my daughters away like
   captives of the sword?

27 Why did you secretly flee and steal away on me, without
   even telling me,
   —for I would have sent you off with joy and with song,
   with drum and with lyre—

28 and you did not even allow me to kiss my grandchildren
   and my daughters?
   You have done foolishly now!

29 It lies in my hand's power to do (all of) you ill!
   But yesterday night the God of your father said to me,
   saying:
   Be on your watch
   from speaking to Yaakov, be it good or ill!

30 Well now, you had to go, yes, go, since you longed, longed
   for your father's house—
   Why did you steal my gods?

31 Yaakov answered and said to Lavan:
   Indeed, I was afraid, for I said to myself: Perhaps you will
   even rob me of your daughters!

---

19 *terafim:* Hebrew obscure; apparently some sort of idols. Others use "house-hold gods."
20 **stole the wits:** Fooled, hoodwinked.
24 **be it good or ill:** Lit. "from good to ill."
28 **kiss:** Upon leaving; "kiss good-bye."
30 **you had to go:** Or "Suppose you had to go."
31 **Indeed, I was afraid:** Yaakov seems to be explaining why he "had to go" first, and then answering Lavan's question in verse 32.

32 With whomever you find your gods—he shall not live;
   here in front of our brothers, (see if) you recognize anything
      of yours with me, and take it!
   Yaakov did not know that Rahel had stolen them.
33 Lavan came into Yaakov's tent and into Lea's tent and into
      the tents of the two maids, but he did not find anything.
   Then he went out of Lea's tent and came into Rahel's tent.
34 Now Rahel had taken the *terafim* and had put them in the
      basket-saddle of the camels, and had sat down upon them.
   Lavan felt all around the tent, but he did not find anything.
35 She said to her father:
   Do not let anger rage in my lord's eyes that I am not able to
      rise in your presence,
   for the manner of women is upon me.
   So he searched, but he did not find the *terafim*.
36 Now Yaakov became enraged and took up quarrel with
      Lavan,
   Yaakov answered, saying to Lavan:
   What is my offense, what is my sin,
   that you have dashed hotly after me,
37 that you have felt all through my wares?
   What have you found from all your household-wares?
   Set it here in front of your brothers and my brothers,
    that they may decide between us two!
38 It is twenty years now that I have been under you:
   your ewes and your she-goats have never miscarried,
   the rams from your flock I never have eaten,
39 none torn-by-beasts have I ever brought you—
   I would make good the loss,
   at my hand you would seek it,
   stolen by day or stolen by night.
40 (Thus) I was:
   by day, parching-heat consumed me, and cold by night,
   and my sleep eluded my eyes.
41 It is twenty years for me now in your house:
   I have served you fourteen years for your two daughters,
      and six years for your animals,
   yet you have changed my wages ten times over.
42 Had not the God of my father,

the God of Avraham and the Terror of Yitzhak,
been-there for me,
indeed, you would have sent me off now, empty-handed!
But God has seen my being afflicted and the toil of my
  hands,
and yesterday night he decided.

43 Lavan gave answer, he said to Yaakov:
The daughters are my daughters,
the children are my children,
the animals are my animals—
all that you see, it is mine!
But to my daughters—what can I do to them today, or to
  their children whom they have borne?

44 So now, come,
let us cut a covenant, I and you,
and let (something here) serve as a witness between me and
  you.

45 Yaakov took a stone and erected it as a standing-pillar.

46 And Yaakov said to his brothers:
Collect stones!
They fetched stones and made a mound.
And they ate there by the mound.

47 Now Lavan called it: *Yegar Sahaduta,*
while Yaakov called it: Gal-Ed.

---

32 **with me:** In my possession.
34 **sat down upon them:** Ridiculing the pagan gods, at least to the audience.   **felt all around:** Recalling the "feeling" of Yitzhak in Chapter 27.
35 **manner of women:** The menstrual period.
37 **felt all through:** Or "rifled."
39 **seek:** I.e., seek restitution.
41 **twenty years:** Yosef will be away from Yaakov for approximately the same
   period of time.
42 **Terror:** The intent of the Hebrew is unclear; it could be something like
   "Yitzhak's champion" or "the One who inspired terror in Yitzhak."
43 **to my daughters:** Others use "for my daughters."
46 **And they ate:** See note to 26:30.
47 ***Yegar Sahaduta:*** Aramaic for "Mound-Witness" (Yaakov's Gal-Ed of the
   next verse). Aramaic was the *lingua franca* of the area from the First Millennium B.C.E. on, and still exists in some forms today.

48 Lavan said:
This mound is witness between me and you from today.
Therefore they called its name: Gal-Ed/Mound-Witness,
49 and also: Mitzpa/Guardpost,
because he said:
May YHWH keep guard between me and you, when we are
    hidden from one another!
50 If you should ever afflict my daughters,
if you should ever take wives besides my daughters . . . !
No man is here with us,
(but) see, God is witness between me and you!
51 And Lavan said to Yaakov:
Here is this mound, here is the pillar that I have sunk
    between me and you:
52 witness is this mound, witness is the pillar
that I will not cross over this mound to you
and you will not cross over this mound and this pillar to
    me,
for ill!
53 May the God of Avraham and the God of Nahor
    keep-justice between us—the God of their father.
And Yaakov swore by the Terror of his father Yitzhak.
54 Then Yaakov slaughtered a slaughter-meal on the mountain
and called his brothers to eat bread.
They ate bread and spent the night on the mountain.
32:1 Lavan (arose) early in the morning, kissed his grandchildren
    and his daughters and blessed them,
and Lavan went to return to his place.

  2 As Yaakov went on his way,
messengers of God encountered him.
  3 Yaakov said when he saw them:
This is a camp of God!
And he called the name of that place:
    Mahanayim/Double-Camp.

  4 Now Yaakov sent messengers on ahead of him to Esav his
    brother in the land of Se'ir, in the territory of Edom,

5 and charged them, saying:
  Thus say to my lord, to Esav:
  Thus says your servant Yaakov:
  I have sojourned with Lavan and have tarried until now.
6 Ox and ass, sheep and servant and maid have become mine.
  I have sent to tell my lord, to find favor in your eyes.
7 The messengers returned to Yaakov, saying:
  We came to your brother, to Esav—
  but he is already coming to meet you, and four hundred
      men are with him!
8 Yaakov became exceedingly afraid and was distressed.
  He divided the people that were with him and the sheep
      and the oxen and the camels into two camps,
9 saying to himself:
  Should Esav come against the one camp and strike it, the
      camp that is left will escape.

Preparations for Esav (32:2–24): As if to portend something momentous,
Yaakov's first act upon setting out for home is an encounter with "messengers of God." From this starting point everything is subsequently a
matter of "two camps" (v.8) or two levels: the divine and the human.
This is the key to understanding the meeting between Yaakov and his
brother in its entirety: Yaakov will have to deal with God before he can
resolve his problem with Esav.

With an obsequiousness whose language reflects both the culture and
the emotional setting, Yaakov prepares a gift for Esav, but finds to his
dismay that his brother is "coming to meet him," with seemingly hostile
intent. Once again stealth (or at least extreme caution) is the rule, with
Yaakov taking elaborate precautions.

49 **when we are hidden:** Even when I cannot verify your behavior.
50 **God:** Or "a god."
54 **bread:** Or more generally, "food."
32:1 **Lavan (arose) . . . :** The verse numbering follows the Hebrew; some English translations number 32:1 as 31:55.
  7 **four hundred men:** A considerable fighting force. Even if the number is
   schematic (as ten times forty), it still represents something formidable.

10 Then Yaakov said:
God of my father Avraham,
God of my father Yitzhak,
O YHWH,
who said to me: Return to your land, to your kindred, and
I will deal well with you!—
11 Too small am I for all the faithfulness and trust that you
have shown your servant.
For with only my rod did I cross this Jordan, and now I
have become two camps.
12 Pray save me from the hand of my brother, from the hand
of Esav!
For I am in fear of him,
lest he come and strike me down, mothers and children
alike!
13 But you, you have said:
I will deal well, well with you,
I will make your seed like the sand of the sea, which is too
much to count!
14 Spending the night there that night,
he took a gift from what was at hand, for Esav his brother:
15 she-goats, two hundred, and kids, twenty,
ewes, two hundred, and rams, twenty,
16 nursing camels and their young, thirty,
cows, forty, and bulls, ten,
she-asses, twenty, and colts, ten;
17 he handed them over to his servants, herd by herd
separately,
and said to his servants:
Cross on ahead of me, and leave room between herd and
herd.
18 He charged the first group, saying:
When Esav my brother meets you
and asks you, saying: To whom do you belong, where are
you going, and to whom do these ahead of you belong?
19 Then say:
—to your servant, to Yaakov, it is a gift sent to my lord, to
Esav,

and here, he himself is also behind us.

20 Thus he charged the second, and thus the third, and thus
all that were walking behind the herds, saying:
According to this word shall you speak to Esav when you
come upon him:

21 You shall say: Also—here, your servant Yaakov is behind
us.
For he said to himself:
I will wipe (the anger from) his face
with the gift that goes ahead of my face;
afterward, when I see his face,
perhaps he will lift up my face!

22 The gift crossed over ahead of his face,
but he spent the night on that night in the camp.

23 He arose during that night,
took his two wives, his two maids, and his eleven children
to cross the Yabbok crossing.

24 He took them and brought them across the river; he
brought across what belonged to him.

25 And Yaakov was left alone—
Now a man wrestled with him until the dawn rose.

26 When he saw that he could not prevail against him,
he touched the socket of his thigh;
the socket of Yaakov's thigh had been dislocated as he
wrestled with him.

---

11 **Too small:** This is the first indication of the change in Yaakov's personality. Now he relies on God (although he still uses his wits, by diplomatically
and strategically preparing for his meeting with Esav).

13 **you have said:** I.e., you have promised. See also note on 31:10. **like the
sand:** In fact, this is God's promise to Avraham, in 22:17.

15: **she-goats . . . :** The gift is a special one, promising increase (females with
their young).

21 **lift up my face:** Or "be gracious to me."

23 **Yabbok:** A traditional natural boundary, it creates a wild gorge which is the
perfect setting for this incident.

25 **left alone:** In a psychological sense Yaakov has not yet crossed the river.

26 **touched:** Perhaps in homage, for the injury had already occurred (Ehrlich).

27 Then he said:
   Let me go,
   for the dawn has risen!
   But he said:
   I will not let you go
   unless you bless me.
28 He said to him:
   What is your name?
   And he said: Yaakov.
29 Then he said:
   Not as Yaakov/Heel-Sneak shall your name be henceforth
      uttered,
   but rather as Yisrael/God-Fighter,
   for you have fought with God and men
   and have prevailed.
30 Then Yaakov asked and said:
   Pray tell me your name!
   But he said:
   Now why do you ask after my name?
   And he gave him farewell-blessing there.
31 Yaakov called the name of the place: Peniel/Face of God,
   for: I have seen God,
   face to face,
   and my life has been saved.
32 The sun shone on him as he crossed by Penuel,
   and he was limping on his thigh.
33 —Therefore the Sons of Israel do not eat the sinew that is
      on the socket of the thigh until this day,
   for he had touched the socket of Yaakov's thigh at the
      sinew.

33:1 Yaakov lifted up his eyes and saw:
     there was Esav coming, and with him, four hundred men!
     He divided the children among Lea, Rahel, and the two
        maids:
   2 he put the maids and their children first,
     Lea and her children behind them,
     and Rahel and Yosef behind them,

The Mysterious Stranger: Struggle at the Yabbok (32:25–33): Unexpectedly there is a break in the narrative. The stage has been set for something mysterious to happen with a nighttime backdrop and accented references to "crossing" (vv.23–24), which clearly refers to more than just the river.

The great wrestling scene at the Yabbok both symbolizes and resolves beforehand Yaakov's meeting with Esav, much as Shakespeare's pre-battle dream scenes (e.g., *Julius Caesar, Richard III, Macbeth*) will do with his characters. Struggle, the motif already introduced in the mother's womb (Chapter 25), returns here, but that is not the only consideration. At issue is Yaakov's whole life and personality, which despite his recent material successes are still under the pall of Esav's curse (27:36). Central, then, is the change of name in verse 29, which suggests both a victorious struggle and the emergence of a new power. This is further supported by the Hebrew plays on sound: *Y'KB* (Yaakov), *YBK* (Yabbok), and *Y'BK* (wrestling).

The story may have originated as the well-known tale of a hero fighting a river divinity, but it clearly has been transformed into something much broader by its position and vocabulary.

Resolution (33:1–17): Once the Yabbok crisis is past, there is hope for reconciliation of the brothers. Even so, Yaakov exercises caution, behaving like a man who is presenting tribute to a king. The narrative is brought full circle in verses 10 and 11, where "face" is once again highlighted and where Yaakov's gift is termed a "token-of-blessing." At last the tension of Yaakov's early life seems resolved.

27 **dawn has risen:** In folklore, supernatural beings often must disappear with the break of day.
28–29 **What is your name?** . . . **Not as Yaakov:** As if to say "You cannot be blessed with such a name!" The "man" in effect removes Esav's curse.
29 **God-Fighter:** The name may actually mean "God fights." Buber further conjectured that it means "God rules," containing the kernel of ancient Israel's concept of itself, but he retained "Fighter of God" in the translation. **God and men:** Others use "beings divine and human."
30 **Now why do you ask:** In folklore the name of a divine being is often withheld, for to know it would be to acquire power over him. See also Judges 13:18: "Now why do you ask after my name? For it is wondrous!"
31 **Peniel/Face of God:** See verse 21, and 33:10, for the important allusions.
32 **The sun shone:** A sign of favor. **Penuel:** A variant spelling of Peniel.
33 **sinew:** The sciatic nerve.

3 while he himself advanced ahead of them.
  And he bowed low to the ground seven times, until he had
    come close to him, to his brother.
4 Esav ran to meet him,
  he embraced him, flung himself upon his neck, and kissed
    him.
  And they wept.
5 Then he lifted up his eyes and saw the women and the
    children, and said:
  What are these to you?
  He said:
  —the children with whom God has favored your servant.
6 Then the maids came close, they and their children, and
    bowed low.
7 Then Lea and her children came close and bowed low.
  Afterward Yosef and Rahel came close and bowed low.
8 He said:
  What to you is all this camp that I have met?
  He said:
  —to find favor in my lord's eyes.
9 Esav said:
  I have plenty, my brother, let what is yours remain yours.
10 Yaakov said:
  No, I pray!
  Pray, if I have found favor in your eyes,
  then take this gift from my hand.
  For I have, after all, seen your face, as one sees the face of
    God,
  and you have been gracious to me.
11 Pray take my token-of-blessing that is brought to you,
  for God has shown me favor—for I have everything.
  And he pressed him, so he took it.
12 Then he said:
  Let us travel on, and I will go on at your side.
13 But he said to him:
  My lord knows
  that the children are frail,
  and the sheep and the oxen are suckling in my care;
  if we were to push them for a single day, all the animals
    would die!

14 Pray let my lord cross on ahead of his servant,
while as for me, I will travel slowly,
at the pace of the gear ahead of me and at the pace of the
children,
until I come to my lord, in Se'ir.
15 Esav said:
Pray let me leave with you some of the people who are
mine.
But he said:
For what reason?
May I only find favor in my lord's eyes!
16 So Esav started back that same day on his journey to Se'ir,
17 while Yaakov traveled to Succot.
He built himself a house there, and for his livestock he
made sheds.
Therefore they called the name of the place: Succot/Sheds.

18 Yaakov came home in peace to the city of Shekhem, which
is in the land of Canaan,
on his homecoming from the country of Aram,
and he encamped facing the city.

Home: Peace and Violence (33:18–34:31): "Yaakov came home in peace
to the city of Shekhem" (33:18) continues the theme of resolution. Not
only has Esav accepted his gift, but Yaakov has arrived home safely, in
fulfillment of his prayer in 28:21. Like Avraham he purchases land;
again like him he builds an altar.

Chapter 34, however, shatters the newly created atmosphere of security and peace ("peaceably disposed" in verse 21 is a bitter twist).
Whereas Avraham and Yitzhak had been able to conclude treaties with
the inhabitants of Canaan, Yaakov winds up in the opposite position.
The text implies, as usual, that Canaanite sexual behavior is odious (v.7,
"such [a thing] is not to be done!"), and this provides the spring for the

33:8 **What to you is:** I.e., What does it mean to you?
    9 **my brother:** The phrase suggests that they are now reconciled.
   15 **leave with you:** Or "station with you," "put at your disposal."   **mine:** Lit.
      "with me."   **For what reason?:** Yaakov still seems cautious.

19 And he acquired the piece of territory where he had spread
   out his tent, from the Sons of Hamor, Shekhem's father,
   for a hundred lambs'-worth.
20 There he set up an altar
   and called it:
   El/God, the God of Yisrael!

34:1 Now Dina, Lea's daughter, whom she had borne to
     Yaakov, went out to see the women of the land.
   2 And Shekhem son of Hamor the Hivvite, the prince of the
     land, saw her:
     he took her and lay with her, forcing her.
   3 But his emotions clung to Dina, Yaakov's daughter—he
     loved the girl,
     and he spoke to the heart of the girl.
   4 So Shekhem said to Hamor his father, saying:
     Take me this girl as a wife!
   5 Now Yaakov had heard that he had defiled Dina his
     daughter,
     but since his sons were with his livestock in the fields,
     Yaakov kept silent until they came home.
   6 Hamor, Shekhem's father, went out to Yaakov, to speak
     with him.
   7 But Yaakov's sons came back from the fields when they
     heard,
     and the men were pained, they were exceedingly enraged,
     for he had done a disgrace in Israel by lying with Yaakov's
     daughter,
     such (a thing) is not to be done!
   8 Hamor spoke with them, saying:
     My son Shekhem—
     his emotions are so attached to your daughter,
     (so) pray give her to him as a wife!
   9 And make marriage-alliances with us:
     give us your daughters, and our daughters take for
     yourselves,
  10 and settle among us!
     The land shall be before you:
     settle down, travel about it, obtain holdings in it!

11 And Shekhem said to her father and to her brothers:
   May I only find favor in your eyes!
   However much you say to me, I will give-in-payment,
12 to whatever extreme you multiply the bride price and the
      marriage gift,
   I will give however much you say to me—
   only give me the girl as a wife!
13 Now Yaakov's sons answered Shekhem and Hamor his
      father with deceit,
   speaking (thus) because he had defiled Dina their sister,
14 they said to them:
   We cannot do this thing,
   give our sister to a man who has a foreskin,
   for that would be a reproach for us!

---

action. Interestingly, Yaakov's sons act somewhat like their father had, "with deceit" (v.13); and love once again leads to an unfortunate end.

The vengefulness and brutality of Yaakov's sons in this story anticipates their later behavior in the Yosef story (Chapter 37); surprisingly, it is for the present crime and not the sale of Yosef that their father condemns them on his deathbed (49:5–7).

The chapter is notable for the latitude it allows its characters to express their thoughts and emotions: Shekhem's desire and love, the sons' anger and cunning, the Hivvites' gullibility and greed, and Yaakov's fear. Like other stories in the Yaakov cycle, it presents us with a somewhat ambiguous situation, where right and wrong are not always simple and the putative heroes are not always heroic.

19 **he acquired:** Like his grandfather Avraham, Yaakov must purchase the land. **lambs'-worth:** Hebrew obscure.
34:1 **to see:** To visit.
   2 **Hamor:** Heb. "ass." Some take the name to prove that they were donkey-drivers, while others see it as an insult to the character.
   7 **disgrace:** A different Hebrew word from the one rendered "disgraced" in 15:2.
   8 **his emotions are so attached:** Speiser uses "has his heart set on." **pray give:** The repetition of "give" suggests a greediness on their part.
   10 **travel about:** Or "trade."
   13 **with deceit:** Another example of a key word in the Yaakov stories; see 27:35 and 29:25.

15 Only on this (condition) will we comply with you:
   if you become like us, by having every male among you
       circumcised.
16 Then we will give you our daughters, and your daughters
       we will take for ourselves,
   and we will settle among you, so that we become a single
       people.
17 But if you do not hearken to us, to be circumcised,
   we will take our daughter and go.
18 Their words seemed good in the eyes of Hamor and in the
       eyes of Shekhem son of Hamor,
19 and the young man did not hesitate to do the thing,
   for he desired Yaakov's daughter.
   Now he carried more weight than anyone in his father's
       house.
20 When Hamor and Shekhem his son came back to the gate
       of their city,
   they spoke to the men of their city, saying:
21 These men are peaceably disposed toward us;
   let them settle in the land and travel about in it,
   for the land is certainly wide-reaching enough for them!
   Let us take their daughters as wives for ourselves, and let
       us give them our daughters.
22 But only on this condition will the men comply with us, to
       settle among us, to become a single people:
   that every male among us be circumcised, as they are
       circumcised.
23 Their acquired livestock, their acquired property and all
       their beasts—will they not then become ours?!
   Let us only comply with them, that they may settle among
       us!
24 So they hearkened to Hamor and to Shekhem his son, all
       who go out (to war) from the gate of his city:
   all the males were circumcised, all who go out (to war) from
       the gate of his city.
25 But on the third day it was, when they were still hurting,
   that two of Yaakov's sons, Shim'on and Levi, Dina's
       full-brothers, took each man his sword,

they came upon the city (feeling) secure, and killed all the
    males,

26 and Hamor and Shekhem his son they killed by the sword.
Then they took Dina from Shekhem's house and went off.

27 Yaakov's other sons came up upon the corpses and
    plundered the city,
because they had defiled their sister.

28 Their sheep, their oxen, their asses—whatever was inside
    the city and out in the field, they took,

29 all their riches, all their little-ones and their wives they
    captured and plundered,
as well as all that was in the houses.

30 But Yaakov said to Shim'on and to Levi:
You have stirred-up-trouble for me,
making me reek among the settled-folk of the land, the
    Canaanites and the Perizzites!
For I have menfolk few in number;
they will band together against me and strike me,
and I will be destroyed, I and my household!

31 But they said:
Should our sister then be treated like a whore?

35:1 Now God said to Yaakov:
Arise,
go up to Bet-El and stay there,
and construct an altar there
to the God/*El* who was seen by you when you fled
    from Esav your brother.

---

19 **desired:** Not the same Hebrew term as in 2:9.   **carried more weight:** I.e.,
was more respected.

21 **peaceably disposed:** Or "friendly," "honest."

24 **all who go out . . . :** I.e., all able-bodied men.

25 **Shim'on and Levi:** They are condemned for this incident by Yaakov in
49:5–7.

27 **Yaakov's other sons:** Lit. "Yaakov's sons."

2 Yaakov said to his household and to all who were with him:
Put away the foreign gods that are in your midst!
Purify yourselves! Change your garments!

3 Let us arise and go up to Bet-El,
there I will construct an altar
to the God who answered me on the day of my distress
—he was with me on the way that I went!

4 So they gave Yaakov all the foreign gods that were in their
hand, along with the sacred-rings that were in their ears,
and Yaakov concealed them under the oak/*ela* that is near
Shekhem.

5 Then they departed.
Now a dread from God lay upon the towns that were
around them,
so that they did not pursue Yaakov's sons.

6 So Yaakov came home to Luz, which is in the land of
Canaan—that is now Bet-El—he and all the people that
were with him.

7 There he built an altar
and called the place:
Godhead/*El* of Bet-El!
For there had the power-of-God been revealed to him,
when he fled from his brother.

8 Now Devora, Rivka's nurse, died.
She was buried below Bet-El, beneath the oak;
they called its name: Allon Bakhut/Oak of Weeping.

9 God was seen by Yaakov again, when he came home from
the country of Aram,
and he gave him blessing:

10 God said to him:
Yaakov is your name,
Yaakov shall your name be called no more,
for your name shall be Yisrael!
And he called his name: Yisrael!

11 God said further to him:
I am God Shaddai.
Bear fruit and be many!

Nation, yes, a host of nations shall come from you,
kings shall go out from your loins!

12 The land
that I gave to Avraham and to Yitzhak,
to you I give it,
and to your seed after you I give the land.

13 God went up from beside him, at the place where he had
spoken with him.

14 And Yaakov set up a standing-pillar at the place where he
had spoken with him, a pillar of stone,
he poured out a poured-offering on it and cast oil upon it.

15 And Yaakov called the name of the place where God had
spoken with him:
Bet-El/House of God!

Home: Blessing and Death (35): Several brief notices round out Yaakov's
return to Canaan. First (vv.1–7) there is the return to Bet-El, where he
builds an altar and has the "foreign" gods of his household people put
away—thus fulfilling his promise in Chapter 28. This passage is built
upon the Hebrew word *El*, God (related actually to an earlier Northwest
Semitic name for a god).

Apparently a second version of Yaakov's name change is recorded in
verses 9–15. As in the case of Avraham, seed and land are promised by
God. The land can be given to him and "to your seed after you" only
upon his return.

Finally, spread out through the chapter are the accounts of three
deaths: Devora, Rivka's nurse (v.8—a veiled reference to Rivka's own
death?), Rahel (vv.16–20), and finally Yitzhak (vv.28–29). Yaakov's
youth is over, with the dramatic break with those close to him in that
period.

35:2 **Change your garments:** Speiser translates this as "Put on new clothes."
  8 **Rivka's nurse, died:** See note to 24:59.
9ff. **God was seen . . . :** Apparently a different version of the Peniel story of
    Chapter 32.
11–12 **I am God Shaddai . . . :** See God's words to Avraham in 17:6.
    13 **at the place where he had spoken with him:** The phrase occurs three times
       here and subsequently, probably to emphasize the sanctity of Bet-El.

16 They departed from Bet-El.
   But when there was still a stretch of land to come to Efrat,
   Rahel began to give birth,
   and she had a very hard birthing.
17 It was, when her birthing was at its hardest,
   that the midwife said to her:
   Do not be afraid,
   for this one too is a son for you!
18 It was, as her life was slipping away
   —for she was dying—
   that she called his name: Ben-Oni/Son-of-My-Woe.
   But his father called him: Binyamin/Son-of-the-Right-Hand.
19 So Rahel died;
   she was buried along the way to Efrat—that is now
      Bet-Lehem.
20 Yaakov set up a standing-pillar over her burial-place,
   that is Rahel's burial pillar of today.

21 Now Yisrael departed and spread his tent beyond
      Migdal-Eder/Herd-Tower.
22 And it was when Yisrael was dwelling in that land: Re'uven
      went and lay with Bilha, his father's concubine.
   And Yisrael heard—

   Now the sons of Yaakov were twelve:
23 The sons of Lea: Yaakov's firstborn, Re'uven; Shim'on,
      Levi and Yehuda, Yissakhar and Zevulun.
24 The sons of Rahel: Yosef and Binyamin.
25 The sons of Bilha, Rahel's maid: Dan and Naftali.
26 The sons of Zilpa, Lea's maid: Gad and Asher.
   These (were) Yaakov's sons, who were born to him in the
      country of Aram.

27 Yaakov came home to Yitzhak his father at Mamre, in the
      town of Arba—that is now Hevron,
   where Avraham and Yitzhak had sojourned.
28 And the days of Yitzhak were a hundred years and eighty
29   years,/ then Yitzhak breathed-his-last.

He died and was gathered to his kinspeople, old and
   abundant in days.
Esav and Yaakov his sons buried him.

36:1 And these are the begettings of Esav—that is Edom.
   2 Esav took his wives from the women of Canaan:
       Ada, daughter of Elon the Hittite, and Oholivama, daughter
   3   of Ana (and) granddaughter of Tziv'on the Hivvite,/ and
       Ba'semat, daughter of Yishmael and sister of Nevayot.
   4 Ada bore Elifaz to Esav,
       Ba'semat bore Re'uel,
   5 Oholivama bore Ye'ush, Ya'lam, and Korah.
       These are Esav's sons, who were born to him in the land of
       Canaan.

Re'uven (35:21–22): The following tiny fragment, concerning Re'uven's
usurping his father's concubine, serves to presage his fall as firstborn
later on. Such an act had symbolic value in biblical society; Avshalom
(Absalom) sleeps with David's concubines as a sign of rebellion and a
desire to attain the crown (II Sam. 16:21–22).

Esav's Descendants (36): The complicated genealogies and dynasties of
this chapter close out the first part of the Yaakov cycle, strictly speaking.
Fitting in the context of a society which lay great store by kinship and
thus by careful remembering of family names, it may also indicate the
greatness of Yitzhak's line, as Chapter 25 had earlier done for Avraham.
Certainly the lists give evidence of a time when the Edomites were more
than merely Israel's neighbors, assuming great importance in historical
recollection (Speiser).

17 **this one too is a son:** This seems to be a breach birth, since the midwife
   already knew that it was a son when "her birthing was at its hardest"—that
   is, before the child had fully emerged.
18 **her life was slipping away:** Or "her life-breath was leaving (her),"—paralleling a similar expression in Ugaritic.   **But his father called him: Binyamin:**
   Given the power of names, it would not have been considered fortuitous for
   a child to begin life with a name such as the one Rahel gives him. **Binyamin:** Trad. English "Benjamin."
19 **Bet-Lehem:** Trad. English "Bethlehem."
29 **Then Yitzhak breathed-his-last:** See the Commentary on 26:1–6.

6 Esav took his wives, his sons and his daughters, and all the
   persons in his household,
   as well as his acquired livestock, all his beasts, and all his
   acquisitions that he had gained in the land of Canaan,
   and went to (another) land, away from Yaakov his brother;
7 for their property was too much for them to settle together,
   the land of their sojourning could not support them, on
   account of their acquired livestock.
8 So Esav settled in the mountain-country of Se'ir—Esav, that
   is Edom.
9 And these are the begettings of Esav, the tribal-father of
   Edom, in the mountain-country of Se'ir:
10 These are the names of the sons of Esav:
   Elifaz son of Ada, Esav's wife, Re'uel, son of Ba'semat,
   Esav's wife.
11 The sons of Elifaz were Teman, Omar, Tzefo, Ga'tam, and
   Kenaz.
12 Now Timna was concubine to Elifaz son of Esav, and she
   bore Amalek to Elifaz.
   These are the sons of Ada, Esav's wife.
13 And these are the sons of Re'uel: Nahat and Zerah,
   Shamma and Mizza.
   These were the sons of Ba'semat, Esav's wife.
14 And these were the sons of Oholivama, daughter of Ana,
   (and) granddaughter of Tziv'on (and) Esav's wife:
   She bore Ye'ush and Ya'lam and Korah to Esav.
15 These are the families of Esav's sons:
   From the sons of Elifaz, Esav's firstborn, are: the Family
   Teman, the Family Omar, the Family Tzefo, the Family
16   Kenaz,/ the Family Korah, the Family Ga'tam, the
   Family Amalek;
   these are the families from Elifaz in the land of Edom, these
   are the sons of Ada.
17 And these are the Sons of Re'uel, Esav's son: the Family
   Nahat, the Family Zerah, the Family Shamma, the
   Family Mizza;
   these are the families from Re'uel in the land of Edom,
   these the Sons of Ba'semat, Esav's wife.

18 And these are the Sons of Oholivama, Esav's wife: the
     Family Ye'ush, the Family Ya'lam, the Family Korah;
   these are the families from Oholivama, daughter of Ana,
     Esav's wife.
19 These are the Sons of Esav and these are their families.
   —That is Edom.

20 These are the sons of Se'ir the Horite, the settled-folk of the
     land:
21 Lotan and Shoval and Tziv'on and Ana and Dishon and
     Etzer and Dishan.
   These are the Horite families, the Sons of Se'ir in the land
     of Edom.
22 The sons of Lotan were Hori and Hemam, and Lotan's
     sister was Timna.
23 And these are the sons of Shoval: Alvan and Manahat and
     Eval, Shefo and Onam.
24 And these are the sons of Tziv'on: Ayya and Ana.
   —That is the Ana who found the *yemim* in the wilderness,
     as he was tending the asses of Tziv'on his father.
25 And these are the sons of Ana: Dishon—and Oholivama was
     Ana's daughter.
26 And these are the sons of Dishon: Hemdan and Eshban and
     Yitran and Ceran.
27 These are the sons of Etzer: Bilhan and Zaavan and Akan.
28 These are the sons of Dishan: Utz and Aran.
29 These are the Horite families: the Family Lotan, the Family
30   Shoval, the Family Tziv'on, the Family Ana,/ the Family
     Dishon, the Family Etzer, the Family Dishan.

36:7 **for their property was too much:** Again recalling Avraham, in his conflict
   with Lot (13:6).
 14 **Tziv'on:** The name means "hyena." Such animal names have long been
   popular in the region and occur a number of times in this chapter (Vawter).
 15 **families:** Others use "chieftains."
 24 *yemim:* Hebrew obscure; some use "hot-springs," "lakes."
 26 **Dishon:** The traditional text uses "Dishan," but see I Chron. 1:41.

These are the families of the Horites, according to their families in the land of Se'ir.

31 Now these are the kings who served as king in the land of Edom, before any king of the Sons of Israel served as king:
32 In Edom, Bela son of Be'or was king; the name of his city was Dinhava.
33 When Bela died, Yovav son of Zerah of Botzra became king in his stead.
34 When Yovav died, Husham from the land of the Temanites became king in his stead.
35 When Husham died, Hadad son of Bedad became king in his stead—who struck Midyan in the territory of Mo'av, and the name of his city was Avit.
36 When Hadad died, Samla of Masreka became king in his stead.
37 When Samla died, Sha'ul of Rehovot-by-the-River became king in his stead.
38 When Sha'ul died, Baal-Hanan son of Akhbor became king in his stead.
39 When Baal-Hanan son of Akhbor died, Hadar became king in his stead; the name of his city was Pa'u, and the name of his wife, Mehetavel daughter of Matred, daughter of Me-Zahav.

40 Now these are the names of the families from Esav, according to their clans, according to their local-places, by their names:
41 The Family Timna, the Family Alvan, the Family Yetet,/ the Family Oholivama, the Family Ela, the Family
42 Pinon,/ the Family Kenaz, the Family Teman, the Family
43 Mivtzar,/ the Family Magdiel, the Family Iram.
   These are the families of Edom according to their settlements in the land of their holdings.

That is Esav, the tribal-father of Edom.

PART IV Yosef
(37–50)

THE STORIES about the last Patriarch form a coherent whole, leading some to dub it a "novella." It stands well on its own, although it has been consciously and artfully woven together into both the Yaakov cycle and the entire book.

Initially the tale is one of family emotions, and it is in fact extreme emotions which give it a distinctive flavor. All the major characters are painfully expressive of their feelings, from the doting father to the spoiled son, from the malicious brothers to the lustful wife of Potifar, from the nostalgic adult Yosef to the grief-stricken old Yaakov. It is only through the subconscious medium of dreams, in three sets, that we are made to realize that a higher plan is at work which will supersede the destructive force of these emotions.

For this is a story of how "ill"—with all its connotations of fate, evil, and disaster—is changed to good. Despite the constant threat of death to Yosef, to the Egyptians, and to Binyamin, the hidden, optimistic thrust of the story is "life," a word that appears in various guises throughout. Even "face," the key word of the Yaakov cycle which often meant something negative, is here given a kinder meaning, as the resolution to Yaakov's life.

A major subtheme of the plot is the struggle for power between Re'uven and Yehuda. Its resolution has implications that are as much tribal as personal, for the tribe of Yehuda later became the historical force in ancient Israel as the seat of the monarchy.

Although many details of the narrative confirm Egyptian practices, those practices actually reflect an Egypt considerably later than the period of the Patriarchs (Redford). Of interest also is the prominence of the number five in the story, a detail that is unexplained but that gives some unity to the various sections of text.

In many ways the Yosef material repeats elements in the Yaakov traditions. A long list could be compiled, but let us at least mention here sibling hatred, exile of the hero, foreign names, love and hate, dreams, and deception—even so detailed as to duplicate the use of a goat-kid. But its focusing on a classic rags-to-riches plot, with the addition of a moralistic theme, make the Yosef story a distinctive and always popular tale, accessible in a way that the more difficult stories of the first three parts of Genesis are not.

37:1 Yaakov settled in the land of his father's sojournings,
   in the land of Canaan.

2 These are the begettings of Yaakov.

  Yosef, seventeen years old, used to tend the sheep along with
     his brothers,
   for he was serving-lad with the sons of Bilha and the sons of
     Zilpa, his father's wives.
   And Yosef brought a report of them, an ill one, to their
     father.
3 Now Yisrael loved Yosef above all his sons,
   for he was a son of old age to him,
   so he made him an ornamented coat.
4 When his brothers saw that it was he whom their father
     loved above all his brothers,
   they hated him,
   and could not speak to him in peace.

5 Now Yosef dreamt a dream, and told it to his brothers
   —from then on they hated him still more—,
6 he said to them:
   Pray hear this dream that I have dreamt:
7 Here,
   we were binding sheaf-bundles out in the field,
   and here, my sheaf arose, it was standing upright,
   and here, your sheaves were circling round and bowing
     down to my sheaf!

8 His brothers said to him:
   Would you be king, yes, king over us?
   Or would you really rule, yes, rule us?
   From then on they hated him still more—for his dreams,
     for his words.

———————

Young Yosef: Love and Hate (37): As has been the pattern with the Avraham and Yaakov cycles, the opening chapter here introduces the key themes of the entire story. These include the father's love, the power of words, dreams, "ill" as a key word (here denoting evil intent but eventually encompassing misfortune, among other concepts), and of course, the brothers' hatred, which at first glance is the motivating force behind the action.

But the initial blame for what happens clearly lies with the father (vv.3–4), and is made unbearable by Yosef's own behavior. In point of fact he is largely responsible for his own downfall, bearing tales about his brothers (v.2) even before Yaakov's preference for him is noted. His insistence on telling his dreams to his brothers must be galling, particularly the second time (v.9), coming as it does after the report that "they hated him still more for his dreams" (v.8).

37:2 **begettings:** In the sense of "family history." As noted above, the Yosef story is a continuation of the Yaakov saga. **seventeen:** Together with 47:28, this provides another example of numerical balance in these stories (see the Commentary on "The Patriarchal Narratives, p. 45). Yosef lives with Yaakov for the first seventeen years of his life and for the last seventeen of his father's. **along with his brothers:** A hint that he would one day "shepherd" (rule) his brothers? The Hebrew is open to that interpretation (Redford). **brought a report:** Or "gossip." Although the doting father's love is crucial, it seems really to be Yosef's own behavior (which precedes the information about his coat) that causes his abuse by the brothers.
   3 **ornamented:** Hebrew obscure; B-R uses "ankle-length."
   4 **hated:** Such a violent emotion nevertheless has once before (with Lea in 29:31) led not to disaster but to the fulfillment of the divine plan (there, the hatred results in the competition to have children). **in peace:** Or "civilly"—again the key Yaakov word, "peace."
   6 **hear:** Which can also mean "understand" in biblical Hebrew.
   8 **king, yes, king . . . rule, yes, rule:** The doubling might reflect the brothers' astonishment and bitterness. See also verse 10.

9 But he dreamt still another dream, and recounted it to his
      brothers,
   he said:
   Here, I have dreamt still (another) dream:
   Here,
   the sun and the moon and eleven stars were bowing down
      to me!
10 When he recounted it to his father and his brothers,
   his father rebuked him and said to him:
   What kind of dream is this that you have dreamt!
   Shall we come, yes, come, I, your mother and your
      brothers,
   to bow down to you to the ground?
11 His brothers envied him,
   while his father remembered the matter.

12 Now his brothers went to tend their father's sheep in
      Shekhem.
13 Yisrael said to Yosef:
   Are not your brothers tending sheep in Shekhem?
   Come, I will send you to them!
   He said to him:
   Here I am.
14 And he said to him:
   Come, pray, look into the well-being of your brothers and
      into the well-being of the sheep,
   and bring me back word.
   So he sent him out from the valley of Hevron, and he came
      to Shekhem.
15 And a man came upon him—here, he was roaming in the
      field;
   the man asked him, saying:
   What do you seek?
16 He said:
   I seek my brothers,
   pray tell me where they are tending-sheep.
17 The man said:
   They have moved on from here,
   indeed, I heard them say: Let us go to Dotan.

Yosef went after his brothers and came upon them in
  Dotan.
18 They saw him from afar,
  and before he had gotten near them, they plotted-cunningly
    against him to cause his death.
19 They said each man to his brother:
  Here comes that dreamer!
20 So now, come, let us kill him and cast him into one of these
    pits
  and say: An ill-tempered beast has devoured him!
  Then we will see what becomes of his dreams!
21 When Re'uven heard it he tried to rescue him from their
    hand, he said:
  Let us not take his life!
22 And Re'uven said to them:
  Do not shed blood!
  Cast him into this pit that is in the wilderness,
  but do not lay a hand upon him!
  —in order that he might save him from their hand, to
    return him to his father.

The key word of the chapter, not surprisingly, is "brother," culminating in Yehuda's ironic words (v.27): "let not our hand be upon him, for
he is our brother. . . ." Shortly afterward Yosef, their "(own) flesh," is
sold into slavery and probable death.

10 **your mother:** The fact that she had died in Chapter 35 does not detract
   from the symbol of the dream.
11 **remembered:** Or "kept in mind."
12 **Shekhem:** In our text this city's name (three times here) reminds the reader
   of the disastrous events of Chapter 34.
13 **Come:** Repeated in verses 20 and 27; it is ironically Yaakov's decision to
   send Yosef to his brothers that sets this part of the plot into action.
14 **well-being:** Heb. *shalom,* translated as "peace" in verse 4 and elsewhere.
15 **a man:** Possibly another divine messenger (like the "man" in 32:25). See
   also the note to 'roaming" in 20:13.
21 **take his life:** Lit. "strike him mortally."

23 So it was, when Yosef came to his brothers,
    that they stripped Yosef of his coat,
    the ornamented coat that he had on,
24 and took him and cast him into the pit.
    Now the pit was empty—no water in it.
25 And they sat down to eat bread.

    They lifted up their eyes and saw:
    there was a caravan of Yishmaelites coming from Gil'ad,
    their camels carrying balm, balsam, and ladanum,
    traveling to take them down to Egypt.
26 Now Yehuda said to his brothers:
    What gain is there
    if we kill our brother and cover up his blood?
27 Come, let us sell him to the Yishmaelites—
    but let not our hand be upon him,
    for he is our brother, our flesh!
    And his brothers listened to him.

28 Meanwhile, some Midyanite men, merchants, passed by;
    they hauled up Yosef from the pit
    and sold Yosef to the Yishmaelites, for twenty pieces of
       silver.
    They brought Yosef to Egypt.

29 When Re'uven returned to the pit:
    here, Yosef was no more in the pit!
    He rent his garments
30 and returned to his brothers and said:
    The child is no more!
    And I—where am I to go?

31 But they took Yosef's coat,
    they slew a goat buck
    and dipped the coat in the blood.
32 They had the ornamented coat sent out
    and had it brought to their father and said:
    We found this;
    pray recognize

whether it is your son's coat or not!

33 He recognized it
and said:
My son's coat!
An ill-tempered beast has devoured him!
Yosef is torn, torn-to-pieces!

34 Yaakov rent his clothes,
he put sackcloth on his loins
and mourned his son for many days.

35 All his sons and daughters arose to comfort him,
but he refused to be comforted.
He said:
No,
I will go down to my son
in mourning, to Sheol!
Thus his father wept for him.

36 Meanwhile, the Midyanites had sold him into Egypt
to Potifar, Pharaoh's court-official,
Chief of the (palace) Guard.

---

25 **bread:** Or "food."

29 **rent his garments:** The tearing of clothing was a customary sign of mourning.

30 **And I . . . :** Heb. *va-ani, ana ani va.* The sound expresses the emotions. **Where am I to go:** I.e., what will become of me?

32 **pray recognize:** See 27:23, where Yitzhak did not "recognize" Yaakov. Yaakov's youth returns to haunt him, in a sense.

33 **My son's coat:** With the omission of "It is," the shock is conveyed more dramatically. Some ancient versions, however, include the phrase. **An ill-tempered beast . . . torn-to-pieces:** The Hebrew breaks into verse structure, with three word-beats per line: *haya ra'a akhalat'hu/ tarof toraf Yosef* (Alter).

34 **many days:** Possibly "years"; at any rate, longer than a normal mourning period (in the Bible, thirty or seventy days) (Jacob).

35 **Sheol:** The biblical underworld; others (and B-R) use "the grave."

36 **Midyanites:** The Hebrew has "Medanites." **court-official:** Lit. "eunuch," a common ancient Near Eastern title for such a position. Originally the term was applied literally, although later on the person was not necessarily a eunuch.

38:1 Now it was at about that time
       that Yehuda went down, away from his brothers
       and turned aside to an Adullamite man—his name was
           Hira.
   2 There Yehuda saw the daughter of a Canaanite man—his
           name was Shua,
       he took her (as his wife) and came in to her.
   3 She became pregnant and bore a son, and he called his
           name: Er.
   4 She became pregnant again and bore a son, and she called
           his name: Onan.
   5 Once again she bore a son, and she called his name: Shela.
       Now he was in Ceziv when she bore him.

   6 Yehuda took a wife for Er, his firstborn—her name was
           Tamar.
   7 But Er, Yehuda's firstborn, was ill in the eyes of YHWH,
           and YHWH caused him to die.
   8 Yehuda said to Onan:
       Come in to your brother's wife, do a brother-in-law's duty
           by her,
       to preserve seed for your brother!
   9 But Onan knew that the seed would not be his,
       so it was, whenever he came in to his brother's wife, he let
           it go to ruin on the ground,
       so as not to provide seed for his brother.
  10 What he did was ill in the eyes of YHWH,
       and he caused him to die as well.
  11 Now Yehuda said to Tamar his daughter-in-law:
       Sit as a widow in your father's house
       until Shela my son has grown up.
       For he said to himself:
       Otherwise he will die as well, like his brothers!
       So Tamar went and stayed in her father's house.
  12 And many days passed.

       Now Shua's daughter, Yehuda's wife, died.
       When Yehuda had been comforted,
       he went up to his sheep-shearers, he and his friend Hira the
           Adullamite, to Timna.

Yehuda and Tamar (38): Chapter 38 has been the subject of many discussions, for it seems to be out of place. It interrupts the story of Yosef at a crucial dramatic spot, and is not chronologically fully consistent with it (Yehuda ages considerably; then we return to Yosef as a seventeen-year-old). Some feel that the suspension in the drama helps to raise tension; others argue that this is the only possible place to put an important tradition about the important brother. While these and other arguments may have their merit, one may discern some significant thematic connections as well, both within the context of the Yosef story and of Genesis as a whole.

The episode first of all demonstrates the growth of Yehuda as a character who is central to the Yosef novella. Already in Chapter 37 he had demonstrated active leadership, albeit in a questionable cause. There he actually saved Yosef's life, in contrast to Re'uven's unsuccessful and ultimately self-centered rescue attempt. As the one who basically assumes responsibility, he will be made to undergo an inner development in the narrative, and again becomes the one to take charge of the youngest son (Binyamin, in Chapters 43 and 44). The missing piece that begins to explain his nobility in this regard (Chapter 44) is the present chapter. Yehuda here learns what it is to lose sons, and to want desperately to protect his youngest. Although his failure to marry off Tamar to the youngest son leads to public humiliation (twice, actually), his response shows that he immediately accepts blame: "She is in-the-right more than I" (v.26). Such an interpretation is further confirmed by the restriction

---

38:1 **away from his brothers:** More than geography seems to be meant. Yehuda begins to change as a person here, in preparation for Chapter 44. Note that the place Adullam assonates with Arabic (*'adula*) "to turn aside."

5 **Ceziv:** The Hebrew root connotes "lying."

6 **Tamar:** The name means "palm tree."

6–7 **firstborn:** Perhaps parallel to the ineffectual firstborn, Re'uven, of the previous chapter.

7 **was ill:** I.e., he was evil, although we are not told specifically how.

8 **a brother-in-law's duty:** It was a well-known practice in biblical times that if a man died without leaving an heir, it was the obligation of his nearest of kin (usually his brother) to marry the widow and sire a son—who would then bear the name of the deceased man (Deut. 25:5–10).

10 **What he did was ill:** Onan dies because he does not fulfill his legal obligation to continue his brother's line. The later interpretation, that his crime was masturbation ("onanism"), has no basis in this text.

11 **Otherwise he will die:** Folk belief often regarded a woman who had outlived two husbands as a bad risk in marriage. The emotion here—a father's fear of losing a young son—will return as central in 42:36.

13 Tamar was told, saying:
Here, your father-in-law is going up to Timna to shear his
  sheep.
14 She removed her widow's garments from her,
covered herself with a veil and wrapped herself,
and sat down by the entrance to Enayim/Two-Wells, which
  is on the way to Timna,
for she saw that Shela had grown up, yet she had not been
  given to him as a wife.
15 When Yehuda saw her, he took her for a whore, for she had
  covered her face.
16 So he turned aside to her by the wayside and said:
Come-now, pray let me come in to you—
for he did not know that she was his daughter-in-law.
She said:
What will you give me for coming in to me?
17 He said:
I myself will send out a goat kid from the flock.
She said:
Only if you give me a pledge, until you send it.
18 He said:
What is the pledge that I am to give you?
She said:
Your seal, your cord, and your staff that is in your hand.
He gave them to her and then he came in to her—and she
  became pregnant by him.
19 She arose and went away,
then she put off her veil from her and clothed herself in her
  widow's garments.
20 Now when Yehuda sent the goat kid by the hand of his
  friend the Adullamite, to fetch the pledge from the
  woman's hand,
he could not find her.
21 He asked the people of her place, saying:
Where is that sacred-prostitute, the one in Two-Wells by
  the wayside?
They said:
There has been no sacred-prostitute here!
22 So he returned to Yehuda and said:

I could not find her; moreover, the people of the place said:
There has been no sacred-prostitute here!
23 Yehuda said:
Let her keep them for herself, lest we become a
laughing-stock.
Here, I sent her this kid, but you, you could not find her.

---

of the word "pledge" to here and 43:9. Yehuda has learned what it means to stake oneself for a principle.

Only after we have been informed of Yehuda's change can the narrative resume with Chapter 39. True to biblical thinking, redemption may start only after the crime has been punished (e.g., the Samson story, where the hero's hair begins to grow immediately after his imprisonment).

Actually the chronology works out quite well. We are told via 41:46, 53–54, that about twenty years elapse between the sale of Yosef and his meetings with the brothers in Egypt; this often signifies a period in biblical parlance and could encompass a generation or a bit less. Since Yehuda was quite possibly a father already in Chapter 37, the present story could well end just before the events reported in Chapter 43—in other words, Yehuda reaches full inner maturity just in time.

The other function of this story seems to be to carry out the major theme of Genesis as we have presented it: continuity and discontinuity between the generations. What is at stake here is not merely the line of one of the brothers, but the line which (as the biblical audience must have been fully aware) will lead to royalty—King David was a descendant of Peretz of verse 29. This should not be surprising in a book of origins; we noted the possible mention of Jerusalem in 14:18. Apparently a popular early theme, connected as we have noted to the power of God in history, continuity/discontinuity is repeated in somewhat similar circumstances in the book of Ruth (which contains the only other mention of "begettings" outside of Genesis and Num. 3:1).

The narrator has woven Chapters 38 and 37 together with great skill. Again a man is asked to "recognize" objects, again the use of a kid, and again a brother (this time a dead one) is betrayed.

18 **seal . . . cord . . . staff:** Individual objects of identification in the ancient Near East, particularly the seal, which served to sign documents. See Speiser.
21 **sacred-prostitute:** Or "cult prostitute," one attached to a shrine in Canaan. Sex in the ancient world was often linked to religion (as part of fertility rites), although the Hebrews sought to sever the tie.

24 Now it was, after almost three New-Moons
   that Yehuda was told, saying:
   Tamar your daughter-in-law has played-the-whore,
   in fact, she has become pregnant from whoring!
   Yehuda said:
   Bring her out and let her be burned!
25 (But) as she was being brought out,
   she sent a message to her father-in-law, saying:
   By the man to whom these belong I am pregnant.
   And she said:
   Pray recognize—
   whose seal and cords and staff are these?
26 Yehuda recognized them
   and said:
   She is in-the-right more than I!
   For after all, I did not give her to Shela my son!
   And he did not know her again.

27 Now it was, at the time of her birthing, that here: twins
      were in her body!
28 And it was, as she was giving birth, that (one of them) put
      out a hand;
   the midwife took and tied a crimson thread on his hand,
      saying:
   This one came out first.
29 But it was, as he pulled back his hand, here, his brother
      came out!
   So she said:
   What a breach you have breached for yourself!
   So they called his name: Peretz/Breach.
30 Afterward his brother came out, on whose hand was the
      crimson thread.
   They called his name: Zerah.

39:1 Now when Yosef was brought down to Egypt,
     Potifar, an official of Pharaoh, and Chief of the Guard, an
        Egyptian man, acquired him from the hand of the
        Yishmaelites who brought him down there.

2 But YHWH was with Yosef, so that he became a man of
   success:
   while he was in the house of his lord the Egyptian,
3 his lord saw that YHWH was with him,
   so that whatever he did, YHWH made succeed in his
   hands.
4 Yosef found favor in his eyes, and he waited upon him;
   he appointed him over his house, and everything belonging
   to him he placed in his hands.
5 And it was, from when he had appointed him over his
   house and over everything that belonged to him,
   that YHWH blessed the Egyptian's house because of Yosef;
   YHWH's blessing was upon everything that belonged to
   him, in the house and in the fields.

Yosef: Rise and Fall (39): This chapter prefigures Yosef's eventual rise to
power and simultaneously chronicles his lowest point, literally and figuratively. The two strands of the plot are woven together into a pattern of
success/authority → imprisonment → success/authority. This also mirrors the larger story, which progresses from favorite son → slavery →
viceroy of Egypt. The integration takes place partly through the medium
of a key word, "hand"—which also occurred four times at the end of
Chapter 38 and thus acts as a further textual connector. Yosef's success is
tied six times to the phrase "in his hands" (vv.3, 4, 6, 8, 22, 23); he is
thrown into prison because of the garments that he left in his mistress's
"hands" (vv.12, 13). Similarly, the movement of the chapter is mirrored
in the word "eyes," which is linked first to the theme of authority (v.4),

27ff. **Now it was . . .** : The scene here rather strikingly recalls Yaakov and Esav
   at birth: twins, the hand reaching out, and the struggle to be first.
29 **breach:** Not in the sense of a "breach birth."
30 **Zerah:** Possibly connoting "red of dawn"—connecting with the crimson
   thread of verse 28 (and possibly paralleling Esav, who was also known as
   Edom, the "Red One").
39:1 **Potifar . . .** : The narrative resumes exactly, almost literally, where it had
   left off in 37:36.
2 **a man of success:** Or "a man blessed by success."
4 **over his house:** Foreshadowing Yosef's eventual position and title (41:40).

6 So he left everything that was his in Yosef's hands,
   not concerning himself about anything with him there,
     except for the bread that he ate.
   Now Yosef was fair of form and fair to look at.

7 Now after these events it was
   that his lord's wife fixed her eyes upon Yosef
   and said:
   Lie with me!
8 But he refused,
   he said to his lord's wife:
   Look, my lord need not concern himself with anything in
     the house, with me here,
   and everything that belongs to him, he has placed in my
     hands.
9 He is no greater in this house than I
   and has withheld nothing from me
   except for yourself,
   since you are his wife.
   So how could I do this great ill?
   I would be sinning against God!
10 Now it was, as she would speak to Yosef day after day, that
   he would not hearken to her, to lie beside her, to be with
   her—
11 so it was, on such a day,
   when he came into the house to do his work,
   and none of the house-people was there in the house—
12 that she grabbed him by his garment, saying:
   Lie with me!
   But he left his garment in her hand and fled, escaping
   outside.
13 Now it was, when she saw that he had left his garment in
   her hand and had fled outside,
14 that she called in her house-people and said to them, saying:
   See! He has brought to us
   a Hebrew man to play around with us!
   He came to me, to lie with me,
   but I called out with a loud voice,
15 and it was, when he heard that I raised my voice and called
   out

that he left his garment beside me and fled, escaping
        outside!
16 Now she kept his garment beside her, until his lord came
        back to the house.
17 Then she spoke to him according to these words, saying:
        There came to me the Hebrew servant whom you brought
        to us, to play around with me;
18 but it was, when I raised my voice and called out,
        that he left his garment beside me and fled outside.
19 Now it was, when his lord heard his wife's words which she
        spoke to him,
        saying: According to these words, your servant did to me!—
        that his anger raged;

---

then to the attempted seduction (v.7), and finally to authority again
(v.21) (Alter).

The chapter also repeats the phrase "And it was" (in one form or
another) some twelve times, as a distinct stylistic pattern.

Yosef's temporary downfall occurs here for reasons beyond literary
balance or suspense. It is in a very real sense the punishment for the
bratty behavior of his adolescence. Once again words (this time not his
own) get him into trouble (vv.17, 19), as they did in 37:8. And once
again a garment is cited as proof of a fabricated crime.

6 **left:** Consigned; see also verse 13 for a play on words. **except for the
   bread that he ate:** Since the Egyptians did not eat with foreigners (see, for
   instance, 43:32). **fair of form and fair to look at:** The only other person
   in the Bible described in exactly these words is Rahel, Yosef's mother
   (29:17). We are thus given an indirect clue about the source of Yaakov's
   doting behavior in the Yosef story.
9 **sinning:** Or "at fault." **against God:** From this point on, it is clear that
   Yosef is no longer the spoiled brat of Chapter 37. At key points in his life
   he consistently makes mention of God as the source of his success and good
   fortune (40:8; 41:16; 45:5, 7, 9).
10 **to lie beside her, to be with her:** A curious expression. Why does not the
   text say, as in verse 7, "to lie with her"? There is an additional irony: "to
   be with" usually refers to God (see verse 2, for example).
14 **play around:** A sexual reference.
15 **beside:** Three times here, the word perhaps suggests to the audience that
   Yosef's garment is all that she will ever get "to lie beside her."

20 Yosef's lord took him and put him in the dungeon house,
in the place where the king's prisoners are imprisoned.
But while he was there in the dungeon house,
21 YHWH was with Yosef and extended kindness to him:
he put his favor in the eyes of the dungeon warden.
22 And the dungeon warden put in Yosef's hands all the
prisoners that were in the dungeon house;
whatever had to be done there, it was he that did it.
23 The dungeon warden did not need to see to anything at all
in his hands,
since YHWH was with him,
and whatever he did, YHWH made succeed.

40:1 Now after these events it was
that the cupbearer and the baker of the king of Egypt fell
afoul of their lord, the king of Egypt.
2 Pharaoh became infuriated with his two officials, with the
chief cupbearer and the chief baker,
3 and he placed them in custody in the house of the chief of
the guard, in the dungeon house, the place where Yosef
was imprisoned.
4 The chief of the guard appointed Yosef for them, that he
should wait upon them.
They were in custody for many days.
5 And then the two of them dreamt a dream, each man his
own dream, in a single night,
each man according to his dream's interpretation,
the cupbearer and the baker of the king of Egypt, who were
imprisoned in the dungeon house.
6 When Yosef came to them in the morning and saw them,
here, they were dejected!
7 So he asked Pharaoh's officials who were with him in
custody in the house of his lord, saying:
Why are your faces in such ill-humor today?
8 They said to him:
We have dreamt a dream, and there is no interpreter for it!
Yosef said to them:
Are not interpretations from God?
Pray recount them to me!

9 The chief cupbearer recounted his dream to Yosef, he said
   to him:
   In my dream—
   here, a vine was in front of me,
10 and on the vine, three winding-tendrils,
   and just as it was budding, the blossom came up,
   (and) its clusters ripened into grapes.
11 Now Pharaoh's cup was in my hand—
   I picked the grapes
   and squeezed them into Pharaoh's cup
   and put the cup in Pharaoh's palm.
12 Yosef said to him:
   This is its interpretation:
   The three windings are three days—

The Rise to Power: Dreams (40:1–41:52): Continued are the themes of
Yosef's success in adversity and skill in interpreting dreams (yet his
father and brother, and not he, had done the interpreting in Chapter
37!). In Chapter 37 dreams had brought about his downfall; here
(Chapter 40) they will help the cupbearer and in Chapter 41 ultimately
save a country, his family, and himself. Yosef's self-assurance and reliance on God, already evident in 39:9, here mean that it will not be long
before he stands at the pinnacle.

Yosef's dramatic rise to power is an old and favorite motif in folklore.
The text colorfully presents Pharaoh's dreams, in great detail, especially
in his emotional retelling. All the more striking then is Yosef's simple
interpretation (41:23–27).

20 **dungeon:** Hebrew obscure.
21 **kindness:** Or "faithfulness," "loyalty." See 32:11.
40:1 **the cupbearer and the baker of the king of Egypt:** The Hebrew has "the
    cupbearer of the king of Egypt and the baker," a common construction in
    biblical Hebrew.
  2 **cupbearer:** Others use "butler."
  4 **appointed Yosef:** As Potifar had "appointed him over his house" (39:4).
  5 **interpretation:** Or "meaning."
  8 **Are not interpretations from God:** Foreshadowing 41:16, "Not I!/ God
    will answer. . . ."
  11 **Pharaoh's cup:** The cup was a common symbol of fate in the ancient Near
    East.

13 in another three days
Pharaoh will lift up your head,
he will restore you to your position
so that you will put Pharaoh's cup in his hand (once more),
according to the former practice, when you were his
    cupbearer.
14 But keep me in mind with you, when it goes well for you,
pray deal kindly with me and call me to mind to Pharaoh,
so that you have me brought out of this house.
15 For I was stolen, yes, stolen from the land of the Hebrews,
and here too I have done nothing
that they should have put me in this pit.
16 Now when the chief baker saw that he had interpreted for
    good,
he said to Yosef:
I too, in my dream—
here, three baskets of white-bread were on my head,
17 and in the uppermost basket, all sorts of edibles for
    Pharaoh, baker's work,
and birds were eating them from the basket, from off my
    head.
18 Yosef gave answer, he said:
This is its interpretation:
The three baskets are three days—
19 in another three days
Pharaoh will lift up your head
from off you,
he will hang you on a tree,
and the birds will eat your flesh from off you.
20 And thus it was, on the third day,
Pharaoh's birthday,
that he made a great drinking-feast for all his servants,
and he lifted up the head of the chief cupbearer and the
    head of the chief baker amidst his servants:
21 he restored the chief cupbearer to his cupbearership,
so that he put the cup in Pharaoh's palm (once more),
22 but the chief baker he hanged,
just as Yosef had interpreted to them.

23 But the chief cupbearer did not keep Yosef in mind,
   he forgot him.

41:1 Now at the end of two years'-time it was
    that Pharaoh dreamt:
    here, he was standing by the Nile-Stream,
   2 and here, out of the Nile, seven cows were coming up,
    fair to look at and fat of flesh,
    and they grazed in the reed-grass.
   3 And here, seven other cows were coming up after them out
      of the Nile,
    ill to look at and lean of flesh,
    and they stood beside the other cows on the bank of the
      Nile.
   4 Then the cows ill to look at and lean of flesh ate up
    the seven cows fair to look at, the fat-ones.
    Pharaoh awoke.
   5 He fell asleep and dreamt a second time:
    here, seven ears-of-grain were going up on a single stalk, fat
      and good,
   6 and here, seven ears, lean and scorched by the east wind,
      were springing up after them.

---

13 **lift up your head:** A parallel expression in Assyrian means "release" or
   "pardon."
14 **with you:** Possibly stressing the personal nature of the plea.
15 **stolen:** The Yaakov motif of Chapters 30–31.
16 **white-bread:** Others use "wicker."
17ff. **eating:** In Pharaoh's dreams of Chapter 41, "eating" comes to symbolize
   the disaster of famine.
19 **hang . . . on a tree:** Others use "impale on a stake."
23 **he forgot him:** Here, as in Potifar's house, initial success gives way to
   failure and continued imprisonment.
41:1 **two years'-time:** Lit. "two years of days."
   2 **cows:** In later (Ptolemaic) Egyptian inscriptions, as here, cows represent
     years.
   5 **fat and good:** Referring to the ears of grain.

7 Then the lean ears swallowed up
the seven ears fat and full.
Pharaoh awoke,
and here: (it was) a dream!

8 But in the morning it was, that his spirit was agitated,
so he sent and had all of Egypt's magicians and all of its
   wise-men called.
Pharaoh recounted his dream to them,
but no one could interpret them to Pharaoh.

9 Then the chief cupbearer spoke up to Pharaoh, saying:
I must call my faults to mind today!

10 Pharaoh was once infuriated with his servants
and placed me in custody, in the house of the chief of the
   guard,
myself and the chief baker.

11 And we dreamt a dream in a single night, I and he,
we dreamt each man according to the interpretation of his
   dream.

12 Now there was a Hebrew lad there with us, a servant of the
   chief of the guard;
we recounted them to him, and he interpreted our dreams
   to us,
for each man according to his dream he interpreted.

13 And thus it was: As he interpreted to us, so it was—
I was restored to my position, and he was hanged.

14 Pharaoh sent and had Yosef called.
They hurriedly brought him out of the pit;
he shaved, changed his clothes, and came before Pharaoh.

15 Pharaoh said to Yosef:
I have dreamt a dream, and there is no interpreter for it!
But I have heard it said of you
that you but need to hear a dream in order to interpret it.

16 Yosef answered Pharaoh, saying:
Not I!
God will answer what is for Pharaoh's welfare.

17 Pharaoh spoke to Yosef:
In my dream—
here, I was standing on the bank of the Nile,

18 and here, out of the Nile were coming up seven cows,

fat of flesh and fair of form,
and they grazed in the reed-grass.

19 And here, seven other cows were coming up after them,
wretched and exceedingly ill of form and lank of flesh,
in all the land of Egypt I have never seen their like for
ill-condition!

20 Then the seven lank and ill-looking cows ate up
the first seven cows, the fat-ones.

21 They entered their body, but you would not know that they
had entered their body, for they were as ill-looking as at
the beginning!
Then I awoke.

22 And I saw (again) in my dream:
here, seven ears were going up on a single stalk, full and
good,

23 and here, seven ears, hardened, lean, and scorched by the
east wind, were springing up after them.

24 Then the lean ears swallowed up
the seven good ears!
Now I have spoken with the magicians, but there is no one
that can tell me the answer!

25 Yosef said to Pharaoh:
Pharaoh's dream is one.
What God is about to do, he has told Pharaoh.

26 The seven good cows
are seven years,
the seven good ears
are seven years,
the dream is one.

---

8 **his dream:** The two dreams function as one, as Yosef explains.

19 **in all the land . . . I have never seen their like:** Pharaoh's description of
his dream is more vivid than the narrator's (vv.1–4).

25 **is one:** Or "has a single meaning."

26ff. **The seven good cows . . . :** Yosef's interpretation is highly structured.
The rhetoric emphasizes the last line of verse 27: after hearing "x are seven
years," three times, we hear "x will be seven years of famine!" See above,
40:19, where "Pharaoh will lift up your head" is followed by "from off
you."

27 And the seven lank and ill-looking cows that were coming
      up after them
   are seven years,
   and the seven ears, hollow and scorched by the east wind,
   will be seven years of famine!
28 That is the word that I spoke to Pharaoh:
   what God is about to do, he has let Pharaoh see.
29 Here,
   seven years are coming
   of great abundance in all the land of Egypt.
30 But seven years of famine will arise after them,
   when all the abundance in the land of Egypt will be
      forgotten.
   The famine will destroy the land,
31 and you will not know of that abundance in the land
   because of that famine afterward,
   for it will be exceedingly heavy.
32 Now as for the twofold repetition of the dream to Pharaoh:
      it means that the matter is determined by God,
   and God is hastening to do it.
33 So now, let Pharaoh select a discerning and wise man,
   and set him over the land of Egypt.
34 Let Pharaoh do this: let him appoint appointed-overseers
      for the land,
   dividing the land of Egypt into five parts during the seven
      years of abundance.
35 Let them collect all kinds of food from these good years
      that are coming,
   and let them pile up grain under Pharaoh's hand as
      food-provisions in the cities, and keep it under guard.
36 So the provisions will be an appointed-reserve for the land
   for the seven years of famine that will occur in the land of
      Egypt,
   so that the land will not be cut off by the famine.
37 The words seemed good in Pharaoh's eyes and in the eyes
      of all his servants,
38 and Pharaoh said to his servants:
   Could we find another like him, a man in whom is the spirit
      of a god?
39 Pharaoh said to Yosef:

Since a god has made you know all this,
there is none as wise and discerning as you;
40 you shall be the One Over My House!
To your orders shall all my people submit;
only by the throne will I be greater than you!
41 Pharaoh said further to Yosef:
See, I place you over all the land of Egypt!
42 And Pharaoh removed his signet-ring from his hand and
placed it on Yosef's hand,
he had him clothed in linen garments and put the gold
chain upon his neck;
43 he had him mount the chariot of his second-in-rank, and
they called out before him: *Avrekh!*/Attention!
Thus he placed him over all the land of Egypt.
44 Pharaoh said to Yosef:
I am Pharaoh,
but without you, no man shall raise hand or foot in all the
land of Egypt!
45 Pharaoh called Yosef's name: *Tzafenat Pane'ah*/The God
Speaks and He Lives.
He gave him Asenat, daughter of Poti Fera, priest of On, as
a wife.
And Yosef's influence went out over all the land of Egypt.

----

34 **let him appoint appointed-overseers:** We already know that Yosef is a
man often entrusted with responsibility—"appointed" (39:4, 40:4). **dividing . . . into five parts:** Hebrew obscure. B-R uses "arm (the land of
Egypt)."
35 **hand:** I.e., supervision.
36 **the land:** I.e., its people.
37 **The words seemed good:** Words now bring about Yosef's rise to power.
40 **the One Over My House:** A title similar to that of Yosef's steward in
43:16ff. **submit:** Hebrew obscure. **only by the throne:** Similar to Yosef's situation in Potifar's house, "He is no greater in this house than I"
(39:9)—but he withholds his wife.
41ff. **all the land of Egypt:** A refrain here, pointing to Yosef's power.
43 *Avrekh*/**Attention:** Hebrew unclear. Some suggest that it is Hebrew for
"bend the knee," others that it resembles an Assyrian title.
45 *Tzafenat-Pane'ah*/ **The God Speaks and He Lives:** An Egyptian name
which is appropriate to the story. Yosef lives, and through him, so do
Egypt, his family, and the future People of Israel. **Yosef's influence:**
Perhaps an idiom, or merely "Yosef went out."

46 Now Yosef was thirty years old when he stood in the
     presence of Pharaoh, king of Egypt.
   Yosef went out from Pharaoh's presence and passed through
     all the land of Egypt.

47 In the seven years of abundance the land produced in
     handfuls.
48 And he collected all kinds of provisions from those seven
     years that occurred in the land of Egypt,
   and placed provisions in the cities.
   The provisions from the fields of a city, surrounding it, he
     placed in it (as well).
49 So Yosef piled up grain like the sand of the sea, exceedingly
     much, until they had to stop counting, for it was
     uncountable.

50 Now two sons were born to Yosef, before the year of famine
     came,
   whom Asenat, daughter of Poti Fera, priest of On, bore to
     him.
51 Yosef called the name of the firstborn:
     Menashe/He-Who-Makes-Forget,
   meaning: God has made-me-forget all my hardships, all my
     father's house.
52 And the name of the second he called:
     Efrayim/Double-Fruit,
   meaning: God has made me bear fruit in the land of my
     affliction.

53 There came to an end the seven years of abundance that
     had occurred in the land of Egypt,
54 and there started to come the seven years of famine, as
     Yosef had said.
   Famine occurred in all lands, but in all the land of Egypt
     there was bread.
55 But when all the land of Egypt felt the famine, and the
     people cried out to Pharaoh for bread,
   Pharaoh said to all the Egyptians:

Go to Yosef, whatever he says to you, do!

56 Now the famine was over all the surface of the earth.
   Yosef opened up all (storehouses) in which there was
      (grain), and gave-out-rations to the Egyptians,
   since the famine was becoming stronger in the land of
      Egypt.

57 And all lands came to Egypt to buy rations, to Yosef,
   for the famine was strong in all lands.

42:1 Now when Yaakov saw that there were rations in Egypt,
   Yaakov said to his sons:
   Why do you keep looking at one another?

 2 And he said:
   Here, I have heard that there are rations in Egypt,
   go down there and buy us rations from there,
   that we may live and not die.

Famine: The Brothers Come (41:53-42:38): Worldwide famine creates the backdrop for the family drama that is about to unfold. The ancients understood famine as sent by the gods, often as punishment; and the events of our text suggest that God is indeed the prime mover here. We are again presented with the characters of Chapter 37, all of whom have somehow changed. Yaakov emerges as more pitiful than ever (a shadow of the wrestler at the Yabbok), Yosef as powerful governor, not only of all Egypt but of his family's destiny as well, and the brothers, remarkably, are repentant (42:21-22). We also see Yosef's emotional side for the first time. He weeps in 42:24, as he will do three times again (43:30; 45:2, 14,15).

46 **thirty:** Yosef will be in power for eighty years (2 × 40), another patterned number.

51 **Menashe:** Trad. English "Menasseh." **made-me-forget:** Yet he does not forget for long, any more than the cupbearer did (Chapter 41).

52 **bear fruit . . . affliction:** Two expressions from the stories about the Patriarchs.

54ff. **Famine occurred in all lands:** The repetition of "all" here brings home the totality of the famine.

42:2 **that we may live and not die:** This becomes a refrain in the story, alternating in meaning between Yosef's family (here and 43:8) and the Egyptians (47:19).

3 So Yosef's brothers went down, ten (of them),
   to buy some rationed grain from Egypt.
4 But Binyamin, Yosef's brother, Yaakov would not send
      with his brothers,
   for he said: Lest harm befall him!
5 The sons of Yisrael came to buy rations among those that
      came,
   for the famine was in the land of Canaan.
6 Now Yosef was the governor over the land, it was he who
      supplied rations to all the people of the land.
   And Yosef's brothers came and bowed low to him, brow to
      the ground.
7 When Yosef saw his brothers, he recognized them,
   but he pretended-no-recognition of them and spoke harshly
      with them.
   He said to them:
   From where do you come?
   They said: From the land of Canaan, to buy food-rations.
8 Now although Yosef recognized his brothers, for their part,
      they did not recognize him.
9 And Yosef was reminded of the dreams that he had dreamt
      of them.
   He said to them:
   You are spies!
   It is to see the nakedness of the land that you have come!
10 They said to him: No, my lord!
   Rather, your servants have come to buy food-rations.
11 We are all of us the sons of a single man,
   we are honest,
   your servants have never been spies!
12 But he said to them:
   No!
   For it is the nakedness of the land that you have come to
      see!
13 They said:
   Your servants are twelve,
   we are brothers,
   sons of a single man in the land of Canaan:

the youngest is with our father now,
and one is no more.

14 Yosef said to them:
It is just as I spoke to you, saying: You are spies!

15 Hereby shall you be tested:
As Pharaoh lives!
You shall not depart from this (place)
unless your youngest brother comes here!

16 Send one of you to fetch your brother,
while (the rest of) you remain as prisoners.
Thus will your words be tested, whether there is truth in
   you or not—
as Pharaoh lives, indeed, you are spies!

17 He removed them into custody for three days.

18 Yosef said to them on the third day:
Do this, and stay alive,
for I fear God:

19 if you are honest,
let one of your brothers be held prisoner in the house of
   your custody,
and as for you, go, bring back rations for the famine-supply
   of your households.

20 Then bring your youngest brother back to me,
so that your words will be proven truthful, and you will not
   die.
They (prepared to) do so.

---

4 **Yosef's brother:** His full brother, as opposed to the others who were
half-brothers.

7 **recognized:** Ironically recalling the brothers' "Pray recognize" of 37:32.
pretended-no-recognition: Others use "pretended to be a stranger."

9 **nakedness:** Vulnerability (strategically).

11 **honest:** They will be, by the end of the chapter (Redford).

13 **twelve:** At last they think of themselves as a unit, "we are brothers!"

16 **tested:** Heb. *bahan*, a different root from the word translated "tested" (*nissa*)
in 22:1. Interestingly, the English "test" and the Hebrew *bhn* originally
meant the refining of metals, separating pure from impure. **or not—:** Or
"(in you.)/ If not. . . ."

21 But they said, each man to his brother:
Truly,
we are guilty:
concerning our brother!
—that we saw his heart's distress
when he implored us,
and we did not listen.
Therefore this distress has come upon us!
22 Re'uven answered them, saying:
Did I not say to you, say: Do not sin against the child!
But you would not listen,
so for his blood—now, satisfaction is demanded!
23 Now they did not know that Yosef was listening, for a
translator was between them.
24 But he turned away from them and wept.
When he was able to return to them, he spoke to them
and had Shim'on taken away from them, imprisoning him
before their eyes.
25 Then Yosef commanded that they fill their vessels with
grain
and return their silver-pieces into each man's sack,
and give them victuals for the journey.
They did so for them.
26 Then they loaded their rations onto their asses and went
from there.
27 But as one opened his sack to give his ass fodder at the
night-camp,
he saw his silver—there it was in the mouth of his pack!
28 He said to his brothers:
My silver has been returned—yes, here in my pack!
Their hearts gave way, and they trembled to one another,
saying:
What is this that God has done to us?
29 They came home to Yaakov their father, in the land of
Canaan,
and told him all that had befallen them, saying:
30 The man, the lord of the land, spoke harshly with us,
he took us for those that spy on the land!

31 Now we said to him: We are honest, we have never been
    spies!
32 We are twelve, brothers all, sons of our father:
    one is no more, and the youngest is now with our father in
    the land of Canaan.
33 Then the man, the lord of the land, said to us:
    Hereby shall I know whether you are honest:
    Leave one of your brothers with me,
    and as for the famine-supply of your households, take it and
    go.
34 But bring your youngest brother back to me,
    so that I may know that you are not spies, that you are
    honest.
    (Then) I will give your brother back to you, and you may
    travel about the land.
35 But it was, when they emptied their sacks: there was each
    man's silver pouch in his sack!
    They looked at their silver pouches, they and their father,
    and became frightened.
36 Yaakov their father said to them:
    It is me that you bereave!
    Yosef is no more,
    Shim'on is no more,

---

21 **guilty:** Perhaps it is the phrase "youngest brother" in Yosef's words (v.20)
    that jars their memory. They must now show responsibility to their father,
    which they had evaded in Chapter 37. **distress. . . . distress:** Another
    example of strict justice in the Bible: the punishment fits the crime.
22 **Re'uven:** A replay of Chapter 37, with Re'uven again making extravagant
    but ineffective declarations. Once again Yehuda will emerge in charge.
23 **translator:** Interpreter.
24 **imprisoning:** Or "fettering." **before their eyes:** As opposed to the sale of
    Yosef, where their presence is not mentioned, strictly speaking.
25 **they fill:** "They" refers to Yosef's servants. **silver-pieces:** Yosef had been
    sold for siver (37:28).
30 **The man:** Used eight times of Yosef in Chapters 42–44, perhaps out of
    ironic anonymity. **harshly:** Paralleling their earlier attitude: they "could
    not speak to him in peace" (37:4).

now you would take Binyamin—
upon me has all this come!
37 Re'uven said to his father, saying:
My two sons you may put to death
if I do not bring him back to you!
Place him in my hands, and I myself will return him to
    you.
38 But he said:
My son is not to go down with you!
For his brother is dead,
and he alone is left!
Should harm befall him on the journey on which you are
    going,
you will bring down my gray hair in grief to Sheol!

43:1 But the famine was heavy in the land.
    2 And so it was, when they had finished eating the rations
        that they had brought from Egypt,
        that their father said to them:
        Return, buy us some food-rations.
    3 But Yehuda said to him, saying:
        The man warned, yes, warned us,
        saying: You shall not see my face unless your brother is
            with you.
    4 If you wish to send our brother with us, we will go down
        and buy you some food-rations.
    5 But if you do not wish to send him, we will not go down,
        for the man said to us: You shall not see my face unless
            your brother is with you.
    6 Yisrael said:
        Why did you deal so ill with me, by telling the man that
            you have another brother?
    7 They said:
        The man asked, he asked about us and about our kindred,
        saying: Is your father still alive? Do you have another
            brother?
        So we told him, according to these words.
        Could we know, know that he would say: Bring your
            brother down?

8 Yehuda said to Yisrael his father:
Send the lad with me,
and we will arise and go,
that we may live and not die,
so we, so you, so our little-ones!

9 I will act as his pledge,
at my hand you may seek him!
If I do not bring him back to you
and set him in your presence,
I will be culpable-for-sin against you all the days (of my
life).

The Test (43–44): Yosef's testing of his brothers is masterful, not only because of the plan itself, but also because of the depth of emotion that the text evokes in its characterizations. It demonstrates how well the whole story has been integrated into the Yaakov material, for here as well as there long conversations are used to reveal complex passions.

Some have questioned the morality of Yosef's actions, seeing that the aged Yaakov might well have died while the test was progressing, without ever finding out that Yosef had survived. But that is not the point of the story. What it *is* trying to teach (among other things) is a lesson about crime and repentance. Only by recreating something of the original situation—the brothers are again in control of the life and death of a son of Rahel—can Yosef be sure that they have changed. Once the brothers pass the test, life and covenant can then continue.

37 **My two sons:** Re'uven is again spouting nonsense. **I myself will return him:** But he did not in 37:22 (Ackerman).
38 **My son is not to go down. . . . you will bring down my gray hair in grief:** Yaakov will indeed "go down," but to Egypt, not to Sheol, to meet his "dead" son. The latter part of the phrase is basically repeated in 44:29 and 44:31, as a key to the father's feelings. **he alone is left:** Of his mother Rahel (see 44:20).
43:3 **my face:** The great confrontation theme of the Yaakov stories returns.
4–5 **send:** Or "release," "let go."
9 **I will act as his pledge/ at my hand you may seek him:** Echoing Yaakov's own language of responsibility in 31:39 ("I would make good the loss/ at my hand you would seek it"). **in your presence:** Literally, "before your face."

10 Indeed, had we not lingered, we would indeed have been
     back twice already!
11 Yisrael their father said to them:
     If it must be so, then, do this:
     Take some of the produce of the land in your vessels
     and bring them down to the man as a gift:
     a little balsam, a little honey, balm and ladanum, pistachio
       nuts and almonds.
12 And silver two times over take in your hand;
     and the silver that was returned in the mouth of your packs,
       return in your hand,
     perhaps it was an oversight.
13 And as for your brother, take him!
     Arise, return to the man,
14 and may God Shaddai give you mercy before the man,
     so that he releases your other brother to you, and Binyamin
       as well.
     And as for me—if I must be bereaved, I must be bereaved!
15 The men took this gift, silver two times over they took in
       their hand
     and Binyamin as well.
     They arose and went down to Egypt
     and stood in Yosef's presence.
16 When Yosef saw Binyamin with them,
     he said to the steward of his house:
     Bring the men into the house, slaughter some
       slaughter-animals and prepare them,
     for it is with me that these men shall eat at noon.
17 The man did as Yosef had said, the man brought the men
     into Yosef's house.
18 But the men were frightened that they had been brought
     into Yosef's house, and said:
     It is because of the silver that was returned in our packs
       before that we have been brought here,
     for (them to) roll upon us, and fall upon us,
     and take us into servitude, along with our asses!
19 They came close to the man, to the steward of Yosef's
     house, and spoke to him at the entrance to the house,
20 they said:

Please, my lord!

We came down, came down before to buy food-rations,

21 but it was, when we came to the night camp and opened
   our packs,

there was each man's silver in the mouth of his pack, our
   silver by its exact weight—

but (here) we have returned it in our hand!

22 And other silver as well we have brought down in our hand,
   to buy food.

We do not know who put back our silver in our packs!

23 He said:

It is well with you, do not be afraid!

Your God, the God of your father, placed a treasure in your
   packs for you—(for) your silver has come in to me.

And he brought Shim'on out to them.

24 Then the man had the men come into Yosef's house
   and gave them water so that they might wash their feet
   and gave them fodder for their asses.

25 They prepared the gift, until Yosef came back at noon,
   for they understood that they were to eat bread there.

26 When Yosef came into the house, they brought him the gift
   that was in their hand, into the house,
   and bowed down to him, to the ground.

27 He asked after their welfare and said:
   Is your old father well, of whom you spoke?
   Is he still alive?

---

11 **Take:** Three times, culminating in the pathetic "And as for your brother,
take him!" (v.13).   **balsam . . . honey, balm and ladanum, pistachio nuts
and almonds:** Another example of concealment in the story. The list includes the cargo of the caravan that carried Yosef away (37:25).

12 **two times over . . . oversight:** Heb. *mishne . . . mishge.*

14 **God Shaddai:** Yaakov uses the same term for God as did his father, when
Yaakov left for Aram (28:3).   **bereaved:** Echoing the fears of his mother
Rivka (27:45).

18 **roll upon us:** Others use "attack us."   **roll upon us, and fall upon us:** The
rhythm reflects the brothers' emotional anguish.

23 **has come in:** I.e., I have received full payment.

27 **well:** Or "at peace"—as before, a key element of the Yaakov stories.

28 They said:
   Your servant, our father, is well, he is still alive—
   and in homage they bowed low.
29 He lifted up his eyes and saw Binyamin his brother, his
      mother's son,
   and he said:
   Is this your youngest brother, of whom you spoke to me?
   And he said:
   May God show you favor, my son!
30 And in haste—for his feelings were so kindled toward his
      brother that he had to weep—
   Yosef entered a chamber and wept there.
31 Then he washed his face and came out, he restrained
      himself, and said:
   Serve bread!
32 They served him by himself and them by themselves and
      the Egyptians who were eating with him by themselves,
   for Egyptians will not eat bread with Hebrews—for that is
      an abomination for Egyptians.
33 But they were seated in his presence:
   the firstborn according to his rank-as-firstborn and the
      youngest according to his rank-as-youngest.
   And the men stared at each other in astonishment over it.
34 He had courses taken to them from his presence,
   and Binyamin's course was five times greater than all their
      courses.
   Then they drank and became drunk with him.
44:1 Now he commanded the steward of his house, saying:
   Fill the men's packs with food, as much as they are able to
      carry,
   and put each man's silver in the mouth of his pack.
  2 And my goblet, the silver goblet, put in the mouth of the
      youngest's pack, along with the silver for his rations.
   He did according to Yosef's word which he had spoken.
  3 At morning light, the men were sent off, they and their
      asses;
  4 they were just outside the city—they had not yet gone far—
   when Yosef said to the steward of his house:

Up, pursue the men, and when you have caught up with
    them, say to them:
Why have you paid back ill for good?
5 Is not this (goblet) the one that my lord drinks with?
And he also divines, yes, divines with it!
You have wrought ill in what you have done!
6 When he caught up with them, he spoke those words to
    them.
7 They said to him:
Why does my lord speak such words as these?
Heaven forbid for your servants to do such a thing!
8 Here, the silver that we found in the mouth of our packs,
    we returned to you from the land of Canaan;
so how could we steal silver or gold from the house of your
    lord?
9 He with whom it is found among your servants, he shall
    die,
and we also will become my lord's servants!
10 He said:
Now as well, according to your words, so be it:
he with whom it is found shall become my servant, but you
    shall be clear.
11 With haste each man let down his pack to the ground, each
    man opened his pack.
12 and then he searched: with the eldest he started and with
    the youngest he finished—
and the goblet was found in Binyamin's pack!

---

29 **Is this:** Or "So this is."
34 **five times:** Others use "many times." Yet the prominence of the number
five throughout the Yosef story, as noted above, should not be overlooked.
44:2 **my goblet:** The ensuing scene is somewhat parallel to Rahel's theft of the
terafim (compare verse 9 with 31:32).
5 **divines:** Cups were used in predicting the future in the ancient Near East;
see note to 40:11. The diviner would examine the shapes made by insoluble
liquids, such as oil in water. **You have wrought ill:** Resembling Laban's
accusation against Yaakov, "You have done foolishly" (31:28).
10 **clear:** Of punishment.

13 They rent their clothes,
each man loaded up his ass, and they returned to the city.

14 Yehuda and his brothers came into Yosef's house
—he was still there—
and flung themselves down before him to the ground.

15 Yosef said to them:
What kind of deed is this that you have done!
Do you not know that a man like me can divine, yes divine?

16 Yehuda said:
What can we say to my lord?
What can we speak, by what can we show ourselves
   innocent?
God has found out your servants' crime!
Here we are, servants to my lord, so we, so the one in
   whose hand the goblet was found.

17 But he said:
Heaven forbid that I should do this!
The man in whose hand the goblet was found—he shall
   become my servant,
but you—go up in peace to your father!

18 Now Yehuda came closer to him and said:
Please, my lord,
pray let your servant speak a word in the ears of my lord,
and do not let your anger rage against your servant,
for you are like Pharaoh!

19 My lord asked his servants, saying: Do you have a father or
   another brother?

20 And we said to my lord: We have an old father
and a young child of his old age,
whose brother is dead,
so that he alone is left of his mother,
and his father loves him.

21 And you said to your servants: Bring him down to me, I
   wish to set my eyes upon him.

22 But we said to my lord:
The lad cannot leave his father,
were he to leave his father, he would die.

23 But you said to your servants: If your youngest brother does
   not come down with you, you shall not see my face again.

24 Now it was, when we went up to your servant, my father,
   we told him my lord's words,
25 and our father said: Return, buy us some food-rations.
26 But we said: We cannot go down;
   if our youngest brother is with us, then we will go down,
   for we cannot see the man's face if our youngest brother is
      not with us.
27 Now your servant, my father, said to us:
   You yourselves know
   that my wife bore two to me.
28 One went away from me,
   I said: For sure he is torn, torn-to-pieces!
   And I have not seen him again thus far.
29 Now should you take away this one as well from before my
      face,
   should harm befall him, you will bring down my gray hair
      in ill-fortune to Sheol!
30 So now,
   when I come back to your servant, my father, and the lad is
      not with us,
   —with whose life his own life is bound up!—
31 it will be, that when he sees that the lad is no more, he will
      die,
   and your servant will have brought down the gray hair of
      your servant, our father, in grief to Sheol!

---

16 **your servants' crime:** Of selling Yosef?
17 **But he said:** "He" is Yosef.   **this:** Enslaving all of the brothers.
18 **Now Yehuda . . . said . . . :** Yehuda's great speech, masterful in its rhetoric, is chiefly aimed at stirring up sympathy for the father; it contains the word "father" fourteen times. Binyamin, whose appearance actually causes Yosef great anguish, is hardly treated as a personality at all.   **you are like Pharaoh:** Lit. "like you is like Pharaoh."
22 **he would die:** "He" refers to Yaakov, although the Hebrew is somewhat ambiguous.
28 **thus far:** A hint that Yosef is still alive, or perhaps a tiny expression of hope.
30 **life:** Heb. *nefesh,* also "emotions" or "feelings."
31 **our father:** Is Yehuda unknowingly including Yosef?

32 For your servant pledged himself for the lad to my father,
   saying: If I do not bring him back to you, I will be
      culpable-for-sin against my father all the days (of my life).
33 So now,
   pray let your servant stay instead of the lad, as servant to
      my lord,
   but let the lad go up with his brothers!
34 For how can I go up to my father, when the lad is not with
      me?
   Then would I see the ill-fortune that would come upon my
      father!

45:1 Yosef could no longer restrain himself in the presence of all
      who were stationed around him,
   he called out:
   Have everyone leave me!
   So no one stood (in attendance upon) him when Yosef made
      himself known to his brothers.
  2 He put forth his voice in weeping:
   the Egyptians heard, Pharaoh's household heard.
  3 Then Yosef said to his brothers:
   I am Yosef. Is my father still alive?
   But his brothers were not able to answer him,
   for they were confounded in his presence.
  4 Yosef said to his brothers:
   Pray come close to me!
   They came close.
   He said:
   I am Yosef your brother, whom you sold into Egypt.
  5 But now, do not be pained,
   and do not let (anger) rage in your eyes that you sold me
      here!
   For it was to save life that God sent me on before you.
  6 For it is two years now that the famine has been in the
      midst of the land,
   and there are still another five years in which there shall be
      no plowing or harvest.
  7 So God sent me on before you

to make you a remnant on earth,
to keep you alive as a great body-of-survivors.
8 So now,
it was not you that sent me here, but God!
He has made me Father to Pharaoh and lord of all his
household and ruler over all the land of Egypt.
9 Make haste, go up to my father and say to him:
Thus says your son, Yosef:
God has made me lord of all Egypt;
come down to me, do not remain!
10 You shall stay in the region of Goshen, you shall be near
me,
you and your sons and the sons of your sons,
your sheep, your oxen, and all that is yours.
11 I will sustain you there,
for there are still five years of famine left
—lest you be as disinherited, you and your household and
all that is yours.
12 Here, your eyes see, as well as my brother Binyamin's eyes,
that it is my mouth that speaks to you!
13 So tell my father of all the weight I carry in Egypt, and of
all that you have seen,
and make haste, bring my father down here!

Reconciliation (45): In revealing his true identity at last, Yosef makes two points: first, that it was all part of God's plan; and second, that the family must immediately prepare for migration to Egypt. Thus the personal story is intertwined with the national one, and the text therefore gives limited time and space to psychological details. The motif of God's plan is stressed by the repetition of "God sent me" (vv.5, 7, 8), while the anticipated bounties of settling in Egypt are brought out by the threefold "good-things of Egypt" (vv.18, 20, 23) and by the repeated exhortation to "come" (vv.18, 19).

45:5 **(anger):** At each other, or referring to each individual's feelings of guilt.
11 **as disinherited:** Or "reduced-to-poverty."
13 **all the weight I carry:** I.e., my importance.

14 He flung himself upon his brother Binyamin's neck and
      wept,
   and Binyamin wept upon his neck.
15 Then he kissed all his brothers and wept upon them.
   After this his brothers spoke with him.

16 The news was heard in Pharaoh's household, they said:
   Yosef's brothers have come!
   It was good in Pharaoh's eyes and in the eyes of his
      servants.
17 And Pharaoh said to Yosef:
   Say to your brothers:
   Do this—
   load your animals and go,
   come back to the land of Canaan;
18 fetch your father and your households
   and come to me!
   I will give you the good-things of the land of Egypt,
   so that you will eat of the fat of the land!
19 And you, you have been commanded:
   Do this—
   take you wagons from the land of Egypt for your little ones
      and your wives,
   and carry your father down
   and come!
20 Let not your eyes look-with-regret on your household-
      wares,
   for the good-things of all the land of Egypt—they are yours!
21 The sons of Yisrael did so,
   Yosef gave them wagons in accordance with Pharaoh's
      orders
   and gave them victuals for the journey.
22 To all of them, each man, he gave changes of clothes,
   but to Binyamin he gave three hundred pieces of silver and
      five changes of clothes,
23 and to his father he sent in like manner:
   ten asses, carrying the good-things of Egypt,
   and ten mares, carrying grain and bread,
   and food for his father, for the journey.

24 Then he sent off his brothers, and they went;
   he said to them:
   Do not be upset on the journey!
25 They went up from Egypt and came to the land of Canaan,
   to Yaakov their father,
26 and they told him, saying:
   Yosef is still alive!
   Indeed, he is ruler of all the land of Egypt!
   His heart failed,
   for he did not believe them.

Migration to Egypt (45:16–47:12): Yaakov's descent to Egypt involves three meetings: with God, with Yosef, and with Pharaoh. The first is God's final revelation to Yaakov. God had previously forbidden Yitzhak to go to Egypt during a famine (26:1–2), but his son may now go as part of the divine plan, his people's destiny. The blessing given to Avraham's children (particularly to Yishmael) is repeated in 46:3, and God will be "with" Yaakov (46:4) on this journey as he has been on others.

The meeting between father and long-lost son is brief but powerful, returning as it does to the "face" motif (46:30). Immediately afterward Yosef gives the family advice on how to demonstrate their usefulness to the Egyptians, and one is struck by the precariousness of their situation in even this best of circumstances.

Yaakov's brief audience with Pharaoh is both moving and pathetic. The Patriarch sums up his life in depressing terms, and it becomes clear that long life (he believes his own to be short), in addition to wealth and fertility, is considered a sign of divine favor.

The actual migration is sketched in a few brief strokes. The list of names in 46:8–27 has been constructed on patterned numbers, with a total of seventy.

15 **his brothers spoke with him:** Which they could not do "in peace" in 37:4.
16 **come:** The verb focuses toward Pharaoh's invitation to follow: "Yosef's brothers have come!" (v.16) to "and come to me" (v.18) to "and come!" (v.19).
18 **good-things:** More precisely, "best-things" ("good" has been retained here to indicate a major theme of the story: good and ill).
20 **Let not your eyes look-with-regret:** Possibly "Do not stint."
22 **but to Binyamin he gave:** The original situation (Chapter 37) is set up once more; this time the brothers do not react adversely to the youngest son's being favored.

27 But when they spoke to him all of Yosef's words which he
      had spoken to them,
   and when he saw the wagons that Yosef had sent to carry
      him down,
   their father Yaakov's spirit came to life.
28 Yisrael said:
   Enough!
   Yosef my son is still alive;
   I must go and see him before I die!

46:1 Yisrael traveled with all that was his
       and came to Be'er-Sheva,
       and he slaughtered slaughter-offerings to the God of his
          father Yitzhak.
   2 And God said to Yisrael in visions of the night,
       he said:
       Yaakov! Yaakov!
       He said:
       Here I am.
   3 Now he said:
       I am *El*/God,
       the God of your father.
       Do not be afraid of going down to Egypt,
       for a great nation will I make of you there.
   4 I myself
       will go down with you to Egypt,
       and I myself
       will bring you up, yes, up again.
       And Yosef will lay his hand on your eyes.

   5 Yaakov departed from Be'er-Sheva.
       Yisrael's sons carried Yaakov their father, their little-ones
          and their wives in the wagons that Pharaoh had sent for
          carrying him,
   6 and they took their acquired livestock and their property
          that they had gained in the land of Canaan
       and came to Egypt,
       Yaakov and all his seed with him,

7 his sons and the sons of his sons with him, his daughters
    and the daughters of his sons;
all his seed he brought with him to Egypt.

8 Now these are the names of the Sons of Israel who came to
    Egypt:
Yaakov and his sons:
Yaakov's firstborn was Re'uven.
9 Re'uven's sons: Hanokh, Pallu, Hetzron, and Carmi.
10 Shim'on's sons: Yemuel, Yamin, Ohad, Yakhin, and
    Tzohar, and Sha'ul the son of the Canaanite-woman.
11 Levi's sons: Gershon, Kehat, and Merari.
12 Yehuda's sons: Er, Onan, Shela, Peretz, and Zerah,
but Er and Onan had died in the land of Canaan.
And Peretz's sons were Hetzron and Hamul.
13 Yissakhar's sons: Tola, Puvva, Yov, and Shimron.
14 Zevulun's sons: Sered, Elon, and Yahl'el.
15 These are the sons of Lea, whom she bore to Yaakov in the
    country of Aram, and also Dina his daughter;
all the persons among his sons and daughters were
    thirty-three.
16 Gad's sons: Tzifyon and Haggi, Shuni and Etzbon, Eri,
    Arodi, and Ar'eli.
17 Asher's sons: Yimna, Yishva, Yishvi, and Beria, and Serah
    their sister.
And Beria's sons: Hever and Malkiel.
18 These are the sons of Zilpa, whom Lavan had given to Lea
    his daughter,
she bore these to Yaakov: sixteen persons.

---

27 **Yosef's words:** In Chapter 37 his words were damaging, but here they are
life-giving.
46:2 **Yaakov! Yaakov!:** Doubled as in 22:11 and other moments of dramatic
revelations in the Bible (e.g., Ex. 3:4).
  4 **lay his hand on your eyes:** I.e., be present at your death.
  8 **Now these are the names . . . :** This phrase opens the book of Exodus,
making that book a resumption of the Genesis narrative.

19 The sons of Rahel, Yaakov's wife: Yosef and Binyamin.

20 To Yosef there were born in the land of Egypt—whom
   Asenat, daughter of Poti Fera, priest of On, bore to him:
   Menashe and Efrayim.

21 Binyamin's sons: Bela, Bekher and Ashbel, Gera and
   Naaman, Ahi and Rosh, Muppim, Huppim, and Ard.

22 These are the sons of Rahel, who were born to Yaakov,
   all the persons were fourteen.

23 Dan's sons: Hushim.

24 Naftali's sons: Yahtze'el, Guni, Yetzer, and Shillem.

25 These are the sons of Bilha, whom Lavan had given to
   Rahel his daughter,
   she bore these to Yaakov: all the persons were seven.

26 All the persons who came with Yaakov to Egypt, those
   going out from his loins, aside from the wives of Yaakov's
   sons:
   all the persons were sixty-six.

27 Now Yosef's sons, who had been born to him in Egypt: the
   persons were two.
   (Thus) all the persons of Yaakov's household who came to
   Egypt were seventy.

28 Now Yehuda he had sent on ahead of him, to Yosef,
   to give directions ahead of him to Goshen.
   When they came to the region of Goshen,

29 Yosef had his chariot harnessed and went up to meet Yisrael
   his father, to Goshen.
   When he caught sight of him
   he flung himself upon his neck
   and wept upon his neck continually.

30 Yisrael said to Yosef:
   Now I can die,
   since I have seen your face, that you are still alive!

31 Yosef said to his brothers and to his father's household:
   I will go up, so that I may tell Pharaoh and say to him:
   My brothers and my father's household, who were in the
   land of Canaan, have come to me.

32 The men are shepherds of flocks,

indeed, they have always been livestock men,
and their sheep and their oxen, all that is theirs, they have
    brought along.
33 Now it will be, when Pharaoh has you called and says:
What is it that you do?
34 Then say: Your servants have always been livestock men,
from our youth until now, so we, so our fathers—
in order that you may settle in the region of Goshen.
For every shepherd of flocks is an abomination to the
    Egyptians.

47:1 So Yosef came and told Pharaoh, he said:
My father and my brothers, their sheep and their oxen and
    all that is theirs, have come from the land of Canaan,
and here, they are in the region of Goshen!
2 Now from the circle of his brothers he had picked out five
    men and had set them in Pharaoh's presence.
3 Pharaoh said to his brothers:
What is it that you do?
They said to Pharaoh:
Your servants are shepherds of flocks, so we, so our fathers.
4 And they said to Pharaoh:
It is to sojourn in the land that we have come,
for there is no grazing for the flocks that are your servants',
for the famine is heavy in the land of Canaan.
So now,
pray let your servants settle in the region of Goshen!
5 Pharaoh said to Yosef, saying:
(So) your father and your brothers have come to you:

---

27 **seventy:** Once again, the "perfect" number.
33 **What is it that you do:** What is your occupation?
34 **every shepherd . . . is an abomination to the Egyptians:** Speiser understands this as a reference to the Hyksos "shepherd kings," who as foreigners ruled Egypt in the mid-Second Millennium (until they were driven out).
47:4 **It is to sojourn:** Are they still sensitive to the accusation in 42:12, "For it is the nakedness of the land that you have come to see"?

6 the land of Egypt is before you;
  in the goodliest-part of the land, settle your father and your
    brothers,
  let them settle in the region of Goshen.
  And if you know that there are able men among them,
  make them chiefs of livestock over what is mine.
7 Yosef brought Yaakov his father and had him stand in
    Pharaoh's presence.
  And Yaakov gave Pharaoh a blessing-of-greeting.
8 Pharaoh said to Yaakov:
  How many are the days and years of your life?
9 Yaakov said to Pharaoh:
  The days and years of my sojourn are thirty and a hundred
    years;
  few and ill-fated have been the days and years of my life,
  they have not attained the days and years of my fathers'
    lives in the days of their sojourn.
10 Yaakov gave Pharaoh a blessing-of-farewell
   and went out from Pharaoh's presence.
11 So Yosef settled his father and his brothers,
   giving them holdings in the land of Egypt,
   in the goodliest-part of the land, in the region of Ra'meses,
     as Pharaoh had commanded.
12 Yosef sustained his father, his brothers, and his father's
     entire household with bread, in proportion to the
     little-ones.

13 But bread there was none in all the land,
   for the famine was exceedingly heavy,
   and the land of Egypt and the land of Canaan were
     exhausted by the famine.
14 Yosef had collected all the silver that was to be found in the
     land of Egypt and in the land of Canaan, from the rations
     that they had bought,
   and Yosef had brought the silver into Pharaoh's house.
15 When the silver in the land of Egypt and in the land of
     Canaan had run out,
   all the Egyptians came to Yosef, saying:
   Come-now, (let us have) bread!

Why should we die in front of you, because the silver is
  gone?
16 Yosef said:
Come-now, (let me have) your livestock, and I will give you
  (bread) for your livestock, since the silver is gone.
17 So they brought their livestock to Yosef, and Yosef gave
  them bread (in exchange) for the horses, the
  sheep-livestock, the oxen-livestock, and the asses;
he got-them-through with bread (in exchange) for all their
  livestock in that year.
18 But when that year had run out, they came back to him in
  the second year and said to him:
We cannot hide from my lord
that if the silver has run out and the animal-stocks are my
  lord's,
nothing remains for my lord except for our bodies and our
  soil!
19 Why should we die before your eyes, so we, so our soil?
Acquire us and our soil for bread,
and we and our soil will become servants to Pharaoh.
Give (us) seed-for-sowing
that we may live and not die,
that the soil may not become desolate!

Yosef the Life-Giver (47:13–26): The events of this section are not attested historically in Egyptian records. Perhaps they have been included
here to confirm Yosef's stature as Rescuer, not only of his family but of
all Egypt as well (see note to 42:2). The description of Yosef's power is
now complete: just as the brothers were ready to "become my lord's
servants" (44:9), so now are the Egyptians (47:25).

Some have seen the episode as an ironic reversal of what is to come in
Exodus, with the Egyptians' enslavement of the Israelites; if so, this
interlude may have been an amusing one to ancient Israelite audiences.

The text uses the repetition of the phrase "to/for Pharaoh" to effectively paint the legal transaction.

8 **days and years:** See the note to 25:7.
9 **in the days of:** Others use "during."
17 **got-them-through:** Lit. "led them."

20 So Yosef acquired all the soil of Egypt for Pharaoh
—for each of the Egyptians sold his field, for the famine
was strong upon them—
and the land went over to Pharaoh.

21 As for the people, he transferred them into the cities, from
one edge of Egypt's border to its other edge.

22 Only the soil of the priests he did not acquire,
for the priests had a prescribed-allocation from Pharaoh,
and they ate from their allocation which Pharaoh had
given them,
therefore they did not sell their soil.

23 Yosef said to the people:
Now that I have acquired you and your soil today for
Pharaoh,
here, you have seed, sow the soil!

24 But it shall be at the ingatherings, that you shall give a fifth
to Pharaoh,
the four other parts being for you
as seed for the field and for your eating-needs, for those in
your households, and for feeding your little-ones.

25 They said:
You have saved our lives!
May we find favor in my lord's eyes: we will become
servants to Pharaoh.

26 And Yosef made it a prescribed-law until this day,
concerning the soil of Egypt: For Pharaoh every fifth
part!
Only the soil of the priests, that alone did not go over to
Pharaoh.

27 Now Yisrael stayed in the land of Egypt, in the region of
Goshen;
they obtained holdings in it, bore fruit, and became
exceedingly many.

28 And Yaakov lived in the land of Egypt for seventeen years.
And the days of Yaakov, the years of his life, were seven
years and a hundred and forty years.

29 Now when Yisrael's days drew near to death,

he called his son Yosef and said to him:
Pray, if I have found favor in your eyes,
pray put your hand under my thigh—
deal with me faithfully and truly:
pray do not bury me in Egypt!
30 When I lie down with my fathers,
carry me out of Egypt, and bury me in their burial-site!
He said:
I will do according to your words.
31 But he said:
Swear to me!
So he swore to him.
Then Yisrael bowed, at the head of the bed.

48:1 Now after these events it was
that they said to Yosef:
Here, your father has taken sick!
So he took his two sons with him, Menashe and
      Efrayim. . . .
2 When they told Yaakov, saying: Here, your son Yosef is
      coming to you,
Yisrael gathered his strength and sat up in the bed.
3 Yaakov said to Yosef:
God Shaddai was seen by me
in Luz, in the land of Canaan;
he blessed me

Yosef's Sons Blessed (48): Yaakov, near to death, blesses his grandsons
(Rahel's!) in moving terms, bringing full circle many of the motifs of his
life. Elder and younger sons are switched by the blind Patriarch, this
time, though, one who is fully aware of their identities. As in both
literature and life, a dying man sees both past (here) and future (the next
chapter) with great clarity, as in a vision.

21 **transferred them:** Hebrew difficult; some read "enslaved them."
24 **a fifth:** Here is the ubiquitous "five" again.

4 and he said to me:
Here, I will make you bear fruit and will make you many,
and will make you into a host of peoples;
I will give this land to your seed after you, as a holding for
   the ages!
5 So now,
your two sons who were born to you in the land of Egypt
before I came to you in Egypt,
they are mine,
Efrayim and Menashe,
like Re'uven and Shim'on, let them be mine!
6 But your begotten sons, whom you will beget after them,
let them be yours;
by their brothers' names let them be called, respecting their
   inheritance.
7 While I—
when I came back from that country,
Rahel died on me,
in the land of Canaan,
on the way, with still a stretch of land left to come to Efrat.
There I buried her, on the way to Efrat—that is now
   Bet-Lehem.
8 When Yisrael saw Yosef's sons, he said:
Who are these?
9 Yosef said to his father:
They are my sons, whom God has given me here.
He said:
Pray take them over to me, that I may give-them-blessing.
10 Now Yisrael's eyes were heavy with age, he was not able to
   see.
He brought them close to him,
and he kissed them and embraced them.
11 Yisrael said to Yosef:
I never expected to see your face again,
and here, God has let me see your seed as well!
12 Yosef took them from between his knees
and they bowed low, their brows to the ground.
13 Yosef took the two of them,
Efrayim with his right-hand, to Yisrael's left,

and Menashe with his left-hand, to Yisrael's right,
and brought them close to him.

14 But Yisrael stretched out his right-hand and put it on the
   head of Efrayim—yet he was the younger!—
   and his left-hand on the head of Menashe;
   he crossed his arms, although Menashe was the firstborn.

15 Then he blessed Yosef and said:
   The God
   in whose presence my fathers walked,
   Avraham and Yitzhak,
   the God
   who has tended me
   ever since I was (born), until this day—

16 the messenger
   who has redeemed me from all ill-fortune,
   may he bless the lads!
   May my name continue to be called through them
   and the name of my fathers, Avraham and Yitzhak!
   May they teem-like-fish to (become) many in the midst of
   the land!

17 Now when Yosef saw that his father had put his right hand
   on Efrayim's head,
   it sat ill in his eyes,
   and he laid hold of his father's hand, to turn it from
   Efrayim's head to Menashe's head.

18 Yosef said to his father:
   Not so, father, indeed, this one is the firstborn, place your
   hand on his head!

48:5 **they are mine:** As it were, adopted.   **Efrayim and Menashe:** Note how
     Yaakov reverses the order of birth; see verses 14, 17–19.
   7 **Rahel died on me:** The memory is still painful to Yaakov, even after many
     years.
  11 **your face:** The final and most powerful occurrence of the term.
  15 **tended:** Or "shepherded."
  16 **redeemed me from all ill-fortune:** Despite his words in 47:9, perhaps
     Yaakov achieves a measure of peace in the end.   **my name continue to be
     called through them:** My line continue through them.   **teem-like-fish:**
     Others use "become teeming (multitudes)."

19 But his father refused and said:
I know, my son, I know—
he too will be a people, he too will be great,
yet his younger brother will be greater than he, and his seed
    will become a full measure of nations!
20 So he blessed them on that day,
saying:
By you shall Israel give-blessings, saying:
God make you like Efrayim and Menashe!
Thus he made Efrayim go before Menashe.
21 Then Yisrael said to Yosef:
Here, I am dying,
but God will be with you,
he will have you return to the land of your fathers.
22 And I, I give you
one portion over and above your brothers,
which I took away from the Amorite,
with my sword, with my bow.

49:1 Now Yaakov called his sons and said:
Gather round, that I may tell you
what will befall you in the aftertime of days.

2   Come together and hearken, sons of Yaakov,
         hearken to Yisrael your father.

3   Re'uven,
         my firstborn, you,
         my might, first-fruit of my vigor!
         Surpassing in loftiness, surpassing in force!
4   Headlong like water—surpass no more!
         For when you mounted your father's bed,
         then you defiled it—he mounted the couch!

5   Shim'on and Levi,
         such brothers,
         wronging weapons are their ties-of-kinship!
6   To their council may my being never come,
         in their assembly may my person never unite!
         For in their anger they kill men,
         in their self-will they maim bulls.

7   Cursed be their anger, that it is so fierce!
Their fury, that it is so harsh!
I will split them up in Yaakov,
I will scatter them in Yisrael.

8   Yehuda,
you—your brothers will praise you,
your hand on the neck of your enemies!
Your father's sons will bow down to you.

9   A lion's whelp, Yehuda—
from torn-prey, my son, you have gone up!
He squats, he crouches,
like the lion, like the king-of-beasts,
who dares rouse him up?

Yaakov's Testament and Death (49): In this ancient piece of poetry, Yaakov addresses his sons, not as they are, but as they will be. There is little resemblance, for instance, between the Binyamin as the beloved and protected youngest son of the Yosef story and the preying wolf of verse 27, but the Benjaminites were later to be known for their military skills. Scholars have therefore seen the entire poem as a retrojection of Israel as it came to be on the days of the Patriarchs.

As in the fuller Yosef narrative, the first three sons are quickly disqualified from active leadership, paving the way for the rise of Yehuda (the tribe from which sprang David and the royal house of Israel). Despite this, Yosef still receives the richest blessing.

The chapter is textually among the most difficult in the Torah. Many passages are simply obscure, leaving the translator to make at best educated guesses.

19 **I know:** Though blind, Yaakov knows exactly what he is doing, unlike his father in Chapter 27.
22 **one portion over and above:** Hebrew unclear. We do not know to what event Yaakov is referring in this entire verse. **took away:** Others use "will take," "must take."
49:4 **when you mounted . . . :** Alluding to 35:21–22.
5 **ties-of-kinship:** Hebrew obscure. Others use "weapons," "swords" (B-R uses "mattocks").
6 **in their anger they kill men:** See 34:25–26.
8 **Yehuda . . . enemies:** Heb. *yehuda/ atta yodukha ahikha/ yadekha al oref oyevekha.*
9 **lion:** Eventually the symbol of the (Judahite) monarchy.

10   The scepter shall not depart from Yehuda,
        nor the staff-of-command from between his legs,
        until they bring him tribute,
        —the obedience of peoples is his.
11   He ties up his foal to a vine,
        his young colt to a crimson tendril;
        he washes his raiment in wine,
        his mantle in the blood of grapes;
12   his eyes, darker than wine,
        his teeth, whiter than milk.

13   Zevulun,
        on the shore of the sea he dwells;
        he is a haven-shore for boats,
        his flank upon Tzidon.

14   Yissakhar,
        a bone-strong ass,
        crouching among the fire-places.
15   When he saw how good the resting-place was,
        and how pleasant was the land,
        he bent his shoulder to bearing
        and so became a laboring serf.

16   Dan,
        his people will mete-out-judgment,
        (to all) of Israel's branches together.
17   May Dan be a snake on the wayside,
        a horned-viper on the path,
        who bites the horse's heels
        so that his rider tumbles backward.

18   I wait-in-hope for your salvation, O YHWH!

19   Gad,
        goading robber-band will goad him,
        yet he will goad at their heel.

20   Asher,
        his nourishment is rich,

he gives forth king's dainties.

21   Naftali,
        a hind let loose,
        he who gives forth lovely fawns.

22   Young wild-ass,
        Yosef,
        young wild-ass along a spring,
        donkeys along a wall.
23   Bitterly they shot at him,
        the archers assailed him,
24   yet firm remained his bow,
        and agile stayed his arms and hands—
        by means of the hands of Yaakov's Champion,
        up there,
        the Shepherd, the Stone of Yisrael.
25   By your father's God—
        may he help you,
        and Shaddai,
        may he give-you-blessing:
        Blessings of the heavens, from above,
        blessings of Ocean crouching below,
        blessings of breasts and womb!

---

10 **until they bring . . . :** Hebrew difficult; others use "until Shiloh comes."
   The phrase is an old and unsolved problem for interpreter and translator
   alike.
11 **colt:** Of an ass.
15 **laboring serf:** The Hebrew *mas 'oved* denotes forced labor.
16 **mete-out-judgment:** Others use "will endure."
18 **I wait-in-hope . . . :** Either a deathbed cry or possibly the cry of a falling
   rider (see the preceding line) (Ehrlich).
19 **goad:** Lit. "attack"; a play on "Gad" (Heb. *gad gedud yegudennu*).
24 **arms and hands:** Lit. "arms of his hands."
25 **Shaddai:** Once again connected to fertility (note the content of the following lines).   **give-you-blessing:** Just as Yaakov had blessed Yosef's sons, so
   Yosef is the only one of the twelve brothers to whom Yaakov applies the
   term.

26   May the blessings of your father transcend
            the blessings of mountains eternal,
            the bounds of hills without age.
            May they fall upon the head of Yosef,
            on the crown of the one-set-apart among his brothers.

27   Binyamin,
            a wolf that tears-to-pieces!
            In the morning he devours prey,
            and then, in the evening, divides up the spoil.

28 All these are the tribes of Israel, twelve,
   and this is what their father spoke to them;
   he blessed them,
   according to what belonged to each as blessing, he blessed
       them.
29 And he charged them, saying to them:
   I am now about to be gathered to my kinspeople;
   bury me by my fathers,
   in the cave that is in the field of Efron the Hittite,
30 at the cave that is in the field of Makhpela, that faces
       Mamre, in the land of Canaan.
   —Avraham had acquired that field from Efron the Hittite,
       as a burial holding.
31 There they buried Avraham and Sara his wife,
   there they buried Yitzhak and Rivka his wife,
   there I buried Lea—
32 an acquisition, the field and the cave that is in it, from the
       Sons of Het.

33 When Yaakov had finished charging his sons,
   he gathered up his feet onto the bed and breathed-his-last,
   and was gathered to his kinspeople.

50:1 Yosef flung himself on his father's face,
   he wept over him and kissed him.
  2 Then Yosef charged his servants, the physicians, to embalm
       his father,
   and the physicians embalmed Yisrael.

3 A full forty days were required for him,
for thus are fulfilled the days of embalming.
And the Egyptians wept for him for seventy days.
4 Now when the days of weeping for him had passed,
Yosef spoke to Pharaoh's household, saying:
Pray, if I have found favor in your eyes,
pray speak in the ears of Pharaoh, saying:
5 My father had me swear, saying:
Here, I am dying—
in my burial-site which I dug for myself in the land of
    Canaan,
there you are to bury me!
So now,
pray let me go up, bury my father, and return.
6 Pharaoh said:
Go up and bury your father, as he had you swear.
7 So Yosef went up to bury his father;
and with him went up all of Pharaoh's servants,
the elders of his household and all the elders of the land of
    Egypt,

Yaakov's Burial (50:1–14): The funeral of Yaakov seems to presage the Exodus from Egypt—here with Pharaoh's permission and a large royal escort (including "chariots and horsemen," who in several generations will pursue Yaakov's descendants into the sea).

Interestingly, the *Iliad* also ends with an elaborate burial scene. The contrast is instructive: the Homeric epic celebrates the deeds and mourns the lost youth of a hero (Hector); Genesis reflects Yosef's standing at court and the desire to bury Yaakov in the land of Canaan, in the family plot. Note too that Genesis has two more scenes, tending to lessen the impact of this impressive funeral sequence.

26 **mountains:** Reading *hararei* for the traditional Hebrew *horei*, "parents" on the basis of Hab. 3:6.
28 **tribes:** Heb. *shevatim*, "staffs," which symbolized the tribes.
31 **Lea:** Not called "my wife." Again the old feelings remain vivid.
33 **breathed-his-last:** Omitted are the "old and abundant in days" that were applied to his father and grandfather.

8 all of Yosef's household,
   his brothers and his father's household.
   Only their little-ones, their sheep, and their oxen did they
      leave behind in the region of Goshen.
9 And along with him went up chariots as well, and horsemen
      as well—
   the company was an exceedingly heavy one.
10 They came as far as Goren Ha-Atad/Bramble
      Threshing-Floor, which is across the Jordan,
   and there they took up lament, an exceedingly great and
      heavy lament,
   and he held mourning for his father, for seven days.
11 Now when the settled-folk of the land, the Canaanites, saw
      the mourning at Bramble Threshing-Floor,
   they said:
   This is such a heavy mourning/*evel* for Egypt!
   Therefore its name was called: Meadow/*avel* of Egypt,
   which is across the Jordan.
12 So his sons did thus for him, as he had charged them:
13 his sons carried him back to the land of Canaan
   and buried him in the cave in the field of Makhpela.
   —Avraham had acquired that field as a burial holding from
      Efron the Hittite, (the field) facing Mamre.
14 Then Yosef returned to Egypt,
   he and his brothers and all who had gone up with him to
      bury his father,
   after he had buried his father.

15 When Yosef's brothers saw that their father was dead, they
      said:
   What if Yosef holds a grudge against us
   and repays, yes, repays us for all the ill that we caused him!
16 So they charged Yosef, saying:
   Your father left-this-charge before his death, saying:
17 Say thus to Yosef:
   Ah, pray forgive your brothers' offense and their sin, that
      they caused you ill!
   Now, pray forgive the offense of the servants of your
      father's God!
   Yosef wept as they spoke to him.

18 And his brothers themselves came, they flung themselves
   down before him and said:
   Here we are, servants to you!
19 But Yosef said to them:
   Do not be afraid! For am I in place of God?
20 Now you, you planned ill against me,
   (but) God planned-it-over for good,
   in order to do (as is) this very day—
   to keep many people alive.
21 So now, do not be afraid!
   I myself will sustain you and your little-ones!
   And he comforted them and spoke to their hearts.

22 So Yosef stayed in Egypt, he and his father's household.
   Yosef lived a hundred and ten years;

The End of the Matter (50:15–26): Drawing out the tension inherent in
the Patriarchs' family relationships to the very end, the text repeats an
earlier situation in Yaakov's life—his brother's feelings of "grudge" and
threats to kill him—in the guise of his sons' fears toward Yosef. Here,
however, there can be no question of personal vengeance, since Yosef
sees the brothers' betrayal of him as but part of a larger purpose. In his
words of verse 20, "God planned-it-over for good . . . to keep many
people alive," the text resolves two of the great hanging issues that have
persisted throughout Genesis: sibling hatred and the threat to genera-
tional continuity.

Left hanging, of course, is the issue of the promised land, since the
narrative concludes "in Egypt," but these final chapters lead to the
assurance that God will "take account" (vv.24–25) of the Sons of Israel,
as they are soon to be termed.

50:9 **heavy:** Three times through verse 11. The root *kbd* connotes "honor,"
    "importance," "weight," and is central here perhaps to emphasize the
    respect shown to Yaakov.
   13 **the cave in the field of Makhpela:** Despite God's continual promise of the
    land throughout the book, this is practically all that the Patriarchs possess
    at the end of Genesis.
   16 **left-this-charge:** Or "commanded."
   22 **a hundred and ten years:** The ideal Egyptian life span.

23 Yosef saw from Efrayim sons of the third generation,
and also the sons of Makhir son of Menashe were born on
   Yosef's knees.
24 Yosef said to his brothers:
I am dying,
but God will take account, yes, account of you,
he will bring you up from this land
to the land about which he swore
to Avraham, to Yitzhak, and to Yaakov.
25 Yosef had the Sons of Israel swear, saying:
When God takes account, yes, account of you,
bring my bones up from here!
26 And Yosef died, a hundred and ten years old.
They embalmed him and they put him in a coffin
in Egypt.

נשלם ספר בראשית

ברוך המחיה והממית

---

23 **born on Yosef's knees:** Considered his own; see 30:3.
24 **brothers:** Presumably meant in the sense of "family."
25 **Sons of Israel:** They are no longer merely the sons of one man but are now
on their way to becoming a people.

SUGGESTIONS FOR FURTHER READING

This list cites selected works in English only. It is intended to supplement *Genesis* with reference to the text of Genesis, ancient Near Eastern background, and a literary approach to the Bible. Included also is material referred to in the Commentary and Notes under authors' names in parentheses. Works written after 1982 (and in a few cases, before that date), while not referred to in the Commentary or Notes, have been added here to supply the reader with some recent and stimulating studies.

Ackerman, James S. "Joseph, Judah and Jacob." In Kenneth R. R. Gros Louis and James S. Ackerman, eds., *More Literary Interpretations of Biblical Narratives* (Nashville, 1982).

Alter, Robert. *The Art of Biblical Narrative* (New York, 1981).

Alter, Robert, and Frank Kermode, eds., *The Literary Guide to the Bible* (Cambridge, MA, 1987).

Andersen, Frances. *The Sentence in Biblical Hebrew* (The Hague, 1974).

Auerbach, Erich. *Mimesis* (New York, 1957).

Bar Efrat, Shimon. *Narrative Art and the Bible* (Sheffield, 1989).

Bird, Phyllis. "Images of Women in the Old Testament," in Rosemary Radford Ruether, *Religion and Sexism* (New York, 1974).

Buber, Martin. *Good and Evil* (New York, 1952).

———. *On the Bible* (New York, 1982).

Cassuto, Umberto. *A Commentary on the Book of Genesis. Part One: From Adam to Noah* (Jerusalem, 1972); *Part Two: From Noah to Abraham* (Jerusalem, 1974).

Culley, Robert. *Studies in the Structure of Hebrew Narrative* (Philadelphia, 1976).

———, ed. "Oral Tradition and Old Testament Studies." *Semeia* 5 (1976).

Damrosch, David. *The Narrative Covenant* (New York, 1987).

Davidson, Robert. *Genesis 1–11 (Cambridge Bible Commentary)* (Cambridge, 1979).

———. *Genesis 12–50 (Cambridge Bible Commentary)* (Cambridge, 1979).

De Vaux, Roland. *Ancient Israel* (New York, 1965).

———. *The Early History of Israel* (Philadelphia, 1978).

Driver, S. R. *The Book of Genesis* (New York, 1926).

Fishbane, Michael, *Text and Texture* (New York, 1979).

Fokkelman, J. P. *Narrative Art in Genesis* (Assen and Amsterdam, 1975).

Fox, Everett. "The Bible Needs to Be Read Aloud." *Response* 33 (Spring 1977).

———. "Can Genesis Be Read As a Book?" *Semeia* 46 (1989).

———. "Franz Rosenzweig as Translator," *Leo Baeck Institute Yearbook* 34 (1989).

———. "The Samson Cycle in an Oral Setting." *Alcheringa: Ethnopoetics* 4, no. 1 (1978).

Frankfort, Henri, et al. *Before Philosophy* (New York, 1951).

Gaster, Theodor H. *Myth, Legend, and Custom in the Old Testament* (New York, 1969).

Geller, Stephen A. "The Struggle at the Jabbok: the Uses of Enigma in a Biblical Narrative," *Journal of the Ancient Near Eastern Society of Columbia University (JANES)* 14 (1982).

Ginzberg, Louis. *The Legends of the Jews* (Philadelphia, 1933).

Glatzer, Nahum N. *Franz Rosenzweig: His Life and Thought* (New York, 1961).

Goldin, Judah. "The Youngest Son or Where Does Genesis 38 Belong," *Journal of Biblical Literature* 96 (1977).

Greenstein, Edward L. "The State of Biblical Studies, or Biblical Studies in a State," in *Essays in Biblical Method and Translation* (Atlanta, 1989).

———. "Theories of Modern Bible Translation," *Prooftexts* III (1983).

———. "The Torah as She is Read," *Response* 47 (Winter 1985).

Gros Louis, Kenneth R. R.; Ackerman, James S.; and Warshaw, Thayer S., eds. *Literary Interpretations of Biblical Narratives* (Nashville, 1974).

Gros Louis, Kenneth R. R., and Ackerman, James S. *More Literary Interpretations of Biblical Narratives* (Nashville, 1982).

Hendel, Ronald. *The Epic of the Patriarch: The Jacob Cycle and the Narrative Traditions of Canaan and Israel* (Atlanta, 1987).

Interpreter's Dictionary of the Bible (New York, 1962).

Jacobson, Dan. *The Story of the Stories* (New York, 1982).

Jeansonne, Sharon Pace. *The Women of Genesis* (Minneapolis, 1990).

Levenson, Jon D. *Creation and the Persistence of Evil* (New York, 1985).

Miller, Alan. "Clause Levi-Strauss and Gen. 37–Ex. 20," in Ronald Brauner, ed., *Shiv'im* (Philadelphia, 1977).

Muffs, Yochanan. "Abraham the Noble Warrior: Patriarchal Politics and Laws of War in Ancient Israel." In Geza Vermes and Jacob Neusner, eds. *Essays in Honor of Yigael Yadin, Journal of Jewish Studies* 33, nos. 1–2 (Spring–Autumn, 1982).

Plaut, W. Gunther. *The Torah: A Modern Commentary.* Volume I: *Genesis* (New York, 1974).

Polzin, Robert M. "The Ancestress of Israel in Danger." *Semeia* 3 (1975).

Redford, Donald. *A Study of the Biblical Story of Joseph* (Leiden, 1970).

Rosenberg, Joel. "The Garden Story Forward and Backward: The Non-Narrative Dimension of Gen. 2–3." *Prooftexts* 1, no. 1 (1978).

———. *King and Kin* (Bloomington, 1986).

Russell, Letty M., ed. *Feminist Interpretation of the Bible* (Philadelphia, 1985).

Sarna, Nahum. *The JPS Torah Commentary: Genesis* (Philadelphia, 1989).

———. *Understanding Genesis* (New York, 1966).

Skinner, John. *Genesis (International Critical Commentary)* (New York, 1910).

Speiser, Ephraim E. *Genesis (The Anchor Bible)* (New York, 1964).

Spiegel, Shalom. *The Last Trial* (New York, 1979).

Steinberg, Naomi. "The Genealogical Framework of the Early Stories in Genesis," *Semeia* 46 (1989).

Sternberg, Meir. *The Poetics of Biblical Narrative* (Bloomington, 1985).

Tedlock, Dennis. "Toward an Oral Poetics." *New Literary History* 7, no. 3 (Spring 1977).

Vawter, Bruce. *On Genesis: A New Reading* (New York, 1977).

Wander, Nathaniel. "Structure, Contradiction, and 'Resolution' in Mythology: Father's Brother's Daughter Marriage and the Treatment of Women in Genesis 11–50," *JANES* 13 (1981).

Williams, James G. *Women Recounted: Narrative Thinking and the God of Israel* (Sheffield, 1982).

Non-English works also referred to in the Commentary and Notes:

Ehrlich, Arnold. *Mikra Ki-Pheshuto* (New York, 1969).

Jacob, Benno. *Das erste Buch der Tora: Genesis* (Berlin, 1931).

Redak (Rabbi David Kimhi). *Perush Redak al Ha-Torah* (Jerusalem, 1975).

EXODUS:
Now These Are the Names

ON THE BOOK OF EXODUS AND ITS STRUCTURE

THE BOOK of Exodus is Israel's second book of origins. Genesis had concerned itself with the beginnings of the world, of human beings and their institutions, and of the people of Israel as a tribal family. Exodus continues this thrust as it recounts the origin of the people on a religious and political level (here inseparable as concepts). A number of biblical ideas receive their fullest early treatment in this book: God's acting directly in history; making himself "known" to both Israelites and foreigners; covenant as a reciprocal agreement between God and humans; law as an expression of total world view; and the use of sacred structure (Tabernacle or "Dwelling") as a vehicle for and expression of perceived truths about the world. In addition, several biblical institutions make their first appearance in Exodus: Passover, Sabbath, rudimentary leadership/ government, and cult/priesthood. All this is presented in a general narrative framework, raising the question as to whether what we have here is story or history. Is Exodus a fanciful reconstruction of what happened to Moshe (Moses) and his generation, riddled with anachronisms? Or is it a faithful and reliable handing-down of eyewitness data which only the cynical or irreligious would doubt?

For the first position there are several supports. We possess virtually no extrabiblical references to the events recorded in our book, either in Egypt or elsewhere. Then, too, there seem to be inconsistencies of time within the story (Chapters 16 and 18 appear to presuppose laws which were given later), and patterns within the telling of the tale that are too symmetrical (the Plagues) or too stereotyped (the constant use of Deuteronomic language) to be simple reporting of fact. Finally, Exodus is lacking in the citation of personal and geographical names, especially as compared to the books that precede and follow (*Genesis* and *Numbers*).

For the second position, that of Exodus as a reliable historical record, there exist no methods of proof other than evaluation of literary form— that is, accepting that oral literature is able to preserve facts without later coloration. But even if it could be shown that Exodus is oral literature—an evaluation which is too sweeping, given the present form of the book—

modern scholarship has come to cast doubt on the absolute historical reliability of oral tradition (see Vansina 1965).

Despite these observations, there is still something unsettling about writing Exodus off as a work of fiction, however pious that fiction may have been. For the rest of the Hebrew Bible abounds in emotional references to the experience of the exodus. At every stage of biblical literature, that experience is invoked for the purpose of directing behavior (see especially Judges 2, I Samuel 8, II Samuel 7, II Kings 17, Nehemiah 9, and Psalm 78; and most of Deuteronomy is rhetorically grounded in it). The entire structure and emotional force of biblical law rest upon such exhortations as "A sojourner you are not to oppress:/ you yourselves know (well) the feelings of the sojourner,/ for sojourners were you in the land of Egypt" (Ex. 23:9) and such situations as that of the Hebrew serf (Ex. 21:1ff.). Apparently the experience of the exodus period was crucial in forming the group consciousness of the Israelites, and ever since it has provided a model from which both later Judaism and Christianity were to draw frequently and profoundly.

A hypothetical analogy, based on American history, may help to shed light on the historicity of Exodus. Imagine a book based on the following outline: first, a section on the American Revolution, with some biographical material on a few of the Founding Fathers, focusing mostly on the outbreak of the war and key battles; second, a description of the Constitutional Convention, including some of the more important speeches and discussions; third, the text of the Constitution itself; and finally, L'Enfant's original blueprints for the building of the new capital, Washington, D.C., interspersed with accounts of the first few presidents' inaugural addresses. What would be the underlying message of such a book? We are certainly dealing here with more than a straight journalistic description of the events, more than a legalistic discussion of constitutional law, and more than a technical presentation for architects. Such a book would actually be presenting the ideals of America's self-image: a nation founded on the willingness to fight for particular rights against Old World tyranny, established under democratic laws based on reason and providing governmental checks and balances, and whose ideals would be embodied in the construction of a brand-new, centrally located capital city that used classically grounded forms of architecture to express grace and reason as the basis for the new society.

Now this portrayal is very simplistic, but it gets its point across (and I would be willing to wager that, somewhere in this country, there exists a school textbook written along these lines). In a similar manner, although with much more weight given to God's role in the process, the book of Exodus unfolds. The dramatic story of Israel's deliverance from bondage, coupled with Moshe's own early development, is only the first part of the book, and accounts for less than half of it. It is followed by several stories of desert wanderings, and then by a presentation of the covenant made between God and Israel at Sinai, against a stunning natural backdrop. The second half of the book enumerates a series of laws which constitute the covenant, and the details of construction of a portable sanctuary designed both to symbolize and actually to accommodate God's presence among the Israelites (with the interruption of a major rebellion). So, like our theoretical American model, Exodus conveys far more than information about events. It is, rather, the narration of a world view, a laying out of different types of texts bearing the *meaning* of Israel's historical experience.

I stress the word "experience" because that is what is at stake here. Human memory is always selective. We remember what we wish to remember, giving weight to particular emotions, sometimes over and above the facts (or, as the poet Maya Angelou puts it autobiographically, "The facts sometimes obscure the truth"). The same thing appears to be true of group memory. What a people remembers of substance is not nearly as important as how they process their experience.

In our Exodus text one can perceive a characteristically Israelite process at work. The book emerges as a mix of historical recollection, mythical processing, and didactic retelling, what Buber and others have called a "saga." What is preserved in the book of Exodus, therefore, is a Teaching (Heb. *Torah*) based on a set of experiences, which became history for ancient Israel. Hence, to understand better the workings of the book, we need to turn to its themes and its structure. This will be more fruitful than trying to find the exact location of the Sea of Reeds or Mount Sinai, or the "Lost Ark," or Moshe's burial site—whose location "no man knows even today" (Deut. 34:6). These have all receded into archeological oblivion. What has survived of ancient Israel is its approach to history and to life, and its literature. In that sense, the book of Exodus is an attempt to distill history and to learn from it, using echoes from the past to shape the present and the future.

When we turn to a closer consideration of the structure of Exodus, we must proceed on the assumption that a work of art stems from both artful and unconscious design. Therefore, any structuring of such a book can only be hypothetical and must not limit itself to ironclad categories.

With that said, a number of potential divisions of our book present themselves. The first emerges from a close look at the subject matter of the text. Strikingly, Exodus appears to be arranged in groups of a few chapters each (bearing in mind that the chapter divisions are historically late), resulting in the following scheme:

1. Prologue in Egypt (Chap. 1)
2. Moshe's Early Life and Call (Chaps. 2–4)
3. Moshe's Mission in Egypt (5:1–7:13)
4. The First Nine Plagues (7:14–10:29)
5. The Tenth Plague and the Exodus (Chaps. 11–13)
6. In the Wilderness I: The Deliverance at the Sea (14:1–15:21)
7. In the Wilderness II: Early Experiences (15:22–18:27)
8. Covenant at Sinai (Chaps. 19–20)
9. The Terms (Laws) and Conclusion of the Covenant (Chaps. 21–24)
10. Details of the Tabernacle (Chaps. 25–27)
11. Details of the Cult (Chaps. 28–31)
12. Rebellion and Reconciliation (Chaps. 32–34)
13. The Building of the Tabernacle, Priestly Vestments (Chaps. 35–39)
14. Conclusion (Chap. 40)

Such a measured shifting of focus helps to maintain the flow of the text and our interest in it.

A glance through this list will also lead to the positing of larger structures. The traditions collected in Exodus fall naturally into both geographical and thematic divisions. The first part of the book takes place in Egypt (1:1–15:21), the second in the wilderness (15:22–40:38); this could alternatively be viewed as the events preceding Mount Sinai (Chaps. 1–17/18) and those that take place there (Chaps. 18/19–40). One could also combine the geographical and thematic aspects, resulting in the structure (1) Israel in Egypt (1:1–15:21), (2) Israel in the Wilderness (15:22–24:18), and (3) Tabernacle and Calf (Chaps. 25–40).

My own preference for structuring Exodus also combines these aspects, as follows:

I. The Deliverance Narrative (1:1–15:21)
II. In the Wilderness (15:22–18:27)
III. Covenant and Law (Chaps. 19–24)
IV. The Blueprints for the Tabernacle and Its Service (Chaps. 25–31)

V. Infidelity and Reconciliation (Chaps. 32–34)
VI. The Building of the Tabernacle (Chaps. 35–40)

These divisions exhibit a great deal of overlapping. In Part I, Israel's life in Egypt (Chap. 1) paves the way for Moshe's early years (Chaps. 2–4), then the account of his mission before Pharaoh and the Plagues (Chaps. 5–13), and the final victory (Chaps. 14–15); Part II is anticipated by some of what happens after the exodus itself (Chap. 14), and leads to Sinai (Chap. 19); the covenant and laws of Part III naturally lead to other prescriptions, this time the building instructions for the Tabernacle (Chaps. 25–31); planning the sacred structure in Part IV is followed by the making of a forbidden construction, the Golden Calf (Chaps. 32–33); and the reconciliation between God and Israel (Chap. 34) restores Israel's capacity to return to the actual building of the Tabernacle, and to complete it (Chaps. 35–40). So despite the presence of what must have been several very diverse traditions behind the final text of Exodus, it has been skillfully woven together to form a coherent whole. In addition to the above structures, it can be said that the book of Exodus rests on several textual backbones, inner structures and recurring themes and motifs that help to create a unified work. These may be listed by category:

1. There are various climaxes which serve to highlight the action—the Encounter at the Bush (Chaps. 3–4), the Tenth Plague and Exodus (12:29–42), the Deliverance at the Sea (14–15:21), the Revelation at Sinai (Chaps. 19–20), the Calf Episode (Chap. 32), and Completion of the Tabernacle (Chap. 40). Anchoring these dramatic scenes, at the center of the book, is the Sinai Revelation. The Binding of Yitzhak (Isaac) in Chapter 22 of Genesis serves much the same focusing function.

2. There exist three strategically placed accounts of God's Presence accompanying the Israelites (13:21–22, 24:15–18, 40:34–38) which share a common vocabulary. Key words in these passages are "move on," "day/night," "cloud," "fire," "dwell," "Glory," "cover," "go up," and "in the eyes of the Children of Israel/before the people" (it should be noted that not every passage uses all of these terms). These words chart God's movement: first, following the Exodus; second, following the concluding of the covenant; and third, following the erection of the Tabernacle, at the end of the book. A variation of these Presence accounts occurs in Numbers 9:15–23, where it rounds out the picture—for it is at this point that the Israelites finally depart from Sinai (having spent about a year there), on their journey toward the Promised Land.

3. Several leading words recur throughout the book and give it a sense of unity:

serve—The Israelites pass from "servitude" to Pharaoh into the "service" of God; laws are given that warn against "serving" other gods, that specify how a "serf" is to be treated, and that detail the "service" (i.e., construction and dismantling) of a sanctuary where God is to be properly "served."

Glory—Liberated from Pharaoh's "stubbornness" (Heb. *koved lev*), the Israelites experience God's "Glory" (Heb. *kavod*) at the Sea of Reeds, and encounter it again at Sinai (Chap. 24) and when the Tabernacle is completed (Chap. 40). When Israel falters in Chapter 32, Moses begs to see God's "Glory" as a sign of reassurance. This is one of the central issues of the book, receiving its clearest formulation in Chap. 17:7—"Is YHWH in our midst, or not?" Without the accompanying Presence, the Israelites can survive neither in Egypt nor in the wilderness. That the book ends with the "Glory" taking up residence in the Tabernacle is a sign that all is well in this regard.

know—The Plagues and the liberation take place so that Egyptian and Israelite alike will acknowledge God as the true ruler (who "knows" the slaves' sufferings). The book as a whole portrays a God who is "known" by his compassion toward the oppressed.

see—God "sees" and rescues the people early in the book (Chap. 3); they "see" his deliverance at the sea (Chap. 14) and the awesome display at Sinai (Chaps. 19–20); the Tabernacle blueprint is given to Moshe to "see" (Chaps. 25ff.).

4. Aside from theme words, there are also several thematic threads that run through the book. These may be listed as well:

distinction—The Israelites learn what it is to be separated out, first for oppression and later for God's service. This process occurs during the Plagues and throughout the legal sections, which are often based on the making of distinctions (the Hebrew word for "holy," *kadosh*, may originally have had this connotation). In general, Exodus is a book that abounds in polarities and distinctions: between God and Pharaoh, life and death, slavery and freedom, Egyptianness and Israeliteness, city and wilderness, visible gods/magic and an invisible God who is not conjurable, doubt and trust.

construction—The Israelites are enslaved as builders of Egyptian cities; they go on to build a society, a calf-god, and a Tabernacle.

rebellion—From the beginning, God and Moshe are often unheeded, as the Israelites seek to maintain or return to their status as dependent slaves in Egypt (Chaps. 2, 5, 14, 15–17, 32).

Sabbath—As a newly freed people, Israel is to adapt to a rhythm of work and sacred cessation, which celebrates both creation and freedom. The Sabbath is at issue immediately after liberation (Chap. 16) and is commanded three times (Chaps. 20, 31, 35); and the account of the Tabernacle's completion echoes the vocabulary of God's completed creation in Genesis 2, a passage which serves as one justification for observing the Sabbath (see Ex. 20:11).

origins—We are told of the beginnings of the new covenant (distinct from that concluded with Abraham), the law system, the cult/priesthood, and the sacred calendar, but with the significant omission of the monarchy.

covenant—God establishes a relationship with the people of Israel: if they will obey him and observe his laws, he will protect them and treat them as his "firstborn son." This form of covenant is different from the ones in Genesis, and plays a significant role in subsequent books of the Bible.

God in History—The God of Exodus actively intervenes to rescue a people, defeating their oppressors in battle; he leads them through the wilderness, meets them, and makes a covenant with them.

5. The above themes are specifically Israelite themes. There are, however, motifs in Exodus that have a more universal ring. One could term these anthropological, since they employ standard aspects of human experience to convey the overall messages of the book.

Fire is used frequently and in varied contexts (at the Burning Bush and later back at Mount Sinai, in the desert trek, in the Tabernacle service, and at the Calf incident), usually to make a statement about God. In contrast to conventional fire gods (e.g., the Norse trickster Loki), the God of Exodus is most often associated with the more positive aspects of fire: constancy, purity, and transformation. The fire at Sinai does not destroy Moshe and the people, but rather turns them into something new. At the same time it should not be forgotten that fire is used regularly to connote anger in the Bible, especially God's, and especially in the later wilderness narratives.

Water appears throughout Exodus, not as a backdrop but as an active medium which most often signifies life and death simultaneously. The Nile, into which the enslaved Hebrews' babies are thrown, gently bears the infant Moshe to safety; the Nile, the giver of life in Egypt, is changed into blood, itself a major signifier of life in the Bible but useless here because it is undrinkable; the Sea of Reeds acts as a passageway of birth for the Israelites but as a graveyard for their Egyptian pursuers. The availability of water becomes a central issue in the wilderness, as an instrument for survival and for the testing of the Israelites' faith. Finally, water creates the ritual purity necessary for the people at Sinai and their priests in the Tabernacle to approach God.

Desert/Wilderness is the scene of the crucial second part of the book. Only in the desert, away from the massive influence of age-old Egyptian culture, can the new Israelite society be forged. Moshe, like many other real-life and fictional heroes, demonstrates this in his own early life. The desert acts as a purifying agent for him, changing the Egyptian prince into a member of his own true people. Similarly, the Israelites begin the process of transformation from bondage to self-rule, a process which is taught in the harsh reality of desert life and which will take an entire generation to complete.

In point of fact, all these media—fire, water, and desert—suggest change as a major concern of the book of Exodus. Our text chronicles the start of Israel's journey as a nation, a transformative journey which takes vastly changed circumstances, a whole generation in time, and indeed several books of recounting to complete. Exodus is very concerned with topography—not for the purposes of historical recollection (as Genesis was, apparently) but as an account of an inner journey. Thus the people travel to the boundary between Egypt and the desert, through the sea, to the great fiery mountain; and we know that they cannot but be on their way to a final goal. That goal, the Promised Land, will not be realized in Exodus, because in this book we stand only at the beginning of the journey. Change does not occur quickly, and the true molding of a people, like that of an individual, requires formative experiences over time. In Exodus, then, the People of Israel begins in adolescence, as it were. It has survived infancy in Genesis, a period marked by constant threats of physical extinction, and must now begin the tortuous process of learning to cope with adulthood—that is to say, peoplehood—in a hostile world.

That process will take us past the present text. Exodus stands at the beginning of a trilogy in the middle of the Torah. It takes us from slavery up to Sinai, inaugurating the law-giving process. Leviticus will concentrate almost exclusively on laws (of "holiness"), never budging geographically, while Numbers will see the conclusion of the Sinai experience and the traveling toward (and actually reaching) the land of Israel. Exodus is thus of great importance in the overall five-book pattern, introducing key elements of the wilderness books: law, institutions, rebellion, and— Moshe himself. It serves as a bridge between the great narratives of Genesis and the priestly code of Leviticus and the wanderings of Numbers (Greenberg 1972 notes how the opening of Exodus points back, to Genesis 46; and the closing points forward, to Numbers 9). It in fact contains elements of all three books.

Exodus is the basis not only of what follows in the Torah, but also sets the stage for the rest of the Hebrew Bible. What Israel understood of its God, and what that God expects of them, are set forth most directly and unforgettably in the memories enshrined in the book of Exodus.

PART I The Deliverance Narrative (1–15:21)

THE FIRST PART of the book of Exodus is presented as a continuation of the Genesis narratives, by abbreviating the genealogy of the immigrant Yaakov from Gen. 46:8–25. We find here the same centrality of God, the same kind of sparse but powerful biographical sketch of the human hero, and a narrative style similar to that of the previous book.

And yet Exodus introduces a new and decisive element into the Hebrew Bible, which becomes paradigmatic for future generations of biblical writers. The book speaks of a God who acts directly in history, blow by blow—a God who promises, liberates, guides, and gives laws to a people. This is, to be sure, an outgrowth of a God who brings the Flood and disperses the Babel generation, but it is also a decisive step forward from a God who works his will in the background, through intrafamily conflicts (which comprise most of Genesis). This deity frees his people, not by subterfuge, but by directly taking on Egypt and its gods. Pharaoh and the Nile, both of which were considered divine in Egypt, are in the end forced to yield to superior power. Surely it is no accident that the ending of Part I—the Song of Moshe at the Sea—hails YHWH as Israel's true king, a king whose acts of "leading," "redeeming," and "planting" his people are exultingly affirmed in the body of the Song.

Part I receives its structural coherence in a number of ways. For one, it encompasses a straight chronological narrative, moving from Israel's enslavement to its liberation and triumph over its oppressors. The ending, Chapter 15, is rhetorically and stylistically fitting (see Gaster 1969), celebrating as it does the mighty deeds of God. For another, Part I carefully paces its climaxes, building up from the Burning Bush to various stages of Plagues, to the Tenth Plague/exodus and finally the great scene at the sea. There are also a number of key words that help to tie together various sections of the narratives: "know," "serve," and "see." All of these go through interesting changes in meaning, through which one can trace the movement of central ideas (see the Commentary).

In the area of vocabulary, David Daube (1963) has made the interesting observation that the Deliverance Narrative uses a number of verbs that occur regularly in biblical law regarding the formal release of a slave: "send free" (Heb. *shale'ah*), "drive out," (*garesh*), and "go out" (*yatzo'*). In addition, the motif of the Israelites' "stripping" the Egyptians (3:22, 12: 36) links up with the regulation of release in Deut. 15:13. " . . . you are not to send him free empty-handed." Daube sees our text as bearing the stamp of Israelite social custom: Pharaoh is made to flout "established social regulations."

Finally, several scholars (Kikawada 1975, Ackerman 1974, Fishbane 1979, and Isbell 1982) have pointed out that the vocabulary of the first few chapters of the book foreshadows the whole of Part I. This use of sound and idea helps to create unity in these narratives (despite their possibly diverse origins), and is also of importance in viewing the biographical material in the first four chapters.

The Early Life of Moshe and Religious Biography

Dominating the early chapters of Exodus, more than the description of bondage itself, is the figure of the reluctant liberator, Moshe. The portrayal of his beginnings contrasts strongly with the classic hero stories of the ancient world.

This is not immediately apparent. Moshe's birth narrative parallels that of King Sargon of Akkad; his flight from Egypt and return as leader are reminiscent of Jephthah and David in the Bible, and of the Syrian king Idrimi (as recounted in Akkadian texts) as well. In addition, half a century ago Lord Raglan attempted to demonstrate common elements in hero biographies by compiling a list of up to thirty key motifs. Those relevant to Moshe include: the father a relative of the mother, an attempt made to kill him at birth, his escape through the action of others, being raised by foster parents, little information about his childhood, his traveling to his "future kingdom" upon reaching adulthood, promulgating laws, losing favor with the deity, dying on the top of a hill, not being succeeded by his children, and a hazy death/burial. Moshe therefore shares with Oedipus, Hercules, Siegfried, and Robin Hood, among others, a host of common elements; his point total according to Raglan's scheme puts him toward the top of the list as an archetypal traditional hero. It must be concluded that, far from being a factual account, his biography is composed largely of literary constructs.

When one looks closer at the biblical portrayal of Moshe, however, the purpose and particularly Israelite thrust of these constructs becomes clear. Almost every key element in Moshe's early life—e.g., rescue from death by royal decree, rescue from death by water, flight into the desert, meeting with God on the sacred mountain—foreshadows Israel's experience in the book of Exodus. The key theme of the distinction between Israel and Egypt, so central to the Plague Narrative and to Israelite religion as a whole, is brought out beautifully in the depiction of Moshe's development from Egyptian prince to would-be liberator to shepherd in the wilderness, the latter an ancestral calling (cf. Nohrnberg 1981, who also discusses Yosef as developing in exactly the opposite direction—from Israelite shepherd boy to Egyptian viceroy, complete with Egyptian appearance, wife, and name). What is important in these early chapters of Exodus, then, is not the customary focus on the young hero's deeds (e.g., Hercules strangling serpents in the cradle) or his fatal flaw (although there is a hint of this too!), but on what he shares with his people, or, more precisely, how he prefigures them.

Another aspect of these stories removes them from the usual realm of heroic biography. Elsewhere in the Bible, individual hero types are at least partially overshadowed by the true central "character": God. This appears to be true in Exodus as well. Moshe develops only so far; he recedes as a full-blown personality during the Plague Narrative, to emerge sporadically in later encounters with the people (e.g., Chapters 16 and 32–33; the portrait expands in the narratives of the book of Numbers). No wonder that later Jewish legend (and further, Christian and Muslim stories as well) found it necessary to fill in the tantalizing hints left by the biblical biographer, with sometimes fantastic tales. But in the Exodus text, it is God who holds sway. In this context, one is reminded that Israelite thinking had room neither for worship of human heroes nor interest in the biography of God (i.e., divine birth and marriage) on the model of surrounding cultures. The biblical portrayal of both God and Moshe has been reduced in our book to only such facts as will illuminate the relationship between Israel and its God. Thus we learn from the Moshe of Exodus much about the people themselves, and about prophecy (cf. Chaps. 3–4); from the God of Exodus, how he acts in history and what he demands of the people. More than that is not easily forthcoming from our text (interestingly, the Passover Haggadah picked up on the Bible's direction and all but omitted Moshe's name in the celebration of the holiday).

As we have suggested, later Jewish legend—some of which may actually be of great antiquity—sought to fill in various aspects of Moshe's life that are missing from the Exodus text. A perusal of Ginzberg (1937) will uncover rich legendary material, dealing with Moshe's childhood, family identity, experience in Midian and elsewhere as a hero. While this material does not always illuminate the biblical story, it does demonstrate how folk belief includes a need for heroes in the classic Raglan mold; the Midrashic portrait of Moshe corresponds nicely to what we find in other cultures.

Turning to stylistic characteristics of these early chapters, we may note that a good deal of repetition occurs, as if further to highlight the themes. Baby Moshe is saved from death twice; three times he attempts acts of opposing oppression; twice (Chaps. 2 and 5) he fails in his attempts to help his enslaved brothers; and twice (Chaps 3 and 6) God reassures him with long speeches that center around the Divine Name. This kind of continuity is artfully literary, but it is also an echo of real life, where people often live out certain themes in patterns.

Finally there is the matter of recurring words. Most important is the telling use of "see," from the loving gaze of Moshe's mother (2:2), through to the auspicious glance of Pharaoh's daughter (2:6), then to Moshe's sympathetic observing of his brothers' plight (2:11); all this seems to be linked to the episode at the Burning Bush, where God "is seen" by the future leader (3:2), and where the climax of this whole development takes place: God affirms that he has "seen, yes, seen the affliction of my people that is in Egypt . . . . and I have also seen the oppression with which the Egyptians oppress them" (3:7, 9). Thus Moshe's biography leads to, and is an outgrowth of, the people's own situation.

In sum, Moshe's early biography leads us to ponder the "growing up" process through which the people of Israel must pass on their way out of Egypt. The narratives that deal with his leadership of the people in the wilderness period, from Exodus 16 on, will help to round out our picture of him as a real personality, with the tragedies and triumphs that are a part of human life but magnified in the case of great individuals.

On the Journey Motif

World literature is dominated by stories involving a journey. More often than not, these tales are framed as quests for holy or magical objects (e.g., the Golden Fleece, the Holy Grail), or for eternal youth/immortality (Gilgamesh). The classic pattern, as Joseph Campbell (1972) has described it, calls for the hero to make a kind of round trip, crossing dangerous thresholds (monsters, giants, unfriendly supernatural beings) both on the way toward the goal and on the way home. Either at the middle or at the end of the journey stands the goal, which often entails meeting with the divine and/or obtaining a magical or life-giving object (e.g., the Golden Fleece).

Such stories mirror our own longings for accomplishment and acceptance, as well as our universal desire to overcome the ultimate enemy, Death. In the hero's triumphs, we triumph; his vanquishing of death cathartically becomes our own.

This mythic substructure has penetrated the biblical tales, but it has been toned down for human protagonists, to suppress the idea of the mortal hero in favor of the divine one. Thus all the Patriarchs except Yitzhak (Isaac) go on fateful long journeys (his is reserved for the three-day trip to Moriah in Genesis 22), yet there is none of the color and adventure that we find, for example, in Greek mythology. Outside of Yaakov's encounter with the mysterious wrestler in Genesis 32, there is little in Genesis to suggest hero tales on the classic mold. In Exodus, too, Moshe makes a significant journey—to Midyan—one might say, within himself, to find his true identity and calling, but it is highly muted, containing virtually no details. The round trip contains two thresholds of death, with Moshe first threatened by Pharaoh's justice (2:15) and, on the way back to Egypt, by God himself (4:24–26). The initial goal is attained at the "mountain of God" "behind the wilderness," where, meeting with divinity amid fire, he is finally able to integrate his own past, present, and future (as he will return to this mountain with the entire people in Chaps. 19ff). At the Burning Bush, the Egyptian prince, the Israelite shepherd, and the Hebrew liberator coalesce, investing Moshe with unique qualifications for his task.

But it is to a larger journey framework that we must look to understand the "hero" content of Exodus, and with it, that of the Torah as a whole. The major journey undertaken is, of course, that of the people of Israel, from slavery to Promised Land. It is also a journey from death to life, from servitude to god-king to the service of God as king; along the way, death serves to purify an entire generation. And yet even this most obvious of journey stories differs markedly from those of gods and heroes so familiar in Western culture. The people of Israel function as a collective antihero, an example of precisley how *not* to behave. They play no active role whatsoever in their own liberation, use neither brawn nor wits to survive in the wilderness, constantly grumble about wanting to return to Egypt, and at both Sinai and the threshold of the Promised Land (in the book of Numbers), their chief form of behavior is first fear and later rebellion.

Moshe's own journeys parallel those of the entire people later on. Like them, he flees from Pharaoh into the wilderness, meets God at flaming Sinai, and has trouble accepting his task but must in the end. Here is where Moshe shines as the true leader: he epitomizes his people's experience and focuses and forges it into something new.

Moshe Before Pharaoh: The Plague Narrative (5–11)

The heart of the Exodus story sets out the confrontation between the visible god-king, Pharaoh, who embodies the monumental culture of Egypt, and the invisible God of Israel who fights for his ragtag people. The drama is conveyed by means of alternating conversations/confrontations and events. The narrator has built his account, bracketed by the early approach of Moshe and Aharon (Aaron) to Pharaoh, which fails (Chap. 5), and the extended construct of the Tenth Plague (11–13); in between fall the schematically arranged first nine plagues.

Three overall stages characterize this latter section. The first is indicated by the oft-repeated demand, "Send free my people, that they may serve me!"; the second is the "hardening" of Pharaoh's heart; and the third, the unleashing of each plague. Further, it can be shown that the plagues are presented via a variety of structures and substructures (see Greenberg 1969 and the chart in Sarna 1986). Some commentators divide them into five thematic groups of two apiece—1 and 2, the Nile; 3 and 4, insects; 5 and 6, disease; 7 and 8, airborne disaster; and 9 and 10, darkness/death (Plaut 1981). Also fruitful is the following threefold division: 1, 4, and 7, God's command to confront Pharaoh in the morning; 2, 5, and 8, God says, "Come to Pharaoh"; 3, 6, and 9, no warning is given to Pharaoh. Yet another grouping of themes is possible (Bar Efrat 1979): 1–3, God vs. the magicians of Egypt; 4–6, stress on the distinction between Israel and Egypt; 7–9, the most powerful plagues.

This utilization of order, symbolized by "perfect" numbers such as 3 and 10, finds a parallel in the creation story of Genesis 1 (where the key number, of course, is 7, 3 + 3 + 1, whereas here we have 3 + 3 + 3 + 1). Both texts display a desire to depict God as one who endows nature and history with meaning. The poetic tradition about the plagues, as represented, for instance, by Psalm 78, was content to describe the plagues in brief, within the setting of a single poem. The narrator of the Pentateuchal traditions, however, has a different point to make, and structured exposition is the best way to do it.

There is another structural tendency that one may observe in the Plague Narrative. Repeating words and motifs comprise over twenty shared and discrete elements in the story. Since the vast majority of these occur by the end of the fourth plague, this leaves the narrator free to develop plagues 7 and 8 with particular intensity, using a full palette of descriptions, with the addition of the theme that these were the worst of their kind ever to take place in Egypt. It will be useful here to list a few of the key words and phrases, and motifs, that can be found in the Plague Narrative:

Words/phrases: Go to Pharaoh; send . . . free; know; throughout the land of Egypt; plead; distinguish; tomorrow; man and beast; not one remained; heavy [i.e., severe] as YHWH had said.

Motifs: Moshe's staff; Aharon as agent; magicians; death.

It is important to note here that the structuring of the plagues is not a perfectly balanced one. The narrative varies between exact repetition of elements and phrases and nonrepetition (Licht 1978). By thus using sounds and ideas in variation, the narrator is able to weave a tale whose message constantly reinforces itself, and which holds the audience's attention without getting tedious.

I have deliberately omitted the question of Pharaoh's heart above, as a separate issue. A host of expressions is used in the text to describe Pharaoh's stubbornness: "harden" (Heb. *hiksha*), "make heavy-with-stubbornness" (*hakhbed*), and "strengthen" (*hehezik/hazzek*), with the resultant "refused" and "did not hearken." This motif is the only one that occurs in all nine plagues, and therefore stands at the very heart of our narrative. When one notes the pattern within—that Pharaoh does the hardening at the beginning, God at the end—the intent begins to become clear. The Plague Narrative is a recounting of God's power, and Pharaoh's stubbornness, which starts out as a matter of will, eventually becomes impossible to revoke. The model is psychologically compelling: Pharaoh becomes trapped by his own refusal to accept the obvious (in biblical parlance, to "know"). Despite the prophetic idea that human beings can be forgiven, we find here another one—that evil leads to more evil, and can become petrified and unmovable.

A final note about the backdrop of these stories. Cecil B. DeMille did it differently, and in the difference lies the gap between Western culture and biblical culture. In the movie *The Ten Commandments* (a strange title, given the actual content of the film!), DeMille's own 1956 remake of his earlier silent film, great stress is put on the physical, visual trappings of Pharaoh's court. Apparently no expense was spared to bring in costumes, sets, and extras, and the result causes the audience to focus on the splendor of Egyptian culture, despite the fact that it is peopled by the villians of the story. In contrast, the Bible says practically nothing about the visual backdrop of the Plague Narrative. Just as Genesis made reference to the mighty culture of Babylonia by parodying it (for instance, in the Babel story of Chapter 11), Exodus strips down Egyptian culture by making it disappear, and by ridiculing its gods. The book saves descriptive minutiae for the Tabernacle (Chaps. 25ff.), preferring to stress the positive and simply to omit what it found as negative. This profoundly "anticultural" stance (see the intriguing analysis by Schneidau 1976) was characteristic of Israel's world view and was a mystery to the Greeks and Romans who centuries later conquered the land; it was to stand the people of Israel in good stead in their wanderings through the centuries.

1:1 Now these are the names of the children of Israel coming to
       Egypt,
    with Yaakov, each-man and his household they came:
2 Re'uven, Shim'on, Levi and Yehuda,
3 Yissakhar, Zevulun and Binyamin,
4 Dan and Naftali, Gad and Asher.
5 So all the persons, those issuing from Yaakov's loins, were
       seventy persons,
    —Yosef was (already) in Egypt.

6 Now Yosef died, and all his brothers, and all that generation.
7 Yet the Children of Israel bore fruit, they swarmed, they
       became many, they grew powerful—exceedingly, yes, ex-
       ceedingly;
    the land filled up with them.

8 Now a new king arose over Egypt, who had not known
       Yosef.
9 He said to his people:

Prologue in Egypt (1): Rather than being presented as a totally separate story, the book of Exodus opens as a continuation of the Genesis saga. This is true both specifically and generally: the first five verses echo and compress the information about the descent of Yaakov's family into Egypt that was given in Gen. 46:8–27, while "Now these are the names" (v.1) recalls the oft-repeated formula "Now these are the begettings," which forms the structural background of Genesis. At the same time one might note that the main subject matter of our chapter, life and death (or, threatened continuity), is central to the thematic content of Genesis (see my *In the Beginning*, "On the Book of Genesis and Its Structure").

Kikawada (1975) and Ackerman (1974) have shown that the opening chapters of Exodus reflect other Genesis material as well. For instance, the five verbs in verse 7 mirror the language of creation (Gen. 1:28 and 9:1–2),

1:1 **children of Israel:** Or "sons," though it should be noted that the Hebrew *b'nei* can denote members of a group in general, not just family. In this verse, "children" has been printed with a lowercase "c"; by verse 7 the whole expression comes to mean a nation, and so a capital "C" has been utilized (Hebrew writing does not make this distinction). **Yaakov:** Trad. English "Jacob."

2–4 **Re'uven, Shim'on, Levi, Yehuda, Yissakhar, Zevulun, Binyamin, Dan, Naftali, Gad, Asher:** Trad. English "Reuben, Simeon, Levi, Judah, Issachar, Zebulun, Benjamin, Dan, Naphtali, Gad, Asher."

5 **issuing:** The same Hebrew verb (*yatzo'*) is later used to describe the Israelites' "going out" of Egypt (e.g., 12:31, 41). **loins:** A figurative expression denoting the genitals. **seventy:** A number expressing perfection or wholeness in the thought of many ancient cultures; see Gen. 46:8–27 for the original passage.

6 **Now Yosef died . . . :** Note the rhythmic lilt of this verse; such devices are often used in biblical style when a key event is portrayed. **Yosef:** Trad. English "Joseph."

7 **Yet:** Despite the disappearance of the politically influential generation of Yosef, the Israelites' success continues (Cassuto 1967). **swarmed:** This verb is usually applied to animals (see Gen. 1:20) (Greenberg 1969). Here the term is positive, as part of God's plan; shortly, it will carry a negative connotation for Pharaoh. **grew powerful:** Others, "grew numerous." This reflects the promise of God to Avraham in Gen. 18:18 (to become "a powerful nation") (Keil and Delitzsch 1968).

8 **a new king:** His name is not given, even though later biblical books do refer to foreign rulers by name. This is perhaps another example of the biblical text's playing down history in favor of stressing the story and its lesson. **who had not known Yosef:** Just as his successor will say "I do not know YHWH" (5:2), and will continue the oppression begun here.

9 **his people . . . this people:** Pharaoh states the case as the conflict between one national entity and another.

Here, (this) people, the Children of Israel, is many-more
   numerous and powerful than we!
10 Come-now, let us use-our-wits against it,
   lest it become many-more,
   and then, if war should occur,
   it too be added to our enemies
   and make war upon us
   or go up away from the land!
11 So they set gang-captains over it, to afflict it with their
   burdens.
   It built storage-cities for Pharaoh—Pitom and Ra'amses.
12 But as they afflicted it, so did it become many, so did it
   burst forth.
   And they felt dread before the Children of Israel.
13 So they, Egypt, made the Children of Israel subservient with
   crushing-labor;
14 they embittered their lives with hard servitude in loam and
   in bricks and with all kinds of servitude in the field—
   all their service in which they made them subservient with
   crushing-labor.

15 Now the king of Egypt said to the midwives of the Hebrews
   —the name of the first one was Shifra, the name of the
   second was Pu'a—
16 he said:
   When you help the Hebrew women give birth, see the supporting-stones:
   if he be a son, put him to death,
   but if she be a daughter, she may live.

where a similar vocabulary of fecundity signals the divine desire to "fill the
earth." It is as if Israel's "becoming many" in Exodus fulfills the plan of
history inaugurated at creation, at the same time reminding us of God's
promise to Avraham, to make his descendants as numerous "as the stars in
the heavens and [as] the sand that is on the shore of the sea" (Gen. 22:17).
   This leads to the predominant issue of Chapter 1: Pharaoh's paranoid
fears about Israel's growth. What for God was a sign of blessing (cf. the
"swarming" of creatures in Gen. 1:20f.) is for Pharaoh a sign of disaster, a
feeling of being overwhelmed by what is alien. The birth of the Israelite

nation is thus placed in a vivid context, completely physical in its description. And because birth, and not the economic aspects of slavery, is central, the actual description of the oppression of the Hebrews has been reduced to a bare minimum here. Contrary to DeMille's spectacular and stereotyped portrayal of the Israelites' sufferings, the Bible limits itself to a few brief verses in the early chapters of the book. The same holds true for parallel depictions of bondage in biblical literature, such as Psalms 78 and 105. It is the experience of being a stranger in Egypt that the Bible has chosen to focus on, rather than on the horrors of slave labor.

In Exodus, the Egyptians cannot stand having aliens among them (this theme has already appeared in Genesis regarding their eating habits—see Gen. 43:32); they dread their presence and fear their increase. A natural plan of attack, to stem the human tide, is genocide. Ironically, because of his fear of war Pharaoh concentrates his worries around the males, ignoring the true source of fecundity. And it is the women in these chapters, as

10 **use-our-wits:** Others, "We must be prudent," "Let us deal shrewdly."
it: The shift from plural to singular to refer to a plural object is not unusual in biblical parlance.   **added:** Heb. *nosaf*, like Yosef (Joseph), whose name is interpreted as "May God add . . . another son" at his birth in Gen. 30:24.   **go up away:** Heb. unclear.

11 **afflict:** Or "oppress."   **Pharaoh:** Heb. *Par'o*. This is an Egyptian title, "(Lord of) the Great House," and not a proper name. One could justifiably translate, as some do, "*the* Pharaoh."

12 **so . . . so:** Heb *ken . . . ken*. Ackerman (1974) interprets this as a rhyming retort to Pharaoh's earlier *pen* ("*lest* he become many more") in 1:10.   **burst forth:** The verb (Heb. *parotz*) is connected to fertility and wealth in Genesis (e.g., 28:14).

13 **crushing-labor:** A rare Hebrew word, here translated according to early rabbinic tradition, *perekh* is used rhetorically three times in Leviticus 25 (vv. 43, 46, and 53), where the Israelites are given laws about how to deal with their impoverished countrymen (v.43, "you are not to oppress him with crushing-labor").

14 **in the field:** In Egyptian accounts, the phrase indicates hard labor.   **all their service . . . :** The Hebrew syntax is difficult. Here the phrase is taken as the object of "they embittered."

15 **midwives of the Hebrews:** The ambiguity of this phrase raises an ancient question: were they Hebrew or Egyptian? The names seem Semitic (and hence un-Egyptian); then, too, the use of "Hebrew" in the Bible usually occurs when a foreigner is talking about Israelites. Yet the women's answer is verse 19 suggests that they are in fact Egyptians. Abravanel notes that Hebrew women would not be likely to kill Hebrew babies.

16 **supporting-stones:** Some suggest that these were stools or other objects on which to support women in labor, while others see them as a reference to the testicles of the newborn males.

17 But the midwives feared God,
   and they did not do as the king of Egypt had spoken to
      them,
   they let the (male) children live.
18 The king of Egypt called for the midwives and said to them:
   Why have you done this thing, you have let the children
      live!
19 The midwives said to Pharaoh:
   Indeed, not like the Egyptian (women) are the Hebrew
      (women),
   indeed, they are lively:
   before the midwife comes to them, they have given birth!
20 God dealt well with the midwives.
   And the people became many and grew exceedingly power-
      ful.
21 It was, since the midwives feared God, that he made them
      households.
22 Now Pharaoh commanded all his people, saying:
   Every son that is born, throw him into the Nile,
   but let every daughter live.

2:1 Now a man from the house of Levi went and took (to wife) a
      daughter of Levi.
  2 The woman became pregnant and bore a son.
   When she saw him—that he was goodly, she hid him, for
      three months.

many commentators have pointed out (see Exum 1983), who play the
major role in beginning the liberation process. The midwives accomplish a
successful coverup; Moshe's mother and sister, and Pharaoh's daughter,
save the future liberator's life. "If she be a daughter, she may live" (v. 16),
along with four other occurrences of "live" in verses 17–22, underscore
the irony and the certainty of Israelite survival. The use of women—a
group that was often powerless in ancient societies—in these stories makes
the eventual victory of the Israelites all the more striking from a traditional
patriarchal point of view (see Ackerman 1982); the motif returns a number
of times in Israelite literature, as with Jael and Judith.
   Failing in his commissioning of special agents (midwives) to carry out
his genocidal plan, Pharaoh finally must enlist "all his people" (v.22), and

shift the scene to a cosmic setting, the Nile. The stage is thus set for the birth, endangering, and rescue of Moshe.

The historically minded reader may ask: Why would the ruler of a society that is (literally) built on slavery destroy his own workforce? Two answers are possible. First, the story is tied to Chapter 2, the survival of Moshe, and thus must be told to that end (a threat to males). Second, the story does not describe a rational fear, but paranoia—paralleling the situation in Nazi Germany of the of the 1930s and 1940s, where Jews were blamed for various economic and political catastrophes not of their own making and were eliminated from a society that could have used their resources and manpower.

Moshe's Birth and Early Life (2:1–22): Picking up from the last phrase of Chapter 1, "let every daughter live," Chapter 2 opens as a story of three daughters (the word occurs six times here), Moshe's real and foster mothers and his sister.

It has long been maintained that the story of Moshe's birth is a classic "birth of the hero" tale, sharing many features with other heroes of antiquity. (See pp. 4ff.) The parallel most often drawn is that of Sargon of Akkad, whose birth story is set in an era before Moshe but was written

17 **feared:** Worshipped or held in awe. This may be a sound-play on "see" in verse 16: *va-yire'u* ("feared") resembles *va-yir'u* ("saw").

19 **lively:** Another form of the Hebrew would mean "animals," and so B-R combined the two ideas in rendering the word as "lively-like-animals."

20–21 **And the people . . .:** The order here seems confused. "And the people . . ." is perhaps out of place, although the thought is not inappropriate for the context.

22 **all his people:** Specialists (the midwives) are not equal to the task of checking the Israelite population explosion, and so the whole Egyptian population must now be enlisted. **Nile:** Heb. *ye'or*, Egyptian *itrw*', "the great river" (cf. Heb. *ha-nahar ha-gadol*, with the same meaning, used for the Euphrates in Gen. 15:18 etc.).

2:1 **a man . . . a daughter:** Moshe's parents are anonymous, unlike the usual king and queen of the hero myth found in other cultures. The namelessness of all the secondary characters in this chapter—sister, Pharaoh's daughter and her maids—helps us to focus on the protagonist and on his name.

2 **she saw him—that he was goodly:** The parallel in Genesis is "God saw the light: that it was good" (Gen. 1:4). **goodly:** Handsome (so Ibn Ezra, among others), although others interpret the Hebrew *tov* as "healthy," given the context. What is important is the Genesis connection just mentioned. **three months:** Another "perfect" number, which will recur with the Israelites' three-month trip to Mount Sinai (see, 19:1).

3 And when she was no longer able to hide him,
   she took for him a little-ark of papyrus,
   she loamed it with loam and with pitch,
   placed the child in it,
   and placed it in the reeds by the shore of the Nile.
4 Now his sister stationed herself far off, to know what would
      be done to him.

5 Now Pharaoh's daughter went down to bathe at the Nile,
   and her girls were walking along the Nile.
   She saw the little-ark among the reeds
   and sent her maid, and she took it.
6 **She opened (it) and saw him, the child:**
   here, a boy weeping!
   She pitied him, and she said:
   One of the Hebrews' children is this!
7 Now his sister said to Pharaoh's daughter:
   Shall I go and call a nursing woman from the Hebrews for
      you,
   that she may nurse the child for you?
8 Pharaoh's daughter said to her:
   Go!
   The maiden went and called the child's mother.
9 Pharaoh's daughter said to her:
   Have this child go with you and nurse him for me,
   and I myself will give you your wages.
   So the woman took the child and she nursed him.

down later; similar elements include being separated from the real parents
through a death threat, and being set adrift on the river. Hallo (in Plaut
1981) cites other parallels in Hittite and Egyptian literature, noting at the
same time that "none of them includes all of the elements of the Moses
birth legend."

   If, as I maintained in the introduction ("On the Book of Exodus and Its
Structure"), most of this material has been collected for didactic and not
for historical purposes, we are entitled to ask what this story was intended
to teach. It cannot simply be written off as an attempt to explain away
Moshe's name and origins. Two elements seem crucial. First, the text as
we have it centers around the activity of women—giving birth, hiding,
watching and adopting Moshe. The female principle of life-giving tri-

umphs over the male prerogatives of threatening and death-dealing; the Nile, source of all life in Egypt, births another child. Second, the story and its continuation to the end of the chapter set up Moshe as a man of two sides: Hebrew and Egyptian. He is at once archetypal victim (of Pharaoh's death decree) and archetypal collaborator, growing up, as he apparently does, in Pharaoh's palace. What are we to make of this two-sided fate and personality? It may well have been intended as a reflex of the people of Israel itself. Often in the Hebrew Bible the hero's life mirrors that of Israel (see Greenstein 1981), and the case of Moshe is a good example. Moshe develops into a Hebrew—that is, he eventually recovers his full identity. This is accomplished, first, through his empathy with and actions on behalf of "his brothers" (vv.11, 12), then through his exile from Egypt, and finally through the purifying life in the wilderness as a shepherd. Thus Moshe's personality changes are wrought by means of separations, and the same process will characterize the coming Plague Narrative (with its emphasis on "distinction" between Egypt and Israel) and the entire Israelite legal and ritual system, which stresses holiness and separation.

The first section of the chapter (vv.1-10) uses a number of repeating words: "take" appears four times, indicative of divine protection; "child,"

3 **little-ark**: The term used to designate the little basket/boat, *teva*, has clearly been chosen to reflect back to Noah's ark in Genesis. The implication is that just as God saved Noah and thus humanity from destruction by water, so will he now save Moshe and the Israelites from the same.
papyrus: A material that floats; it was also used in biblical times for writing, including biblical texts.   **in the reeds**: Another foreshadowing; when Moshe grows up, he will lead the liberated people through the Sea of Reeds. The word *suf* (reeds) appears to be a loan-word from Egyptian.

4 **to know**: Better English would be "to learn." This first occurrence of the Hebrew word *yado'a* foreshadows the later theme of the Egyptians' and the Israelites' coming to "know" (or "acknowledge") God's power. For the moment, and in the story that follows, the issue is one of revealing information—Moshe's fate (2:4) and the discovery of his crime (2:14).

5 **Pharaoh's daughter**: Her station is important, for it enables Moshe to be saved and to be brought up in the Egyptian palace (useful both for his political future and for literary irony of situation).   **girls**: Maidservants.

6 **She opened . . . boy!**: The emphatic, halting syntax of the narrative brings out the visual drama of seeing, taking, opening, and identifying.
One of the Hebrews' children: How does she know that? The simplest explanation lies in the situation itself and not in any identifying marks. Who else but a Hebrew, under the threat of losing her baby, would set such a child adrift?   **is this**: Or "must this be."

8 **Go**: In biblical Hebrew, a verb repeated from a question is the equivalent of "Yes," for which there was no other expression.

10 The child grew, she brought him to Pharaoh's daughter,
    and he became her son.
    She called his name: Moshe/He-Who-Pulls-Out;
    she said: For out of the water *meshitihu*/I-pulled-him.

11 Now it was some years later, Moshe grew up;
    he went out to his brothers and saw their burdens.
    He saw an Egyptian man striking a Hebrew man, (one) of
        his brothers.
12 He turned this-way and that-way, and seeing that there was
        no man (there),
    he struck down the Egyptian
    and buried him in the sand.
13 He went out again on the next day, and here: two Hebrew
        men fighting!
    He said to the guilty-one:
    For-what-reason do you strike your fellow?
14 He said:
    Who made you chief and judge over us?
    Do you mean to kill me
    as you killed the Egyptian?
    Moshe became afraid and said:
    Surely the matter is known!

15 Pharaoh heard of this matter and sought to kill Moshe.
    But Moshe fled from Pharaoh's face and settled in the land
        of Midyan;
    he sat down by a well.

seven times (Greenberg 1969); and "see," which as I have mentioned, will recur meaningfully in Chapter 3. There is also a threefold motif of death threat in the chapter: at birth, on the Nile, and at the hand of the avenging Pharaoh. Isbell (1982) notes several items of vocabulary (e.g., "deliver," "feared," "amidst the reeds") that return in the victory account at the Sea of Reeds (Chap. 14).

From the other two accounts here (vv. 11–14 and 15–22), we learn all we need to know about Moshe's early personality: he is Hebrew-identifying but Egyptian-looking; concerned with justice, but impetuous and violent in pursuit of that goal. It is also ominous that his first contacts with the

Israelites end in rejection, since that will so often be his experience with them later on. The doubly unsatisfactory situation of confused identity and impetuous means must be rectified, and it is exile that accomplishes it. The Midianite wilderness transforms Moshe into shepherd, foreigner,

10 **grew:** His age is not mentioned, but weaning may be inferred (cf. Gen. 21:8) as the appropriate boundary, and hence the child was probably around three (DeVaux 1965).   **he became her son:** A formulaic expression for legal adoption.   **Moshe/He-Who-Pulls-Out:** Trad. English "Moses." *Mss* is a well-attested name in ancient Egypt, meaning "son of" (as in Ra'amses—"son of Ra"—in Ex. 1:11). Thus it is quite appropriate that Pharaoh's daughter names her adopted son in this manner. However, there is an explicit irony here, as Buber (1958) and others have pointed out. The princess, in a Hebrew folk etymology (one based on sound rather than on the scientific derivation of words), thinks that the name Moshe recalls her act of "pulling out" the baby from the Nile. But the verb form in *moshe* is active, not passive, and thus it is Moshe himself who will one day "pull out" Israel from the life-threatening waters of both slavery and the Sea of Reeds.

11 **some years later:** Heb. *yamim*, lit. "days," can mean longer periods of time, and often years. Here the narrative skips over what it considers unimportant, and we are presented with a young man, who already has strong identity and opinions.   **his brothers:** Occurring twice in this verse, this phrase can only mean that Moshe was aware of his background, and concerned with the plight of the Israelites (Heb. *r'h b-*, "see" with a specific preposition, indicates not only observation but sympathy).

12 **no man (there):** Although some have interpreted this as "no man around to help," the expression taken in context would seem to indicate that Moshe was afraid of being seen. This incident reveals Moshe's concern and early leanings toward being a liberator, but also demonstrates his youthful lack of forethought. In fact, it will take God, not Moshe's own actions, to set the liberation process in motion.   **struck down:** This is the same verb (Heb. *hakkeh*) that the narrator used in verse 11 to describe the fatal beating received by the Israelite slave.

13 **Hebrew men fighting:** A rhyme in Hebrew, *anashim 'ivriyyim nitzim*.

14 **Who made you chief . . . :** One hears here echoes of Moshe's later experiences with his "hard-necked" people, which commences in the book of Exodus (Greenberg 1969).   **judge:** Or "ruler." I have retained "judge" here in order not to lose the connection with 5:21.

15 **Moshe fled . . . and settled:** The details about what must have been a psychologically important journey are not spelled out, as the narrative rushes toward its first great climax in Chapter 3. More important than the journey motif is that of exile, brought out tellingly in verse 22.   **settled . . . sat:** Adding the "settle down" of verse 21, we hear a threefold use of *yashov*, perhaps to stress Moshe's new life.

16 Now the priest of Midyan had seven daughters;
    they came, they drew (water) and they filled the troughs,
    to water their father's sheep.
17 Shepherds came and drove them away.
    But Moshe rose up, he delivered them and gave-drink to
        their sheep.
18 When they came (home) to Re'uel their father, he said:
    Why have you come (home) so quickly today?
19 They said:
    An Egyptian man rescued us from the hand of the shepherds,
    and moreover he drew, yes, drew for us and watered the
        sheep.
20 He said to his daughters:
    So-where-is-he?
    For-what-reason then have you left the man behind?
    Call him, that he may eat bread (with us)!

21 Moshe agreed to settle down with the man,
    and he gave Tzippora his daughter to Moshe.
22 She gave birth to a son,
    and he called his name: Gershom/Sojourner There,
    for he said: A sojourner have I become in a foreign land.

23 It was, many years later,
    the king of Egypt died.
    The Children of Israel groaned from the servitude,
    and they cried out;
    and their plea-for-help went up to God, from the servitude.
24 God hearkened to their moaning,
    God called-to-mind his covenant with Avraham, with Yitz-
        hak, and with Yaakov,

father, and seer—in short, into a son of the Patriarchs (see also "On the Journey Motif," above).

Incredibly, the man whose activity is to span four whole books has, it seems, half his life (or, according to the chronology of 7:7, two-thirds of his life!) described in a single chapter. Typical of biblical storytelling, much has been compressed and left out, but enough is told to establish the person who is to come.

God Takes Notice (2:23–25): Chapter 2 ends on a note that looks forward and backward simultaneously. The fourfold "God" plus verb (vv.24–25) echo the same structure at Creation's first day (Gen. 1:3–5), and suggest that he puts his concern for the people of Israel on a par with his concern

16 **priest of Midyan:** This title has spawned extensive theorizing about the origins of Mosaic religion (sometimes called the "Kenite Hypothesis" after the Kenites, a tribe of smiths connected to Moshe's father-in-law and spoken of favorably at a number of points in the Bible). It has been suggested that Moshe learned the rudiments of his religious or legal system from this source. We do not have enough evidence to make a positive judgment on this theory; biographically, it does make sense for Moshe to marry into a holy family of some sort. **seven daughters:** The requisite "magic" number, as in a good folk tale.

19 **An Egyptian man:** Moshe would have been recognizable as such from his manner of dress and lack of facial hair. In addition, he is not yet fully an Israelite, spiritually speaking.

20 **So-where-is-he:** This is one word in the Hebrew (*ve-ayyo*). The whole verse stands in ironic contrast to Moshe's earlier treatment (v. 14) at the hand of "his brothers" (Childs 1974). There, he was rejected; here, his host cannot welcome him quickly enough. **for-what-reason:** Similarly, this is one Hebrew word (*lamma*). **bread:** As often in both the Bible and other cultures, "bread" is here synonymous with "food."

21 **Tzippora:** Trad. English, "Zipporah." The name means "bird"; such animal names are still popular among Bedouin.

22 **Gershom/Sojourner There:** Related to the Hebrew *ger*, "sojourner" or resident alien. The name more accurately reflects the sound of the verb *garesh*, "drive out" (so Abravanel), which plays its role in the Exodus stories (and in Moshe's recent experience in the narrative). As my student Nancy Ginsberg once pointed out, this naming of sons to express the feelings about exile has already occurred in a more personally positive context—with Yosef (see Gen. 41:50–52). **A sojourner . . . in a foreign land:** The King James Version phrase, "a stranger in a strange land," is stunning, but the Hebrew uses two different roots (*gur* and *nakhor*).

23 **The king of Egypt died./ The Children of Israel groaned:** The change in regime does not prove beneficial to the suffering slaves, but makes it possible for Moshe to return to Egypt, thus impelling the narrative along and reestablishing the link between Moshe and his people. **cried out:** The same verb (Heb. *tza'ok*) is used to describe the "hue and cry" of Sodom and Gomorra (Gen. 18:20; see also the note to 22:22, below).

23–24 **groaned . . . cried out . . . plea-for-help . . . moaning:** As in 1:7, four phrases describe the Israelites' actions. Note also the double use of "from the servitude."

24 **Avraham, Yitzhak, Yaakov:** Trad. English "Abraham, Isaac, Jacob."

25 God saw the Children of Israel,
   God knew.

3:1 Now Moshe was shepherding the flock of Yitro his father-
      in-law, priest of Midyan.
    He led the flock behind the wilderness—
    and he came to the mountain of God, to Horev.   *sinai usually*
                                                     by Deuts.
  2 And YHWH's messenger was seen by him
    in the flame of a fire out of the midst of a bush.
    He saw:
    here, the bush is ablaze with fire,
    and the bush is not consumed!
  3 Moshe said:
    Now let me turn aside
    that I may see this great sight—
    why the bush does not burn up!
  4 When YHWH saw that he had turned aside to see,
    God called to him out of the midst of the bush,
    he said:
    Moshe! Moshe!
    He said:
    Here I am.

for creation of light (connoting "good" in folklore). In addition, the four
verbs used here play a prominent role in the entire Deliverance Narrative,
as Isbell (1982) has shown.

At the Bush: The Call (3:1–4:17): The great revelation scene in these two
chapters, so much a classic in the literature of the West, comes as somewhat of a surprise in the close context of our story. Nothing in Exodus so
far has prepared us for such a religious, inward vision on the part of
Moshe; and indeed, Genesis itself contains no meeting between God and a
human being of such a dramatic character. Adam and Avraham converse
with God; Yaakov experiences him, to be sure, in dreams and in the guise
of a wrestler; but nowhere thus far does one find a biblical hero encounter-
ing God with such intensity and purity of vision.
    The shepherd, now in the service of his father-in-law, the "priest,"
comes upon the "mountain of God," "behind the wilderness." The results
are those of an unintended or half-intended journey. Moshe, who had fled
previously, finds himself at the utmost reaches of the wilderness, almost

like Jonah in the bowels of the boat or of the great fish. The sight that Moshe is granted is of unclear nature, but it involves fire, with all its pregnant associations: passion, purity, light, mystery (Greenberg 1969), and here, inextinguishability.

God's initial speech (vv.6–10) contains all the elements basic to the Deliverance Narrative: it identifies him as the ancestral deity, establishes his compassion for the oppressed people, demonstrates his resolve to rescue them, and ends with the commissioning of Moshe to be his emissary. Central here is the verb *see*, whose threefold occurrence (vv.7 and 9) ties together the threads of the previous parts of Moshe's story (see above).

The entire scene is the model for the "call" of the biblical prophet, with

25 **knew:** Others, "took notice," but *yado'a* needs to be noticed throughout the book as a key word.

3:1 **Now Moshe was shepherding . . .:** The Hebrew syntax indicates the beginning of an entirely new story. **shepherding:** A symbol of great power in the ancient Near East; witness the enduring image of King David, sprung from shepherding roots, and of course that of Jesus. **Yitro:** Trad. English "Jethro." It is not clear why other names (Re'uel, Hovav) are also associated with him. The name, if Semitic, means "excellence." **behind:** Others, "to the west side of," "to the far side of," or simply "into," although the word seems to convey a certain mystery. Fairy tales often portray the hero's going deep into a forest and the like. **mountain of God:** Sinai is so designated only several times subsequently in the Pentateuch, suggesting perhaps biblical religion's reluctance to make of it a shrine of permanence. **Horev:** Another name for Sinai, principally used in Deuteronomy (but also twice more in Exodus, 17:6 and 33:6). A related Hebrew root, *harev*, means "dry."

2 **YHWH's messenger:** Traditionally "angel," but the English word stems from the Greek *angelos*, which means "messenger." In Genesis, God appears in somewhat human guise (cf. Chap. 18), and "messenger" indicates an unspecified manifestation of God, open to wide interpretation. **in the flame:** Others, "as a flame." **bush:** Jewish tradition identifies it as a thornbush, but the precise plant remains unknown. The bush, called *s'neh* in Hebrew, perhaps has the added function here of providing assonance with *Sinai*. **the bush is ablaze . . . the bush is not consumed:** The use of tense (plus the opening "here") conveys the immediacy of the vision. **not consumed:** The symbolism of the imperishable bush is left open for the reader; commentators suggest variously Israel and God himself.

3 **let me turn aside:** Despite Moshe's apparent retirement from intervening on behalf of his brothers in Egypt, his reaction here seems active, not passive. He does not shirk from seeking out the strange sight. **burn up:** The same Hebrew verb (*bi'er*) as the one translated as "blaze" above.

4 **Moshe! Moshe!:** The name is repeated for emphasis, as in Gen. 22:11. **Here I am:** The classic response of biblical heroes; see Gen. 22:1, 11; I Sam. 3:4.

5 He said:
Do not come near to here,
put off your sandal from your foot,
for the place on which you stand is holy ground!
6 And he said:
I am the God of your father,
the God of Avraham,
the God of Yitzhak,
and the God of Yaakov.
Moshe concealed his face,
for he was afraid to gaze upon God.
7 Now YHWH said:
I have seen, yes, seen the affliction of my people that is in
    Egypt,
their cry have I heard in the face of their slave-drivers;
indeed, I have known their sufferings!
8 So I have come down
to rescue it from the hand of Egypt,
to bring it up from that land
to a land, goodly and spacious,
to a land flowing with milk and honey,
to the place of the Canaanite and the Hittite,
of the Amorite and the Perizzite,
of the Hivvite and the Yevusite.
9 So now,
here, the cry of the Children of Israel has come to me,
and I have also seen the oppression with which the Egyp-
    tians oppress them.
10 So now, go,
for I send you to Pharaoh—
bring my people, the Children of Israel, out of Egypt!
11 Moshe said to God:
Who am I
that I should go to Pharaoh,
that I should bring the Children of Israel out of Egypt?
12 He said:
Indeed, I will be-there with you,
and this is the sign for you that I myself have sent you:
when you have brought the people out of Egypt,
you will (all) serve God by this mountain.

its emphasis on God's speaking to the fledgling prophet amid a vision and the motif of refusal; of the call scenes in the Bible, this is the longest and most memorable in its starkness. A man is called by God to return to society and serve as God's spokesperson—despite any opposition he may encounter and despite his personal shortcomings. Moshe's reluctance, indeed his almost obsessive need to turn down the commission, is as much indicative of the general nature of prophecy (cf. Elijah and Jeremiah) as it is of Moshe's own personality. The prophet must be prepared "to uproot and tear down, to destroy and overthrow, to build and plant" (Jer. 1:10), and to stand tall against kings if necessary (Jer. 1:13). So it comes as no surprise that the call is met with less than enthusiasm. And this refusal also teaches something about Israel's political conceptions. With such a response as this, there can be no question of personal ambition or inner lust for power. The prophet does what he does out of compulsion: he is driven by forces that he perceives as external to him.

In our text, Moshe refuses the commission five times, and five times God counters. In four of these cases the assurance is given that God will "be-there" with him (3:12, 14; 4:12, 15), and the use of that verb carries in its essence one of the most significant motifs of the Bush Narrative: the interpretation of God's name.

5 **put off your sandal from your foot:** A common form of respect in the ancient East, still practiced by Muslims in worship.
6 **the God of your father:** Hearkening back to the personal and family relationships with God in Genesis (see, for instance, Gen. 26:24, 31:42, 32:10). **Avraham . . .:** The text stresses the Patriarchs, reminding both Moshe and the reader of the promises made to them in Genesis.
7 **I have seen . . . heard . . . known:** Echoing the narrative above, 2:24–25. **the affliction of my people:** Heb. *'oni 'ammi*. **my people:** This fateful designation signals the beginning of the liberation process. The Golden Calf story (Chaps. 32ff.) provides a tragic variation on this phrase.
8 **I have come down:** The phrase indicates God's intervention in human affairs (as, negatively, in Gen. 11:7). **a land flowing with milk and honey:** Or with "goats' milk and date-syrup." This description of Canaan is repeated many times in the three subsequent books of the Pentateuch, but is not found in Genesis. **Canaanite . . . Hittite** [etc.]: These names are the Bible's designation for the indigenous peoples of Canaan at the time of the Israelite conquest. Biblical lists contain varying numbers of peoples, from six to ten.
12 **this is the sign:** The thought is not entirely clear. It may signify that liberation signals Israel's birth as a people, and therefore Moshe's legitimacy as well. **(all):** "You" is plural here. **by:** As opposed to "upon," since the people will not be allowed to trespass its sacred boundaries (see 19:12).

13 Moshe said to God:
Here, I will come to the Children of Israel
and I will say to them:
The God of your fathers has sent me to you,
and they will say to me: What is his name?—
what shall I say to them?

14 God said to Moshe:
EHYEH ASHER EHYEH / I will be-there howsoever I will
    be-there.
And he said:
Thus shall you say to the Children of Israel:
EHYEH/I-WILL-BE-THERE sends me to you.

15 And God said further to Moshe:
Thus shall you say to the Children of Israel:
YHWH,
the God of your fathers,
the God of Avraham, the God of Yitzhak, and the God of
    Yaakov,
sends me to you.
That is my name for the ages,
that is my title (from) generation to generation.

16 Go,
gather the elders of Israel
and say to them:
YHWH, the God of your fathers, has been seen by me,
the God of Avraham, of Yitzhak, and of Yaakov,
saying:
I have taken account, yes, account of you and of what is
    being done to you in Egypt,

17 and I have declared:
I will bring you up from the affliction of Egypt,
to the land of the Canaanite and of the Hittite,
of the Amorite and of the Perizzite,
of the Hivvite and of the Yevusite,
to a land flowing with milk and honey.

18 They will hearken to your voice,
and you will come, you and the elders of Israel, to the king
    of Egypt
and say to him:
YHWH, the God of the Hebrews, has met with us—

so now, pray let us go a three days' journey into the wilderness
and let us make slaughter-offerings to YHWH our God.
19 But I, I know
that the king of Egypt will not give you leave to go,
not (even) under a strong hand.
20 So I will send forth my hand
and I will strike Egypt with all my wonders which I will do
in its midst—
after that he will send you free!
21 And I will give this people favor in the eyes of Egypt;
it will be that when you go, you shall not go empty-handed:

When Moshe asks God for his name in 3:13, he asks for more than a title
(Buber and Rosenzweig 1936). In the context of Egyptian magic, knowing
the true name of a person or a god meant that one could coerce him, or at
the very least understand his true essence. Moshe foresees that the slaves
will want to be able to call on this power that has promised to deliver
them.

God's answer is one of the most enigmatic and widely debated statements in the Hebrew Bible (the reader will want to consult Childs 1974 for
a full bibliography). What does *ehyeh asher ehyeh* mean? One's suspicions
are aroused from the outset, for the answer is alliterative and hence already

13 **What is his name?:** See Comentary above. B-R: "What is behind his
name?"
14 **EHYEH ASHER EHYEH** . . .: The syntax is difficult. Others, "I am
that I am."
15 **title:** Others, "memorial."
16 **elders:** They are the holders of political power in such a tribal society.
taken account: As per Yosef's promise in Gen. 50:24.
18 **pray let us go:** Interestingly, the initial request made of Pharaoh is not for
emancipation but for permission to observe a religious festival. It eventually becomes clear that Israel cannot be Israel until it is free of Egyptian
hegemony. **make slaughter-offerings:** Offer slaughtered animals to
God.
21 **you shall not go empty-handed:** The despoiling of the Egyptians is reminiscent of obtaining booty in war. At the same time, there is probably a
legal background to this (Daube 1961): the furnishing of a freed slave with
provisions. The follow-up to the despoiling, intended or not, is God's
command that, in Israel's future observance of religious festivals in the
Promised Land, "no one is to be seen in my presence empty-handed" (Ex.
23:15).

22 each woman shall ask of her neighbor and of the sojourner in
        her house
    objects of silver and objects of gold, and clothing,
    you shall put (them) on your sons and on your daughters—
    so shall you strip Egypt!
4:1 Moshe answered, he said:
    But they will not trust me, and will not hearken to my
        voice,
    indeed, they will say: YHWH has not been seen by
        you . . . !
  2 YHWH said to him:
    What is that in your hand?
    He said:
    A staff.
  3 He said:
    Throw it to the ground!
    He threw it to the ground, and it became a snake,
    and Moshe fled from its face.
  4 YHWH said to Moshe:
    Send forth your hand! Seize it by its tail!
    —He sent forth his hand, took hold of it, and it became a
        staff in his fist—
  5 So that they may trust that YHWH, the God of their fathers,
        the God of Avraham, the God of Yitzhak, and the God of
        Yaakov, has been seen by you.
  6 YHWH said further to him:
    Pray put your hand in your bosom!
    He put his hand in his bosom, then he took it out,
    and here: his hand was leprous, like snow!
  7 Now he said:
    Return your hand to your bosom!
    —He returned his hand to his bosom, then he took it out
        of his bosom,
    and here: it had returned (to be) like his (other) flesh.
  8 So it shall be, if they do not trust you, and do not hearken to
        the voice of the former sign,
    that they will put their trust in the voice of the latter sign.
  9 And it shall be, if they do not put their trust in even these
        two signs, and do not hearken to your voice:

then take some of the water of the Nile
and pour it out on the dry-land,
and the water that you take from the Nile will become blood
  on the dry-land.
10 Moshe said to YHWH:
Please, my Lord,
No man of words am I
not from yesterday, not from the day-before, not (even)
  since you have spoken to your servant,
for heavy of mouth and heavy of tongue am I.

not easy to pin down; the poetics of the phrase indicate both importance
and vagueness or mystery. There is some scholarly consensus that the
name may mean "He who causes (things) to be" or perhaps "He who is."
Buber and Rosenzweig, taking an entirely different tack (of which one
occasionally finds echoes in the scholarly literature), interpret the verb
hayoh as signifying presence, "being-*there*," and hence see God's words as
a real answer to the Israelites' imagined question—an assurance of his
presence. The B-R interpretation has been retained here, out of a desire to
follow them on at least this significant point of theology, and out of my

22 **ask from:** Others, "borrow." **strip:** Here the verb (*natzel*) means
    "strip," perhaps punning on a different form used in verse 8 which means
    "rescue."

4:1 **answered . . . said:** This coupling of verbs is common in Ugaritic and
    Hebrew to denote a new thought on the speaker's part (Cassuto 1967).

6 **bosom:** Others, "upper folds of (his) cloak." **leprous:** Others, "en-
    crusted with snowy scales." According to Cassuto (1967), leprosy was a
    disease common in Egypt. It also was taken as a sign from God, often of
    wrongdoing on the part of the victim.

8 **voice:** Meaning "message," as in Ugaritic usage. **sign:** These were often
    required or used by prophets in the Bible (see the discussion in Deut.
    13:2ff.) (Greenberg 1969).

9 **blood:** Since the Nile was regarded as divine by the Egyptians, not only
    would such a plague be miraculous and devastating, but it would also be a
    direct swipe at the Egyptian religion.

10 **no man of words am I:** Yet this is exactly the quality that Moshe's mission
    requires! (Greenberg 1969). Similarly, Jeremiah (1:6) seeks to evade the
    call, although his refusal is based more on inexperience than on lack of
    eloquence. **yesterday . . . the day-before:** A Hebrew idiom for "the
    past." **heavy of mouth and heavy of tongue:** The nature of Moshe's
    speech impediment is not clear. Curiously, writes Buber (1958), it is the
    stammerer whose job it is to bring down God's word to the human world.

11 YHWH said to him:
    Who placed a mouth in human beings
    or who (is it that) makes one mute or deaf
    or open-eyed or blind?
    Is it not I, YHWH?
12 So now, go!
    I myself will be-there with your mouth
    and will instruct you as to what you are to speak.
13 But he said:
    Please, my Lord,
    pray send by whose hand you will send!
14 YHWH's anger raged against Moshe,
    he said:
    Is there not Aharon your brother, the Levite—
    I know that *he* can speak, yes, speak well,
    and here, he is even going out to meet you;
    when he sees you, he will rejoice in his heart.
15 You shall speak to him,
    you shall put the words in his mouth!
    I myself will be-there with your mouth and with his mouth,
    and will instruct you as to what you shall do.
16 He shall speak for you to the people,
    he, he shall be for you a mouth, and you, you shall be for
        him a god.
17 And this staff, take in your hand,
    with which you shall do the signs.

18 Moshe went and returned to Yitro his father-in-law
    and said to him:
    Pray let me go and return to my brothers that are in Egypt,
    that I may see whether they are still alive.

feeling that it also fits the smaller context. For of the several times that
Moshe tries to wriggle out of his mission, God answers him all but once
with the same verb, in the same meaning: "I will be-there with you" (note
the parallel between Moshe and the people again).

    It is, however, also possible that *ehyeh asher ehyeh* is a deliberately vague
phrase, whose purpose is antimagical and an attempt to evade the question
(Rosenzweig speaks of this as well), as if to suggest that possession of the
true name cannot be used to coerce this God. In this interpretation, it
would follow that, just as God is magicless (see v.20), he is nameless, at
least in the conventional sense of religion. On the other hand, the name

YHWH, however it may have been vocalized throughout the history of the text, did function as a name in ancient Israel (and possibly outside of Israel as well). It was used in oaths (e.g., Gen. 22:16, II Sam. 12:5), and later, in the Second Temple period, limited in public pronunciation to the high priest on the Day of Atonement. As happens frequently in the history of religion, if we follow a concept long enough it transforms back to the beginning, often in an opposite meaning, and so when the use of YHWH is traced through the Middle Ages one finds it turned into a magical name at the hands of Jewish mystics.

To return to the Bush Narrative as a whole: these chapters introduce a number of important words that will recur throughout the entire Liberation Narrative. These include "trust," "hearken to (my) voice," "staff," "heavy," "go out," "strong," "send," and "blood" (see Isbell 1982). It should also be mentioned that several key words occur in multiples of 7 from 2:23 to 4:31 (Cassuto 1967): "see" (7), "send" (7), "go" (14), "mouth" (7), "speak/word" (Heb. *dabber/davar;* 7). This vocabulary in particular focuses the story around major aspects of prophecy.

In the end, what does Moshe have with which to return from the mount of vision? In the DeMille film version his face and personality clearly change; in the biblical text, however, he comes back with a word—the divine promise—and a staff, "with which you shall do the signs" (4:17). He had previously been a man whose lack of tolerance for injustice produced violence; now he is armed with words and a wonder-working object—not a sword or a helmet, but a shepherd's staff.

The Journey Back (4:18–31): It is clear that something has been inserted into the normal course of our narrative. What follows verse 20 should be verse 27; Moshe, ready to go back to Egypt, is met by Aharon in the wilderness, and they subsequently announce their mission to the Children of Israel. However, the editor has prefaced the brothers' meeting, first

13 **pray send by whose hand you will send!**: That is, find someone else!
14 **raged:** Literally, burned, the normal biblical metaphor for anger. **Aharon:** Trad. English "Aaron." This is the first mention of the brother whom we later find out was the firstborn. **the Levite:** Why this designation here? Some theorize that it means "joiner," while others seen it as a tracing of Levite roots as spokespeople in Israel. The phrase could also be translated as, "Is not your brother Aharon the Levite?"
15 **you shall put. . .:** Moshe is to Aharon as God is to a prophet; the latter is to serve principally as a mouthpiece.
16 **a god:** Others, "an oracle."
18 **Yitro:** Here his name appears as *Yeter* in Hebrew. **Pray let me go:** B-R: "Now I will go." **my brothers:** This concern has not been heard from Moshe during his years in Midyan, nor has he mentioned his past at all. **whether they are still alive:** Reminiscent of Yosef's cry in Gen. 45:3, "Is

Yitro said to Moshe:
Go in peace!

19 Now YHWH said to Moshe in Midyan:
Go, return to Egypt,
for all the men who sought (to take) your life have died.

20 So Moshe took his wife and his sons and mounted them
upon an ass, to return to the land of Egypt,
and Moshe took the staff of God in his hand.

21 YHWH said to Moshe:
When you go to return to Egypt,
see:
All the portents that I have put in your hand, you are to do
before Pharaoh,
but I will make his heart strong-willed, so that he will not
send the people free.

22 Then you are to say to Pharaoh:
Thus says YHWH:
My son, my firstborn, is Israel!

23 I said to you: Send free my son, that he may serve me,
but you have refused to send him free,
(so) here: I will kill your son, your firstborn!

24 Now it was on the journey, at the night-camp,
that YHWH encountered him and sought to make him die.

25 Tzippora took a flint and cut off her son's foreskin,
she touched it to his legs and said:
Indeed, a bridegroom of blood are you to me!

26 Thereupon he released him.
Then she said, "a bridegroom of blood" upon the circum-
cision-cuttings.

27 Now YHWH said to Aharon:
Go to meet Moshe in the wilderness!
He went, he encountered him at the mountain of God
and he kissed him.

28 And Moshe told Aharon all YHWH's words with which he
had sent him
and all the signs with which he had charged him.

with a warning to Moshe that his mission will be strongly resisted by
Pharaoh, and a warning that Moshe is to deliver to Pharaoh. Then follows
a bizarre episode, which, like the Name passage discussed above, has
provoked centuries of comment and attempts to explain it. What are we to
make of the circumcision story here, especially the last scene, which is
unclear not only in import but in details such as pronouns as well?

Buber (1958) explains it as an event that sometimes occurs in hero
stories: the deity appears as "divine demon" and threatens the hero's life.
Perhaps this underlines the dangerous side of contact between the human
and the divine. But there seem to be other reasons for the passage's
inclusion at this point in the text. First, it serves as an end bracket to
Moshe's sojourn in Midyan. As mentioned earlier, Moshe flees Egypt
under pain of death (2:15); here, on his return, he is in mortal danger once
more. Second, our passage seems to be an *inclusio* or bracketing passage
for the entire Plague Narrative (Kosmala 1962, and others). This is confirmed by the use of verses 21–23 as an introduction. God, designating
Israel his firstborn and alluding to the future killing of Pharaoh's/Egypt's
firstborn sons, demonstrates his power as life-taker, to be pacified or

my father still alive?" Note that Moshe says nothing to Yitro about what
happened to him on the mountain.

19 **all the men:** Moshe need no longer fear for his life at Pharaoh's hands, but
he will shortly be threatened by God himself (see vv. 24–26).

20 **mounted them upon an ass:** A stereotyped biblical way of describing
setting out on a journey. **staff of God:** In standard hero stories, one
would expect to hear a good deal more about this object, which would
normally possess magical powers. Here, as usual, such a motif has been
suppressed. It surfaces later in Jewish legend, in full mythical garb. The
staff is mentioned in this verse, possibly, to provide a dramatic conclusion
to the entire revelation account: Moshe sets out for Egypt armed, as it
were, with a token from God. This was the missing piece in his activity in
Egypt.

21 **portents:** Signs, wonders. **send free:** Others, "let . . . go."

22 **Thus says YHWH:** A formula often used by the prophets to open their
pronouncements. The context is similar as well: the prophets stand frequently against the kings of Israel and Judah, arguing for an end to
oppression. **my firstborn:** The use of this image is a statement of emotional force, not actual primacy of birth or antiquity, as Israel was a
comparative latecomer in the ancient Near East.

24 **to make him die:** To kill him; the means is not specified, but one could
surmise that illness is meant.

25 **his:** Whose? Presumably those of Moshe, who is then "released" by God.

26 **released him:** Or "relaxed (his hold upon) him." **circumcision-
cuttings:** Others, "on account of the circumcision," "because of the circumcision," "referring to the circumcision."

29 Moshe and Aharon went,
   they gathered all the elders of the Children of Israel,
30 and Aharon spoke all the words which YHWH had spoken
      to Moshe,
   he did the signs before the people's eyes.
31 The people trusted,
   they hearkened
   that YHWH had taken account of the Children of Israel,
   that he had seen their affliction.
   And they bowed low and did homage.

5:1 Afterward Moshe and Aharon came and said to Pharaoh:
   Thus says YHWH, the God of Israel:
   Send free my people, that they may hold-a-festival to me in
      the wilderness!
 2 Pharaoh said:
   Who is YHWH, that I should hearken to his voice to send
      Israel free?
   I do not know YHWH,
   moreover, Israel I will not send free!
 3 They said:
   The God of the Hebrews has met with us;
   pray let us go a three days' journey into the wilderness,
   and let us make-slaughter-offering to YHWH our God,
   lest he confront us with the pestilence or the sword!
 4 The king of Egypt said to them:
   For-what-reason, Moshe and Aharon,
   would you disrupt the people from their tasks?
   Go back to your burdens!
 5 Pharaoh said:
   Here, too many now are the people of the land,
   and you would have them cease from their burdens!
 6 So that day Pharaoh commanded the slave-drivers of the
      people and its officers, saying:
 7 You are no longer to give straw to the people to make the
      bricks as yesterday and the day-before;
   let it be them that go and gather straw for themselves!
 8 But the (same) measure of bricks that they have been mak-
      ing, yesterday and the day-before,
   you are to impose on them,

turned away only by a ceremonial blood-smearing—parallel to the Israel-ites' smearing of blood on their doorposts when their own firstborn are threatened by the Tenth Plague (12:12-13).

Two final points should be noted here. First, it is with the act of his son's circumcision that Moshe finally becomes a true Israelite (that, after all, was the major term of God's covenant with Abraham in Genesis 17). Similarly, Yehoshua (Joshua), Moshe's successor, will circumcise the next generation of Israelites in the process of conquering the Promised Land (Josh. 5:2). And second, it is telling, again, that the person who saves Moshe's life in adulthood is a woman. In a sense, Moshe's early life is now over, having come full circle.

Before Pharaoh (5:1-6:1): Moshe and Aharon's initial efforts to free the people—even temporarily for an act of worship—are unsuccessful, as foretold in the previous chapter. But even though God had predicted failure, we are still left with a portrait of clashing human wills: the libera-tors', the king's, and the reluctant people's. The narrative appears to be a set-up for the second major revelation of God to Moshe (Chapter 6), which, preceded by expressions of doubt on both Moshe's part and that of

31 **The people trusted . . .:** For the first time in the Torah, Israel responds to God's promises in a positive manner, something which will rarely hap-pen again. The vocabulary and attitude form an *inclusio* (a bracket) with the end of the Liberation Narrative, 14:30-31 (cf. the verbs "trust" and "see").

5:1 **hold-a-festival:** Or "observe a pilgrimage-festival." The Hebrew *hag* is still echoed in the great pilgrimage of Islam, the hajj, in which worship-pers make (sometimes long) journeys to Mecca.

2 **Who is YHWH:** This attitude recalls an earlier obstacle to the liberation process, "Who am I" of Moshe (3:11). **I do not know YHWH:** Collo-quially, "I care not a whit for YHWH!" To Pharaoh's pointed challenge, the entire narrative that follows is an answer (cf. 14:4, 18).

3 **pray let us go:** A milder phrase than the earlier "Send free my people!" **three days' journey:** Either the magical 3 again, or a standard biblical way of describing a journey (see Gen. 22:4). **lest he confront us:** In the ancient world the gods demanded sacrifices at specified times. "Confront" and "sword" also occur in verses 20-21, nicely balancing this section of narrative.

4 **For-what-reason:** Heb. *lamma,* as distinct from *maddu'a* ("why," with similar meaning).

5 **too many:** Echoing 1:9ff. (Fishbane 1979). **the people of the land:** This phrase occurs here in its wider usage, i.e., the common folk, as opposed to what is found in Gen. 23:7, where the term indicates the landed nobility.

6 **slave-drivers:** In several Semitic languages *nagos* denotes "pressing" or "overpowering" (Ullendorff 1977), hence "driving" here.

you are not to subtract from it!
For they are lax—
therefore they cry out, saying: Let us go, let us make-
   slaughter-offering to our God!

9 Let the servitude weigh-heavily on the men!
They shall have to do it, so that they pay no more regard to
   false words!

10 The slave-drivers of the people and its officers went out
and said to the people, saying:
Thus says Pharaoh:
I will not give you straw:

11 You go, get yourselves straw, wherever you can find (it),
indeed, not one (load) is to be subtracted from your servitude!

12 The people scattered throughout all the land of Egypt,
gathering stubble-gatherings for straw.

13 But the slave-drivers pressed them hard, saying:
Finish your tasks, each-day's work-load in its day, as when
   there was straw!

14 And the officers of the Children of Israel, whom Pharaoh's
   slave-drivers had set over them, were beaten,
they said (to them):
For-what-reason have you not finished baking your allocation as yesterday and the day-before,
so yesterday, so today?

15 The officers of the Children of Israel came and cried out to
   Pharaoh, saying:
Why do you do thus to your servants?

16 No straw is being given to your servants, and as for bricks—
   they say to us, Make (them)!
Here, your servants are being beaten, and the fault is your
   people's!

17 But he said:
Lax you are, lax,
therefore you say: Let us go, let us make-slaughter-offering
   to YHWH—

18 so now, go—serve;
no straw will be given to you,
and the full-measure in bricks you must give back!

19 The officers of the Children of Israel saw that they were in
   an ill-plight,

having to say: Do not subtract from your bricks each-day's
    work-load in its day!
20 They confronted Moshe and Aharon, stationing themselves
    to meet them when they came out from Pharaoh,
21 they said to them:
    May YHWH see you and judge,
    for having made our smell reek in the eyes of Pharaoh and in
       the eyes of his servants,
    giving a sword into their hand, to kill us!
22 Moshe returned to YHWH and said:
    My Lord,

the people, harks back to the concerns voiced at the Burning Bush. There
is also a forward-looking figure, Pharaoh, who is a prototype for other
foreign rulers and enemies in the Bible who challenge God (Greenberg
1969).

Chapter 5 contains the Bible's most extended description of the conditions of Egyptian bondage. Not surprisingly, the root "serve" occurs
seven times in verses 9 to 21 (Greenberg 1969), and sound variations on
the Hebrew *ra'* ("ill/evil") three times (vv. 19–23).

9 **so that they pay:** Others, "Let them pay" (Greenberg 1969).

10 **Thus says Pharaoh:** An ironic transformation of the prophetic formula
noted in verse 1 above, "the language of redemption turned sour" (Greenberg).

14 **beaten:** The same Hebrew verb as "striking" in 2:11–13.

16 **your people's:** Heb. *'ammekha*, which some read *'immakh* ("with you").

18 **go—serve:** This phrase will be repeated three times during the Plague
Narratives (10:8, 24; 12:31), with a different meaning: Go serve God!
Pharaoh cannot wait to free the Israelites! (Greenberg 1969).

19–21 **saw . . . see:** In these negative usages it is as if the earlier redemptive
theme of God's "seeing" has gone awry. But all is righted below, in 6:1
("Now you will see . . .").

21 **having made our smell reek:** An expression meaning the causing of hatred or horror. **giving a sword into their hand:** This scenario often
occurs historically with liberators; initial attempts fail or are rejected.
Here we have a replay of Moshe's earlier efforts (note the use of "judge"
there as well, in 2:14). The tension in this chapter may be said to revolve
around whether God's sword (v. 3) or Pharaoh's will prevail.

22 **My Lord:** The Hebrew *Adonai* is used often in the Bible for pleading
one's case, as before a king (see Gen. 18:27, 30, 31, 32; 19:18, and Ex.
3:10).

for-what-reason have you dealt so ill with this people?
For-what-reason have you sent me?

23 Since I came to Pharaoh to speak in your name, he has dealt
   only ill with this people,
and rescued—you have not rescued your people!

6:1 YHWH said to Moshe:
Now you will see what I will do to Pharaoh:
for with a strong hand he will send them free,
and with a strong hand he will drive them out of his land.

2 God spoke to Moshe,
he said to him:
I am YHWH.

3 I was seen by Avraham, by Yitzhak, and by Yaakov
as God Shaddai,
but (by) my name YHWH I was not known to them.

4 I also established my covenant with them,
to give them the land of Canaan,
the land of their sojournings, where they had sojourned.

5 And I have also heard the moaning of the Children of Israel,
whom Egypt is holding-in-servitude,
and I have called-to-mind my covenant.

6 Therefore,
say to the Children of Israel:
I am YHWH;
I will bring you out
from beneath the burdens of Egypt,
I will rescue you
from servitude to them,
I will redeem you
with an outstretched arm, with great (acts of) judgment;

7 I will take you
for me as a people,
and I will be for you
as a God;
and you shall know
that I am YHWH your God,
who brings you out
from beneath the burdens of Egypt.

8 I will bring you

into the land (over) which I lifted my hand (in an oath) to
   give to Avraham, to Yitzhak, and to Yaakov.
I will give it to you as a possession,
I, YHWH.

The Promise Renewed (6:2–13): Greenberg (1969) and others have noted
how this section in many respects recapitulates God's speeches at the
Bush. Once again God assures Moshe that he has "heard" and "recalled"
the Israelites and their old covenant; once again he promises to act ("bring
out" resounds four times); once again the promise is linked to an interpretation of God's name; and once again Moshe expresses doubt as to whether
he will be believed or listened to (v.12).

   Why the repetition? Perhaps here, as elsewhere, to double is to emphasize. Also, just as Moshe initially failed as a self-appointed liberator in
Chapter 2, only to be sought out by God in the wilderness, he fails as a
leader here as well, followed by God's reassuring speech. There can be no
question from whence the liberation comes.

22–23 **this people . . . this people . . . your people:** Note Moshe's brilliant use
   of psychology in dealing with God, similar to what he will do again in
   32:11–13.
   23 **to speak in your name:** The issue of God's name will become paramount
   in the passage following.
   6:1 **out of his land:** The phrase is also used in connection with "sending free"
   in 6:11, 7:2, and 11:10.
   2 **I am YHWH:** An authority formula in the ancient Near East (as in Gen.
   41:44, where it refers to an earlier Pharaoh) (Greenberg 1969).
   3 **Shaddai:** Heb. obscure; traditionally translated "Almighty," while some
   understand it as "of the mountains." In Genesis the name is most often
   tied to promises of human fertility (see 17:12); a possibly related Hebrew
   word means "breasts." **was not known:** Others, "did not make
   known."
   6ff. **I will bring . . .:** God's answer comprises verbs of action: "bring out,"
   "rescue," "redeem," "take," and "give." The Hebrew rhymes (*ve-heveti
   etkhem. . . . ve-hitzalti etkhem . . .*).
   6–7 **beneath. . . . beneath:** A more vivid image than merely rescuing them.
   7 **I will take you . . .:** This covenant language recalls the vocabulary of
   marriage in many societies ("take you," "be for/to you"). **you shall
   know:** The verb "know" in the ancient Near East is often part of covenant
   (treaty) language, and so Moshe's task is not only to force Pharaoh to
   acknowledge God, but also to bring the Israelites into a special relationship with God (see Chaps. 19ff).
   8 **(over) which I lifted my hand . . .:** The promise of the land forms the
   backbone of the book of Genesis, which ends with it as well (Gen. 50:24).

9 Moshe spoke thus to the Children of Israel.
But they did not hearken to Moshe,
out of shortness of spirit and out of hard servitude.

10 YHWH spoke to Moshe, saying:
11 Go in, speak to Pharaoh king of Egypt,
that he may send free the Children of Israel from his land.
12 Moshe spoke before YHWH, saying:
Here, (if) the Children of Israel do not hearken to me,
how will Pharaoh hearken to me?
—and I am of foreskinned lips!
13 YHWH spoke to Moshe and to Aharon,
and charged them to the Children of Israel and to Pharaoh
king of Egypt,
to bring the Children of Israel out of the land of Egypt.

14 These are the heads of their father-households:
The sons of Re'uven, firstborn of Israel: Hanokh and Pallu,
Hetzron and Karmi,
these are the clans of Re'uven.
15 And the sons of Shim'on: Yemuel, Yamin, Ohad, Yakhin
and Tzohar, and Sha'ul the son of the Canaanite-woman,
these are the clans of Shim'on.
16 Now these are the names of the Sons of Levi according to
their begettings:
Gershon, Kehat and Merari.
Now the years of Levi's life were seven and thirty and a
hundred years.
17 The sons of Gershon: Livni and Shim'i, according to their
clans.
18 And the sons of Kehat: Amram, Yitzhar, Hevron and
Uzziel.
Now the years of Kehat's life were three and thirty and a
hundred years.
19 And the sons of Merari: Mahli and Mushi.
These are the Levite clans, according to their begettings.
20 Amram took himself Yokheved his aunt as a wife,
she bore him Aharon and Moshe.
Now the years of Amram's life were seven and thirty and a
hundred years.

21 Now the sons of Yitzhar: Korah, Nefeg and Zikhri.

22 And the sons of Uzziel: Mishael, Eltzafan and Sitri.

23 Aharon took himself Elisheva daughter of Amminadav,
     Nahshon's sister, as a wife.
     She bore him Nadav and Avihu, Elazar and Itamar.

24 Now the sons of Korah: Assir, Elkana and Aviasaf; these are
     the Korahite clans.

25 Elazar son of Aharon took himself one of Putiel's daughters
     for himself as a wife,
     she bore him Pin'has.
     These are the heads of the Levite father-groupings accord-
     ing to their clans.

The Genealogy of Moshe and Aharon (6:14–27): At this tension-filled moment in the narrative, in the face of Moshe's self-doubt and the possible
collapse of his mission, there is an unlikely break, at least by Western
storytelling standards. Apparently the genealogy has been inserted to but-
tress Moshe and Aharon's claim to represent the people before the Egyptian crown, and to stress their Levite ancestry (which solidly establishes
them within the priestly class in Israel). Significantly, the genealogy of
Yaakov's sons ends with the third, Levi, and the rest of the list enumerates
the Levite clans. More significantly, the ages mentioned are composed of
patterned numbers such as 3, 7, 30, and 100. As in Genesis, this betokens
a concept of order and meaning in history.

9   **shortness of spirit:** Others, "impatience" (so Ramban), "shortness of
     breath" (so Rashi). Also notable is Walzer's (1985) suggestion of "dispirit-
     edness." A parallel Ugaritic phrase probably means "wretched."

12 **spoke before:** Appealed to (Orlinsky 1970).   **of foreskinned lips:** Either
     Moshe had some physical defect, as legend has it, or he is alluding to his
     difficulties as a public speaker (cf. 4:10). The use of "foreskinned" may
     express the biblical idea that things in their natural state require sanctify-
     ing, as can be seen with firstborn humans and animals, first-fruits, food,
     sexuality, etc.

14 **father-households:** Tribal units, listed according to the name of the an-
     cestor. **sons:** Heb. *banim*, translated above as "children," but here
     clearly referring to the males.

16 **seven and thirty and a hundred years:** Here, and in verse 18 and 20, the
     life spans of Moshe's family members are composed of "perfect" numbers
     in combinations and multiples, as if to say that biography as well as group
     history has a preordained meaning.

25 **Pin'has:** Trad. English "Phinehas." He will play an important role in
     Num. 25:7 as a zealot for the new faith. The name is Egyptian in origin.

26 That is (the) Aharon and Moshe to whom YHWH said:
   Bring the Children of Israel out of the land of Egypt by
   their ranks;

27 those (were they) who spoke to Pharaoh king of Egypt, to
   bring the Children of Israel out of Egypt,
   that Moshe and Aharon.

28 So it was on the day that YHWH spoke to Moshe in the land
   of Egypt,

29 YHWH spoke to Moshe, saying:
   I am YHWH;
   speak to Pharaoh king of Egypt all that I speak to you.

30 Moshe said before YHWH:
   If I am of foreskinned lips,
   how will Pharaoh hearken to me?

7:1 YHWH said to Moshe:
   See, I will make you as a god for Pharaoh,
   and Aharon your brother will be your prophet.

 2 **You are to speak all that I command you,**
   And Aharon your brother is to speak to Pharaoh
   so that he may send free the Children of Israel from his land.

 3 But I,
   I will harden Pharaoh's heart,
   I will make my signs and my portents many in the land of
   Egypt:

 4 Pharaoh will not hearken to you,
   so I will set my hand against Egypt,
   and I will bring out my ranks,
   my people, the Children of Israel,
   from the land of Egypt, with great (acts of) judgment;

 5 the Egyptians will know that I am YHWH,
   when I stretch out my hand over Egypt
     and bring the Children of Israel out from their midst.

 6 Moshe and Aharon did
   as YHWH had commanded them, thus they did.

 7 Now Moshe was eighty years old, and Aharon was eighty-
   three years old, when they spoke to Pharaoh.

 8 YHWH said to Moshe and to Aharon, saying:

 9 When Pharaoh speaks to you, saying: Give, you, a portent,
   then say to Aharon:

Take your staff and throw it down before Pharaoh: Let it
  become a serpent.
10 Moshe and Aharon came to Pharaoh,
  they did thus, as YHWH had commanded,
  Aharon threw down his staff before Pharaoh and before his
    servants, and it became a serpent.
11 Pharaoh too called for the wise men and for the sorcerers,
  that they too, the magicians of Egypt, should do thus with
    their occult arts,

Thus legitimated, Moshe and Aharon can return to the task at hand. It
would seem, then, that the passage is speaking to the Israelites, both in
Egypt and in the audience of later generations.

The Mission Renewed (6:28–7:13): As preparation for the next meeting with
Pharaoh, Moshe is once more reminded that the king will not listen to him.
Taking a page from his speech at the Bush, God instructs Moshe and
Aharon to use the "sign" that had previously served to convince the people:
snake magic. Yet despite Aharon's one-upping the Egyptian magicians in
the warm-up for the plagues, Pharaoh remains unconvinced. This episode

26 **by their ranks:** The term has a military ring, and is used frequently in the
  Bible with that connotation.
7:1 **as a god.** Or "oracle," as mentioned in the note to 4:16.
  5 **when I stretch out my hand:** In the Plague Narrative, Moshe and Aharon
    will do the actual stretching out of hands (see 7:19, 8:1, 12; 9:22; 10:12,
    21; and the climactic passage in 14:16, 26).
  6 **Moshe and Aharon did/ as YHWH had commanded them, thus they
    did:** This construction can be broken up in two ways (with, for instance,
    the break at "them"), a syntactical usage found fairly frequently in bibli-
    cal texts (cf. 39:43). The wording recalls the Flood Narrative in Genesis,
    with the same emphasis: the hero obeys God without question.
  7 **eighty . . . eighty-three:** Another set of "perfect" numbers, this time
    using 40 (and 3) as the base. It occurs here due to the biblical practice of
    mentioning age to "mark . . . a milestone in life's journey" (Greenberg
    1969).
  9 **Give, you, a portent:** That is, "Prove yourselves by working a miracle"
    (Hyatt 1971).   **your staff:** It is not clear whether the staff is the aforemen-
    tioned one of Moshe, or part of another tradition, connected to Aharon.
    serpent: Heb. *tanin*, a word indicating a reptile, with possible mythologi-
    cal overtones (as in "dragon").
  11 **occult arts:** Whereas Aharon needs none, since God performs the miracle
    (Greenberg 1969).

12 they threw down, each-man, his staff, and these became
     serpents.
   But Aharon's staff swallowed up their staffs.
13 Yet Pharaoh's heart remained strong-willed, and he did not
     hearken to them,
   as YHWH had spoken.

14 YHWH said to Moshe:
   Pharaoh's heart is heavy-with-stubborness—he refuses to
     send the people free.
15 Go to Pharaoh in the morning, here, he goes out to the Nile,
   station yourself to meet him by the shore of the Nile,
   and the staff that changed into a snake, take in your hand,
16 and say to him:
   YHWH, the God of the Hebrews, has sent me to you, saying:
   Send free my people, that they may serve me in the wilder-
     ness!
   But here, you have not hearkened thus far.
17 Thus says YHWH:
   By this shall you know that I am YHWH:
   here, I will strike—with the staff that is in my hand—upon
     the water that is in the Nile,
   and it will change into blood.
18 The fish that are in the Nile will die, and the Nile will reek,
   and the Egyptians will be unable to drink water from the
     Nile.
19 YHWH said to Moshe:
   Say to Aharon:
   Take your staff
   and stretch out your hand over the waters of Egypt,
   over their tributaries, over their Nile-canals, over their
     ponds and over all their bodies of water,
   and let them become blood!
   There will be blood throughout all the land of Egypt—in the
     wooden-containers, in the stoneware.
20 Moshe and Aharon did thus, as YHWH had commanded
     them.
   He raised the staff and struck the water in the Nile, before
     the eyes of Pharaoh and before the eyes of his servants,
   and all the water that was in the Nile changed into blood.

21 The fish that were in the Nile died, and the Nile reeked,
   and the Egyptians could not drink water from the Nile;
   the blood was throughout all the land of Egypt.
22 But the magicians of Egypt did thus with their occult arts,

helps to prepare for what follows, and indeed contains a virtual glossary of
Exodus words. Some of these are: "speak," "send," "harden," "heart,"
"sign/portent," "hand," "bring out," "know," "staff," "hearken,"
"midst."

First Blow (7:14–25): The first plague uses elements and words common
to many subsequent plagues; in addition to those just mentioned, it introduces "refuse" and "reek" and "throughout all the land of Egypt." More
important is the choice of site and object for the curse: the Nile (a god in

12 **swallowed up:** Leaving no doubt as to whether optical illusion or sleight
   of hand is involved.
14 **heavy-with-stubbornness:** In the Plague Narrative, the root *kaved*,
   "heavy," occurs ten times—five times referring to Pharaoh's heart and
   five referring to the plagues themselves. The latter are perhaps seen as the
   direct outcome of the former.
15 **he goes out to the Nile:** Many interpretations have been proposed for this
   action, which must have had some significance for the biblical narrator. It
   remains unclear whether Pharaoh is involved in a religious rite or a function of state. More charming is the suggestion by Rashi, the medieval
   Hebrew commentator, that Pharaoh went secretly to the river in order to
   relieve himself—so that the Egyptians would not see him as less than a
   god.
17 **change:** Continuing the theme of transformation found in the scene with
   the snake. Overall, the change from slavery to liberation and to responsible society is a major theme in Exodus.
19 **wooden-containers . . . stoneware:** It is unclear what is meant. The
   context seems to suggest "even in their kitchen utensils," reflected in the
   present translation. On the other hand, virtually everywhere in the Bible
   that "wood and stone" occur as a pair in the singular, they refer to idols;
   Cassuto (1967) speaks of the Egyptians' bathing their idols and thus sees
   the passage as another example of Exodus' denigrating Egyptian religion.
20 **He raised the staff:** "He" refers to Aharon. **struck:** The first
   "stroke"—that is the Hebrew term (*makka*) used for what we know in
   English as a "plague."
21 **throughout all the land of Egypt:** One of the refrains used in this section
   of the book (see "On the Book of Exodus and Its Structure," p. xxix).

and Pharaoh's heart remained strong-willed, and he did not
  hearken to them,
as YHWH had spoken.
23 So Pharaoh turned and came into his house, neither did he
  pay any mind to this.
24 But all Egypt had to dig around the Nile to drink water,
  for they could not drink from the waters of the Nile.
25 Seven days were fulfilled, after YHWH had struck the Nile.

26 YHWH said to Moshe:
Come to Pharaoh and say to him:
Thus says YHWH:
Send free my people, that they may serve me!
27 **Now if you refuse to send them free,**
here, I will smite your entire territory with frogs.
28 The Nile will swarm with frogs;
they will ascend, they will come
into your house, into your bedroom, upon your couch,
into your servants' houses, in among your people,
into your ovens and into your dough-pans;
29 onto you, onto your people, onto all your servants will the
  frogs ascend!
8:1 YHWH said to Moshe:
Say to Aharon:
Stretch out your hand with your staff, over the tributaries,
  over the Nile-canals, and over the ponds,
make the frogs ascend upon the land of Egypt!
2 Aharon stretched out his hand over the waters of Egypt,
the frog-horde ascended
and covered the land of Egypt.
3 Now the magicians did thus with their occult arts—
they made frogs ascend upon the land of Egypt.
4 Pharaoh had Moshe and Aharon called
and said:
Plead with YHWH, that he may remove the frogs from me
  and from my people,
and I will send the people free, that they may make-
  slaughter-offering to YHWH!
5 Moshe said to Pharaoh:
Be praised over me:

> For when shall I plead for you, for your servants, for your
>   people,
> to cut off the frogs from you and from your houses,
> (so that) only in the Nile will they remain?
> 6 He said:
> For the morrow.
> He said:
> According to your words, (then)!
> In order that you may know
> that there is none like YHWH our God.

Egypt), water (source of life for the Egyptians but earlier source of death for the Hebrew babies), and blood (sign of life and death). No more effective choice could have been made for this first demonstration of the far-reaching power of the Israelite God.

As with the first six plagues, the threat is long and the actual carrying-out brief. Note the relationship, at the end of the episode, between the uncaring Pharaoh and his own people, who have to scratch for water.

Second Blow (7:26–8:11): The second plague is linked to the first by a number of elements: the Nile, the magicians, and of course, Pharaoh's disregard of the threats after it is all over. It is also a full narrative,

25   **YHWH had struck the Nile:** Even though Aharon did the "striking," it becomes clear here that the brothers are only agents.

27   **frogs:** A symbol of fertility in Egyptian culture (the goddess Heket), and so the plague might be regarded as an assault on the Egyptian gods again (Casuto 1967). There may also be an ironic hint here of the "swarming" of the Israelites in 1:7.

28   **ovens:** A place which, because of its dryness, would be most unlikely to harbor them (Childs 1974).

8:2   **frog-horde:** The Hebrew uses a collective singular here (likewise with "insects" in 8:17ff. and "locusts" in 10:4ff.); all other "frogs" in this plague receive the standard plural.

3   **the magicians did thus:** The theme of Israel's distinctiveness, so prominent in these stories, is delayed. Here the magicians can do the same tricks as their Hebrew counterparts, although, as noted above, they require the aid of "occult arts."

5   **Be praised over me:** Others, "Have the advantage over me." The sense is that Pharaoh will be allowed to choose the precise time of the frogs' removal.

6   **In order that you may know:** The intent of Moshe's words in verse 5 is now revealed: precise timing, even when chosen at will, demonstrates God's total power.

7 The frogs shall remove from you, from your houses, from
   your servants, from your people,
   —only in the Nile shall they remain.
8 Moshe and Aharon went out from Pharaoh,
   Moshe cried out to YHWH
   on account of the frogs that he had imposed upon Pharaoh.
9 And YHWH did according to Moshe's words:
   the frogs died away, from the houses, from the courtyards,
   and from the fields.
10 They piled them up, heaps upon heaps, and the land reeked.
11 But when Pharaoh saw that there was breathing-room,
   he made his heart heavy-with-stubbornness, and did not
   hearken to them,
   as YHWH had spoken.

12 YHWH said to Moshe:
   Say to Aharon:
   Stretch out your staff and strike the dust of the land,
   it will become gnats throughout all the land of Egypt!
13 They did thus,
   Aharon stretched out his hand with his staff and struck the
   dust of the ground,
   and gnats were on the man and on beast;
   all the dust of the ground became gnats throughout all the
   land of Egypt.
14 Now the magicians did thus with their occult arts, to bring
   forth the gnats, but they could not,
   the gnats were on man and on beast.
15 The magicians said to Pharoah:
   This is the finger of a god!
   But Pharaoh's heart remained strong-willed, and he did not
   hearken to them,
   as YHWH had spoken.

16 YHWH said to Moshe:
   (Arise) early in the morning, station yourself before Pharaoh—here, he goes out to the water,
   and say to him:
   Thus says YHWH:
   Send free my people, that they may serve me!
17 Indeed, if you do not send my people free,

here, I will send upon you, upon your servants, upon your
   people, upon your houses—
insects,
the houses of Egypt will be full of the insects,
as well as the ground upon which they are!

containing most of the formal aspects of the plagues within itself (see "The
Plague Narrative," above).

The threat of this plague breaks into poetry in a striking passage (v.28)
which uses repeating prepositions. The frogs are literally everywhere.
Also, for the first time Pharaoh asks that God be entreated—that is, he
finally acknowledges his existence (as against which, see 5:2).

Third Blow (8:12–15): With the third plague, the curse becomes more
intimate, affecting the bodies of all living creatures in Egypt (cf. the
refrain in vv.13–14, "on man and on beast"). The narrative uses the
briefest plague formula here, without introduction or warning to Pharaoh.
Yet it results in an Egyptian effort to end the siege, as the magicians term
the plague "the finger of a god" (v.15).

Fourth Blow (8:16–28): Despite its similarity to the previous plague (insects), number four introduces a new and important element into the tale:
the idea that God makes a distinction between Egypt and Israel. It also
involves protracted bargaining between Moshe and Pharaoh over the issue
of allowing the Israelites to worship God.

9 **from the houses . . .:** The threefold repetition of "from" paints a vivid
   picture of the end of this plague. The dead frogs recede like water drying
   up.
12 **gnats:** Other translations vary here. There are many traditions, but it
   seems clear that some kind of small insect is indicated (Hyatt 1971).
15 **the finger of a god:** That is, God's direct intervention in human affairs.
   The only other occurrence of this expression is in Exodus (31:18) and in
   the text that retells that story, Deut. 9:10. In the latter cases it refers to the
   divine writing on the two tablets of Testimony.
17 **upon you . . .:** Similar to the refrain of 7:28–29, with regard to the frogs;
   here, "upon" occurs four times in one line. **insects:** As in the last
   plague, there are many opinions as to what these were (e.g., gnats, gad-
   flies, mosquitos); Bekhor Shor understands the "mixture" (the literal
   meaning of the Hebrew term used here, *'arov*) as one of wild animals.

18 But I will make distinct, on that day, the region of Goshen,
       where my people is situated,
     so that there will be no insects there,
     in order that you may know that I am YHWH in the land;
19 I will put a ransom between my people and your people—
     on the morrow will this sign occur.
20 YHWH did thus,
     heavy insect (swarms) came into Pharaoh's house, into the
       houses of his servants, throughout all the land of Egypt,
     the land was in ruins in the face of the insects.
21 Pharaoh had Moshe and Aharon callled
     and said:
     Go, make-slaughter-offering to your god in the land!
22 Moshe said:
     It would not be wise to do thuswise:
     for Egypt's abomination is what we slaughter-offer for our
       God;
     if we were to slaughter Egypt's abomination before their
       eyes,
     would they not stone us?
23 Let us go a three days' journey into the wilderness,
     and we shall make-slaughter-offering to YHWH our God, as
       he has said to us.
24 Pharaoh said:
     I will send you free,
     that you may make-slaughter-offering to YHWH your God
       in the wilderness,
     only: you are not to go far, too far!
     Plead for me!
25 Moshe said:
     Here, when I go out from you, I will plead with YHWH,
     and the insects will remove from Pharaoh, from his servants,
       and from his people, on the morrow,
     only: let not Pharaoh continue to trifle (with us),
     by not sending the people free to make-slaughter-offering to
       YHWH!
26 Moshe went out from before Pharaoh and pleaded with
       YHWH.
27 And YHWH did according to Moshe's words,

he removed the insects from Pharaoh, from his servants and
  from his people,
not one remained.

28 But Pharaoh made his heart heavy-with-stubbornness this
     time as well,
and he did not send the people free.

9:1 YHWH said to Moshe:
Come to Pharaoh and speak to him:
Thus says YHWH, the God of the Hebrews:
Send free my people, that they may serve me!

Fifth Blow (9:1–7): Although this plague spares humans, it is nevertheless
described as "heavy" (v.3). The narrative uses a play-on-words as well:
the Hebrew for pestilence (*dever*) echoes that for thing (*davar*).

18 **region**: Lit., "land" (see Gen. 45:10).   **in the land:** That is, as an active
   force.
19 **ransom:** Heb. *pedut*, usually emended to *pelut*, "distinction," to bring the
   phrase into consonance with verse 18 and with the entire plague section in
   general.
20 **in ruins:** The verb "ruin" (Heb. *shihet*) is often used in the Bible in
   connection with punishment for sin (see, for example, Gen. 6:11–12;
   19:13, 29).
22 **wise . . . thuswise:** Heb. *nakhon . . . ken.* **Egypt's abomination:** In
   Cassuto's (1967) view, there are two possibilities here: either the animals
   in question were venerated as holy by the Egyptians, or they were actually
   thought of as gods, in which case the Hebrew phrase would be quite
   derogatory (so too Rashi).   **stone:** A widely used form of execution in
   biblical times (e.g., 17:4; 19:13; 21:28, 29, 32 below). It was apparently
   used for very severe crimes, and often connected, logically, to the anger of
   the populace (Greenberg 1962).
24 **only: you are not to go far, too far:** Heb. *rak harhek lo tarhiku.*
27 **not one remained:** Similar words will be used of the Egyptians, drowned
   in the Sea of Reeds (14:28).

2 If you refuse to send (them) free, and continue to hold-on-
strongly to them,
3 here, YHWH's hand will be on your livestock in the field,
on the horses, on the asses, on the camels, on the oxen, (and)
on the sheep—
an exceedingly heavy pestilence!
4 And YHWH will make-a-distinction between the livestock
of Israel and the livestock of Egypt:
there will not die among all that belong to the Children of
Israel a thing!
5 YHWH set an appointed-time, saying:
On the morrow, YHWH will do this thing in the land.
6 YHWH did that thing on the morrow—
all the livestock of Egypt died,
but of the livestock of the Children of Israel, there died not
one.
7 Pharaoh sent to inquire, and here: there had not died of the
livestock of the Children of Israel even one.
But Pharaoh's heart remained heavy-with-stubbornness,
and he did not send the people free.

8 YHWH said to Moshe and to Aharon:
Take yourselves fistfuls of soot from a furnace
and let Moshe toss it heavenward before Pharaoh's eyes,
9 it will become fine-dust on all the land of Egypt,
and on man and on beast, it will become boils sprouting into
blisters,
throughout all the land of Egypt!
10 They took the soot from a furnace and stood before Pharaoh, and Moshe tossed it heavenward,
and it became boil-blisters, sprouting on man and on beast.
11 Now the magicians could not stand before Moshe because of
the boils,
for the boils were upon the magicians and upon all Egypt.
12 But YHWH made Pharaoh's heart strong-willed, and he did
not hearken to them,
as YHWH had said to Moshe.
13 YHWH said to Moshe:

Get-up-early in the morning, station yourself before Pharaoh and say to him:
Thus says YHWH, the God of the Hebrews:
Send free my people, that they may serve me!
14 Indeed, this time I will send all my blows upon your heart,
and against your servants, and against your people,
so that you may know that there is none like me throughout
all the land;
15 indeed, by now I could have sent out my hand and struck
you and your people with the pestilence,
and you would have vanished from the land;
16 however, just on account of this I have allowed you to with-
stand,
to make you see my might,
and in order that they might recount my name throughout
all the land.

Sixth Blow (9:8–12): Just as in the previous "short" plague, number 3, the
magicians come to the fore. No longer do they cry to Pharaoh; they cannot
even take the stage!

Seventh Blow (9:13–35): Long like its corresponding predecessors (numbers 1 and 4), the seventh plague prefaces its occurrence with an emphatic
introduction by God, and its warning gives God-fearing Egyptians a
chance to save themselves (vv.19–21), something new. The description of
the plague itself is fraught with spectacle, presaging Sinai with its use of
thunder and fire. There is also the ominous note, twice in the text (vv.18,
24), that such a plague was unique in Egyptian annals. The plagues, at
least for the Egyptians, now transcend the realms of normal, explainable
experience, as well as of historical recollection.

9:2 **hold-on-strongly:** Both Pharaoh's obduracy and his stranglehold on the
slaves are described with the same verbal root.
5 **an appointed-time:** As before (8:5–6), equally striking to the plague itself
is its precise removal at the time promised.
8 **soot:** The transformation from soot to fine-dust and then boils reflects a
poetic justice, paralleling bricks baked in a kiln (Cassuto 1967). It also
reflects the biblical concept of disease as punishment. **toss:** Moshe will
later "toss" the blood of the covenant on the freed Israelites (24:8).
16 **land:** Others, "earth."

17 (But) still you set yourself up over my people, by not sending them free—

18 here, around this time tomorrow I will cause to rain down an
exceedingly heavy hail,
the like of which has never been in Egypt from the days of
its founding until now!

19 So now:
send (word): give refuge to your livestock and to all that is
yours in the field;
all men and beasts who are found in the field and who have
not been gathered into the house—
the hail will come down upon them, and they will die!

20 Whoever feared the word of YHWH among Pharaoh's servants had his servants and his livestock flee into the
houses,

21 but whoever did not pay any mind to the word of YHWH
left his servants and his livestock out in the field.

22 YHWH said to Moshe:
Stretch out your hand over the heavens:
Let there be hail throughout all the land of Egypt,
on man and on beast and on all the plants of the field,
throughout the land of Egypt!

23 Moshe stretched out his staff over the heavens,
and YHWH gave forth thunder-sounds and hail, and fire
went toward the earth,
and YHWH caused hail to rain down upon the land of
Egypt.

24 There was hail and a fire taking-hold-of-itself amidst the
hail,
exceedingly heavy,
the like of which had never been throughout all the land of
Egypt since it had become a nation.

25 The hail struck, throughout all the land of Egypt, all that
was in the field, from man to beast;
all the plants of the field the hail struck, and all the trees of
the field it broke down;

26 only in the region of Goshen, where the Children of Israel
were, was there no hail.

27 Pharaoh sent and had Moshe and Aharon called

and said to them:

This-time I have sinned!

YHWH is the one-in-the-right, I and my people are the ones-in-the-wrong!

28 Plead with YHWH!

For enough is the God-thunder and this hail!

Let me send you free—do not continue staying here!

29 Moshe said to him:

As soon as I have gone out of the city, I will spread out my hands to YHWH,

the thunder will stop and the hail will be no more—

in order that you may know that the land belongs to YHWH.

30 But as for you and your servants,

I know well that you do not yet stand-in-fear

before the face of YHWH, God!

31 —Now the flax and the barley were stricken, for the barley was in ears and the flax was in buds,

32 but the wheat and the spelt were not stricken, for late (-ripening) are they.—

33 Moshe went from Pharaoh, outside the city, and spread out his hands to YHWH:

the thunder and the hail stopped, and the rain no longer poured down to earth.

34 But when Pharaoh saw that the rain and the hail and the thunder had stopped,

he continued to sin: he made his heart heavy-with-stubbornness, his and his servants'.

20 **Whoever feared . . .:** The focus now shifts to the Egyptians in general (at least some of them), who now suspect the real source of their troubles, whereas only the magicians recognized it previously.

24 **fire taking-hold-of-itself:** Heb. difficult; others, "lightning flashed back and forth," "lightning flashing through it." **the like of which had never been:** The phrase here foreshadows the final plague (11:6).

27 **one-in-the-right . . . ones-in-the-wrong:** The terms are drawn from the world of legal, not religious, terminology.

28 **enough is:** Or "enough of their being. . . ."

29 **spread out my hands:** In entreaty.

31 **Now the flax . . .:** An editorial comment, to explain how much harm was done (Cassuto 1967: they used it for cloth and for food).

35 Pharaoh's heart remained strong-willed, and he did not send
    the Children of Israel free,
  as YHWH had spoken through Moshe.

10:1 YHWH said to Moshe:
    Come to Pharaoh!
    For I have made his heart and the heart of his servants
        heavy-with-stubbornness,
    in order that I may put these my signs amongst them
  2 and in order that you may recount in the ears of your son
        and of your son's son
    how I have toyed with Egypt,
    and my signs, which I have placed upon them—
    that you may know that I am YHWH.
  3 Moshe and Aharon came to Pharaoh, they said to him:
    Thus says YHWH, the God of the Hebrews:
    How long will you refuse to humble yourself before me?
    Send free my people, that they may serve me!
  4 But if you refuse to send my people free,
    here, on the morrow I will bring the locust-horde into your
        territory!
  5 They will cover the aspect of the ground, so that one will not
        be able to see the ground,
    they will consume what is left of what escaped, of what
        remains for you from the hail,
    they will consume all the trees that spring up for you from
        the field,
  6 they will fill your houses, the houses of all your servants,
        and the houses of all Egypt,
    as neither your fathers nor your fathers' fathers have seen
    from the day of their being upon the soil until this day.
    He turned and went out from Pharaoh.
  7 Pharaoh's servants said to him:
    How long shall this one be a snare to us?
    Send the men free, that they may serve YHWH their God!
    Do you not yet know that Egypt is lost?
  8 Moshe and Aharon were returned to Pharaoh,
    and he said to them:
    Go, serve YHWH your God!
    —Who is it, who is it that would go?

9 Moshe said:

With our young ones, with our elders we will go,
with our sons and with our daughters,
with our sheep and with our oxen we will go—
for it is YHWH's festival for us.

10 He said to them:

May YHWH be thus with you, the same as I mean to send
  you free along with your little-ones!
You see—yes, your faces are set toward ill!

11 Not thus—go now, O males, and serve YHWH, for that is
  what you (really) seek!
And they were driven out from Pharaoh's face.

12 YHWH said to Moshe:

Stretch out your hand over the land of Egypt for the locust-
  horde,
and it will ascend over the land of Egypt, consuming all the
  plants of the land, all that the hail allowed to remain.

Eighth Blow (10:1–20): Anticipating Pharaoh's eventual capitulation, the Egyptians now urge their king to release the Israelites, before Egypt is truly "lost" (v.7). The request occurs before the plague does. This longest plague is in many ways the most devastating of all, affecting as it does the very soil itself. Here the last two plagues are anticipated (v.15, "the ground became dark"; and v.17, "this death"), and the previous one is echoed (vv.6, 14, with the reference to past history). Also foreshadowed, in the locusts' removal, is the final victory at the Sea of Reeds (Chap. 14), through the mention of the location and the use of a powerful wind.

10:2 **toyed:** Others, "dealt harshly with," "made fools of."
  5 **aspect:** Lit., "eye." **not be able to see:** Foreshadowing the next plague, darkness (Plaut 1981).
  8 **Who is it:** Pharaoh qualifies his approval with conditions.
  9 **Moshe said . . .:** The answer is rhythmical, almost ritual. **With our young ones . . .:** The addition of children and animals to the request of Moshe makes Pharaoh suspect that they will not come back.
  10 **May YHWH be thus with you:** That is to say, may he not be with you! **your faces are set toward ill:** You have evil intentions; "your evil intentions are written on your faces" (Abravanel).
  11 **O males:** And only the males.

13 Moshe stretched out his staff over the land of Egypt,
and YHWH led an east wind against the land
all that day and all night;
when it was morning, the east wind had borne in the locust-
horde.

14 The locust-horde ascended over all the land of Egypt,
it came to rest upon all the territory of Egypt,
exceedingly heavy;
before it there was no such locust-horde as it, and after it
will be no such again.

15 It covered the aspect of all the ground, and the ground
became dark,
it consumed all the plants of the land, and all the fruit of the
trees that the hail had left;
nothing at all green was left of the trees and of the plants of
the field, throughout all the land of Egypt.

16 Quickly Pharaoh had Moshe and Aharon called
and said:
I have sinned against YHWH your God, and against you!

17 So now,
pray bear my sin just this one time!
And plead with YHWH your God,
that he may only remove this death from me!

18 He went out from Pharaoh and pleaded with YHWH.

19 And YHWH reversed an exceedingly strong sea wind
which bore the locusts away and dashed them into the Sea of
Reeds,
not one locust remained throughout all the territory of
Egypt.

20 But YHWH made Pharaoh's heart strong-willed, and he did
not send the Children of Israel free.

21 YHWH said to Moshe:
Stretch out your hand over the heavens,
and let there be darkness over the land of Egypt;
they will feel darkness!

22 Moshe stretched out his hand over the heavens,
and there was gloomy darkness throughout all the land of
Egypt, for three days,

23 a man could not see his brother, and a man could not arise
from his spot, for three days.

But for all the Children of Israel, there was light in their
  settlements.
24 Pharaoh had Moshe called and said:
Go, serve YHWH,
only your sheep and your oxen shall be kept back,
even your little-ones may go with you!
25 Moshe said:
You must also give slaughter-animals and offerings into our
  hand, so that we may make-them-ready for YHWH our
  God!
26 Even our livestock must go with us, not a hoof may remain
  behind:
for some of them we must take to serve YHWH our God;
we—we do not know how we are to serve YHWH
until we come there.
27 But YHWH made Pharaoh's heart strong-willed, so that he
  would not consent to send them free.
28 Pharaoh said to him:
Go from me!
Be on your watch:
You are not to see my face again,
for on the day that you see my face, you shall die!

Ninth Blow (10:21–29): Little is new here; darkness foreshadows the final
plague, death. Yet at the end of the brief episode, as well as in 11:8, we are
given a glimpse into the human element, as Moshe and Pharaoh rage in
anger against each other.

19 **sea wind:** The story is told from the perspective of the land of Israel,
   where such a wind means a west wind (Plaut 1981). **wind . . . not
   one . . . remained:** Foreshadowing the incident at the Sea of Reeds
   (14:21, 28).
21 **they:** The Egyptians.
24 **only your sheep and your oxen:** Pharaoh still tries to salvage some control
   of the situation.
28 **Go from me!:** Others, "Out of my sight!," "Leave my presence." **on
   the day . . . you shall die:** The expression is similar to the one used in
   reference to Yosef in Gen. 43:3, 5. Despite the finality of the language
   here, the confrontation between Moshe and Pharaoh continues in 11:4–8
   and 12:31–32.

29 Moshe said:
You have spoken well,
I will not henceforth see your face again.

11:1 YHWH said to Moshe:
I will cause one more blow
to come upon Pharaoh and upon Egypt;
afterward he will send you free from here.
When he sends you free, it is finished—he will drive, yes,
 drive you out from here.
2 Pray speak in the ears of the people:
They shall ask, each man of his fellow, each woman of her
 fellow, objects of silver and objects of gold.
3 And YHWH gave the people favor in the eyes of Egypt,
while the man Moshe was (considered) exceedingly great in
 the land of Egypt,
in the eyes of Pharaoh's servants and in the eyes of the
 people.
4 Moshe said:
Thus says YHWH:
In the middle of the night
I will go forth throughout the midst of Egypt,
5 and every firstborn shall die throughout the land of Egypt,
from the firstborn of Pharaoh who sits on his throne
to the firstborn of the maid who is behind the handmill,
and every firstborn of beast.
6 Then shall there be a cry throughout all the land of Egypt,
the like of which has never been, the like of which will never
 be again.
7 But against all the Children of Israel, no dog shall even
 sharpen its tongue, against either man or beast,
in order that you may know that YHWH makes a distinction
 between Egypt and Israel.
8 Then all these your servants shall go down to me,
they shall bow to me, saying:
Go out, you and all the people who walk in your footsteps!
And afterward I will go out.
He went out from Pharaoh in raging anger.

9 YHWH said to Moshe:
Pharaoh will not hearken to you,
in order that my portents may be many in the land of Egypt.
10 Now Moshe and Aharon had done all the portents in Pharaoh's presence,
but YHWH had made Pharaoh's heart strong-willed, and he
had not sent the Children of Israel free from his land.

The Final Warning (11:1–10): What seems to be the introduction to the
last plague is made up of motifs common to several of the previous ones. It
also reintroduces the idea of despoiling the Egyptians, which had been
mentioned in Moshe's original commission (3:21–22)—so we know that
redemption is at hand. Artfully, the specification of what "one more
blow" is, is delayed until verse 5. In addition, there is the motif of Moshe's
greatness/fame among the Egyptians, which would appear to be a suppressed remnant of the story (in the face of the desire to glorify God as the
hero). The section ends (vv.9–10) with a summary of the entire Plague
Narrative— or at least of what is to be learned from it.

11:3 **Moshe was (considered) exceedingly great:** Interestingly, at this point in
the narrative it is Moshe and not God who is glorified (see also the note to
verse 8, below).

4 **the middle of the night:** As so often in folklore. The Hebrew word for
"middle" (*hatzi*) is different from the one used for "midst" on the next
line (*tavekh*).

6 **cry:** See also 12:30. The cry of the Egyptians echoes that of the Children
of Israel in 3:7, 9.

7 **sharpen:** Heb. obscure. **no dog:** Much less the "bringer-of-ruin" of
verse 13!

8 **in raging anger:** Somewhat uncharacteristically, the story of this last confrontation reports the emotions of both Moshe and Pharaoh. For a change
we get a glimpse of the human side of the drama.

9–10 **Pharaoh will not hearken . . .:** These two verses serve as a summary of
the entire Plague Narrative. They also help to smoothe out the transition
to Chapter 12.

10 **from his land:** The last occurrence of this phrase.

12:1 YHWH said to Moshe and to Aharon in the land of Egypt,
    saying:

2 Let this New-Moon be for you the beginning of New-
    Moons,
    the beginning-one let it be for you of the New-Moons of the
      year.

3 Speak to the whole community of Israel, saying:
    On the tenth day of this New-Moon
    they are to take them, each-man, a lamb, according to their
      father-households, a lamb per household.

4 Now if there be too few in the house for a lamb,
    he is to take (it), he and his neighbor who is near his house,
      by the assessment according to the (total number of)
      persons;
    each-man according to what he can eat you are to assess for
      the lamb.

5 A whole, male, year-old lamb shall be yours, from the sheep
    and from the goats are you to take it.

6 It shall be for you in safekeeping, until the fourteenth day of
    this New-Moon,
    and they are to butcher it—the whole assembly of the com-
      munity of Israel—at twilight.

7 They are to take some of the blood and put it onto the two
    posts and onto the lintel,
    onto the houses in which they eat it.

8 They are to eat the flesh on that night, roasted in fire,
    and *matzot,*
    with bitter-herbs they are to eat it.

9 Do not eat any of it raw, or boiled, boiled in water,
    but rather roasted in fire, its head along with its legs, along
      with its innards.

10 You are not to leave any of it until morning;
    what is left of it until morning, with fire you are to burn.

11 And thus you are to eat it:
    your hips girded, your sandals on your feet, your sticks in
      your hand;
    you are to eat it in trepidation—
    it is a Passover-Meal to YHWH.

12 I will proceed through the land of Egypt on this night

The Tenth Blow in Its Context: With Chapter 12 the narrative leaves the realm of storytelling and enters that of ritual. What has so far been recounted as a story now takes on the aspect of commemorative ceremony. Instead of proceeding from warning (11:1, 4–8) to plague (12:29–30), the tenth plague account has been embedded in a setting of the lengthy de-

12:1 **in the land of Egypt:** The text thereby establishes the antiquity of the ritual.

2 **Let this . . . be . . . let it be:** The rhetoric helps to focus attention on this important section.   **beginning-one:** At least one form of the ancient Hebrew calendar began in the spring; the Torah begins its ritual calendar according to its ritual beginning at Passover. It is significant that the new year of nature and that of the nation's birth coalesce. For extensive discussion of Exodus and the biblical calendar, see Sarna 1986.

3 **whole community of Israel:** This term, "community" (Heb. *'eda*), is used somewhat interchangeably with a host of others in the Torah to indicate the leadership (often, the elders) of the people (Weinfeld 1972a).   **tenth:** there is a parallel important day in the fall, on the tenth day of the seventh month—Yom Kippur, the Day of Atonement (see Lev. 16:29).   **father-households:** See the note to 6:14.

5 **whole:** Or "hale" (Heb. *tamim*), that is, physically unblemished. This primary physical meaning often gives way to a spiritualized one, in reference to human beings (Job, for instance, is described as *tamim*, variously translated as "blameless" and "perfect" in Job 1:1).

6 **you . . . they:** The change in the subject of the sentence, from second to third person, is not unusual in biblical Hebrew.   **fourteenth day:** Close to the full moon.   **at twilight:** Lit., "between the evening-hours." This time is mentioned elsewhere (e.g., 16:12; 29:39, 41; and several places in Numbers) in connection with the sacrifices made by the priests. This perhaps implies that we have here the unusual situation (at least in ancient Israel) of the head of the household performing a priestly function.

8 **roasted in fire:** Not raw or boiled, since what seems to be meant is an imitation of standard sacrifices.   **matzot:** Sing. *matza*, the flat, unleavened bread that resembled present-day "Syrian bread."   **with bitter-herbs:** Others, "on bitter herbs." Gaster (1949) notes the long-standing use of such cathartics as purifiers or demon-ridders (e.g., garlic) in folk cultures. Later Jewish tradition speaks to the herbs as a symbol of the bitterness of Egyptian bondage.

9 **legs . . . innards:** That is, completely consumed.

10 **you are not to leave any of it until morning:** Again, as in the removal of leaven, what is meant is complete destruction.

11 **your hips girded . . .:** Prepared for travel. Passover is still observed in this manner by some Jews originating in Arab lands.   **in trepidation:** Others, "in haste," but the element of fear is also contained in the verb (Heb. *hafoz*).

and strike down every firstborn in the land of Egypt, from
man to beast,
and on all the gods of Egypt I will render judgment,
I, YHWH.

13 Now the blood will be a sign for you upon the houses where
you are:
when I see the blood, I will pass over you,
the blow will not become a bringer-of-ruin to you, when I
strike down the land of Egypt.

14 This day shall be for you a memorial,
you are to celebrate it as a festival-celebration for YHWH,
throughout your generations, as a law for the ages you are to
celebrate it!

15 For seven days, *matzot* you are to eat,
already on the first day you are to get rid of leaven from your
houses,
for anyone who eats what is fermented—from the first day
until the seventh day—: that person shall be cut off from
Israel.

16 And on the first day, a calling-together of holiness,
and on the seventh day, a calling-together of holiness shall
there be for you,
no kind of work is to be made on them,
only what belongs to every person to eat, that alone may be
made-ready by you.

17 And keep the (Festival of) *matzot!*
For on this very day
I have brought out your ranks from the land of Egypt.
Keep this day throughout your generations as a law for the
ages.

18 In the first (month), on the fourteenth day of the New-
Moon, at evening, you are to eat *matzot*,
until the twenty-first day of the month, in the evening.

19 For seven days, no leaven is to be found in your houses,
for whoever eats what ferments, that person shall be cut off
from the community of Israel,
whether sojourner or native of the land.

20 Anything that ferments you are not to eat;
in all your settlements, you are to eat *matzot*.

scription of a festival, thus shifting the time sense of the narrative. The enactment of the ceremony is important both for the characters in the story and for the participants in the audience of later generations. Likewise, the description of the actual leaving of Egypt is followed, not by a detailing of the route or what happened next, but by a series of regulations concerning who may eat the Passover meal (12:43–51) and by rules concerning the dedication of the firstborn (13:1–16).

By means of such editing, the final text was obviously meant to move the Exodus story, with all its historical aspects, into what historians of religion call "mythical time." In our text, history becomes present event; the hearer is no longer "in the audience" but actually acts out the story. That immediacy is meant is demonstrated by the threefold occurrence of the phrase "on this/that very day" (vv.17, 41, 51), which also serves to unite the various parts of the text around the tenth plague and the exodus.

The mixture of law and narrative that we find in Chapters 12 and 13 sets the stage for the Sinai scenes that will take place later in the book (Chaps. 19ff.), and indeed for the rest of the Pentateuch.

The Passover Ritual (12:1–28): The festival depicted in this chapter is, in the opinion of many scholars, a combination of two ancient holy days: a Shepherds' Festival, in which each spring a lamb was sacrificed to the deity in gratitude and for protection of the flock, and a celebration of the barley harvest, at which time all leaven/fermentation products were

13 **pass over:** The exact meaning of Hebrew *paso'ah* is in dispute. Some interpret it as "protect"; others, including Buber (1958), relate it to "limp," suggesting a halting dance performed as part of the ancient festival (perhaps in imitation of the newborn spring lambs). It is possible that there are homonyms here, and that the text is playing on them.

14 **celebrate it as a festival-celebration:** Or "make a pilgrimage" (see the note to 5:1).

15 **seven days:** Similar to the great fall festival, Sukkot, mentioned in Lev. 23:24. **leaven . . . fermented:** the removal of these elements is commonly found in agricultural societies (for more, see Gaster 1949, 1969). **from the first . . . that person . . .:** The two phrases occur in reversed order in the Hebrew.

16 **a calling-together of holiness:** Others, "a holy convocation." It is not entirely clear what is meant. **calling-together . . . no kind of work:** The same rules apply to the fall festival (Lev. 23:33–43). **on them:** The first and seventh days.

17 **matzot:** This probably describes a festival separate from the one connected to the lambs, as indicated above.

20 **not to eat . . . to eat matzot:** The section ends with an emphatic doublet.

21 Moshe had all the elders of Israel called and said to them:
   Pick out, take yourselves a sheep for your clans, and butcher
      the Passover-animal.

22 Then take a band of hyssop, dip (it) in the blood which is in
      the basin,
   and touch the lintel and the two posts with some of the blood
      which is in the basin.
   Now you—you are not to go out, any man from the entrance
      to his house, until morning.

23 YHWH will proceed to deal-blows to Egypt,
   and when he sees the blood on the lintel and on the two
      posts,
   YHWH will pass over the entrance,
   and will not give the bringer-of-ruin (leave) to come into
      your houses to deal-the-blow.

24 You are to keep this word
   as a law for you and for your sons, into the ages!

25 Now it will be,
   when you come to the land which YHWH will give you, as
      he has spoken,
   you are to keep this service!

26 And it will be,
   when your sons say to you: What does this service (mean) to
      you?

27 then say:
   It is the slaughtered-meal of Passover to YHWH,
   who passed over the houses of the Children of Israel in
      Egypt,
   when he dealt-the-blow to Egypt and our houses he rescued.
   The people did homage and bowed low.

28 And the Children of Israel went and did
   as YHWH had commanded Moshe and Aharon, thus they
      did.

29 Now it was in the middle of the night:
   YHWH struck down every firstborn in the land of Egypt,
   from the firstborn of Pharaoh who sits on his throne
   to the firstborn of the captive in the dungeon,
   and every firstborn of beast.

30 Pharaoh arose at night,

he and all his servants and all Egypt,
and there was a great cry in Egypt;
for there is not a house in which there is not a dead man.

avoided (although see Ginsberg [1982], who theorizes a shepherds' festival
with *matza*). Each has numerous parallels in other cultures (see Gaster
1949). What has apparently happened here is that the two days have been
fused together and imbued with historical meaning. In addition, rites that
were originally protective in function have been reinterpreted in the light
of the Exodus story. But whatever its origin, Passover as described in our
text bespeaks a strong sense of Israelite tribal community and of distinctiveness. And it is distinctiveness, which played such an important role in
Israelite religion, that is singled out here, with the striking penalty for
transgressing the boundaries of the festival—being "cut off" (probably
death). One also notes the repetition of the phrase "a law for the ages"
(vv.14, 17, 24). Passover, then, is central both to the Exodus story and to
Israelite ideas as a whole (see Sarna 1986 for a detailed discussion).

Tenth Blow and Exodus (12:29–42): The final blow falls. This most horri-
fying of all the plagues, and the reaction to it, are described in only two
verses, whereas the rest of the narrative concerns itself with preparations
for and actual description of the exodus. Note how, as above, the narrative
is surrounded by ritual concerns—trying to explain the subsequent reason

22 **hyssop:** The leaves are known for having a cooling effect (but some
   understand the Hebrew *'ezov* as meaning "marjoram"). **entrance:** Lit.,
   "opening." This spot of entrance often serves as a figurative threshold in
   folklore; here, it is the separation point between life and death, Israelites
   and Egyptians, home and the outside world. Later, it functions as the
   place of revelation or contact with the holy (e.g., 33:10).
23 **pass over:** Or, following the comments on verse 13, above, "skip over."
25 **service:** Ritual; the Israelites have begun their transformation from serfs
   to divine servants, underscored by the recurrence of "service" in 12:26
   and 13:5.
26 **when your sons say:** This framework is used frequently in Deuteronomy
   (e.g., Deut. 6:20).
27 **when he . . .:** The chiastic structure (*A-B/B-A;* here, a verb-noun/noun-
   verb) ends the speech, a device common in biblical style (Andersen 1974).
29 **captive in the dungeon:** Cf. verse 5, "the maid who is behind the handmill"; both phrases express the idea of the lowest person in the society.
30 **for there is not a house:** The omission of the perfect tense expresses the
   immediacy of the situation.

31 He had Moshe and Aharon called in the night
   and said:
   Arise, go out from amidst my people, even you, even the
      Children of Israel!
   Go, serve YHWH according to your words,
32 even your sheep, even your oxen, take, as you have spoken,
      and go!
   And bring-a-blessing even on me!
33 Egypt pressed the people strongly, to send them out quickly
      from the land,
   for they said: We are all dead-men!
34 So the people loaded their dough before it had fermented,
      their kneading-troughs bound in their clothing, upon
      their shoulders.
35 Now the Children of Israel had done according to Moshe's
      words:
   they had asked of the Egyptians objects of silver and objects
      of gold, and clothing;
36 YHWH had given the people favor in the eyes of the Egyp-
      tians,
   and they let themselves be asked of.
   So did they strip Egypt.

37 The Children of Israel moved on from Ra'amses to Sukkot,
   about six hundred thousand on foot, menfolk apart from
      little-ones,
38 and also a mixed multitude went up with them,
   along with sheep and oxen, an exceedingly heavy (amount
      of) livestock.
39 Now they baked the dough which they had brought out of
      Egypt into *matzot* cakes, for it had not fermented,
   for they had been driven out of Egypt, and were not able to
      linger,
   neither had they made provisions for themselves.

40 And the settlement of the Children of Israel which they had
      settled in Egypt was thirty years and four hundred years.
41 It was at the end of thirty years and four hundred years,
   it was on that very day:
   All of YHWH's ranks went out from the land of Egypt.

42 It is a night of keeping-watch for YHWH,
   to bring them out of the land of Egypt;
   that is this night for YHWH,
   a keeping-watch of all the Children of Israel, throughout
      their generations.

for eating unleavened bread (which had not been done in verses 15f., above). There also returns the important motif of despoiling ("stripping") Egypt.

The section ends (vv.40–42) with a dramatic summary of Israel's sojourn in Egypt and the importance of the Passover festival, built on repeti-

31 **according to your words:** Pharaoh has never thus conceded before, and so we know that this time he is sincere. The same change of heart is indicated in the next verse, "And bring a blessing even on me!"

31-32 **even . . . .:** The fourfold use of "even" here shows that Pharaoh is finally not hedging. He gives permission for *all* the Israelites to leave, without preconditions.

33 **Egypt pressed the people strongly:** Contrasting with Pharaoh's "strong-willed heart" of 10:27 and previously.

34 **their kneading-troughs bound:** To explain why only *matza* was baked; see verse 39, below.

37 **moved on:** The Hebrew (*naso'a*) literally means "pulled out their tent pegs." **six hundred thousand . . . menfolk:** That is, there were over 600,000 men of military age (over twenty). Extrapolating from this several million slaves strains the credulity; one might accept either the explanation put forth in Plaut (1981) that *elef* means, not "thousand," but "troop/contingent" (of nine or ten men each), or Cassuto's (1967) designation of the number as a "perfect" or folkloric one, built on the numerical system of 6/60. For a full discussion Sarna (1986).

38 **mixed multitude:** This is the usual translation in English. The Hebrew is *'erev rav,* "riffraff." **heavy:** Their wealth is a counterpart to Pharaoh's previously "heavy" heart (and "heavy" plagues).

39 **were not able to linger,/ neither had they made provisions:** It comes almost as a surprise to the Israelites. Here there can be no question of military victory, as in a coup; history depends on the incursion of God.

40 **thirty years and four hundred years:** The numbers are patterned as usual; although this total disagrees with Gen. 15:13, for instance (which reckons it as 400 years), the differences seem to be more over which patterned numbers to use and not historical exactitude.

42 **keeping-watch:** Reflecting the play on words in the Hebrew *shamor,* by including ideas of both "guarding" and "observing." Cassuto (1967) sees *shamor* as a shepherd's term, appropriate here. Note again, in the tense structure, the conflation of narrative and contemporary ritual.

43 YHWH said to Moshe and Aharon:
    This is the law of the Passover-meal:
    Any foreign son is not to eat of it.
44 But any man's serf who is acquired by money—if you have
    circumcised him, then he may eat of it.
45 Settler and hired-hand are not to eat of it.
46 In one house it is to be eaten,
    you are not to bring out of the house any of the flesh,
    outside.
    And you are not to break a bone of it.
47 The entire community of Israel is to do it.
48 Now when a sojourner sojourns with you, and would make
    the Passover-meal to YHWH,
    every male with him must be circumcised, then he may
    come-near to make it, and will be (regarded) as a native of
    the land.
    But any foreskinned-man is not to eat of it.
49 One Instruction shall there be for the native and for the
    sojourner that sojourns in your midst.

50 All the Children of Israel did
    as YHWH commanded Moshe and Aharon, thus they did.

51 It was on that very day,
    (when) YHWH brought the Children of Israel out of the
    land of Egypt by their ranks,
13:1 YHWH spoke to Moshe, saying:
2   Hallow to me every firstborn,
    breacher of every womb among the Children of Israel, of
    man or of beast,
    it is mine.
3   Moshe said to the people:
    Remember this day,
    on which you went out from Egypt, from a house of serfs,
    for by strength of hand YHWH brought you out from here:
    no fermentation is to be eaten.
4   Today you are going out, in the New-Moon of Ripe-Grain.
5   And it shall be,
    when YHWH brings you to the land of the Canaanite,

tion ("four hundred thirty years," "a night . . . for YHWH," "keeping-watch"). Again, a past event is made immediate for the audience. The powerful religious tones of story and ceremony are established by the threefold reference to night as the setting for both (vv.29–31).

Who May Make Passover (12:43–50): Continuing the immediacy of ritual, the narrative pauses where one would expect it to talk about the Israelites' route, to specify carefully that partaking of the Passover meal, and indeed being a part of the community in general, requires circumcision on the part of the participant. In essence, it creates the new Israelite nation, on the heels of common participation in a historical event. This small passage has been inserted between two occurrences of the same phrase ("that very day"), an editorial device often used in biblical literature.

Passover and the Firstborn (12:51–13:16): To close out the text's celebration of the exodus event, the editor includes a peroration on the firstborn. This too is a reinterpretation of earlier religious practices. Many ancient cultures selected the firstborn as an object for sacrifice to the gods—whether firstborn of fruit, of animals, or of human beings—the grounds for this being that the firstborn represents the best that nature has to offer

43 **foreign son:** Or "foreigner." The English here echoes Hebrew usage and the English idea of "native son" (Edward Greenstein, personal communication).

46 **outside:** Into that area which has the function of being the realm of death in the story. **you are not to break a bone:** As if to violate its perfection, since the bone was identified as symbolic of the whole (viz., the same Hebrew word used for "bone" and "essence, person"). The biblical idea, found in reference to all animal sacrifices, is that only unblemished ("whole" or "hale") animals may be used for such purposes. In Gaster's (1969) view, the prohibition in this verse was originally instituted to ensure a full flock.

48 **come-near:** This verb (Heb. *karev*) is often used in connection with the priestly cult.

49 **Instruction:** Or "teaching," "priestly ruling." The same word later refers to Moshe's fuller "teaching," and eventually to the entire Pentateuch.

51 **that very day:** The phrase serves to bridge the two chapters here (Plaut 1981).

13:2 **Hallow:** Make holy. **breaches:** Opens. This should not be confused with a so-called breach birth.

3 **Remember:** Here and again at 20:8, the Hebrew verbal form is an emphatic one.

4 **ripe-grain:** Heb. *aviv*. The month later took on a Babylonian name (Nisan), as did all the months of the Jewish calendar.

of the Hittite, of the Amorite, of the Hivvite and of the
  Yevusite,
which he swore to your fathers to give you,
a land flowing with milk and honey,
you are to serve this service, in this New-Moon:
6 For seven days you are to eat *matzot*,
and on the seventh day (there is): a festival to YHWH.
7 *Matzot* are to be eaten for the seven days,
nothing fermented is to be seen with you, no leaven is to be
  seen with you, throughout all your territory.
8 And you are to tell your son on that day, saying:
It is because of what YHWH did for me, when I went out of
  Egypt.
9 It shall be for you for a sign on your hand and for a memorial
  between your eyes,
in order that YHWH's Instruction may be in your mouth,
that by a strong hand did YHWH bring you out of Egypt.
10 You are to keep this law at its appointed-time from year-day
  to year-day!
11 It shall be,
when YHWH brings you to the land of the Canaanite, as he
  swore to you and to your fathers,
and gives it to you,
12 you are to transfer every breacher of a womb to YHWH,
every breacher, offspring of a beast that belongs to you,
the males (are) for YHWH.
13 Every breacher of an ass you are to redeem with a lamb;
if you do not redeem (it), you are to break-its-neck.
And every firstborn of men, among your sons, you are to
  redeem.
14 It shall be
when your son asks you on the morrow, saying: What does
  this mean?
You are to say to him:
By strength of hand YHWH brought us out of Egypt, out of
  a house of serfs.
15 And it was
when Pharaoh hardened (his heart) against sending us free,
that YHWH killed every firstborn throughout the land of
  Egypt,

from the firstborn of man to the firstborn of beast.
Therefore I myself slaughter-offer to YHWH every breacher
    of a womb, the males,
and every firstborn among my sons I redeem.
16 It shall be for a sign on your hand and for headbands be-
    tween your eyes,
for by strength of hand YHWH brought us out of Egypt.

(see Gen. 49:3, where Jacob's firstborn is "beginning of my strength"). The idea of strength is played upon in the reinterpretation of sacrifice: four times, including at the end of the passage, we are told that the firstborn is to be consecrated, "for by strength of hand YHWH brought you out of Egypt" (vv.3, 9, 14, 16).

The chapter has a few notable characteristics. For one, the eating of *matzot* has been integrated into the firstborn material; for another, the language is unmistakably reminiscent of Deuteronomy (vv.5 and 11, "it shall be [a refrain here]/when YHWH brings you to the land of the Canaan-ite . . .)"; see Deut. 6:10, 7:1, etc.). This has led some scholars to point to a relatively late date for the material, supporting the idea that Israel in its

9 **sign . . . memorial:** This may have been figurative originally; it became taken literally and gave rise to the phylacteries (*tefillin*) in rabbinic Juda-ism. Notable in this verse is how the body is pressed into the service of memory ("hand . . . eyes . . . mouth"). Rashi draws attention to the par-allel idea of the Song of Songs: "Set me as a seal upon your heart . . . upon your arm" (Song 8:6).

10 **year-day:** Heb. *yamim;* the rendering follows B-R, which took the expres-sion to denote both "year to year" and specifically the holiday.

11–12 **It shall be . . . every breacher:** Returning to the subject of verse 2.

12 **for YHWH:** That is, for sacrifice to him.

13 **ass:** Not one of the "pure" animals fit for sacrifice, and hence its substitu-tion ("redeeming") by a lamb. **break-its-neck:** Others, "decapitate." The intent seems to be that if the animal is not redeemed, one is not allowed to benefit economically from it (Plaut 1981). **firstborn of men . . . redeem:** In this case the male child is symbolically transferred to God; child sacrifice was of course abhorrent to the Bible (see Gen. 22). To this day religious Jews "redeem" their firstborn sons with money given to charity, thirty days after birth (*Pidyon Ha-Ben*).

14 **What does this mean?:** Lit., "What is this?"

16 **headbands:** Others, "frontlets." The meaning is unclear; see the discus-sions in Plaut (1981) and Tigay (1982), from which the present translation is taken.

17 Now it was, when Pharaoh had sent the people free,
    that God did not lead them by way of the land of the Philis-
        tines, which indeed is nearer,
    for God said to himself:
    Lest the people regret it, when they see war,
    and return to Egypt!
18 So God had the people swing about by way of the wilderness
        at the Sea of Reeds.
    And the Children of Israel went up armed from the land of
        Egypt.
19 Now Moshe had taken Yosef's bones with him,
    for he had made the Children of Israel swear, yes, swear,
        saying:
    God will take account, yes, account of you—so bring my
        bones up from here with you!
20 They moved on from Sukkot and encamped in Etam at the
        edge of the wilderness.
21 Now YHWH goes before them,
    by day in a column of cloud, to lead them the way,
    by night in a column of fire, to give light to them,
    to (be able to) go by day and by night.
22 There does not retire
    the column of cloud by day
    or the column of fire by night
    from before the people!

14:1 YHWH spoke to Moshe, saying:
    2 Speak to the Children of Israel,
       that they may turn back and encamp before Pi ha-Hirot,
           between Migdol and the sea,

sixth-century B.C.E. exile in Babylonia looked back to recast the past in its
own image. At any rate, memory is clearly important here, with two
passages stressing the continuity of commemoration through the following
generations (vv.8–10 and 14–16).

The Route and the Escort (13:17–22): The initial exit from Egypt highlights
an ominous fact about the Israelites: God is well aware of their weaknesses
and leads them by a detour, lest they "see war" and seek to recover the
familiar security of being serfs. The section also explains what they are

doing out of the way of the logical route to Canaan (the place names are difficult to identify, but the general stress is clear), and sets up the great final victory of the next chapter.

Two other elements of weight enter in this brief passage. One concerns Yosef's bones, which leave Egypt with his descendants. The body of Yosef seems to anchor early Israelite history: its mummification brings the Genesis stories to a close, its journey here links up Israel's patriarchal past with the radically new deliverance from bondage, and its final interment in the land of Israel formally closes out the conquest of the land under Yehoshua (Joshua) (Josh. 24:32).

Another unifying motif is that of God's accompanying the journeying Israelites in the form of cloud and fire. This passage is the first of what I have called the "Presence Accounts" described in "On the Book of Exodus and Its Structure," above.

At the Sea of Reeds (14): The liberation account ends with two literary masterpieces: the semi-poetic story of Israel's miraculous passage through the Sea of Reeds along with God's smashing of the Egyptian war machine, and the song of triumph that follows in Chapter 15. Taken together, they form a natural conclusion to what has gone before and a bridge to what follows. Chapter 14 marks the Israelites' last contact with the Egyptians, and the beginning of their desert journey.

17 **lead them . . . regret:** A play on words: Heb. *naham . . . yinnahem.*
   way: Some take this to be a proper noun or name: "The Way/Road of the Land of the Philistines." **land of the Philistines:** That is, along the Mediterranean coast.

18 **Sea of Reeds:** Not "Red Sea," which came from an ancient translation. It has more recently been suggested that the term (Heb. *suf*) can be read "End [*sof*] Sea," that is, the Sea at the End of the World. This mythological designation is attractive, given the cosmically portrayed events of the next chapter, but is not provable. The exact location, in any event, has not been established with certainty. **armed:** Heb. (*hamush*) unclear. The present rendering is supported by ancient versions; Plaut (1981) raises the possibility of "groups of five/fifty."

19 **he had made the Children of Israel swear:** See Gen. 50:25. The bones will be reburied, marking the end of the conquest of Canaan, in Josh. 24:32.

21 **YHWH goes before them:** Others, "went before them." The Hebrew idiom here means "to lead," especially in war, and is the classic biblical description of a king. **column of cloud:** Heb. *'ammud 'anan.*
   cloud . . . fire: These are seen as physical manifestations of God's presence, and are brought back in the narrative at Sinai (19:16, 18).

14:2 **Pi ha-Hirot:** The location is unknown.

before Baal-Tzefon, opposite it, you are to encamp by the
    sea.
3 Now Pharaoh will say of the Children of Israel:
    They are confused in the land! The wilderness has closed
        them in!
4 I will make Pharaoh's heart strong-willed, so that he pursues
        them,
    and I will be glorified through Pharaoh and all his forces,
    so that the Egyptians may know that I am YHWH.
    They did thus.
5 Now the king of Egypt was told that the people fled,
    and Pharaoh's heart and (that of) his servants changed re-
        garding the people, they said:
    What is this that we have done, that we have sent free Israel
        from serving us?
6 He had his chariot harnessed,
    his (fighting-) people he took with him,
7 and he took six hundred selected chariots and every (kind
        of) chariot of Egypt,
    teams-of-three upon them all.
8 YHWH made the heart of Pharaoh king of Egypt strong-
        willed, so that he pursued the Children of Israel,
    while the Children of Israel were going out with (their) hand
        upraised.
9 The Egyptians pursued them and overtook them encamped
        by the sea,
    all of Pharaoh's chariot-horses, his riders, and his forces,
    by Pi ha-Hirot, before Baal-Tzefon.
10 As Pharaoh drew near, the Children of Israel lifted up their
        eyes:
    Here, Egypt moving up after them!
    They were exceedingly afraid.
    And the Children of Israel cried out to YHWH,
11 they said to Moshe:
    Is it because there are no graves in Egypt
    that you have taken us out to die in the wilderness?
    What is this that you have done to us, bringing us out of
        Egypt?
12 Is this not the very word that we spoke to you in Egypt,

saying: Let us alone, that we may serve Egypt!
Indeed, better for us serving Egypt
than our dying in the wilderness!

As if the actual exodus were not dramatic enough, the narrator or editor has included a battle scene at this point in the text. As before, the principal combatants are God and Pharaoh, and as before, we begin with God's hardening the monarch's heart (v.4) to teach him a final lesson ("I will be glorified"). In that vein, some of the plague motifs are repeated, making Chapter 14 a fitting conclusion to the Deliverance account stylistically and thematically (see also Isbell 1982). At the same time the story includes a foreshadowing of Israel's behavior in the wilderness for the next two years, with a detailed account of their complaints against Moshe (and God's miraculous response).

God appears in this story in his most warlike garb, and temporarily resembles many of the gods of antiquity (Cross 1973 uses the term "the divine warrior," relating it to Northwest Semitic imagery). This is not unusual for the Bible, and seems appropriate here, given the climactic nature of the events and the general context of the Deliverance Narrative. Otherwise, the Hebrew God was conceived of as the originator of all

4   **be glorified through:** The Hebrew uses the same stem (*khd*) earlier in the narrative, as if to suggest that Pharaoh's "heaviness" (stubborness) is answered, not only by "heavy" (severe) plagues, but by God, showing his "heaviness" (glory) at the sea. I did not find a solution in English to the unified use of the one root in Hebrew—a frustrating defeat, given the principles of this translation.

5   **told that the people fled:** As if they were not expecting it; now it is obvious that the Israelites are not leaving simply to observe a religious festival (Plaut 1981).

6   **(fighting-) people:** This reading is supported by Num. 31:32 and Josh. 8:1 (Childs 1974).

7   **six hundred:** A nice counterpart of the 600,000 (or 600 units of) Israelite males mentioned previously.   **teams-of-three:** Others, "officers," "warriors," "a picked team."

8   **(their) hand upraised:** Others, "defiantly," "in triumph."

11–12   **they said. . . . wilderness:** The Israelites' complaint has been shaped into a great rhetorical paragraph, with the people's first "grumbling" against Moshe an ominous foreshadowing of what will occur throughout the wanderings. In this construction, the longed-for "Egypt" is repeated five times, and the unknown "wilderness" twice. Note also the stress on Moshe: "you have taken us out. . . . you have done to us."

13 Moshe said to the people:
    Do not be afraid!
    Stand fast and see
    YHWH's deliverance which he will work for you today,
    for as you see Egypt today, you will never see it again for the
        ages!
14 **YHWH will make war for you, and you—be still!**
15 YHWH said to Moshe:
    Why do you cry out to me?
    Speak to the Children of Israel, and let-them-move-forward!
16 And you—
    hold your staff high, stretch out your hand over the sea
    and split it!
    The Children of Israel shall come through the midst of the
        sea upon the dry-land.
17 But I,
    here, I will make Egypt's heart strong-willed,
    so that they come in after them,
    and I will be glorified through Pharaoh and all his forces,
    his chariots and his riders;
18 the Egyptians shall know that I am YHWH,
    when I am glorified through Pharaoh, his chariots and his
        riders.
19 The messenger of God that was going before the camp of
        Israel moved on and went behind them,
    the column of cloud moved ahead of them
    and stood behind them,
20 coming between the camp of Egypt and the camp of Israel.
    Here were the cloud and the darkness,
    and (there) it lit up the night;
    the-one did not come near the-other all night.
21 Moshe stretched out his hand over the sea,
    and YHWH caused the sea to go back
    with a fierce east wind all night,
    and made the sea into firm-ground;
    thus the waters split.
22 The Children of Israel came through the midst of the sea
        upon the dry-land,
    the waters a wall for them on their right and on their left.
23 But the Egyptians pursued and came in after them,

things, good and evil, and was of course not compartmentalized into limited tasks as were other gods of neighboring cultures.

From a formal point of view, the sea narrative is among the most formulaic in the Hebrew Bible. That is, it is built entirely upon several phrases that repeat throughout the text, stressing its major themes. These include: God's "making Pharaoh's heart strong-willed" (vv.4, 8, 17); God's "being glorified" through what he does to the Egyptians (vv.4, 17, 18); Israel's going "upon dry-land" (vv.16, 22, 29); the waters' "returning" (vv.26, 27, 28); Israel's marching "through/into the midst of the sea" (vv.16, 22, 23, 27, 29); Pharaoh's "chariots and riders" (vv.17, 18, 23, 26, 28); and a description of the standing waters, "the waters a wall for them to their right and to their left" (vv.22, 29); see also the refrain, "before Pi ha-Hirot . . . before Baal-Tzefon" (v.4) and "by Pi ha-Hirot, before Baal-Tzefon" (v.9). The text is thus much more than a journalistic account of what happened: it is a rhythmic retelling of an experience, strongly conditioned by traditional (probably oral) Israelite forms of storytelling.

The ending (vv.29–31) betrays the influence of Deuteronomy. Using language that mirrors the end of the entire Torah (Deut. 34), the text speaks of seeing, fearing, hand, eyes, and the unique-to-Deuteronomy phrase "Moshe his servant" (see Deut. 34:5). Significantly, then, the final narrative of Israel's relationship to Egypt is cast as a classic ending in general.

What exactly happened at the sea? As I indicated in "On the Book of Exodus and Its Structure," above, such a point is unanswerable, and may not have a great bearing on the meaning of our text. Scholars have scrambled their brains for decades, trying either to reconstruct precisely what

13 **Moshe said . . .:** There follow four rapid-fire verbs of command, to quiet the complaints. **Stand fast and see:** Heb. *hityatzevu u-re'u*. **deliverance:** A word meaning "rescue," but extending to circumstances that appear miraculous to those who experience them.

15–16 **YHWH said . . .:** God echoes Moshe, issuing four commands.

15 **let-them-move-forward:** Countering the "Egypt moving up after them" of verse 10.

16 **and split it!:** As if that were as natural an act as stretching out one's hand!

20 **and (there) it lit up:** Heb. unclear; some read the verb as coming from a different root, meaning "cast a spell on," which, however, weakens the theme of distinction mentioned earlier.

21 **fierce east wind:** Looking back to the "east wind" that rid Egypt of the locusts in 10:13, and forward to God's "fierce-might" in 15:2, after the triumph at the sea. **firm-ground:** In the Flood Narrative, another story of deliverance (and death) by water, the same word appears as a sign that all is well. Similarly, the "dry-land" of the next verse appears in Gen. 8:14.

all of Pharaoh's horses, his chariots and his riders,
into the midst of the sea.

24 Now it was at the morning-watch:
YHWH looked out against the camp of Egypt in the column
    of fire and cloud,
and he stirred up the camp of Egypt,

25 he loosened the wheels of his chariots and made them to
    drive with heaviness.
Egypt said:
I must flee before Israel,
for YHWH makes war for them against Egypt!

26 Then YHWH said to Moshe:
Stretch out your hand over the sea,
and the waters shall return
upon Egypt—upon its chariots and upon its riders.

27 Moshe stretched out his hand over the sea,
and the sea returned, at the face of morning, to its original-
    place,
as the Egyptians were fleeing toward it.
And YHWH shook the Egyptians in the midst of the sea.

28 The waters returned,
they covered the chariots and the riders of all of Pharaoh's
    forces that had come after them into the sea,
not even one of them remained.

29 But the Children of Israel had gone upon dry-land, through
    the midst of the sea,
the waters a wall for them on their right and on their left.

30 So YHWH delivered Israel on that day from the hand of
    Egypt;
Israel saw Egypt dead by the shore of the sea,

31 and Israel saw the great hand that YHWH had wrought
    against Egypt,
the people feared YHWH,
they trusted in YHWH and in Moshe his servant.

15:1 Then sang Moshe and the Children of Israel
this song to YHWH,
they uttered (this) utterance:

        I will sing to YHWH,
        for he has triumphed, yes, triumphed,

"natural" event this "really" was (e.g., tides, tidal wave), or to identify the exact location of the "Sea of Reeds." While such matters are important to the historian, the Bible itself concentrates on the theme of the story. The narrator was concerned to demonstrate God's final victory and to portray Israel's escape in terms of a birthing (through a path, out of water), and these themes had the most influence both on later biblical tradition and on the generations of inspired Jews and Christians that heeded them.

The Song of God as Triumphant King (15:1–21): Moshe's famous Song at the Sea provides a natural boundary in the book of Exodus. It sets off the Egypt traditions from those of Sinai and the wilderness, and brings to a spectacular close the saga of liberation. This is borne out even in scribal tradition, still observed in the writing of Torah scrolls today, where the Song is written out with different spacing from the preceding and following narrative portions.

A poem is necessary at this point in the story, to provide emotional exultation and a needed break before the next phase of Israel's journey in the book. The Song manages to focus the Israelites' (the audience's?) intense feelings in a way that neither the ritual of Chapters 12–13 nor even the semi-poetic description of God's miraculous intervention in Chapter 14 can do. Only poetry is capable of expressing the full range of the people's emotions about what has happened. This is similar to the effect of the great poems that occur toward the end of Genesis (Chap. 49, the Blessing of Yaakov) and Deuteronomy (Chaps. 32–33, the Song and Blessing of Moshe).

A major concern of the poet is God's kingship, with which he ends the poem (a one-liner—"Let YHWH be king for the ages, eternity!"—contrasting with the doublets and triplets in the body of the poem). This is no accident, nor is it inappropriate; since Chapters 4 and 5 the story of

24 **morning-watch:** Before sunrise; the biblical night was divided into three "watches." **stirred up:** Others, "threw into panic." The phrase is used in the Bible to describe God's effect on his enemies (e.g., Josh. 10:10, Jud. 4:15, I Sam. 7:10) (Hyatt 1971).

25 **heaviness:** Again, possibly a play on Pharaoh's "heaviness" (stubbornness) and God's "glory."

27 **face:** Or "turning," which, however, would have clashed with the frequent "returning" (another Hebrew verb) in these verses. **original-place:** Others, "bed," "normal depth."

30–31 **saw . . . saw:** The key verb again, echoing back not only to verse 13 but to various narratives throughout the book.

15:1 **uttered (this) utterance:** Giving a wider range of meaning for the Hebrew *va-yomeru le'mor*. **triumphed:** A rendering based on Ugaritic.

the horse and its charioteer
he flung into the sea!

2   My fierce-might and strength is YAH,
     he has become deliverance for me.

     This is my God—I honor him,
     the God of my father—I exalt him.

3   YHWH is a man of war,
     YHWH is his name!

4   Pharaoh's chariots and his forces
     he hurled into the sea,
     his choicest teams-of-three
     sank in the Sea of Reeds.
5   Oceans covered them,
     they went down in the depths
     like a stone.

6   Your right-hand, O YHWH,
     majestic in power,
     your right-hand, O YHWH,
     shattered the enemy.

7   In your great triumph
     you smashed your foes,
     you sent forth your fury,
     consumed them like chaff.

8   By the breath of your nostrils
     the waters piled up,
     the gushing-streams stood up like a dam,
     the oceans congealed in the heart of the sea.

9   Uttered the enemy:
     I will pursue,
     overtake,
     and apportion the plunder,
     my greed will be filled on them,

            my sword I will draw,
            my hand—dispossess them!
10   You blew with your breath,
            the sea covered them,
            they plunged down like lead
            in majestic waters.

11   Who is like you among the gods, O YHWH!
            who is like you, majestic among the holy-ones,
            Feared-One of praises, Doer of Wonders!

12   You stretched out your right-hand,
            the Underworld swallowed them.

Exodus has revolved around just who shall be king (God or Pharaoh) and just who shall be served. By the end of Chapter 14 this is no longer an issue. The victorious YHWH can now be acclaimed as king, while we hear nothing further of Pharaoh. (Has he drowned or merely been written out of the story? Later generations of Jews enjoyed giving him a role in the world to come: he stands at the gate of Hell, admonishing evildoers as they enter; see Ginzberg 1937.)

    The attempts to recover what happened at the sea through the poem are doomed to failure, considering that the piece is constructed out of two traditional stories, the victory at the sea and the later conquest of Canaan (vv.1–12, 13–17). Further, it is set in cosmic terms. The words "Oceans"

   2 **strength:** Others, "song."   **YAH:** A shortened form (YH) of the name of God (YHWH), and found often in biblical names (e.g., Uriah).
   3 **man of war:** Or "warrior."
   6 **right-hand:** As elsewhere in the ancient and medieval world, the right hand was symbolic of strength.
   8 **piled up:** Heb. root *'rm*, found only here.
   9 **Uttered the enemy . . .:** The Hebrew uses alliteration, as well as a concentration on "I/my," to express the vividness and urgency of the enemy's greed: *'amar 'oyev/ 'erdof 'asig/ 'ahallek shallal.* I have tried to use alliterative English words ("uttered. . . . enemy/I. . . . overtake . . . and apportion") and at least to hint at the poetic force of the Hebrew.   **greed:** The Hebrew (*nefesh*) means "seat of feelings, emotions"; trad. "soul."
  11 **among the gods:** The sea is the scene of YHWH's final triumph over the gods of Egypt, as it were.
  12 **Underworld:** Others, "earth."

13   You led in your faithfulness
      your people redeemed,
      guided (them) in your fierce-might
      to your holy pasture.

14   The peoples heard,
      they shuddered;
      frenzy seized
      Philistia's settlers,
15   and then, terrified,
      Edom's chieftains,
      Moav's "rams"—
      trembling did seize them;
      then melted away
      all Canaan's settlers.

16   There fell upon them
      dread and anguish;
      before your arm's greatness
      they grew dumb like stone.

      Until they crossed—your people, O YHWH,
      until they crossed—the people you fashioned.
17   You brought them, you planted them
       on the mount of your heritage,
       foundation of your (royal) seat
       which you prepared, O YHWH,
       the Holy-Place, O Lord,
       founded by your hands.

(Heb. *tehomot*; vv.5, 8) and "breath" (*ru'ah*; v.8) recall the primeval chaos
at the beginning of Creation itself (Gen. 1:2). This technique is characteristic of much of ancient/religious literature: a great event is told in a way
that reflects the beginnings of the gods/the world (this may include statements about the end of the world as well).
   It should be noted that some scholars point out the close resemblance
between God's victory here and scenes in other ancient Near Eastern
literatures that portray the triumph of a storm god over a sea god. So

however historical the events in Chapters 14–15 may have been, in their biblical retelling they have been patterned after antecedents in myth.

Much has been written concerning the structure of the Song (see, e.g., Cassuto 1967, Cross 1973, and Lichtenstein 1984). I will mention only a few points here. The vocabulary of the poem is extremely concentrated. Major ideas are expressed by clusters of key verbs. Note, for instance, the grouping of "flung," "hurled," "plunged," "shattered," "smashed," "consumed"—a veritable lexicon of military victory. A number of verbs describe divine leadership ("led," "guided," "brought"), and God's establishment of the Israelites in Canaan ("planted," "founded"). The fear of the Canaanites (of Israel and its God) is graphically expanded to "shuddered," "seized with frenzy," "terrified," "seized with trembling," "melted away," ". . . dread and anguish," and "grew dumb." Finally, there are a number of nouns that express weight (cf. Heb. *kaved*, previously discussed): "stone," "dam," and "lead."

The overall effect of the poem is of fierce pride at God's victory, and exultant description of the destruction and discomfort of enemies, whether Egyptian or Canaanite. This general tone parallels many ancient war poems; what is characteristically Israelite about it is God's choosing and leading a people. Therefore the last verse goes far beyond the celebration of a single military victory. The Song constitutes the founding of a theocratic people.

Scholars have long noted the archaic style of the Song, which uses forms characteristic of early biblical Hebrew. Its tone is for this reason even more exalted than is usual in biblical poetry. An imaginative reflection of the effect can be found in Daiches (1975), who paraphrases the Song in the style of early English epic poetry.

Two sections have been appended to the end of the poem. First there is the poetically remarkable summary of the narrative in verse 19, notable for the fact that it is composed wholly from phrases used in Chapter 14. There follows a women's repetition/performance of at least part of the Song complete with dance. Some scholars see this as the "original" form of the poem. Of equal interest is the characterization of Miryam as a "prophet-

13 **holy pasture:** A shepherd's term, which could indicate the entire land of Canaan, and hence support the background of the Conquest in the poem (Childs 1974).

14–15 **Philistia . . . Edom . . . Moav:** Israel's later (and hostile) neighbors, to the west and east.

15 **"rams":** Perhaps, as in Ugaritic usage, a technical term for "chieftains."

17 **mount . . . foundation . . . holy-place:** Probably the Jerusalem Temple of later times, although the entire land is sometimes referred to as "mount of your inheritance" (see Deut. 3:25) (Hertz 1960).

18   Let YHWH be king
        for the ages, eternity!

19 For Pharaoh's horses came with (their) chariots and riders
        into the sea,
    but YHWH turned back the sea's waters upon them,
    and the Children of Israel went upon the dry-land
    through the midst of the sea.

20 Now Miryam the prophetess, Aharon's sister, took a timbrel
        in her hand,
    and all the women went out after her, with timbrels and with
        dancing.
21 Miryam chanted to them:

        Sing to YHWH,
        for he has triumphed, yes, triumphed,
        the horse and its charioteer
        he flung into the sea!

ess." But there may be a structural reason for her appearance as well: the
enterprise of deliverance from Egypt began with a little girl at the Nile,
watching through the reeds to make sure her baby brother would survive;
it ends with the same person, now an adult, a "prophetess" celebrating the
final victory at the Sea of Reeds.

    20 **Miryam the prophetess:** Trad. English "Miriam." This is the first time
        in the narrative that she is mentioned by name, and also the first appear-
        ance of a "prophetess" in the Hebrew Bible.

PART II In the Wilderness

(15:22–18:27)

T HE WILDERNESS narratives in the Torah must have been extraordinarily important to the narrator/editor, as evidenced by their placement at this point in Exodus. Why did he/they see fit to insert here material which, chronologically at least, would fit better at a later point—for instance, in the book of Numbers (which reports essentially the same sort of incidents)?

The answer comes from several quarters. The wilderness stories embody a key process for the Torah story: Israel's passage from enslaved childhood to troubled adolescence, with a hopeful glance toward adulthood (the Promised Land). This process starts immediately after liberation; indeed, it is its direct result. Further, the three "desert themes" prominent in Chapters 15–18—"grumbling" against God and Moshe, hostile neighbors, and early self-government—are appropriate to include before the meeting at Sinai, in that they demonstrate dramatically the people's need for reassurance, protection, group solidarity, and institutions (whereby they can live harmoniously). These narratives, therefore, lay out Israel's precarious position and create the hope for a cure. It is only later on in the Torah, in the book of Numbers, that we will discover that the growing-up process in the wilderness could not be accomplished in a single generation.

The portrait of a people (or of an individual, as is often the case in religious literature) undergoing transformation in a place outside of normal geographic/cultural boundaries is a well-known phenomenon in traditional stories. Anthropologist Victor Turner (1969) speaks of the "liminal" experience, where the protagonist or initiant is separated spiritually and geographically from his origins in order to be changed into something new (see Fredman 1983, Cohn 1981). This is paralleled by the process of pilgrimage in the world of ritual, as can still be observed among many communities of the world to this day. The desert is the site of liminality par excellence: it is a harsh place that contains none of the succoring elements of human civilization, yet at the same time it leads the wanderer into truer communication with nature and the divine, metacultural forces of the universe. It is a place of betwixt and between, which mirrors the experiencer's psychological state. In the case of Israel, later biblical sources speak of the wilderness period with striking force, either as an example of the people's long-standing and deeply ingrained rebelliousness (e.g., Psalm 95), or fondly, as a kind of honeymoon period between God and Israel (e.g., Jer. 2:2). In both cases what is evoked is only a stage on the way, and not the final goal (see Talmon 1966).

Transformation always involves both life and death, and so it is not surprising that a characteristic theme of the stories before us is lack of food and/or water. The opening episodes of the section (15:22–17:7) comprise three scenes of "grumbling" about the difficulties of survival (with the structure: water–food–water), with a unique biblical twist: God and the people "testing" each other. And so the transformation depends very much on God's action on the people's behalf (twice he has to "instruct" them—the very verb from which the term "Torah" is derived). The suspension of the life process, or at least its imperiling, is notable also in the fact that, in contrast to the fertility of the Israelites in Egypt, "the trek narrative does not relate a single birth" (Cohn 1981). This is especially striking given the strong birth image of Israel at the Sea of Reeds, which is still in the reader's mind as the section opens.

22 Moshe had Israel move on from the Sea of Reeds,
      and they went out to the Wilderness of Shur.
      They traveled through the wilderness for three days, and
         found no water.
23 They came to Mara,
      but they could not drink water from Mara, because it was
         mar/bitter.
      Therefore they called its name Mara.
24 The people grumbled against Moshe, saying:
      What are we to drink?
25 He cried out to YHWH,
      and YHWH directed him (to some) wood

which he threw into the water, and the water became
    sweet.—

There he imposed law and judgment for them, and there he
    tested them.

26 He said:

If you will hearken, yes, hearken to the voice of YHWH
    your God,

and what is right in his eyes will do,

giving-ear to his commandments

and keeping all his laws:

all the sicknesses which I have imposed upon Egypt, I will
    not impose upon you;

for I am YHWH, your healer.

Grumbling I (15:22-27): The first of the wilderness narratives is linked to what has gone before via the theme of water. Fresh from their rescue from death at the sea, the Israelites look for water in the desert and find the discovery of unpotable water intolerable. The key word, especially for the many later wilderness traditions such as we find in Numbers, is "grumbled" (Heb. *lyn*), which leads to God's nurturing of the people. Strangely, the theme of undrinkable water recalls the beginning of the plague sequence in Egypt (7:20-21).

Right away in this first desert episode we are told the purpose of Israel's journey: God is testing them, to see if they will "hearken" to what he bids them to do. The language is in the style of Deuteronomy. One should also mention the idea of "law and judgment," indicating another crucial desert theme: Israel's ability or inability to govern itself.

The account ends with an abundance of water in verse 27.

22 **Shur:** Some translate as "Wall" (of Egypt)—the outer fortified boundary of the country, and hence the edge of civilization.

24 **grumbled:** Others, "murmured," which is, however, more alliterative than the Hebrew itself (*va-yilonu*).

25 **There he imposed law and judgment:** Others, "There he made for them statute and ordinance," etc. The force is not clear, but the phrase seems to fit in with the overall section, which, as I have noted, concerns itself with the Israelites' early government.

26 **sicknesses . . . upon Egypt:** A recurring theme in the Torah; see the curse in Deut. 28:60.

27 They came to Elim;
there were twelve springs of water
and seventy palms,
and they camped there by the water.

16:1 They moved on from Elim, and they came, the whole community of the Children of Israel, to the Wilderness of Syn,
which is between Elim and Sinai,
on the fifteenth day of the second New-Moon after their
going-out from the land of Egypt.
2 And they grumbled, the whole community of the Children of
Israel, against Moshe and against Aharon in the wilderness.
3 The Children of Israel said to them:
Would that we had died by the hand of YHWH in the land
of Egypt,
when we sat by the flesh pots,
when we ate bread till (we were) sated!
For you have brought us into this wilderness
to bring death to this whole assembly by starvation!
4 YHWH said to Moshe:
Here, I will make rain down upon you bread from the heavens,
the people shall go out and glean, each day's amount in its
day,
in order that I may test them, whether they will walk according to my instruction or not.
5 But is shall be on the sixth day:
when they prepare what they have brought in,
it shall be a double-portion compared to what they glean day
after day.
6 Moshe and Aharon said to all the Children of Israel:
In the evening
you will know
that it is YHWH who brought you out of the land of Egypt;
7 in the morning
you will see the Glory of YHWH:
when he hearkens to your grumblings against YHWH—
what are we, that you grumble against us?
8 Moshe said:
Since YHWH gives you

flesh to eat in the evening,

and in the morning, bread to sate (yourselves);

since YHWH hearkens to your grumblings which you
   grumble against him—

what are we:

not against us are your grumblings, but against YHWH!

9 Moshe said to Aharon:

Say to the whole community of the Children of Israel:

Come-near, in the presence of YHWH,

for he has hearkened to your grumblings!

10 Now it was, when Aharon spoke to the whole community of
   the Children of Israel,

they faced the wilderness,

and here:

the Glory of YHWH could be seen in the cloud.

11 YHWH spoke to Moshe, saying:

Grumbling II (16): Moving now halfway (in terms of time) to their Sinai
destination, the people encounter a new lack: food. This reintroduces the
"testing" motif (v.4), with its built-in answer: God provides quails and
mahn (trad. English "manna"). The story is full-blown, and its repeating
vocabulary sets forth the issues clearly: "grumble" occurs seven times,
and "command/commandments" four times, linked to the idea of testing.

27 **Elim:** Lit., "terebinths" (great trees already mentioned in Gen. 12:6 and
   18:1). **twelve springs . . . seventy palms:** Once again the numbers are
   obviously typological.

16:1 **whole community:** See the note to 12:3. **Syn:** Pronounced "seen." The
   present spelling has been adopted to avoid the unfortunate associations of
   the sound "sin" in English.

3 **Egypt . . . flesh pots . . .:** Notice the endings of each line, which can be
   grouped into two clusters: "Egypt . . . flesh pots . . . sated" versus
   "wilderness . . . starvation."

4 **YHWH said:** Notice how God's answer is totally devoid of anger, for the
   dissatisfaction of the people is to provide them with a "test." **them . . .
   they:** The pronouns are collective singular in Hebrew.

5 **a double-portion:** For the Sabbath, when no gleaning is permitted.

7 **what are we:** The issue is not between Israel and its human leaders, but
   really between them and God.

8 **bread:** See the note to 2:20.

9 **Come-near:** See the note to 12:48.

12 I have hearkened to the grumblings of the Children of
      Israel—
   speak to them, and say:
   At twilight you shall eat flesh,
   and in the morning you shall be sated with bread,
   and you shall know
   that I am YHWH your God.
13 Now it was in the evening
   a horde-of-quail came up and covered the camp.
   And in the morning
   there was a layer of dew around the camp;
14 and when the layer of dew went up,
   here, upon the surface of the wilderness,
   something fine,
   scaly,
   fine as hoar-frost upon the land.
15 When the Children of Israel saw it
   they said each-man to his brother:
   Mahn hu/what is it?
   For they did not know what it was.
   Moshe said to them:
   It is the bread that YHWH has given you for eating.
16 This is the word that YHWH has commanded:
   Glean from it, each-man according to what he can eat,
   an *omer* per capita, according to the number of your persons,
   each-man, for those in his tent, you are to take.
17 The Children of Israel did thus,
   they gleaned, the-one-more and the-one-less,
18 but when they measured by the *omer*,
   no surplus had the one-more, and the-one-less had no short-
      age;
   each-man had gleaned according to what he could eat.
19 Moshe said to them:
   No man shall leave any of it until morning.
20 But they did not hearken to Moshe,
   and (several) men left some of it until morning;
   it became wormy with maggots and reeked.
   And Moshe became furious with them.
21 They gleaned it morning after morning, each-man in accor-
      dance with what he could eat,

but when the sun heated up, it melted.

22 Now it was on the sixth day

that they gleaned a double-portion of bread, two *omers* for
(each) one.

All the exalted-ones of the community came and told it to
Moshe.

Indeed, this long story poses the question central to all the wilderness
narratives: ". . . whether they will walk according to my instruction or
not" (v.4).

The manna was important in early Israelite tradition as a witness to
God's nurturing, as attested by the end of the chapter with its ritual
prescriptions regarding it (vv.32–34; note the threefold repetition of
"safekeeping"). But it also sets up an emphasis on a more permanent
institution in Israelite culture: the Sabbath. One notion that this passage
may convey is the antiquity and importance of the Sabbath, preceding the
laws of Sinai as it does here. Also at issue is whether the Israelites can
follow simple rules laid down by God.

14 **something fine:** The *mahn* (trad. English "manna"), described again in
verse 31, below, possibly refers to insect secretions found on the branches
of certain Sinai plants. The question has been asked, however, as to
whether the amount so produced would under normal circumstances be
sufficient to feed a large population—hence the text itself stresses the
divine element, and any attempt to explain it scientifically misses the point
of the biblical story.

15 **Mahn hu:** A folk etymological corruption of the Hebrew *mah hu*, although
there is some support for this form in other Semitic languages. A playful
rendering might be "whaddayacallit" or "what's-its-name."

16 **omer:** A dry measure, approximately 2 ⅓ liters or 2 dry quarts.

17 **the-one:** Or "some of them."

18 **no surplus . . . no shortage:** In the tradition of miracle stories, exactly
the right amount is found for each person.

19 **No man shall leave any of it until morning:** Like the Passover sacrifice in
12:10 and 34:25, or the festival-offering in 23:18. The idea may be not to
disturb the perfection of the offering by risking putrefaction.

22 **exalted-ones:** Or "princes."

23 He said to them:
It is what YHWH spoke about:
tomorrow is a Sabbath/Ceasing, a Sabbath of Holiness for
   YHWH.
Whatever you wish to bake—bake, and whatever you wish
   to boil—boil;
and all the surplus, put aside for yourselves in safekeeping
   until morning.
24 **They put it aside until the morning, as Moshe had
   commanded,**
and it did not reek, neither were there any maggots in it.
25 Moshe said:
Eat it today,
for today is a Sabbath for YHWH,
today you will not find it in the field.
26 For six days you are to glean,
but on the seventh day is Sabbath, there will not be (any) on it.
27 But it was on the seventh day
that some of the people went out to glean, and they did not
   find.
28 YHWH said to Moshe:
Until when will you refuse to keep my commandments and
   my instructions?
29 (You) see
that YHWH has given you the Sabbath,
therefore on the sixth day, he gives you bread for two days.
Stay, each-man, in his spot;
no man shall go out from his place on the seventh day!
30 So the people ceased on the seventh day.
31 Now the House of Israel called its name: *Mahn.*
—It is like coriander seed, whitish,
and its taste is like (that of) a wafer with honey.—
32 Moshe said:
This is the word that YHWH has commanded:
An *omer*-full of it for safekeeping throughout your generations,
in order that they may see the bread that I had you eat in the
   wilderness
when I brought you out of the land of Egypt.
33 Moshe said to Aharon:
Take a vat and put an *omer*-full of *mahn* in it,

and put it aside in the presence of YHWH, in safekeeping throughout your generations.

34 As YHWH had commanded Moshe, Aharon put it aside before the Testimony, in safekeeping.

35 And the Children of Israel ate the *mahn* for the forty years, until they came to settled land,
the *mahn* they ate, until they came to the edge of the land of Canaan.

36 Now an *omer*—a tenth of an *efa* it is.

17:1 They moved on, the whole commmunity of the Children of Israel, from the Wilderncss of Syn,
by their moving-stages, at YHWH's bidding.
They encamped at Refidim,
and there is no water for the people to drink!

2 The people quarreled with Moshe, they said:
Give us water, that we may drink!
Moshe said to them:
For-what do you quarrel with me?
For-what do you test YHWH?

Grumbling III (17:1–7): With the third wilderness story we return to the water theme. This time the element of "quarreling" with Moshe is added, in addition to the portrayal of Moshe's eroding patience (v.4). Otherwise it is a variation on the basic theme (notice, for instance, the similarities between 16:3 and 17:3). The ending is ominous, reversing the previously held idea of God's testing Israel.

23 **It is what YHWH spoke about:** Although this speech is not mentioned in a previous text. This may support the position that the story was originally placed after Chapter 20 (which contains the command to observe the Sabbath). **Ceasing:** The root meaning of the Hebrew *shabbat*, "Sabbath."

24 **it did not reek:** Since this time they followed God's orders.

28 **you:** Plural, referring to the people.

31 **Now . . . honey:** A parenthetical comment. For another biblical description of the manna, see Num. 11:8.

34 **Testimony:** The tablets of the covenant mentioned in 25:21 and 31:18; their citing seems out of place here, but it should be borne in mind that the Torah is not always chronological, as was already recognized by medieval commentators.

17:2 **For-what:** Why. Notice how the text equates quarreling with Moshe and testing YHWH. **quarrel:** A verb that often denotes a legal case in biblical texts.

3 The people thirsted for water there,
and the people grumbled against Moshe, and said:
For-what-reason then did you bring us up from Egypt,
to bring death to me, to my children and to my livestock by
thirst?

4 Moshe cried out to YHWH, saying:
What shall I do with this people?
A little more and they will stone me!

5 YHWH said to Moshe:
Proceed before the people,
take some of the elders of Israel with you,
and your staff with which you struck the Nile, take in your
hand,
and go!

6 Here, I stand before you there on the rock at Horev,
you are to strike the rock, and water shall come out of it, and
the people shall drink.
Moshe did thus, before the eyes of the elders of Israel.

7 And he called the name of the place: *Massa*/Testing, and
Meriva/Quarreling,
because of the quarreling of the Children of Israel,
and because of their testing of YHWH, saying:
Is YHWH among us, or not?

8 Now Amalek came and made war upon Israel in Refidim.

9 Moshe said to Yehoshua:
Choose us men,
and go out, make war upon Amalek!
On the morrow I will station myself on top of the hill, with
the staff of God in my hand.

10 Yehoshua did as Moshe had said to him,
to make war against Amalek.
Now Moshe, Aharon and Hur went up to the top of the hill.

11 And it was, whenever Moshe raised his hand, Israel prevailed, and whenever he set down his hand, Amalek
prevailed.

12 Now Moshe's hands are heavy;
so they took a stone and placed it under him, and he sat
down on it,
while Aharon and Hur supported his hands, one on this-side
and one on that-side.

So his hands remained steadfast, until the sun came in.

13 And Yehoshua weakened Amalek and his people, with the
   edge of the sword.

14 YHWH said to Moshe:
   Write this as a memorial in an account
   and put it in Yehoshua's hearing:
   Yes, I will wipe out, wipe out the memory of Amalek from
   under the heavens!

War with Amalek (17:8–16): In addition to testing/grumbling, conflict
with foreigners is a significant wilderness theme (see Num. 20–24). It is
perhaps for this reason that it has been included in the pre-Sinai traditions. Its placement here may depend on its use of Moshe's staff; the
previous narrative ended with the use of that object, and such linkage was
a known form of composition in ancient literature.

The tradition about Israel's relationship with Amalek, however brief,
persists as an important one in the Bible. Saul, Israel's first king, is
commanded by God to wipe out the Amalekites, as punishment for their
opposition of Israel in our passage (I Sam. 15), and centuries later, Ha-
man, the evil Persian councillor who proposes to exterminate the Jews of
his country, is portrayed as a descendant of the Amalekite king (Esther
3:1).

Our story, however, is no mere military report, but also a tradition
about the power of the "staff of God." In another culture, indeed in later
Midrashic literature, such a theme would receive Excalibur-like treatment, but the Bible suppresses the magical side and simply uses it as a
tool, expressing God's continuing deliverance of Israel.

3 **me:** Personalizing the complaint.

6 **you are to strike the rock:** See Num. 20:2–13 for the famous variation on
   this story that proves to be Moshe's undoing.

7 **saying:** Meaning or signifying.

9 **Yehoshua:** Trad. English "Joshua." The name means "God delivers."
   He appears subsequently as Moshe's personal attendant, but it is significant that the first mention of him is in a military context, since he will
   ultimately command the invasion of Canaan.

10 **Hur:** He is mentioned again in 24:4 as Aharon's assistant in the governing
   of the people during Moshe's absence.

12 **sun came in:** Set.

13 **weakened:** Disabled or defeated.

14 **account:** Or "document." **wipe out the memory:** The command demonstrates the depth of Israel's animosity toward Amalek.

15 Moshe built an altar
    and called its name: YHWH My Banner.
16 He said:
    Yes,
    Hand on YAH's throne!
    War for YHWH against Amalek
    generation after generation!

18:1 Now Yitro, the priest of Midyan, Moshe's father-in-law,
        heard
      about all that God had done for Moshe and for Israel his
        people,
      that YHWH had brought Israel out of Egypt.
   2 Yitro, Moshe's father-in-law, took
      Tzippora, Moshe's wife—after she had been sent home—
   3 and her two sons,
      of whom the first-one's name was Gershom/Sojourner
        There, for he had said: I have become a sojourner in a
        foreign land,
   4 and the name of the other was Eliezer/God's-Help, for: the
        God of my father is my help, he rescued me from Pha-
        raoh's sword;
   5 Yitro, Moshe's father-in-law, came with his sons and his
        wife to Moshe, to the wilderness, where he was encamped,
      at the mountain of God.
   6 He (had it) said to Moshe:
      I, your father-in-law Yitro, am coming to you, and your wife
        and her two sons with her.
   7 Moshe went out to meet his father-in-law,
      he bowed and kissed him, and each-man asked after the
        other's welfare;
      then they came into the tent.
   8 Moshe related to his father-in-law
      all that YHWH had done to Pharaoh and to Egypt on Is-
        rael's account,
      all the hardships that had befallen them on the journey,
      and how YHWH had rescued them.
   9 And Yitro was jubilant because of all the good that YHWH
      had done for Israel, that he had rescued him from the land
      of Egypt.

10   Yitro said:
      Blessed be YHWH,
      who has rescued you from the hand of Egypt and from the
        hand of Pharaoh,
      who has rescued the people from under the hand of Egypt.

The New Society: Yitro's Visit (18): Israel finally reaches the "mountain of God," but this, remarkably, is subordinated to the fact that Moshe and the people meet up with Yitro, whom we recall from Chapters 2–4. The designation "father-in-law" recurs throughout this chapter (thirteen times), perhaps playing up the importance of the relationship in Israelite society. The real concern of the story, however, is Moshe's early attempt to set up a functioning judicial system in Israel (hence the key word *davar*, ten times, translated here as "matter" in the sense of "legal matter"). The chapter thus

15   **altar:** B-R use "slaughter-site" to reflect the Hebrew root *zavo'ah* in this
      word *(mizbe'ah)*, and I originally followed them in *In the Beginning*. How-
      ever, this is not fully acceptable, since by the time of the Bible, not only were
      grain and other nonanimal products offered up on Israelite altars, but the
      slaughtering of animals for sacrifices took place near and not on them.
      Hence the familiar English "altar" (which stems from a Latin word denoting
      "high place") will have to suffice. Where *zavo'ah* occurs in our text as a verb,
      I have retained the translation "slaughter."
16   **Hand on:** Cassuto (1967) suggests "monument to," following the mean-
      ing of *yad* in I Sam. 15:12, II Sam. 18:18, and other instances.   **throne:**
      Heb. *kes*, either a corruption of the more standard *kisse* or, most probably,
      a scribal error for *nes*, "banner," as in verse 15.
18:3 **he:** Moshe, in 2:22, above.
   4 **Eliezer:** This is the first and only time we hear of this son.   **he rescued
      me from Pharaoh's sword:** Here, as sometimes occurs in the biblical text,
      we learn of earlier events or emotions. Moshe's emotional makeup while
      he was in Midyan (Chaps. 2–4) thus becomes a little clearer.
   5 **at the mountain of God:** Another important fact has been casually slipped
      in at this point, again probably from a narrative taking place later. In the
      next chapter Israel's arrival at Sinai will be more dramatically heralded.
   8 **YHWH had rescued them:** The verb was used above in relation to
      Moshe, and is a key repeating word in this chapter. Thus the experience of
      leader and people unite again, and the narrative of deliverance comes full
      circle. Moshe had begun his mission at Sinai, as a member of Yitro's
      household, and now the latter meets him in Sinai, on the brink of the
      confirmation of 3:12 ("you will serve God on this mountain").
   9 **jubilant:** Heb. *va-yihd*, from *hdy*, a rare verb.
  10 **who has rescued the people:** There is obviously a redundancy in this
      verse, based perhaps on a scribal error.

11 (So) now I know:
yes, YHWH is greater than all gods—
yes, in just that matter in which they were presumptuous
   against them!
12 Yitro, Moshe's father-in-law, took an offering-up and
   slaughter-animals for God,
and Aharon and all the elders of Israel came to eat bread
   with Moshe's father-in-law, in the presence of God.
13 Now it was on the morrow:
Moshe sat to judge the people,
and the people stood before Moshe from morning until
   evening.
14 When Moshe's father-in-law saw all that he had to do for the
   people,
he said:
What kind of matter is this that you do for the people—
why do you sit alone, while the entire people stations itself
   around you
from morning until evening?
15 Moshe said to his father-in-law:
When the people comes to me to inquire of God,
16 —when it has some legal-matter, it comes to me—
I judge between a man and his fellow
and make known God's laws and his instructions.
17 Then Moshe's father-in-law said to him:
Not good is this matter, as you do it!
18 You will become worn out, yes, worn out, so you, so this
   people that are with you,
for this matter is too heavy for you,
you cannot do it alone.
19 So now, hearken to my voice,
I will advise you, so that God may be-there with you:
Be-there, yourself, for the people in relation to God.
You yourself should have the matters come to God;
20 You should make clear to them the laws and the instructions,
you should make known to them the way they should go,
   and the deeds that they should do;
21 but you—you are to have the vision (to select) from all the
   people
men of caliber, fearing God,

men of truth, hating gain,
you should set (them) over them
as chiefs of thousands, chiefs of hundreds, chiefs of fifties,
   and chiefs of tens,
22 so that they may judge the people at all times.
So shall it be:
every great matter they shall bring before you,
but every small matter they shall judge by themselves.
Make (it) light upon you, and let them bear (it) with you.

serves as a good prelude to Sinai, which will include far-ranging legal material (despite the fact that some scholars see it as an insertion from a later
period—cf. verse 16, "God's laws and his instructions").

It has been noted (Cohn 1981) that the "trek narratives" in Exodus and
Numbers have been laid out evenly, with six "stations" between Egypt
and Sinai and another six between Sinai and the land of Israel. Thus here,
Israel has come to the mid-point of its journey. In another perspective,
Moshe himself has come full circle, returning to both the spot and the man
in whose presence the mature adult phase of his life had begun.

11 **in just that matter:** Heb. difficult; others either omit this phrase altogether, or use complex English constructions to reproduce it (e.g., "for he
did this to those who treated Israel arrogantly," "for he has routed the
mighty foes of his folk"). **they were presumptuous:** The Egyptians.

12 **in the presence of God:** An expression that usually carries a cultic meaning (Levine 1974).

14 **all that he had to do:** Compare verses 8 and 9, where the great "doing" of
God is accomplished with ease. Perhaps a contrast is being drawn between
divine and human deeds; Moshe cannot do the "all" that God can.

18 **heavy:** Again the key word that was mentioned earlier (see the note to
14:4); it aids in linking up stories, as it has occurred in 17:12.

21 **the vision (to select):** The verb "see" in Hebrew (*ra'oh*) also has the
connotation of "select" (cf. Gen. 22:8). **caliber:** A term often used in a
military context (see Jud. 11:1, 18:2).

22 **at all times:** That is, in minor matters—as we would say, "everyday
affairs."

23 If you do (thus in) this matter
   when God commands you (further), you will be able to
      stand,
   and also this people will come to its place in peace.
24 Moshe hearkened to the voice of his father-in-law,
   he did it all as he had said:
25 Moshe chose men of caliber from all Israel,
   he placed them as heads over the people,
   as chiefs of thousands, chiefs of hundreds, chiefs of fifties,
      and chiefs of tens.
26 They would judge the people at all times:
   the difficult matters they would bring before Moshe,
   but every small matter they would judge by themselves.
27 Moshe sent his father-in-law off,
   and he went home to his land.

23 **stand:** Endure.
27 **sent . . . off/ . . . went . . . to his land:** A stock biblical farewell passage
   (see Num. 24:25, for instance).

PART **III** The Meeting and
Covenant at Sinai
(19–24)

T HE NARRATIVE has returned to its source. At Sinai it had been
foretold that when Pharaoh "sends you free, you will serve God on this
mountain," and it is at Sinai that Moshe and the people now arrive. The
fateful public meeting between the deity and the amassed human community will betoken the formal change of masters: the people, no longer
enslaved by the Egyptian crown, now swear fealty to their divine Lord,
who imposes rules of conduct upon them in return for his protection and
their well-being.

The settings for these events of covenant-making and law-giving are
appropriately impressive. The mountain naturally functions as a bridge
between heaven and earth (with only Moshe allowed to ascend!), but it is
additionally accompanied on this occasion by the powerful manifestations
of smoke, fire, cloud, thunder, lightning, and trumpet blasts. To try and
pin down exactly to what natural phenomena the story alludes, be they
volcano, earthquake, or the like, is somewhat beside the point; what
speaks through the text is the voice of an overwhelming experience. Indeed, as Greenberg (1972) points out, the account in Chapter 19 may have
been deliberately left ambiguous and contradictory, showing that the editor wished to include all the received traditions about the event.

At the same time, it should be noted that the Sinai revelation resembles
the appearance of the storm-god Baal in Canaanite texts, especially in the
combining of thunder/lightning and earthquake. Psalm 18:8 portrays a
similar scene. So as varied as the phenomena accompanying God's appearance here are, they conform to a known literary pattern (Greenstein
1984c).

As mentioned previously, Sinai stands geographically at the center of
the Israelite wanderings. As the textual center of the book of Exodus as

well, it anchors the people of Israel on their journey toward the fulfillment of their destiny. But that function is purely a mythic one. Sinai never became an important biblical cult site, and the only later story to take place there, that of Elijah in I Kings 20, clearly stems from the desire to draw a parallel between Elijah and Moshe. The Hebrews apparently could not conceive of God's abiding place's being located outside the land of Israel. On the other hand, it was necessary to demonstrate that Israel's laws and institutions arose, not out of normal settled political and economic circumstances, but rather as the direct gift and stipulation of God himself (see Cohn 1981), and hence the choice of a site wholly removed from the great culture centers of the ancient Near East: the monolithic culture of Egypt, the ancestral heritage of Mesopotamia, and the fertility-based society the people were to encounter in Canaan. Sinai, the originating point of Israel as a self-defined community, had to start everything anew, on a stage in which all other considerations had been stripped away.

Early in the history of biblical exegesis (the Midrash) it was noted that the events on Sinai resemble the conclusion of a marriage ceremony. Such an idea may even have been in the minds of the transmitters of the Exodus traditions. Indeed, the entire book is remarkably reminiscent of a pattern of rescue—courting—wedding with stipulations—home planning—infidelity—reconciliation—and final "moving in" (these stages fit into the general Part divisions I have used throughout the book). Lest this appear to be too Western a model, let it be noted that such analogies occur in the writings of the prophets, where the relationship between God and Israel is likened to that between husband and wife. This constitutes Israel's version of what Joseph Campbell (1972) has termed "sacred marriage" in hero stories—not, as classically, the hero's successful wooing of a goddess or semi-divine creature, but an intimate relationship established between God and his people. As such, it is unique in the ancient world.

On Covenant

Marriage may be one imaginative model for the Sinai experience, but it was covenant that the writers wished to stress above all in these chapters. Here we observe a fascinating phenomenon that occurs again and again in biblical religion: an institution well known in the secular world is given a religious emphasis in the Bible. For covenant (others, "pact") was a widespread form of political bonding in the ancient Near East. Kings and vassals, from Anatolia to Assyria, regularly aligned themselves in treaties involving either freewill granting of privileges or an agreement of mutual obligations between parties. A number of texts laying out the stipulations and ceremonies particular to covenant-making in the ancient Near East have been recovered, and study of them is helpful for an understanding of what we have in Exodus 19–24. Three things are clear. First, the stylistic pattern in our chapters resembles what is found in Hittite treaty texts (Mendenhall 1954); second, the Exodus passages use narrative to express these events, not merely a list of conditions; third, and most important, no other ancient society, so far as we know, conceived of the possibility that a *god* could "cut a covenant" with a people. This last fact leads to the observation that, for Israel, the true king was not earthly but divine—despite the later establishment of a monarchy (Weinfeld 1972b). Hence the narrator's concentration on these chapters, especially considering the dramatic nature of what had gone before (Chaps. 1–15).

The covenant found in Exodus and subsequently in the Torah differs substantively from the two described in Genesis. Noah (Gen. 9) and all living creatures had been promised no further universal destruction, with the stipulation that human beings were not to eat meat with blood or commit willful murder. Avraham, too (Gen. 15, 17), was the recipient of a covenant: God would give him land and descendants, and Avraham was to attend to the circumcision of all his males (yet this is more sign than stipulation). What these early events have in common is the aspect of bestowal—God acts and promises, and human beings are the passive recipients. Exodus introduces the notes of mutuality and conditionality. Both parties are now to have a stake in the agreement, and it can be broken by either (as in Chapter 32; contrast this with the promise to Noah in Gen. 8:21–22, "I will never doom the soil again . . . never shall [natural processes] cease," and Gen. 9:11, "Never again shall there be Deluge. . . .") From the Creator God we have moved to the God of History, who enters into a fateful relationship with the people of Israel (for more on this, see Sarna 1986).

On Biblical Law

A century of modern Bible scholarship has led to far-reaching changes in the perceptions of biblical law. Initial archeological findings, which often included legal documents, had led comparativists to see in the biblical material a pale reflection of its Mesopotamian antecedents. The Code

of Hammurabi, for instance, was deemed the source of some of the Exodus material. These early judgments have given way to a view that places
more emphasis on what is distinctive about the biblical laws.

For our purposes here, several brief points should be made, drawn from
recent research; the reader may find them explored at greater depth in the
essays by Greenberg (1970), Greenstein (1984), Paul (1970), and Sarna
(1986), and the work of Sonsino (1980). Expressions of law in the ancient
Near East, especially in documents from Mesopotamia, reveal a strong
economic underpinning, tied to class structure. They also have at times a
personal or political function. Hammurabi, for instance, presents his code
with the express purpose that the gods and men may see what a just king
he is. The laws are listed by category, with religion occupying its own
sphere. Finally, the king acts as the enforcer of the laws, having received
them from a god—who is nevertheless not their ultimate source. Law
exists in the Mesopotamian texts as an abstract value, designed for the
smooth functioning of society.

By way of contrast, Hebrew law, as typified by our chapters, displays
very different concepts and concerns. Class is hardly alluded to, reflecting
a totally different kind of society economically but also expressing an ideal
that began in the Genesis creation story with the common ancestor of the
human race. The laws are presented as the terms of the covenant (our
section is often termed the "Book of the Covenant"), and the motivation
behind them is portrayed as historical/psychological (". . . for you were
sojourners in the land of Egypt"). Strikingly, the biblical regulations, not
only here but in the other major collections as well (in Leviticus and
Deuteronomy), blur the distinctions between religious and secular, and
treat all law as a matter directly related to God. He is perceived as the
source of laws; they are the expression of his will; and breaking them is a
direct affront to and act of rebellion against him (contrast, for example,
the modern American view).

The key concept behind much of biblical law seems to be that of Ex.
19:6, to make of the people of Israel "a holy nation." This expression,
which appears nowhere else in the Bible, combines a secular notion (the
Hebrew goy, meaning a political body, a state) with a sacral one: this
people is to transform all of its life into service of God. There is, therefore,
no subject in the code before us—slavery, social relations, torts, cult, or
diet—that is not of immediate concern to the biblical God. The first part
of 19:6, "a kingdom of priests" (Buber: "a king's-retinue of priests"),
would seem to suggest that despite the clear existence of a priestly group in

ancient Israel, the ideal approached a more democratic form of religious expression.

This leads us to posit a final question: Are the materials in Ex. 21–24 (and other texts in the Torah that enumerate laws) to be taken as actual regulations or cases, or as something else, rather more didactic? We have little evidence for the former view, and in fact other ancient Near Eastern legal documents such as the Hammurabi Code seem to point in the other (didactic) direction. Given the nature of Torah literature, where narrative has a teaching function rather than a purely historical one, it seems plausible that the legal texts as well were intended to elucidate principles of Israelite belief—to present, as it were, a world view. The other possibility, more in keeping with the history of law, is Daube's (1947) view that "many ancient codes regulate only matters as to which the law is dubious or in need of reform or both." In other words, law in day-to-day Israel was regulated by established precedents, and certainly not by Exodus 21–23, in the main. But in this case, too, our text would be instructive of the biblical mentality. For a fuller treatment of biblical law and its context in the ancient Near East, see Sarna 1986.

Any attempt to describe this section structurally is bound to run into a roadblock; perhaps precisely because of the Bible's desire *not* to distinguish between various categories of life, we do not have a watertight structure. Suffice it to say that, overall, most sections in these chapters begin with the general proposition "When . . ." (Heb. *ki*), and break down the issue under discussion into subsections begining with "If . . ." (Heb. ' *im*), a pattern found commonly in other legal systems as well. Beyond this, and the observation that there are some general categories and logical connections (for which, see the Commentary), one striking stylistic device in the Hebrew should be pointed out. From 21:5 through 23:24 a double verb form appears (infinitive absolute followed by the imperfect) fully twenty-seven times. The effect of this device, which is rhetorically emphatic, is to give a sense of coherence to what are otherwise quite diverse laws.

19:1 On the third New-Moon after the going-out of the Children
        of Israel from the land of Egypt,
      on that day
      they came to the Wilderness of Sinai.
   2 They moved on from Refidim and came to the Wilderness of
        Sinai,
      and encamped in the wilderness.
      There Israel encamped, opposite the mountain.
   3 Now Moshe went up to God,
      and YHWH called out to him from the mountain,
      saying:
      Say thus to the House of Yaakov,
      (yes,) tell the Children of Israel:
   4 You yourselves have seen
      what I did to Egypt,
      how I bore you on eagles' wings and brought you to me.
   5 So now,
      if you will hearken, yes, hearken to my voice
      and keep my covenant,
      you shall be to me a special-treasure from among all peoples.
      Indeed, all the earth is mine,
   6 but you, you shall be to me
      a kingdom of priests,
      a holy nation.
      These are the words that you are to speak to the Children of
        Israel.
   7 Moshe came, and had the elders of the people called,
      and set before them these words, with which YHWH had
        charged him.
   8 And all the people answered together, they said:
      All that YHWH has spoken, we will do.
      And Moshe reported the words of the people to YHWH.
   9 YHWH said to Moshe:
      Here, I am coming to you in a thick cloud,
      so that the people may hear when I speak with you,
      and also that they may have trust in you for ever.
      And Moshe told the words of the people to YHWH.
  10 YHWH said to Moshe:
      Go to the people,

make them holy, today and tomorrow,
let them wash their clothes,

The Meeting and the Covenant (19): The account of God's revelation at Sinai, like the narrative of the tenth plague and exodus, is embedded in a wider setting. After the covenant has been elucidated, the people assent; preparations are made to meet God; and the brief initial meeting is followed by more preparations, including stern warnings against trespassing on the mountain's sanctity. When one takes Chapter 20 into account, the effect of all this is anything but smooth, from a narrator's point of view, and I would agree with Greenberg (1969) that this may be deliberate—stemming from a desire either to include every tradition about this key event that was available to the editor(s), or else to suggest that such things are impossible to describe in normal language and logical sequence (Buber [1968], in another context, once referred to the Creation story of Genesis 1

19:1 **On the third:** The Hebrew omits the usual connecting *vav* ("now," "and," or "but"), and thus signals the start of a new narrative.

2 **There Israel encamped:** The repetition, as in 14:2, suggests poetry, perhaps a remnant of what Cassuto (1967) terms an epic literature here. The rhetorical force alerts the reader that something important is about to follow.

2-3 **the mountain:** It is not necessary to mention its name.

3 **Say thus . . . /(yes,) tell . . .:** A formulaic opening of a speech, highlighting this important address.

4 **eagles' wings:** Most commonly in Western culture, be it ancient Rome, Imperial Europe, the United States, or even Nazi Germany, the eagle is the symbol of strength, independence, and loftiness. Yet here in the Bible it functions primarily as a symbol of God's loving protection—see the nurturing eagle image in Deut. 32:11.

6 **but you:** Or "and you." **kingdom of priests:** Buber (1949) interprets the phrase as meaning a "royal-retinue" around the king, based on the usage in I Chron. 18:17 and II Sam. 8:18.

8 **All . . . we will do:** This phrase, with variations, is repeated in 24:4 and 24:7 to frame the entire covenant and law-giving account.

9 **thick cloud:** Some interpret the cloud as a massive aura, others as a shield to protect mortals from the brilliant divine "Glory" (Heb. *kavod*). **so that the people may hear:** Or "hearken" (i.e., obey). One would expect "so that the people may see," following upon the last phrase, but the narrator apparently wants to make clear that "you saw no image" (Deut. 4:12).

10 **wash:** The Hebrew verb (*kabbes*) is used for the washing of objects, not of people (which is expressed by *rahotz*).

11 that they may be ready for the third day,
for on the third day
YHWH will come down before the eyes of all the people,
upon Mount Sinai.
12 Fix-boundaries for the people round about, saying:
Be on your watch against going up the mountain or against
touching its border!
Whoever touches the mountain—he is to be put-to-death,
yes, death;
13 no hand is to touch him,
but he is to be stoned, yes, stoned, or shot, yes, shot,
whether beast or man, he is not to live!
When the (sound of the) ram's-horn is drawn out, they may
go up on the mountain.
14 Moshe went down from the mountain to the people,
he made the people holy, and they washed their clothes,
15 then he said to the people:
Be ready for three days; do not approach a woman!
16 Now it was on the third day, when it was morning:
There were thunder-sounds, and lightning,
a heavy cloud on the mountain
and an exceedingly strong trumpet sound.
And all of the people that were in the camp trembled.
17 Moshe brought the people out toward God, from the camp,
and they stationed themselves beneath the mountain.
18 Now Mount Sinai smoked all over,
since YHWH had come down upon it in fire;
its smoke went up like the smoke of a furnace,
and all of the mountain trembled exceedingly.
19 Now the trumpet sound was growing exceedingly stronger
—Moshe kept speaking,
and God kept answering him in the sound (of a voice)—
20 and YHWH came down upon Mount Sinai, to the top of
the mountain.
YHWH called Moshe to the top of the mountain,
and Moshe went up.
21 YHWH said to Moshe:
Go down, warn the people
lest they break through to YHWH to see, and many of them
fall;

as a "stammering account"). In any event, the entire description of the fateful meeting between God and the Israelites at Sinai is confined to a mere four verses (19:16–19). This stands in blatant contrast to other ancient Near Eastern traditions, which would have treated such an event with epic length and poetic diction (see, for intance, Deut. 32, or Psalm 78). So here, as in the opening chapter of Genesis, all has been stripped down, focusing attention on the covenant rather than on the mysterious nature of God.

In that vein, it must be observed that the narrative centers around speaking, words, and sounds, keeping the visual to a minimum (in line with the warning in Deut. 4:2: "The sound of words you heard/ a form you did not see/ only a sound-of-a-voice") It also abounds in terms connoting warning and boundaries/separateness—the text contains three sets of warnings: verses 10–13, 21–22 (introducing the phrase "burst out," which refers to God's potential destructiveness if the boundaries are violated), and 24. This recalls Moshe's own experience at Sinai earlier (cf. 3:5). And the number 3 gives the story the same touch of meaning provided by the numbers in Genesis; Israel arrives at the mountain three months after the exodus and meets God on the third day after their preparations.

As Cassuto (1967) points out, the chapter does not begin with "Now it was . . ." (Heb. va-yehi), a normal marker for continuing a previous narrative. The Sinai material thus presents itself in utter newness. To use the previously cited wedding analogy: this text betokens a new relation-

13 **no hand is to touch him:** As if his contact with holiness would somehow contaminate him—a common idea in much of ancient society, and put forth with particular force throughout Leviticus. **shot:** With bow and arrows.

15 **do not approach a woman:** The need for the people to be in a state of ritual purity precludes sexual contact.

16 **morning:** Perhaps to convey that there was nothing deceptive or dreamlike about this event, which was to be seen as a large-scale group experience (and hence a large-scale group commitment). **trumpet:** Perhaps, as part of an ancient Near Eastern convention, heralding the approach of YHWH as a warring storm-god (see the Commentary, above). **trembled:** Note how both people and mountain (v. 18) seem to be in synchrony with one another (yet some scholars emend the text!).

18 **like the smoke of furnace:** A standard biblical way of describing extensive smoke (see Gen. 19:28, which uses "dense-smoke").

19 **sound (of a voice):** Some interpret as "thunder," which is often described biblically as the "voice of God" (in Psalm 18:14 and in Ugaritic literature as well). But the emphasis in the revelation of these chapters seems to be on God's voice and the clarity of his words.

21 **fall:** That is, die, because of too-close contact with the divine.

22 even the priests who approach YHWH must make themselves holy,
  lest YHWH burst out against them.
23 But Moshe said to YHWH:
  The people are not able to go up to Mount Sinai,
  for you yourself warned us, saying: Fix boundaries for the
    mountain and make it holy!
24 YHWH said to him:
  Go, get down,
  and then come up, you and Aharon with you,
  but the priests and the people must not break through to go
    up to YHWH, lest he burst out against them.
25 Moshe went down to the people and said to them

20:1 God spoke all these words,
  saying:

  2 I am YHWH your God,
    who brought you out
    from the land of Egypt, from a house of serfs.

  3 You are not to have
    any other gods
    before me.
  4 You are not to make yourself a hewn-image
    or any figure
    that is in the heavens above, that is on the earth beneath,
      that is in the waters beneath the earth;
  5 you are not to bow down to them,
    you are not to serve them,
    for I, YHWH your God,
    am a jealous God,
    calling-to-account the iniquity of the fathers upon the sons,
      to the third and the fourth (generation)
    of those that hate me,
  6 but showing loyalty to the thousandth
    of those that love me,
    of those that keep my commandments.

ship between God and Israel, however well they have known one another previously.

Also notable in Chapter 19 is the emphasis on movement: going up (Heb. *'aloh*) and down (*yarod*) (see also 24:15-18). This movement serves to bridge the gap, usually great, between heaven and earth; but note that it is Moshe, and not the people, who does the ascending and descending.

Structurally, verses 20-25 appear to have been added, to emphasize the warning theme. They also delay the pronouncement of the "Ten Commandments," creating thereby a more dramatic effect with the appearance of the latter. But it seems clear that considerable editing has taken place.

The Ten Words (The Decalogue) (20:1-14): This section, among the most famous and important in all of religious literature, is set in dramatic tone. Its rhetoric could hardly be more striking. In a form relatively rare in ancient Near Eastern legal documents, a god sets forth demands, with no punishments listed. This "apodictic" form seems to indicate that the Ten Words function as a preamble to the actual laws of Chapters 21-23, by laying forth the major principles on which Israel's relationship to God is to be based (as is to be expected, the secondary literature on Chapter 20 is enormous; see Childs 1974 for a bibliography).

The numbering of the ten differs slightly in the Jewish and Christian traditions, with the main divergences coming in the split of verses 2-3 (or 3-4, as here); see Cassuto (1967). There are also different opinions on the overall structure of the "Commandments." Jewish tradition separates out those that treat the relationship between God and human beings (vv.2-11, numbers 1-5) and those that involve human society alone (vv.12-14, numbers 6-10), although it should be kept in mind that all offenses in

22 **lest YHWH burst out:** Lest God slay them with fire or plague. One recalls the demonic character of God portrayed in 4:24ff. The phrase is repeated in verse 24 for emphasis.

25 **and said to them:** The Hebrew is ambiguous; did Moshe report God's previous speech to them, or the following (Decalogue)? I have left this verse without final punctuation to express the unresolved nature of the question.

20:3 **before me:** Or "besides me." "Before" may connote "to affront," as in literally "in my face."

4 **figure . . .:** A representation of an animal or person.

5 **jealous:** The Hebrew word (*kanna*) has a cognate meaning in Arabic, "red (with dye)," so an interesting English analogy, expressing facial color changes, would be "livid" (from the Latin "color of lead"). **the third and the fourth (generation):** A long time (Plaut 1981).

6 **the thousandth:** That is, forever (Plaut 1981).

7 You are not to take up
the name of YHWH your God
to a delusion,
for YHWH will not clear him
that takes up his name to a delusion.

8 Remember
the Sabbath day, to hallow it.
9 For six days, you are to serve, and are to make all your
    work,
10 but the seventh day
is Sabbath for YHWH your God:
you are not to make any kind of work,
(not) you, nor your son, nor your daughter,
(not) your servant, nor your maid, nor your beast,
nor your sojourner that is within your gates.
11 For in six days
YHWH made
the heavens and the earth,
the sea and all that is in it,
and he rested on the seventh day;
therefore YHWH gave the seventh day his blessing, and he
    hallowed it.

12 Honor
your father and your mother,
in order that your days may be long
on the soil that YHWH your God is giving you.

13 You are not to murder.

You are not to adulter.

You are not to steal.

You are not to testify
against your fellow as a false witness.

14 You are not to desire
the house of your fellow,
you are not to desire the wife of your fellow,
or his servant, or his maid, or his ox, or his ass,
or anything that is your fellow's.

15 Now all of the people were seeing
   the thunder-sounds,
   the flashing-torches,
   the trumpet sound,
   and the mountain smoking;

ancient Israel were seen as affronts to God. This division might be borne out by stylistic considerations, for the last five, of course, begin "You are not to . . ." and numbers 2–4 all use the Hebrew word *ki* ("for") to express reasons or results of the initial stipulations (vv.5, 7, 11, with the substitution of "in order that" in verse 12).

Other notable stylistic aspects here include the fact that "you" is always singular, and that numbers 2–4 and 6–10 are all put in the negative.

Several other features of the "Decalogue" are unique: the prohibition against worshipping images, which would have had a strange ring in the ancient world; the Sabbath as a holy day on which not even servants, farm animals, or noncitizens are to work, equally unprecedented in its time and place; and, strangest of all, the final prohibition against desiring (another person's property).

The language and the content of the Decalogue, then, cooperate to create a lofty and challenging ethical code, which both the people of Israel and the Western world in general have struggled with ever since. The reader may wish to consult Buber's stimulating essays (1968, 1948) "The Words on the Tablets" and "What Are We to Do about the Ten Commandments?"

Aftermath (20:15–23): The verses that follow the Decalogue highlight an important aspect of the Sinai tradition: its occurrence in a public setting.

7 **take up . . . to a delusion:** Use for a false purpose. The traditional translation, "take in vain," limits its scope unnecessarily. **clear:** To acquit or hold innocent.

13 **You are not to . . .:** Closer to the Hebrew rhythmically would be a sequence like "No murder!/ No adultery!" etc., or "Murder not!/ Adulter not!" etc. **murder:** Some interpreters view this as "killing" in general, while others restrict it, as I have done here. **steal:** Ancient Jewish tradition understood this as a reference to kidnapping (see Lauterbach 1976). **adulter:** The English has been tailored to fit the Hebrew rhythm of the last five "commandments," all of which begin with *lo* ("no") and a two-syllable command.

14 **desire:** Trad. "covet." Another possibility is "yearn for."

15 **were seeing:** Others, "perceived." The use of the Hebrew participle again emphasizes immediacy. **flashing-torches:** Perhaps a poetic description of lightning.

when the people saw,
they faltered
and stood far off.

16 They said to Moshe:
You speak with us, and we will hearken,
but let not God speak with us, lest we die!

17 Moshe said to the people:
Do not be afraid!
For it is to test you that God has come,
to have his fear be upon you,
so that you do not sin.

18 The people stood far off,
and Moshe approached the stormy-darkness where God
was.

19 YHWH said to Moshe:
Say thus to the Children of Israel:
You yourselves have seen
that it was from the heavens that I spoke with you.

20 You are not to make beside me
gods of silver, gods of gold you are not to make for yourselves!

21 An altar of soil, you are to make for me,
you are to slaughter upon it
your offerings-up, your well-being-sacrifices,
your sheep and your oxen!
At every place
where I cause my name to be recalled
I will come to you
and bless you.

22 But if an altar of stones you make for me,
you are not to build it smooth-hewn,
for if you hold-high your iron-tool over it, you will have
profaned it.

23 And you are not to ascend my altar by ascending-steps,
that your nakedness not be laid-bare upon it.

21:1 Now these are the judgments that you are to set before
them:

2 When you acquire a Hebrew serf,
   he is to serve for six years,
   but in the seventh he is to go out at liberty, for nothing.

Verses 15–18 could fit nicely after 19:20a; the Decalogue would then follow 20:18. Yet it seems to have been important for the narrator to stress (v.19) that God spoke to the people as a whole, not merely secretly in a revelation to a visionary or priest. To emphasize this point, the verb *ra'oh*, "see/perceive," occurs seven times in verses 15–19. Verse 19 also serves as a framework for the entire Revelation episode, recalling as it does the language of 19:4. Israel now has two reasons for obeying God: he brought them out of Egyptian bondage and he talked to them "from the heavens" (v.19).

The rest of the chapter functions as an introduction to the general body of the legislation that begins in the next chapter. Like Israel's other law collections in Leviticus and Deuteronomy, it starts with rules pertaining to worship.

On the Laws: The reader should bear in mind again that the section headings used in the Commentary are for reference only. This is especially true for Chapters 21–24, where the final form of the Hebrew text discourages distinguishing between different types of offenses (see p. 105, "On Biblical Law").

Laws Regarding Israelite Serfdom (21:1–11): Given the importance of the root "serve" in the book of Exodus, it is fitting that the Covenant Code

18 **stormy-darkness:** Heb. *'arafel*, frequently used in conjunction with *'anan*, "cloud."
21 **of soil:** Cf. verse 22. The altar was to be made of natural materials.
   well-being–sacrifices: Others, "peace-offerings"; but see Orlinsky (1970). **you:** Here, second personal singular, as well as through verse 23.
22 **profaned:** In folklore, iron was said to drive out the soul of the stone—that is, rob it of its essence (Driver 1911).
23 **that your nakedness:** To make sure that the priests' genitals not be uncovered during the rites; the Egyptians wore rather short skirts (Plaut 1981). Note again the desexualizing of religion.
21:1 **judgments:** Others, "judicial decisions," "rules." See Daube (1947).
   2 **you:** Singular, to stress the perspective of the buyer.   **Hebrew:** Cassuto (1967) suggests that the term here has a wide meaning: a member of a bondman class (Akkadian *Hapiru*) found all over the ancient Near East.
   for nothing: Without paying redemption money (Cassuto 1967).

3 If he came by himself, he is to go out by himself;
   if he was the spouse of a wife, his wife is to go out with him.
4 If his lord gives him a wife, and she bore him sons or
     daughters,
   the wife and those she bore are to remain her lord's, and he
     is to go out by himself.
5 But if the serf should say, yes, say:
   I love my lord, my wife and my children, I will not go out at
     liberty!,
6 his lord is to have him approach God's-oracle,
   and then he is to have him approach the door or the post;
   his lord is to pierce his ear with a piercer,
   and he is to serve him forever.

7 When a man sells his daughter as a handmaid,
   she is not to go out as serfs go out.
8 If she is displeasing in the eyes of her lord, who designated
     her for himself,
   he is to have her redeemed;
   to a foreign people he has not the power to sell her,
   since he has betrayed her.
9 But if it is for his son that he designates her,
   according to the just-rights of women he is to deal with her.
10 If another he takes for himself,
   (then) her board, her clothing, or her oil he is not to diminish.
11 If these three (things) he does not do for her,
   she is to go out for nothing, with no money.

12 He that strikes a man, so that he dies,
   is to be put-to-death, yes, death.
13 Now should he not have lain in wait (for him), but should
     God have brought him opportunely into his hand:
   I will set aside for you a place where he may flee.

open with this theme. In verses 1–6 the text considers the case of the
native serf, a status rather like that of the indentured servant in early
American history. Immediately, the act of releasing such an individual—
providing for his "going out"—is stipulated. "For they are my servants,
whom I brought forth out of the land of Egypt" (Lev. 25:42). While the
institution of serfdom existed of necessity in ancient Israel, it could not be

tolerated as a permanent and fully dehumanizing one (on the other hand, these regulations deal with natives, not with foreigners). Note the use of seven here, as the number of perfection and limit—the servant goes free after seven years, just as the land rests every seven years (23:10–11).

The second case (vv.7–11) deals with a woman whose poverty-stricken father sells her as a servant. Here, too, there is an attempt to soften the conditions and to humanize what appears as essentially a property situation in the ancient world.

Capital Crimes of Violence (21:12–17): Four situations involving grave crimes are cited in this section, each ending with the pronouncement of the death penalty in rhetorical form (Heb. *mot yumat*, "He is to be put-to-death, yes, death"): murder, striking one's parents, kidnapping, and denigrating one's parents. Our society has in general supported the first and third of these; but the regulations concerning father and mother do not accord with twentieth-century Western practice, and point up well the enormous importance of the parent–child relationship in ancient Israel (already suggested by "Honor your father and your mother" in the Ten Words). That relationship was often used to describe the one between God and Israel, and thus obedience is an important theme in the covenant as a whole.

3 **by himself:** I.e., as an unmarried man.
4 **and she bore him . . .:** The birth of children changes the situation, and the wife must now remain behind, in bondage, with the children.
5 **say, yes, say:** Or "declare."
6 **God's-oracle:** Others, "God," "the judges."   **door . . . post:** It is not clear whether the sanctuary or the master's house is meant.   **pierce his ear:** The symbolism of this act is not clear. Gaster (1969) theorizes that it establishes the serf's permanent bond to his master's house, through the blood on the doorpost.
7 **handmaid:** In this instance, a free woman is bound over to be a slave.   **as serfs go forth:** As we saw above. In Cassuto's (1967) view, now that she has a new status (that of wife), she may not be so easily disposed of.
8 **he has betrayed her:** He has not married her off, as was intended in the sale.
10 **her board:** "Her" refers to the first woman, mentioned in verse 8.   **her oil:** So Paul (1970), on the basis of Mesopotamian parallels. Others, "marital-relations."
11 **with no money:** Again, without having to pay redemption money.
12 **put-to-death:** Stronger than simply saying "die."
13 **opportunely:** Accidentally.   **a place where he may flee:** The so-called cities of refuge (see Num. 35:9–34, Deut. 19:1–12).

14 But when a man schemes against his fellow, to kill him with
  cunning,
 from my very altar you are to take him away, to die!

15 And he that strikes his father or his mother,
 is to be put-to-death, yes, death.

16 And he that steals a man,
 whether he sells him or whether he is found in his hand,
 is to be put-to-death, yes, death.

17 And he that reviles his father or his mother,
 is to be put-to-death, yes, death.

18 When men quarrel, and a man strikes his fellow with a stone
  or with (his) fist, yet he does not die, but rather takes to
  his bed:
19 If he can rise and walk about outside upon his crutch,
 he that struck (him) is to go clear,
 only: he is to make good for his resting-time, and provide-
  that-he-be-healed, yes, healed.

20 When a man strikes his serf or his handmaid with a rod, so
  that he dies under his hand,
 it is to be avenged, yes, avenged;
21 nonetheless, if for a day or two-days he endures,
 it is not to be avenged, for he is his own "money."

22 When two men fight and deal a blow to a pregnant woman,
  so that her children abort-forth, but (other) harm does not
  happen,
 he is to be fined, yes, fined, as the woman's spouse imposes
  for him,
 but he is to give it (only) according to assessment.
23 But if harm should happen,
 then you are to give life in place of life—
24 eye in place of eye, tooth in place of tooth, hand in place of
25 hand, foot in place of foot,/burnt-scar in place of burnt-
  scar, wound in place of wound, bruise in place of bruise.

26 When a man strikes the eye of his serf or the eye of his
    handmaid, and ruins it,
  he is to send him free at liberty for (the sake of) his eye;
27 if the tooth of his serf or the tooth of his handmaid he breaks
    off,
  he is to send him free at liberty on account of his tooth.

Injuries (21:18–32): The vocabulary of verbs in these verses outlines the
subject at hand: "quarrel," "strike," "contend," "harm," "strike,"
"break-off," "give." The text treats a number of extenuating circumstances, imposing penalties of varying degrees. The case of a caused abor-
tion is especially highlighted (vv.22–25), and in a famous verse (25), the
law-giver breaks into rhetoric in order to stress that punishments be scru-
pulously fair. Also notable is the regulation concerning the goring ox
(vv.28–32), where an *animal* is made to pay the death penalty, since it has
destroyed the most sacred thing of all—life itself. Both of the latter cases
have received exhaustive treatment in the scholarly literature (see Sarna
1986).

14 **from my very altar:** Even the traditional concept of sanctuary will not aid
    such a man.
15 **strikes:** Some interpret this as "strikes dead." But the wording does not
    warrant this here (cf. 21:12), and such a society would in any case be
    supportive of this kind of severe penalty in reference to not "honoring"
    (see 20:12) parents. This is further supported by verse 17, below.
17 **reviles:** Others, "belittles," "insults."
18 **fist:** Some ancient versions read "club" or "spade."
19 **to make good . . . healed:** But he is not liable for criminal action.
20 **avenged:** The exact punishment is not specified, but it sounds like death.
21 **it is not . . . "money":** "He has human rights, but not those of a free
    man" (Plaut 1981). Alternatively, Cassuto (1967) suggests that the master
    has lost his own money thereby.
22 **assessment:** As agreed by the judges.
23 **you:** Singular.   **life in place of life:** This has historically been taken to
    indicate a kind of strict Hebrew vengeance, as in the current expression
    "an eye for an eye." But the passage (note, by the way, its length) may
    have been meant as a contrast to the Babylonian system, where the rich
    could in essence pay to get out of such situations. In Israel this could not
    be done, and thus we are dealing not with strict justice but with strict
    fairness.

28 When an ox gores a man or a woman, so that one dies,
   the ox is to be stoned, yes, stoned, and its flesh is not to be
      eaten,
   and the owner of the ox is to be clear.
29 But if the ox was (known as) a gorer from yesterday and
      the day-before, and it was so designated to its owner,
   and he did not guard it,
   and it causes the death of a man or of a woman,
   the ox is to be stoned, and its owner as well is to be put-
      to-death.
30 If a purging-ransom is established for him,
   he is to give it as a redemption for his life, all that is imposed
      for him.
31 Whether it is a son it gores or a daughter it gores,
   according to this (same) judgment it is to be done to him.
32 If (it is) a serf the ox gores, or a handmaid,
   silver—thirty *shekels*—he is to give to his lord, and the ox is
      to be stoned.

33 When a man opens up a pit, or when a man digs a pit, and
      does not cover it up, and an ox or an ass falls into it,
34 the owner of the pit is to pay, the worth-in-silver he is to
      restore to its owner, and the dead-animal is to remain his.
35 When a man's ox deals-a-blow to his fellow's ox, so that it
      dies,
   they are to sell the live ox and split its worth-in-silver, and
      the dead-animal they are also to split.
36 Yet if it was known that it was a goring ox from yesterday
      and the day-before, and its owner did not guard it,
   he is to pay, yes, pay, an ox in place of the ox, and the
      dead-animal is to remain his.

37 (Now) when a man steals an ox or a lamb, and slaughters it
      or sells it,
   five cattle he is to pay in place of the ox, and four sheep in
      place of the lamb;
22:1 if in (the act of) digging through, the stealer is caught and is
      struck down, so that he dies,
   there is to be on his account no bloodguilt;

2 (but) if the sun shone upon him,
   bloodguilt there is on his account;
   he is to pay, yes, pay—if he has nothing, he is to be sold
      because of his stealing.
3 (Now) if what was stolen is found, yes, found in his hand,
      whether ox, or ass, or lamb, (still) alive,
   twofold he is to pay.

4 When a man has a field or a vineyard grazed in,
   and sends his grazing-flock free, so that it grazes in
      another's field,
   the best-part of his field, the best-part of his vineyard he is
      to pay.

Property (21:33–22:14): These regulations cover various damages to property, commonly through negligence. The key word here is "pay" (Heb. *shallem*, denoting restitution); also repeated are "fellow" and "God's-oracle."

28 **When an ox gores . . .:** The ox may be taken here as the paradigm of the domestic animal. The secondary literature on this law and its parallels is enormous. **its flesh is not to be eaten:** Since the ox has not been properly slaughtered for eating or sacrificial purposes, and possibly also because it is connected with the taking of another life (carnivores are forbidden food in the Bible).

30 **purging-ransom:** Others, "expiation payment." This functions as a way out of his being put to death (as in the case of the firstborn son, in Chap. 12).

37 **(Now) . . . lamb:** In most English translations, this verse is labeled 22:1, and hence 22:1 here appears as 22:2 elsewhere. **five cattle . . . four sheep:** In contradistinction to the case of a stolen animal that is found alive (v.3, above), where the payment is only twofold.

22:1 **digging through:** Secretly, at night; the owner presumably has neither the time nor the light to examine the situation rationally. This issue is still a matter of considerable debate in many state legislatures in America. **no bloodguilt:** He is not considered a murderer.

2 **if the sun shone:** Then the owner could have restrained himself from killing the man.

4–5 **grazed . . . blaze:** The Hebrew is perhaps a pun on *b'r*, which is used for both verbs. Some take the entire case to refer to burning.

5 When fire breaks out and reaches thorn-hedges, and a
   sheaf-stack or the standing-grain or the (entire) field is
   consumed,
   he is to pay, yes, pay, he that caused the blaze to blaze up.

6 When a man gives silver or goods to his fellow for safekeeping, and it is stolen from the man's house;
   if the stealer is found, he is to pay twofold;
7 if the stealer is not found, the owner of the house is to
   come-near God's-oracle,
   (to inquire) if he did not send out his hand against his fellow's property.
8 Regarding every matter of misappropriation,
   regarding oxen, regarding asses, regarding sheep, regarding
   garments, regarding any kind of loss about which one can
   say: That is it!—
   before God's-oracle is the matter of the two of them to come;
   whomever God's-oracle declares guilty, is to pay twofold to
   his fellow.
9 When a man gives his fellow an ass or an ox or a lamb, or any
   kind of beast, for safekeeping,
   and it dies, or is crippled or captured, no one seeing (it
   happen),
10 the oath of YHWH is to be between the two of them,
   (to inquire) if he did not send out his hand against his fellow's property;
   the owner is to accept it, and he does not have to pay.
11 But if it was stolen, yes, stolen away from him,
   he is to pay it back to its owner.
12 If it was torn, torn-to-pieces,
   he is to bring it as evidence; what was torn, he does not have
   to pay back.
13 When a man borrows it from his fellow, and it is crippled or
   it dies:
   (if) its owner was not with it, he is to pay, yes, pay;
14 if its owner was with it, he does not have to pay.
   If it was hired, its hiring-price is received.

15 When a man seduces a virgin who has not been spoken-for
   and lies with her,
   (for) the marrying-price he is to marry her, as his wife.

16 If her father refuses, yes, refuses to give her to him,
   silver he is to weigh out, according to the marriage-price of
      virgins.

17 A sorceress you are not to let live.

Laws Concerning Social Relations and Religious Matters (22:15–23:19): A
great variety of offenses is covered in this section: rape, oppression, tale-
bearing, unjust sentencing, and bribery, among others. Yet the category is
not so neatly drawn; interspersed with these are laws concerning what we
would consider religious affairs: sorcery, idolatry, blasphemy, and the
sacred calendar. Once again the implication seems to be that all of these
areas are of immediate concern to God, regardless of how they are labeled
or pigeonholed.

Stylistically there is also great variety, as categorical prohibitions (22:18)
alternate with pleas (23:5–6) and positive commands (23:10–12). A number of times the justification for the law is given in the text itself (e.g.
22:20, 26; 23:7, 8, 9, 11, 12), with the operative word being "for." (Such a

5 **pay:** Yet not necessarily the "best-part," as in verse 4.
6 **stealer:** The Hebrew form (*ganav*) indicates a professional thief, not a
   casual one.
7 **the owner of the house:** That is, the temporary guardian of the goods.
8 **say:** Others, "allege."
9 **crippled or captured:** Heb. *nishbar o nishbe.*
10 **oath of YHWH:** It functions like a lie-detector test.   **he does not:** The
   guardian, as above.
12 **torn-to-pieces:** A technical term for "devoured by a wild animal" (Daube
   1947); cf. Gen. 37:33.   **he does not have to pay:** Since this could happen
   to anyone.
14 **he does not have to pay:** It is assumed that he did his best to protect his
   charge.   **its hiring-price is received:** The rental price covers the loss.
15 **spoken-for:** Lit., "paid for." Others, "betrothed," but it is not clear that
   there was such an institution as betrothal in biblical Israel (Orlinsky
   1970).
16 **marriage-price of virgins:** As in many cultures, biblical society prized a
   virgin as a bride.
17 **sorceress:** The specifying of women here seems to indicate their involve-
   ment in this practice in ancient Israel. Magic as such was forbidden (see
   the famous story of the "witch of Endor" in I Sam. 28) all over the Bible,
   as an attempt to manipulate God's world behind his back, as it were.
   you: Singular, and so basically through verse 29. The exceptions, verse 21
   and the end of verse 24, may simply be stylistic variations.   **not to let
   live:** An unusual Hebrew phrase, perhaps for emphasis.

18 Anyone who lies with a beast
   is to be put-to-death, yes, death.

19 He that slaughter-offers to (other) gods is to be made-taboo.
   Only to YHWH alone!

20 Now a sojourner you are not to maltreat, you are not to
      oppress him,
   for sojourners were you in the land of Egypt.

21 Any widow or orphan you are not to afflict.
22 Oh, if you afflict, afflict them . . . !
   For (then) they will cry, cry out to me,
   and I will hearken, hearken to their cry,
23 my anger will rage
   and I will kill you with the sword,
   so that your wives become widows, and your children,
      orphans!

24 If you lend money to my people, to the afflicted-one (who
      lives) beside you,
   you are not to be to him like a creditor,
   you are not to place on him excessive-interest.

25 If you take-in-pledge, yes, pledge, the cloak of your fellow,
   before the sun comes in, return it to him,
26 for it is his only clothing,
   it is the cloak for his skin,
   in what (else) shall he lie down?
   Now it will be that when he cries out to me,
   I will hearken,
   for a Compassionate-One am I!

27 God you are not to revile,
   one exalted among your people you are not to curse.

28 Your full fruit of your trickling-grapes, you are not to delay.

   The firstborn of your sons, give to me.

29 Do thus with your ox, with your sheep:
    for seven days let it be with its mother, (and) on the eighth
        day, give it to me!

30 Men of holiness are you to be to me!
    Flesh that is torn-to-pieces in the field, you are not to eat;
    to the dogs you are to throw it.

23:1 You are not to take up a delusive rumor.
      Do not put your hand (in) with a guilty person, to become a
          witness for wrongdoing.

verse is called a "motive clause," and is characteristically although not exclusively biblical; see Sonsino 1980.)

Most notable about this section is the full use that it makes of rhetoric. Several key laws are accompanied by an emotional appeal—e.g., "Oh, if you afflict, afflict them. . . !" (22:22); "for it is his only clothing . . . in what (else) shall he lie down?" (v.26); "for a Compassionate-One am I"

18 **lies with a beast:** Interestingly, Hittite law distinguishes between some animals in this regard, while Israelite law does not. Just as the Bible has essentially excised mythology concerning half-gods and half-humans, or half humans/animals such as the Sphinx, so the spheres are not to mix in real life.

27 **God . . . one exalted:** Here God and ruler are equated, as later in the story of Naboth's vineyard in I Kings 21:10 ("You cursed God and the king").

28 **Your full fruit . . .:** Heb. difficult. Cassuto (1967) cites a parallel Hittite law. **give to me:** Paralleling 13:13 (Cassuto 1967).

29 **eighth day:** Circumcision also takes place on the eighth day, reflecting either a belief that the young are more viable by then, or a symbolic number (7 + 1). Others suggest that it takes seven days for the impurity of birth to be expunged (cf. Lev. 12:2).

30 **Men of holiness:** The idea is continued in Leviticus, where Chapters 19ff. have come to be known as the "Holiness Code," a collection of varied laws dealing with different aspects of human conduct. **Flesh that is torn-to-pieces:** Leviticus 17:15 and 22:8 forbid the eating of an animal that has been slain by another. **to the dogs:** The force of the idea is similar in both Hebrew and English.

23:1 **You:** Singular through verse 12, except for the second and third lines of verse 9. **delusive:** Insubstantial, not based on fact. **Do not put your hand in:** That is, do not throw your weight toward, side with.

2 You are not to go after many (people) to do evil.

   And you are not to testify in a quarrel so as to turn aside
       toward many—(and thus) turn away.
3 Even a poor-man you are not to respect as regards his quarrel.

4 (Now) when you encounter your enemy's ox or his ass stray-
       ing, return it, return it to him.
5 (And) when you see the ass of one who hates you crouching
       under its burden, restrain from abandoning it to him—
   unbind, yes, unbind it together with him.

6 You are not to turn aside the rights of your needy as regards
       his quarrel.

7 From a false matter, you are to keep far!
   And (one) clear and innocent, do not kill,
       for I do not acquit a guilty-person.

8 A bribe you are not to take,
       for a bribe blinds the open-eyed,
       and twists the words of the just.

9 A sojourner, you are not to oppress:
       you yourselves know (well) the feelings of the sojourner,
       for sojourners were you in the land of Egypt.

10 For six years you are to sow your land and to gather in its
       produce,
11 but in the seventh, you are to let it go and to let it be,
       that the needy of your people may eat,
       and what they (allow to) remain, the wildlife of the field may
           eat.
   Do thus with your vineyard, with your olive-grove.

12 For six days you are to make your labor,
       but on the seventh day, you are to cease,
       in order that your ox and your ass may rest
       and the son of your handmaid and the sojourner may
           pause-for-breath.

13 In all that I say to you, keep watch!
   The name of other gods, you are not to mention,
   it is not to be heard in your mouth.

14 At three points you are to hold-festival for me, every year.
15 The Festival of *matzot* you are to keep:
   for seven days you are to eat *matzot*, as I commanded you,
   at the appointed-time of the New-Moon of Ripe-Grain—
   for in it you went out of Egypt,
   and no one is to be seen in my presence empty-handed;
16 and the Festival of the Cutting, of the firstlings of your
      labor, of what you sow in the field;
   and the Festival of Ingathering, at the going-out of the year,

(v.26); and "you yourselves know (well) the feelings of the sojourner"
(23:9).

No passage in these chapters, and indeed throughout the entire Torah,
can easily surpass vv. 21–23 (as I have mentioned above), with their
appeal to language and emotions alike. So at the core of the legal concerns
here is the protection of the powerless.

2 **quarrel:** Legal dispute. **many:** Or "the majority." **turn away:** Referring to either turning the judgment in favor of the wicked, or else the
  "turning" of justice itself.
3 **respect:** Others, "prefer." Contrast this idea with verse 6.
5 **abandoning . . . unbind:** That same Hebrew root, *'azov*, is used for both.
  It is also possible that the text is the result of a scribal error, and some read
  the second verb as *'azor*, "help."
8 **open-eyed:** Here, the equivalent of "wise."
9 **oppress:** Recalling the oppression suffered at the hands of the Egyptians
  in 3:9.
12 **pause-for-breath:** Later (31:17), God himself is portrayed as having
   needed to rest after his work of creation.
13 **you:** Plural. **name . . . it:** Understood as plural.
14 **you:** Singular.
15 **in my presence empty-handed:** No one is to make a religious pilgrimage
   on these occasions without bringing "gifts" (sacrifices).
16 **Festival of the Cutting:** The wheat harvest and that of first-fruits, occurring in the third month, usually in early June (also known as Shavu'ot,
   "Weeks"). **Festival of Ingathering:** The final (grape) harvest, in the
   seventh month in late September or early October (also known as Sukkot,
   "Booths").

when you gather in your labor's (harvest) from the field.
17 Three times in the year
are all your males to be seen
in the presence of the Lord, YHWH.

18 You are not to slaughter-offer with anything fermented my
blood offering.

The fat of my festive-offering is not to remain overnight,
until morning.

19 The choicest firstlings of your soil, you are to bring to the
house of YHWH your God.

You are not to boil a kid in the milk of its mother.

20 Here, I am sending a messenger before you
to watch over you on the way,
to bring you to the place that I have prepared.
21 Be on your watch in his presence,
and hearken to his voice,
do not be rebellious against him,
for he is not able to bear your transgressing,
for my name is with him.
22 So then, hearken, hearken to his voice,
and do all that I speak,
and I will be-an-enemy to your enemies,
and I will be-an-adversary to your adversaries.
23 When my messenger goes before you
and brings you
to the Amorite, the Hittite, the Perizzite, and the Canaanite,
the Hivvite and the Yevusite,
and I cause them to vanish:
24 you are not to bow down to their gods,
you are not to serve them,
you are not to do according to what they do,
but: you are to tear, yes, tear them down,
and are to smash, yes, smash their standing-stones.
25 You are to serve YHWH your God!

Toward the end (23:10–19), emphasis shifts to the festivals of Israel, with a special focus on the agricultural setting. As a result the general scholarly consensus is that these laws could not be wilderness regulations, but refer instead to life after the conquest of Canaan. Be that as it may, the fact that this section ends with ritual concerns provides a rounding-out of the entire body of Exodus legislation, which, as I noted above, began with worship as its subject (20:20ff.).

Finally, the ending passage is notable for its numerical layout—two sets of seven (years and days) and one of three (times a year).

Epilogue: The Future Conquest (23:20–33): It would not be suitable, given the grave nature of the covenant, to end the legal passages merely with a particular law, and so our narrator appends a long speech, in the style of Deuteronomy, warning the Israelites, first, to follow God's messenger, and second, not to assimilate with the nations they are about to conquer. The Deuteronomic themes are classic: "being on your watch," smashing Canaanite idols, God's removing disease from the faithful Israelites, and the spelling-out of Israel's future borders.

17 **be seen in the presence of . . . YHWH:** A technical expression for one's appearing at the sanctuary (Plaut 1981).   **the Lord, YHWH:** Some see this title as a polemic against the Canaanite Baal, whose name means "master" or "lord."

18 **with anything leavened:** Excluding bread and honey (cf. Lev. 2:11) from the offering, possibly since these were included by the Canaanites (Cassuto 1967), or because the sacrifice was to be kept as "natural" as possible.

19 **You are not to boil . . . :** This law occurs three times in the Torah, and so must have been of particular importance. Despite this, interpreters disagree as to its origins and meaning. Some see it as directly opposing a Canaanite practice; others, as parallel to the law in Deuteronomy (22:6–7) against taking the mother bird along with her young. It also keeps the separation between milk (life-giving) and blood (life-taking); it was thus understood in Jewish mystical tradition of the Middle Ages. The phrase is also cited by Talmudic sages as a basis for the separation of milk and meat in postbiblical Jewish dietary laws (*kashrut*).

20 **a messenger:** As sometimes occurs with this word, it is not entirely clear what the distinction is between God and messenger. Here, however, the context seems to require a separate being, whether an angel or Moshe himself.

21 **my name is with him:** Or "in him"; "my authority rests with him" (Clements 1972).

22 **be-an-enemy:** The Hebrew expresses this idea with one verb, without auxiliary.

23 **to the Amorite . . . :** To their land, Canaan.

24 **standing-stones:** Possibly, phallic representations of Canaanite gods.

♭ and he will give-blessing to your food and your water;
I will remove sickness from amongst you,

26 there will be no miscarrier or barren-one in your land,
(and) the number of your days I will make full.

27 My terror I will send on before you,
I will stir up all the peoples among whom you come,
I will give all your enemies to you by the neck.

28 I will send Despair on before you
so that it drives out the Hivvite, the Canaanite and the Hittite from before you.

29 I will not drive them out from before you in one year,
lest the land become desolate
and the wildlife of the field become-many against you.

30 Little by little will I drive them out from before you,
until you have borne-fruit and possessed the land.

31 And I will make your territory
from the Sea of Reeds to the Sea of the Philistines,
from the Wilderness to the River.
For I give into your hand the settled-folk of the land, that
you may drive them out from before you.

32 You are not to cut with them or with their gods any covenant,

33 they are not to stay in your land, lest they cause you to sin
against me,
indeed, you would serve their gods—
indeed, that would be a snare to you.

24:1 Now to Moshe he said:
Go up to YHWH,
you and Aharon, Nadav and Avihu, and seventy of the
elders of Israel,
and bow down from afar;

2 Moshe alone is to approach YHWH,
but they, they are not to approach,
and as for the people—they are not to go up with him
(either).

3 So Moshe came
and recounted to the people all the words of YHWH and all
the judgments.

> And all the people answered in one voice, and said:
> All the words that YHWH has spoken, we will do.
> 4 Now Moshe wrote down all the words of YHWH.
> He (arose) early in the morning,
> he built an altar beneath the mountain
> and twelve standing-stones for the twelve tribes of Israel.

Also to be remarked are the sevenfold repetition of "before you" as a stylistic unifying device, and the ending theme of serving YHWH as opposed to "their gods."

Sealing the Covenant (24:1–11): To close out the account of covenant-making which began back in Chapter 19, the text recounts a formalized ceremony which has many points of contact with what was generally done throughout the ancient Near East when a covenant was "cut." Twice Moshe reads God's words to the people, and twice (vv.3, 7) they give their assent. This is no imposing of laws by a dictator, but a freely accepted, "signed, sealed, and delivered" agreement cemented by blood, the signifier of life itself.

26 **no miscarrier:** No distinction is made here between human and animal, and presumably both would share in the blessing.

27 **terror . . . stir up:** Heb. *'emati . . . hammati.* **stir up:** As in 14:24, above, describing God's routing of the Egyptians. **give all your enemies to you by the neck:** I.e., they will be routed by you, their backs turned.

28 **Despair:** Others, "hornet"; the Hebrew implies both.

29 **I will not drive them out . . . in one year:** This is the situation at the beginning of the book of Judges (after the Conquest); apparently Yehoshua did not finish the job, and so various (later) biblical texts attempt to explain the reason for this.

31 **Sea of the Philistines:** The Mediteranean. **Wilderness:** The southland or Negev. **the River:** The Euphrates, in the north. **drive them out:** Heb. *gerashtemo* is an archaic form (such as we find in 15:17—*tevi'emo ve-titta'emo*), used perhaps for reasons of rhythm.

32 **cut . . . any covenant:** A common Semitic idiom for concluding a treaty (see Gen. 15), perhaps stemming from a ritual. The parties would pass between the halves of sacrificed animals, perhaps implying that such would be the penalty for any party that would break the agreement.

24:1 **Nadav and Avihu:** Aharon's first two sons. **seventy:** The "perfect" number with which the book of Exodus began.

4 **standing-stones:** As distinct from the phallic stones mentioned in 23:24, these functioned as boundary markers and memorials.

5 Then he sent the (serving-) lads of the Children of Israel,
  that they should offer-up offerings-up, slaughter slaughter-
    meals, well-being-offerings for YHWH—bulls.
6 Moshe took half of the blood and put it in basins,
  and half of the blood he tossed against the altar.
7 Then he took the account of the covenant
  and read it in the hearing of the people.
  They said:
  All that YHWH has spoken, we will do and we will hearken!
8 Moshe took the blood, he tossed it on the people
  and said:
  Here is the blood of the covenant
  that YHWH has cut with you
  by means of all these words.

9 Then went up
  Moshe and Aharon, Nadav and Avihu, and seventy of the
    elders of Israel.
10 And they saw
   the God of Israel: beneath his feet
   (something) like work of sapphire tiles,
   (something) like the substance of the heavens in purity.
11 Yet against the Pillars of the Children of Israel, he did not
     send forth his hand—
   they beheld Godhood
   and ate and drank.

12 Now YHWH said to Moshe:
   Go up to me on the mountain
   and remain there,
   that I may give you tablets of stone:
   the Instruction and the Command
   that I have written down, to instruct them.
13 Moshe arose, and Yehoshua his attendant,
   and Moshe went up to the mountain of God.
14 Now to the elders he said:
   Stay here for us, until we return to you;
   here, Aharon and Hur are with you—
   whoever has a legal-matter is to approach them.

15 So Moshe went up the mountain,
   and the cloud covered the mountain;
16 the Glory of YHWH took up dwelling on Mount Sinai.
   The cloud covered it for six days,
   and he called to Moshe on the seventh day from admidst the
     cloud.
17 And the sight of the Glory of YHWH
   (was) like a consuming fire
   on top of the mountain
   in the eyes of the Children of Israel.

As representatives of the people, Moshe, Aharon, Aharon's sons, and seventy elders ascend Mount Sinai, and, most remarkably, "see" God in some sort of vision—without, as one might expect, their being destroyed. They also eat and drink, as was customary in the sealing of the agreement (and often done in business to this day; see Gen. 31:44–54).

Moshe Ascends Alone (24:12–18): Finally, Moshe leaves the people, in order to receive the laws in permanent (stone) form. He "goes up" the mountain four times (or, most likely, is on his way up). In order to give his absence the weight it needs—so that the people will grow restless, setting up the situation that produces the Golden Calf in Chapter 32—the text will now turn to a completely different matter for fully seven chapters.

The ending of this section anticipates the ending of the book of Exodus, with its mention of God's "glory," "dwelling," "fire," and "day/night."

5 **lads:** Or "youths"; the Hebrew term (*na'ar*) is analogous to "apprentice."
7 **hearing:** Lit., "ears." **and we will hearken:** this is an addition to the "we will do" of 19:8. In Deuteronomy "hearken" is often found connoting "obey."
10 **work of sapphire tiles:** Others, "pavement." Childs (1974) notes parallel Ugaritic texts to this description. **purity:** In Ugaritic, this word has an association of clarity or brightness, especially as regards precious stones (see "pure gold" in the Tabernacle account: 24:11, 17, 24, 31, 39, below).
11 **Pillars:** Apparently a technical term for the representatives of the people (Buber 1958: "corner-joints"). **send forth his hand:** Kill them. **beheld:** Heb. *hazoh*, often used in connection with prophetic vision (see Isaiah 1:1).
12 **them:** The Children of Israel.
17 **like a consuming fire:** In contrast to Moshe's striking positive experience of God in Chapter 3, where the bush burned but was not consumed, the Israelites experience him through fear.

18 Moshe came into the midst of the cloud
    when he went up the mountain.
    And Moshe was on the mountain
    for forty days and forty nights.

18 **forty:** Another meaningful number, reminiscent of the Flood. It is echoed
    in Elijah's later experience on the same summit (I Kings 19:8).

PART IV The Instructions for the Dwelling and the Cult (25–31)

Despite the importance of all that has preceded, the section of Exodus we now encounter occupies a significant amount of text, and therefore commands our attention, in the overall scheme of the book. It may seem puzzling to modern readers that a book that purports to be about a people's origins should choose to fill a third of its pages with a detailed description of a sanctuary, down to the last piece of tapestry and the last ritual vessel. Yet it is an indication of the "Tabernacle's" centrality in Israel's idea system that the story of its construction dominates the last half of Exodus.

Several factors may help to explain. First, the system of animal and grain sacrifices, or cult, was as important in ancient Israel as it was elsewhere in antiquity, as the chief means of formally expressing religious feeling. Indeed, the Bible traces this institution back to the beginning of human history, to Cain and Abel (Gen. 4:3–4). The cult's centrality survived the railings of the Prophets and the destruction of Solomon's Temple, and was still strong enough in late antiquity to provoke a severe crisis when its chief site, the Second Temple, fell to the Romans in the year 70 C.E. The latter event was a crux upon which the creation of classical Judaism took place, and the process was a painful one. So the opinion that many moderns have, that animal sacrifice was a barbaric custom, is quite beside the point as far as ancient Israel was concerned.

Second, there is the great theme of the book of Exodus, "Is YHWH in our midst or not?" (17:7), to which our account gives a resounding positive answer. The book of Exodus traces not only the journey of the people of Israel from Egypt to Sinai, but also the journey of God to rescue the people and to dwell ("tabernacle") among them (Greenberg 1972). A detailed presentation of God's "residence," as it were, is meant to convey

EXODUS

the assurance that the people are led by God himself. This further supports the biblical image of the divine king, who dwells among his subjects and "goes before" them.

Third, the Israelites shared with their neighbors the idea that a victorious God, following his triumph, was to be honored by his enthronement in a human-built structure (see Hallo, in Plaut 1981). Thus the last half of Exodus, far from trailing off into obscure priestly details, fits a well-known mold in its contemporary environment.

A final explanation of the prominence of the Tabernacle sections may be found in their intimate connection with the idea of the Sabbath. The "blueprint" chapters, 25–31, end with an extended passage on observing the Sabbath; the construction chapters, 35–40, begin with a brief passage on the prohibition of work on the holy day. These structural aspects suggest (as the ancient rabbis also saw) that cessation from work here means precisely from the tasks of construction, and that once a week human beings must step back from their own creating to acknowledge the true "work" of creation. Chapters 25–40, including the Golden Calf narrative, bring out these ideas through their use of refrainlike phrases, especially the repetition of one key word: "make" (Heb. 'asoh). The entire section is an object lesson in what the Bible deems it proper for human beings to make, and is a vehicle of contrast between God's creation and human attempts to reach the divine. Israel is engaged in the making of the Tabernacle (notice how "build," which would make more sense, is not used); when the time comes for the work to be put aside temporarily, they are to "make" the Sabbath. To these observations may be added the long-observed fact that the vocabulary of the Tabernacle's completion ("finished," "work," "blessed") recalls the completion of Creation in Gen. 2:1–4. Thus we are taught that Israel, through its religious life as typified by Sabbath and cult, becomes a partner in the process of Creation, either by imitating the divine act or by celebrating it.

Other peoples, to be sure, recall the beginning of the world in ritual and story, so it is important to make an anthropological observation. The purpose of all sanctuaries is to build a bridge to the divine, to link up with the forces that transcend human beings. It is perceived that certain places are particularly appropriate for this (folklore terms such places "the navel of the earth"), and, by extension, sanctuaries firmly anchor that inherent holiness. What the Tabernacle account initially accomplishes, most notably in its closing chapter (40), is to transfer a topographic "bridge" to a human-made and portable one. With the completion of this Dwelling, we find God resident neither on Sinai nor in the later Jerusalem, but rather

368

accompanying the people "upon all their travels" (40:38). The sacred center here thus moves; it is a portable anchor that establishes stability wherever it goes. The vitality that surrounded this idea is still to be seen in the successors of the Hebrew Bible, classical Judaism and Christianity, for whom, respectively, Torah and Cross provide a center that is at once movable and stabilizing.

But the sacred center, for biblical religion, finds equal expression in *time*. While the Dwelling account seems obsessed with matters of space, its setting among the Sabbath passages stresses more the concept of time. Such an aspect already begins to make itself felt in 24:16, where Moshe, on Sinai to receive the laws, waits for six days while the "cloud" covers the mountain, and is able to ascend only on the seventh day, at God's summons. We are thus left, paradoxically, with a structure (Dwelling) which at first glance uses many well-known art forms and religious motifs common to the ancient Near East, but which is a total departure from them via its connection with the Sabbath—an institution with no known equivalent in the ancient world. The Dwelling account presents us with a people for whom sacred time takes precedence over sacred space (for more on these themes, see Sarna 1986).

There have been many attempts, textually and artistically, to reconstruct the Tabernacle on the basis of our text here, the rationale being that surely so much detail as we find here will serve as the guidelines for an an actual structure. Rabbinic and medieval Jewish commentators, as well as modern scholars, have expended considerable energy to that end. But in fact none of the reconstructions has succeeded, for, as with narrative, the text is as much message as description. The text's main concern, it seems, is for the Dwelling to reflect holiness, in its choice of measurements and materials (see Haran 1985). The layout of the Dwelling expresses aesthetic ideas of perfection, through various symmetrical proportions (see Appendix A); the materials are graded such that the closer one gets to God (in the "Holiest Holy-Place"), the more precious the metal. In addition, both the colors used and the types of workmanship employed are similarly graded. In a general way, the intent of the narrator seems to have been close to the intent of the great cathedral builders of the Middle Ages: to reflect divine perfection and order in the perfection and order of a sacred structure.

The Dwelling, as described in Exodus, resembles other ancient Near Eastern sanctuaries in many particulars (for which, see the Commentary below), as well as strongly reflecting aspects of the later Temple of Solomon (I Kings 6–7). Some scholars have also likened it to a Bedouin tent (Heb. *shakhen* seems to be an archaic verb for "to tent"), appropriate to desert conditions. It is perhaps all three, a coalescing of Israel's ideas of the cult from a variety of historical and religious settings. That the Dwelling was viewed as historical is clear from biblical tradition itself (see II Sam. 7:6, for instance). But one should keep in mind that it is also a paradigmatic model, that helps to round out the overall scheme of Exodus. The book traces the progress of the people of Israel from servitude (to Pharaoh) to service (of God), and uses the human activity of building to do so. Thus, as Exodus opens, the Israelites are forcibly made to build royal storage cities; as the book ends, the people complete a structure through which they may serve the divine king.

Finally, there is the sequence of description in these chapters: the text begins with the blueprint for the holiest object, the "coffer" (ark), and proceeds through the structure in descending order of holiness. After the building instructions themselves are given, a number of related matters are treated, chief among them the attire of the priests and the ceremony consecrating the priests. The establishment of the cult, like that of the system of justice, is thus viewed as the command of God rather than the result of the need or request of human beings (contrast this with the "requested" monarchy in I Samuel 8).

25:1 Now YHWH spoke to Moshe, saying:
    2 Speak to the Children of Israel,
          that they may take me a raised-contribution;
          from every man whose heart makes-him-willing, you are to
             take my contribution.
    3 And this is the contribution that you are to take from them:
          gold, silver, and bronze,
    4 violet, purple, worm-scarlet, byssus, and goats'-hair,
    5 rams' skins dyed-red, dugongs' skins,
          acacia wood,
    6 oil for lighting,
          spices for oil of anointing and for fragrant smoking-incense,
    7 onyx stones, stones for setting
          for the *efod* and for the breastpiece.
    8 Let them make me a Holy-Place
          that I may dwell amidst them.

9 According to all that I grant you to see,
  the building-pattern of the Dwelling and the building-
      pattern of all its implements,
  thus are you to make it.

The "Contribution" (25:1–9): In the first seven verses of this opening section dealing with the Dwelling, the Israelites' contribution toward the structure is described in detail; but only in verse 8 is the purpose of this activity made clear. Despite the concreteness of the description, however, the actual blueprints, as it were, are shown to Moshe by God, and are not recorded in the text. Architects in the creative sense are superfluous here.

Moderns want to know where the Israelites procured such materials as gold and silver in quantity (see Chapter 38), or how they acquired the skills necessary for the fine artisanry involved (e.g., weaving, dyeing, manufacture of incense, and the setting of jewels). These questions, while logical in a historical setting, do not take the Bible on its own terms. The text appears to present the awed report of the Dwelling and its construction without leaving room for totally practical issues (just as Genesis 4 deals with Cain and his descendants without being concerned with the origins of Cain's wife).

25:2 **raised-contribution:** A collective noun (Plaut 1981). The image is a common one, as in English "raise money."

4 **violet:** The exact color is not certain; others, "blue." What does seem clear is that this was precious, probably because the dye was difficult to extract from its natural setting, and was the color of royalty (viz., "royal purple") (Milgrom 1983). The same color was used on the fringes commanded as a memorial garment in Num. 15:37–38. **worm-scarlet:** Others, "crimson." The dye was produced by crushing the shell of a certain insect, and hence the two-word Hebrew name. **byssus:** Fine linen (Heb. *shesh*, a loan word from Egyptian), as opposed to the plain *bad* (linen) of 28:42.

5 **dugongs':** The identification of *tahash* with this walruslike animal is not certain, but the skin is known to be suitable for purposes such as the one in this passage, as opposed, for instance, to dolphin skin. **acacia:** This particular tree, well suited for construction, is found most often in the Bible in reference to the Tabernacle.

6 **anointing:** For consecrating priests (e.g., 29:7) and kings (e.g., I Sam. 10:1). **fragrant smoking-incense:** See 30:34–38, below.

7 **for setting:** In the high priest's breastpiece (see 28:17–21, below). **efod:** An important garment of the high priest (see 28:6ff., below). **breastpiece:** Hung on the *efod* (see 28:15ff., below).

8 **Holy-Place:** Others, "sanctuary."

10 They are to make
    a coffer of acacia wood,
    two cubits and a half its length,
    a cubit and a half its width,
    and a cubit and a half its height.
11 You are to overlay it with pure gold,
    inside and outside you are to overlay it,
    and are to make upon it a rim of gold all around.
12 You are to cast for it four rings of gold
    and are to put them upon its four feet,
    with two rings on its one flank
    and two rings on its second flank.
13 You are to make poles of acacia wood
    and are to overlay them with gold
14 and are to bring the poles into the rings on the flanks of the
        coffer,
    to carry the coffer by (means of) them.
15 In the rings of the coffer are the poles to remain,
    they are not to be removed from it.
16 And you are to put in the coffer
    the Testimony that I give you.

17 You are to make a purgation-cover of pure gold,
    two cubits and a half its length
    and a cubit and a half its width.

The Coffer (25:10–16). The coffer or ark was a cult object of major importance in premonarchic and early monarchic Israel. In our text it contains
the "Testimony" (i.e., the tablets with the Ten Words); in Josh. 3:14–15
it precedes the people into the Promised Land; in I Sam. 4:11–5:12 it is
captured in battle but mysteriously wreaks havoc among the enemy (hence
its cinematic offspring *Raiders of the Lost Ark*). Finally, David's transporting of it to Jerusalem (II Sam. 6) marks the formal establishment of that
city as a holy one and as the capital of Israel.

In Exodus the coffer literally plays a central role. It stands in the innermost recesses of the Tabernacle, at the sacred center. Considering what the coffer contained—tablets with God's words on them rather than statues of gods—it addresses the primacy of divine word over divine representation in ancient Israelite thought.

The Purgation-Cover (25:17–22): *Kapporet* here could indicate simply "cover," yet its function goes beyond mere protection. The name of this central part of the above-cited central cult object may be a play on words. The Hebrew verb *kapper*, which occurs again later in these texts (see 29:33–37), often means "purge" or "purify"; earlier translators rendered it as "expiate" or even "propitiate," and the *kapporet* as "mercy-seat" or "propitiatory." The *kapporet* was apparently the holiest spot in the Israelite cult system, and it was there that God was said to speak his will to the people. This idea represents a remarkable shrinking and intimatizing process: the God who spoke to the assembled people, amid thunder, fire, and trembling earth at Sinai, now communicates with them from an area roughly the size of a small desk or table. In addition, there is a shift from a one-time event (Sinai) to the permanent fact of a sanctuary—a development which will later be repeated in Solomon's Temple.

10 **coffer:** Others, "ark." The Hebrew word *aron*, like "ark," means a chest or box, and is also used of Yosef's "coffin" in Gen. 50:20. I have used a different word here so as not to confuse it with Noah's ark (Heb. *teva*).
cubits: The cubit was a common measure in the ancient world, conceived of as the length of a man's forearm. The biblical cubit existed in two versions, measuring between 17½ and 20½ inches. **two cubits and a half . . .:** Thus the proportions of the coffer are 5:3:3.
11 **a rim of gold all around:** Heb. *zer zahav saviv.*
16 **testimony:** B-R, seeking to connect *'edut* ("Testimony") with the sound of *mo'ed* ("appointment"), translate these two terms as "representation" and "presence." The tablets bear the name "testimony" because they "testify" or bear witness to God's relationship with the Israelites. It should also be noted that Akkadian *'adu*, cognate with our *'edut*, means "treaty," somewhat like the Hebrew *berit* ("covenant"), which is often found parallel to *'edut* in the Bible (DeVaux 1965).
17 **purgation-cover:** Heb. *kapporet.* There are two long-held traditions of translating this word: "expiation" or "mercy-seat" and plain "cover." I have kept both ideas in the present rendering. The *kapporet* was used for the purpose of obtaining forgiveness from God (see Lev. 16:13–15), and also served symbolically as God's "footstool" to the throne represented by the coffer. Such symbolism is in line with ancient Near Eastern practice, as is the keeping of the covenant documents within the footstool.

18 You are to make two winged-sphinxes of gold,
   of hammered-work are you to make them,
   at the two ends of the purgation-cover.

19 Make one sphinx at the end here
   and one sphinx at the end there;
   from the purgation-cover are you to make the two sphinxes,
   at its two ends.

20 And the sphinxes are to be spreading (their) wings upward
   with their wings sheltering the purgation-cover,
   their faces, each-one toward the other;
   toward the purgation-cover are the sphinxes' faces to be.

21 You are to put the purgation-cover on the coffer, above it,
   and in the coffer you are to put
   the Testimony that I give you.

22 I will appoint-meeting with you there
   and I will speak with you
   from above the purgation-cover,
   from between the sphinxes that are on the coffer of Testi-
       mony—
   all that I command you
   concerning the Children of Israel.

23 You are to make a table of acacia wood,
   two cubits its length,
   a cubit its width,
   and a cubit and a half its height;

24 you are to overlay it with pure gold.
   You are to make a rim of gold for it, all around,

25 you are to make for it a border, a handbreadth all around,
   thus you are to make a rim of gold for its border, all around.

26 You are to make for it four rings of gold
   and are to put the rings at the four edges, where its four legs
       (are).

27 Parallel to the border are the rings to be,
   as holders for the poles, to carry the table.

28 You are to make the poles of acacia wood, and are to overlay
       them with gold,
   that the table may be carried by (means of) them.

29 You are to make its plates and its cups,

its jars and its bowls, from which (libations) are poured;
of pure gold are you to make them.
30 And you are to put on the table
the Bread of the Presence, in my presence, regularly.

The Table (25:23–30): The table and its implements, like some of the other features of the Tabernacle, are holdovers from a more blatantly pagan model, where the gods were seen to be in need of nourishment. By thus using conventions of worship common throughout the ancient Near East, Israel expressed its desire to serve God, even while it was aware that he was not the sort of deity who requires food and drink. It might also be mentioned that another common object found in ancient sanctuaries, a bed, has intentionally been omitted from our structure.

18 **winged-sphinxes:** Others, "cherubim," which, however, is too reminiscent of chubby-cheeked baby angels in Western art. In Mesopotamian temples, these mythical figures in sculpture served as guardians; so too at the end of the Garden of Eden story in Gen. 3:24. See Albright (1961).
19 **here . . . there:** Or "on one side . . . on the other side"; at either end.
from: Or "out of"; others, "of one piece with." This one-piece construction is a frequent feature of the objects associated with the Tabernacle.
20 **toward the purgation-cover:** Facing downward, as if to avoid the direct presence of God.
22 **appoint-meeting:** The Hebrew verb refers to fixing a time, and is not the same as the earlier "meeting" (5:3). Exodus speaks of the "Tent of Appointment" from Chapter 27 on; it is unclear as to whether the Tabernacle itself or a separate structure is meant.   **from above the purgation-cover,/ from between the sphinxes:** So this was seen as the precise spot of God's presence in the Tabernacle.
27 **as holders for the poles:** Heb. *le-vatim le-vaddim*. *Batim* are literally "housings."
29 **plates . . . cups . . . jars . . . bowls:** Translations vary considerably on these terms. Haran (1985) cites several (e.g., "plates, bowls, dishes, cups," "ladles, jars, saucers, beakers").
30 **Bread of the Presence:** Trad. English "shewbread."   **regularly:** Not "perpetually," as earlier interpreters understood.

31 You are to make a lampstand of pure gold;
    of hammered-work is the lampstand to be made, its shaft
      and its stem;
    its goblets, its knobs and its blossoms are to be from it.
32 Six stems issue from its sides,
    three lamp-stems from the one side,
    and three lamp-stems from the second side:
33 three almond-shaped goblets on the one stem, with knobs
      and blossoms,
    and three almond-shaped goblets on the other stem, with
      knobs and blossoms—
    thus for the six stems that issue from the lampstand;
34 and on the lampstand (itself) four almond-shaped goblets,
      with their knobs and their blossoms,
35 a knob beneath two stems, from it,
    a knob beneath two stems, from it,
    and a knob beneath two stems, from it,
    for the six stems that issue from the lampstand.
36 Their knobs and their stems are to be from it,
    all of it hammered-work, of pure gold.
37 You are to make its lamps, seven (of them),
    you are to set up its lamps so that they light up (the space)
      across from it.
38 And its tongs and its trays (shall be) of pure gold.
39 (From) an ingot of pure gold they are to make it, together
      with all these implements.
40 Now see
    and make,
    according to their building-pattern which you are granted to
      see upon the mountain.

26:1 Now the dwelling you are to make
      from ten tapestries
      of twisted byssus, violet, purple and worm-scarlet (yarn),
      with sphinxes, of designer's making, you are to make it.
   2 The length of each one tapestry (shall be) twenty-eight by
        the cubit,
      and the width, four by the cubit
      of each one tapestry,
      one measure for all of the tapestries.

The Lampstand (25:31–40): Despite the wealth of detail lavished on this striking symbol, its exact construction, like that of the Dwelling in general, remains unclear. The vocabulary used for its constituent parts comes from the realm of plants: shaft, stems, blossoms, almond shapes, etc. Indeed, the major latent symbol behind the lampstand is the tree—which appears in many forms and in almost all religions (Meyers 1976). The tree as a symbol is to be found throughout human culture, in such diverse settings as Native American stories and Norse myths; in the ancient Near East it specifically connoted permanence, growth, and majesty—in other words, a reflection of the divine. If one adds to this range of meanings the function of the lampstand—illumination (which often implies not only the giving of physical light but also, as the English phrase has it, enlightenment)—the lampstand will be seen to emerge as an object with considerable evocative power. All these meanings may not have been immediately obvious and conscious to the ancient pilgrim or worshipper, but they periodically surfaced; the lampstand was ancient Judaism's symbol of preference (judging from synagogue ruins) and not the "Star of David," which, as Gershom Scholem (1972) has shown, was a medieval mystical addition.

The importance of the lampstand in our text is indicated by verse 40, where the motif of God's revealing the structure of a sacred object on the mountain is resumed. Its significance is also attested by its major material of construction: pure gold.

The Dwelling Proper (26:1–14): The text describes the network of tapestries or curtains that comprise the structure itself, in two layers (vv.1–6 and 7–12), with two additional layers mentioned (v.14). The outer layers function to protect the inner ones from the elements, while the inner ones, true to the gradations of holiness previously mentioned, are more elaborate.

31 **shaft . . . stem:** Meyers (1976) interprets this as a hendiadys (two Hebrew words that yield a composite meaning), "thickened shaft." **knobs . . . blossoms:** Others, "calyxes . . . petals."
33 **almond-shaped:** Like the shape of the almond flower.
35 **from it:** See the note to verse 19, above.
38 **tongs:** Others, "snuffers."
26:1 **the dwelling:** In this context it signifies the inside portion of the Tabernacle; lowercase is used here to distinguish it from the entire structure. **tapestries:** Others, "curtains," "cloths." **designer's making:** According to the designer's craft.

3 Five of the tapestries are to be joined, each-one to the other,
and five tapestries joined, each-one to the other.
4 You are to make loops of violet
on the edge of one tapestry, at the end of the one joint;
and thus you are to make at the edge of the end tapestry, at
the second joint.
5 Fifty loops are you to make on the first tapestry,
and fifty loops are you to make at the end of the tapestry that
is at the second joint,
the loops opposite, each-one from the other.
6 You are to make fifty clasps of gold
and you are to join the tapestries, each-one to the other, with
the clasps,
so that the dwelling may be one-piece.
7 You are to make the tapestries of goats'-hair for a tent over
the dwelling,
eleven tapestries you are to make them.
8 The length of each one tapestry (shall be) thirty by the cubit,
and the width, four by the cubit,
for each one tapestry,
one measure for the eleven tapestries.
9 You are to join five of the tapestries separately
and six of the tapestries separately,
but you are to double over the sixth tapestry, facing the tent.
10 You are to make fifty loops at the edge of the one tapestry,
the end-one, at the joint,
and fifty loops at the end of the second joining tapestry.
11 You are to make clasps of bronze, fifty,
and you are to bring the clasps into the loops, so that you
join the tent together,
that it may become one-piece.
12 And as for the extension that overlaps in the tapestries of the
tent,
half of the overlapping tapestry you are to extend over the
back of the dwelling.
13 The cubit over here and the cubit over there of the overlap,
in the long-part of the tapestries of the tent,
is to be extended over the sides of the tent over here and over
there, in order to cover it.

14 You are to make a covering for the tent of rams' skins dyed-
      red,
   and a covering of dugongs' skins, above it.

15 You are to make boards for the Dwelling
   of acacia wood, standing-upright;
16 ten cubits, the length of a board,
   and a cubit and a half, the width of each one board;
17 with two pegs for each one board, parallel one to the other,
   thus are you to make for all the boards of the Dwelling.
18 And you are to make the boards for the Dwelling:
   twenty as boardwork on the Negev border, southward,
19 and forty sockets of silver are you to make beneath twenty of
      the boards,
   two sockets beneath each one board for its two pegs
   and two sockets beneath each other board for its two pegs;
20 and for the second flank of the Dwelling, on the northern
      border, twenty as boardwork,
21 with their forty sockets of silver,
   two sockets beneath each one board,
   and two sockets beneath each other board.
22 And for the rear of the Dwelling, toward the sea, you are to
   make six boards,

The Framework (26:15–30): The rigid part of the Tabernacle structure, while described in some detail, leaves room for many questions about specifics (e.g., how exactly did the boards fit together? was there one corner board or two? is the text perhaps describing planks or frames?) What is most important, as mentioned above, is the sense of proportion and approach to the divine implied by symmetrical numbers.

   9 **double over:** Since it overlaps (see vv. 12–13).
   4 **covering:** A different Hebrew verb (*kasse*) from the one translated by "purgation-cover" (*kapper*).
   15 **boards:** Some interpret as "beams" or "frames." See the discussion of the possibilities in Haran (1965).
   17 **pegs:** Others, "tenons," a more technical architectural term. **parallel:** Heb. obscure.
   18 **Negev:** The desert southland of Israel.
   22 **the sea:** The Mediterranean, and hence the west, from the perspective of one living in the land of Israel.

23 and two boards you are to make for the corners of the
    Dwelling, at the rear,
24 so that they may be of twin-use, (seen) from the lower-end,
    and together may be a whole-piece, at the top, toward the
        first ring;
    thus shall it be for the two of them,
    for the two corners shall they be.
25 Then there are to be eight boards with their sockets of silver,
        sixteen sockets,
    two sockets beneath each one board,
    and two sockets beneath each other board.
26 You are to make running-bars of acacia wood,
    five for the boards of Dwelling's one flank
27 and five bars for the boards of the Dwelling's second flank,
    and five bars for the Dwelling's flank at the rear, toward the
        sea.
28 And the middle bar (shall be) amidst the boards, running
    from end to end.
29 Now the boards you are to overlay with gold,
    their rings you are to make of gold, as holders for the bars,
    and are to overlay the bars with gold.
30 So erect the Dwelling, according to its plan,
    as you have been granted to see upon the mountain.

31 You are to make a curtain
    of violet, purple, worm-scarlet and twisted byssus;
    of designer's making, they are to make it, with winged-
        sphinxes.
32 You are to put it on four columns of acacia,
    overlaid with gold, their hooks of gold,
    upon four sockets of silver;
33 and you are to put the curtain beneath the clasps.
    You are to bring there, inside the curtain,
    the coffer of Testimony;
    the curtain shall separate for you
    the Holy-Place from the Holiest Holy-Place.
34 You are to put the purgation-cover
    on the coffer of Testimony;
    in the Holiest Holy-Place.

35   You are to place the table outside the curtain,
       and the lampstand opposite the table on the south flank of
          the Dwelling,
       but the table you are to put on the north flank.
36   You are to make a screen for the entrance to the tent,
       of violet, purple, worm-scarlet and twisted byssus,
       of embroiderer's making;
37   you are to make for the screen five columns of acacia,
       you are to overlay them with gold, their hooks of gold,
       and are to cast for them five sockets of bronze.

27:1 You are to make the altar of acacia wood,
       five cubits in length
       and five cubits in width;
       square is the altar to be,
       and three cubits its height.
   2   You are to make its horns on its four points,

The Curtain and the Screen (26:31–37): Two hangings separate different parts of the Tabernacle: the curtain, which closes off the inner sanctum; and the screen, which separates tent and courtyard.

The Altar (27:1–8): As Cassuto (1967) points out, Israelite worship, like that in surrounding cultures, would have been unthinkable without an altar for animal sacrifices. The one described here is a compromise between permanence and portability: it was hollow for transporting, to be filled in with earth at each encampment.

   As with the lampstand, the exact construction of the object is to proceed along lines given to Moshe by God at Sinai.

   24   **of twin-use:** Used for two purposes? The exact meaning here has been
         long debated, with many sketches as to what the corners of the Tabernacle
         might have looked like.   **toward the first ring:** Heb. obscure.
   26   **running-bars:** Horizontal bars designed to hold the structure together.
   33   **Holiest Holy-Place:** Trad. "Holy of Holies."
   27:2 **horns:** Many altars have been dug up in the area, both Israelite and
         non-Israelite in origin, fitting this description. The origin and purpose of
         the "horns" is not clear. We do know that when an Israelite wanted to be
         granted asylum, for instance, he could grasp the horns of the altar (see I
         Kings 1:50ff.).

from it are its horns to be;
and you are to overlay it with bronze.

3 You are to make its pails for removing-its-ashes,
its scrapers, its bowls, its forks and its pans—
all of its implements, you are to make of bronze.

4 You are to make for it a lattice,
as a netting of bronze is made,
and are to make on the netting four rings of bronze
on its four ends;

5 you are to put it beneath the ledge of the altar, below,
so that the netting (reaches) to the halfway-point of the altar.

6 You are to make poles for the altar,
poles of acacia wood,
and are to overlay them with bronze.

7 Its poles are to be brought through the rings,
so that the poles are on the two flanks of the altar when they
carry it.

8 Hollow, of planks, are you to make it;
as he has granted you to see it on the mountain, thus are they
to make it.

9 You are to make the courtyard of the Dwelling:
on the Negev border, southward,
hangings for the courtyard, of twisted byssus,
a hundred by the cubit, the length on one border;

10 with its columns, twenty, their sockets, twenty, of bronze,
the hooks of the columns and their binders, of silver.

11 And thus on the northern border, lengthwise,
hangings a hundred (cubits) in length,
with its columns, twenty, their sockets, twenty, of bronze,
the hooks of the columns and their binders, of silver.

12 And (along) the width of the courtyard on the sea border
hangings of fifty cubits,
with its columns, ten, their sockets, ten.

13 And (along) the width of the courtyard on the eastern
border, toward sunrise,
fifty cubits,

14 namely: fifteen cubits of hangings for the shoulder-piece,
their columns, three, their sockets, three,

15 and for the second shoulder-piece, fifteen (cubits) of hang-
    ings,
   their columns, three, their sockets, three,
16 and for the gate of the courtyard, a screen of twenty cubits,
   of violet, purple, worm-scarlet and twisted byssus, of em-
    broiderer's making,
   their columns, four, their sockets, four.
17 All the columns of the courtyard all around are attached
    with silver, their hooks of silver,
   their sockets of bronze,
18 —the length of the courtyard, a hundred by the cubit, the
    width, fifty by fifty, the height, five cubits of twisted
    byssus,
   their sockets of bronze.
19 All the implements of the Dwelling for all its service (of
    construction),
   and all its pins, and all the pins of the courtyard,
   —bronze.

The Courtyard (27:9–19): Returning to the Tabernacle structure, the outer
courtyard is laid out, composed of hangings and columns. Again, the
numbers fit meaningfully together. Since we are dealing with the extrem-
ity of the Dwelling, the material used is the least precious: bronze.

3 **scrapers . . . bowls . . . forks . . . pans:** As in 25:29, above, the exact
   identification of these objects is not known.
4 **lattice . . . netting:** To let air through and facilitate burning (Cassuto
   1967).
7 **poles:** In contrast to those of the coffer, these were apparently removable.
   The altar was of lesser sanctity than the coffer, and it was not deemed as
   crucial that no human hand touch it.
8 **Hollow:** And thus easily transportable, to be filled with dirt every time it
   was set up.
9 **twisted byssus:** Heb. *shesh moshzar.*
10 **binders:** Others, "rods."
14 **shoulder-piece:** That is the literal Hebrew; "side" would be acceptable
   idiomatically.
19 **service (of construction):** Not worship (divine service), but rather a term
   referring to the Levites' setting up and dismantling of the Tabernacle
   (Milgrom 1983). **pins:** Others, "pegs."

20 Now you,
    command the Children of Israel,
    that they may take you
    oil of olives, clear, beaten,
    for the light,
    to set up for a lamp, regularly.
21 In the Tent of Appointment,
    outside the curtain that is over the Testimony,
    Aharon and his sons are to arrange it,
    from evening until morning
    in the presence of YHWH—
    a law for the ages, into your generations,
    on the part of the Children of Israel.

28:1 Now you, have come-near to you
    Aharon your brother and his sons with him,
    from amidst the Children of Israel,
    to be-priests for me;
    Aharon,
    Nadav and Avihu, Elazar and Itamar, the sons of Aharon.
  2 You are to make garments of holiness for Aharon your
        brother,
    for glory and for splendor.
  3 So you, speak to each who is wise of mind
    whom I have filled with the spirit of practical-wisdom,
    that they may make Aharon's garments,
    to hallow him, to be-priest for me.
  4 And these are the garments that they are to make:
    breastpiece and *efod* and tunic,
    braided coat,
    wound-turban and sash.
    So they are to make garments of holiness
    for Aharon your brother and for his sons,
    to be-priests for me.
  5 And they, they are to take gold, violet, purple, worm-scarlet
        and byssus.

  6 They are to make the *efod*
    of gold, of violet and of purple, of worm-scarlet and of
        twisted byssus,
    of designer's making.

The Oil (27:20–21): The transition from structure to human institution (the priesthood) is accomplished by both the opening formula here, "Now you. . . ," and by the oil itself, which is here used for light but which will soon be spoken of (Chap. 29) as a major agent in the anointing of the priests.

The Priestly Garments (28:1–5): As in the opening section on the Tabernacle itself (25:1–9), we are now given a listing of what is to come, the clothing in which the priests will perform their sacred functions. The purpose of the objects is mentioned again, this time at both the beginning and the end of the section.

In virtually all traditional religions such garments are of great importance, often signalling the status of the wearer as representative of the community (hence Aharon's breastpiece in this chapter). An additional function, stressed in our account, is that the garments somehow reflect God himself, through the use of certain colors and/or materials. That the term "glory" is used to indicate their function—a key term in the book, and always applied to God, never to Moshe, for instance—signals what is at stake.

The Efod (28:6–12, 13–14): This garment, which here seems to be a kind of apron worn only by the high priest, is mentioned elsewhere in the Bible in connection with worship (e.g., Judges 8:27), but with unclear meaning. Even here, the exact nature of the *efod* is not entirely certain; but what *is* cited is its function as the setting for the stones that symbolize the twelve tribes of Israel in God's presence. This is followed by a description of chains, whose use is mentioned immediately thereafter.

20 **beaten:** Crushed until the substance is pure.
21 **Tent of Appointment:** See the note to 25:22, above. DeVaux (1965) translates as "Tent of Rendezvous," and Moffatt (in his 1926 Bible translation) as "Trysting Tent," but these are too romantic in English, even in view of what I have said about the relationship between God and Israel.
arrange: Or "set up."
28:1 **be-priests:** One translation possibility was to coin an English verb, "to priest."
2 **glory . . . splendor:** Others, "dignity and magnificence," but retaining "glory" for *kavod* enables one to see in the priest's garb a reflection of the divine splendor.
3 **wise of mind:** Idiomatically, "skilled" or "talented." **practical-wisdom:** Wisdom in biblical literature most often denotes worldly wisdom or artisanry, not abstract intellectual prowess.

7 Two shoulder-pieces, joined, it is to have, at its two ends,
   and it is to be joined.
8 The designed-band of its *efod*, which is on it,
   according to its making, is to be from it,
   of gold, of violet, of purple, of worm-scarlet and of twisted
     byssus.
9 You are to take two onyx stones
   and are to engrave on them the names of the Children of
     Israel,
10 six of their names on the one stone,
   and the names of the six remaining-ones on the second
     stone,
   corresponding to their begettings.
11 Of stone-cutter's making, with seal engravings,
   you are to engrave the two stones,
   with the names of the Children of Israel;
   surrounded by braids of gold are you to make them.
12 You are to place the two stones on the shoulder-pieces of the
     efod,
   as stones of remembrance for the Children of Israel.
   Aharon is to bear their names in the presence of YHWH
   on his two shoulders,
   for remembrance.

13 You are to make braids of gold
14 and two chains of pure gold,
   (like) lacings are you to make them, of rope-making,
   and are to put the rope chains on the braids.

15 You are to make the breastpiece of Judgment
   of designer's making,
   like the making of the *efod* are you to make it,
   of gold, of purple, of worm-scarlet and of twisted byssus are
     you to make it.
16 Square it is to be, doubled-over,
   a span its length and a span its width.
17 You are to set-it-full with a setting of stones,
   four rows of stones—
   a row of carnelian, topaz and sparkling-emerald, the first
     row,

18 the second row: ruby, sapphire, and hard-onyx,
19 the third row: jacinth, agate, and amethyst,
20 the fourth row: beryl, onyx, and jasper.
    Braided with gold are they to be in their settings.
21 And the stones are to be with the names of the Children of
    Israel,
    twelve with their names,
    (with) signet engravings, each-one with its name, are they to
    be,
    for the twelve tribes.
22 You are to make, on the breastpiece, laced chains, of rope
    making, of pure gold;
23 and you are to make, on the breastpiece, two rings of gold;
    you are to put the two rings on the two ends of the breast-
    piece.

The Breastpiece (28.15–30): The central garment in this section is the
breastpiece, which seems to be some sort of woven pouch or bag. On the
outside it displays precious stones, each one engraved with the name of an
Israelite tribe; inside, it holds the oracular objects known as *Urim* and
Tummin (see the note to verse 30, below). In this passage, which is cast in
poetic form, the narrator appears to be drawing our attention to the specific function of the garments. Verses 29 and 30 repeat the phrase "over
his/Aharon's heart" (three times), "in the presence of YHWH" (three
times), and "regularly" (twice) to make clear their importance: Aharon
represents the people whenever he officiates in the sanctuary, and bears
the emblem of this office upon his very heart.

8 **designed-band:** Perhaps resembling a belt.
10 **begettings:** Birth order.
11 **braids:** Others, "mesh," "checkered-work."
12 **for remembrance:** For a visible symbol.
16 **a span:** A measure taken to be the distance between the outstretched
    thumb and the little finger, half a cubit or about nine inches.
17–20 **carnelian . . . jasper:** The exact identification of many of these stones is
    uncertain. The reader will find a different list in virtually every Bible
    translation.

24 And you are to put the two ropes of gold on the two rings
   at the ends of the breastpiece;
25 and the two ends of the two ropes, you are to put on the two
      braids
   and you are to put them on the shoulder-piece of the *efod*,
      facing frontward.
26 You are to make two rings of gold,
   and are to place them on the two ends of the breastpiece, on
      its edge, which is across from the *efod*, inward,
27 and you are to make two rings of gold,
   and are to put them on the two shoulder-pieces of the *efod*,
      below, facing frontward, parallel to its joint, above the
      designed-band of the *efod*.
28 They are to tie the breastpiece from its rings to the rings of
      the *efod*
   with a thread of violet,
   to be (fixed) on the designed-band of the *efod;*
   the breastpiece is not to slip from the *efod*.
29 So Aharon is to bear
   the names of the Children of Israel
   on the breastpiece of Judgment
   over his heart,
   whenever he comes into the Holy-Place
   for remembrance, in the presence of YHWH,
   regularly.
30 And you are to put
   in the breastpiece of Judgment
   the *Urim* and the *Tummim,*
   that they may be over Aharon's heart,
   whenever he comes into the presence of YHWH.
   So Aharon is to bear
   the breastpiece of Judgment for the Children of Israel
   over his heart
   in the presence of YHWH,
   regularly.

31 You are to make the tunic for the *efod*
   all of violet.
32 Its head-opening is to be in its middle;

there shall be a seam for its opening, all around, of weaver's
   making,
like the opening for armor is it to be for him, it is not to be
   split.
33 You are to make on its skirts
   pomegranates of violet, purple, and worm-scarlet,
   on its skirts, all around,
   and bells of gold amidst them, all around:
34 bell of gold and pomegranate,
   bell of gold and pomegranate,
   on the skirts of the tunic, all around.

The Tunic (28:31–35): Aharon's tunic or shirt is notable for its design of
bells and pomegranates, but even more for its protective function, supplied by actual bells, of maintaining the proper distance between Aharon
and God in the sanctuary.

29 **over his heart:** Or "upon his heart," three times here. A similar idea
   occurs in later Judaism, which interpreted Deut. 6:8 ("you shall bind
   them as a sign upon your hand, and they shall serve as bands between your
   eyes") literally. The resulting *tefillin* ("phylacteries"), leather straps with
   small boxes containing the relevant Deuteronomy passages, worn during
   weekdays morning prayers, include a text that is worn on the arm in such
   a way as to point to the heart.
30 **Urim . . . Tummim:** Oracular objects, used for divining God's plans (e.g.
   learning if it was the right time to go into battle). Their exact shape and
   mode of operation are the subject of much scholarly debate (see Cassuto
   1967, for instance). In I Sam. 28:6, *Urim* are equated with dreams and
   prophets as a means of answering human queries. B-R, following Luther,
   translate the terms as "Lichtende und Schlichtende" ("lights and perfec-
   tions"), a possible literal but unclear translation. It is also worth noting
   that *Urim* begins with the first letter of the Hebrew alphabet, and *Tummim*
   the last, giving rise to the possibility that the names themselves are
   symbolic.
31 **tunic:** Others, "robe."
32 **armor:** Or "coat of mail."   **split:** Or "splittable."
33 **pomegranates:** Cassuto (1967) notes that these were a common ornamen-
   tal device in the ancient world, and a symbol of fertility (as in Song of
   Songs 6:7, 11; 8:2).   **bells:** Their use is explained in verse 35, "so that he
   [Aharon] does not die." Bells serve to drive away demons or to warn of
   human approach in many cultures; see Gaster (1969) for parallels.
34 **bell of gold and promegranate:** In alternating design.

35 It is to be (put) on Aharon, for attending,
    that its sound may be heard
    whenever he comes into the Holy-Place in the presence of
        YHWH, and whenever he goes out,
    so that he does not die.

36 You are to make a plate of pure gold
    and are to engrave on it signet engravings:
    Holiness for YHWH.
37 You are to place it on a thread of violet,
    that it may be on the turban;
    on the forefront of the turban is it to be.
38 It is to be on Aharon's brow.
    So Aharon is to bear
    the iniquity of the holy-offerings that the Children of Israel
        offer-as-holy,
    all their gifts of holiness;
    it is to be on his brow
    regularly,
    for (receiving) favor for them, in the presence of YHWH.

39 You are to braid the coat with byssus;
    you are to make a turban of byssus,
    and a sash you are to make, of embroiderer's making.
40 And for the sons of Aharon, you are to make coats,
    you are to make them sashes
    and caps you are to make for them,
    for glory and for splendor.
41 You are to clothe in them Aharon your brother, and his sons
        with him,
    you are to anoint them,
    you are to give-mandate to them,
    and you are to hallow them,
    that they may be-priests for me.
42 You are to make them breeches of linen
    to cover the flesh of nakedness;
    from the hips to the thighs are they to extend.
43 They are to be on Aharon and on his sons,
    whenever they come into the Tent of Appointment
    or whenever they approach the altar

to attend at the Holy-Place,
that they do not bear iniquity and die
—a law for the ages, for him and for his seed after him.

29:1 Now this is the ceremony
that you are to make for them

The Head-Plate (28:36–38): Foremost among the symbols on Aharon's garments is what he bears on his brow: a band with the words "Holiness for YHWH." It serves as a symbol of his efforts to obtain forgiveness on behalf of the Israelite people, one of his primary functions as priest. This function extends to cover even unintentional transgressions, such as accidents in the handling of sacred cultic objects.

Other Priestly Garments (28:39–43): These include remaining vestments for Aharon and his sons, to the end that "they do not bear iniquity and die" (v.43)—a major concern of the priesthood, which viewed all impurities as ritually dangerous before God. Note the solemn ending of this passage:"—a law for the ages, for him and for his seed after him."

The Investiture Ceremony (29:1–45): Although the text still has a number of Tabernacle items to discuss, viz., the incense and its altar, other objects, and the commissioning of the artisans for the construction work, it natur-

36 **plate:** Lit., "flower" or "gleamer," perhaps alluding to its shining quality, or to its shape of some kind.
38 **to bear/ the iniquity of the holy-offerings:** To atone for accidental violations of purity concerning sacrifices brought by the people. This is a classic concern of priests.
40 **caps:** Of less splendor than Aharon's turban, but constructed along the same lines (wound cloth).
41 **give-mandate:** Lit., "fill the hand." The term indicates induction into office; possibly something was put into the inductee's hand symbolizing their new status. *Mandatus* in Roman law is similar, and hence the present translation. Plaut (1981) also points out that this expression in Akkadian means "to appoint." **anoint . . . give mandate . . . hallow:** "A rising trilogy of near synonyms" (Plaut 1981).
42 **breeches . . . to cover . . . nakedness:** As previously (20:23), any hint of sexuality is separated from the cult.
29:1 **ceremony:** Lit., "matter." The actual implementation of the ceremony is recounted in Lev. 8:13ff. So unlike the rest of the Tabernacle material, (Chaps. 35–40), this ritual is delayed.

to hallow them, to be-priests for me:
Take a steer, a young-one of the herd, and rams, two, hale,

2 and bread of *matza* and flat cakes of *matza*, mixed with oil,
   and wafers of *matza*, dipped in oil,
of fine-ground wheat are you to make them.

3 **You are to put them in one basket**
and are to bring-them-near in the basket,
along with the steer and along with the two rams.

4 And Aharon and his two sons
   you are to bring-near to the entrance of the Tent of Appoint-
      ment
   and are to wash them with water.

5 You are to take the garments
   and are to clothe Aharon—
in the coat, in the tunic of the *efod*, in the *efod* and in the
      breastpiece;
you are to robe him in the designed-band of the *efod*,

6 you are to place the turban on his head,
   and are to put the sacred-diadem of holiness on the turban.

7 You are to take the oil for anointing
   and are to pour it on his head, anointing him.

8 And his sons, you are to bring-near
   and are to clothe them in coats;

9 you are to gird them with a sash, Aharon and his sons,
   and are to wind caps for them.
   It shall be for them as priestly-right,
   a law for the ages.
   So you are to give-mandate to Aharon and to his sons:

10 You are to bring-near the steer, before the Tent of Appoint-
      ment.
   and Aharon and his sons are to lay their hands on the head of
      the steer.

11 You are to slay the steer in the presence of YHWH,
   at the entrance of the Tent of Appointment,

12 and are to take some of the blood of the steer
   and are to put it on the horns of the altar with your finger,
   but all the rest of the blood, you are to throw against the
      foundation of the altar.

13 You are to take all the fat that covers the innards,

with what hangs over the liver, the two kidneys and the fat
  that is on them,
and turn-them-into-smoke on the altar.

14 And the flesh of the steer, its skin and its dung,
  you are to burn with fire, outside the camp;
  removal-of-sin it is.

15 And the first ram, you are to take,
  and Aharon and his sons are to lay their hands on the head of
    the ram.

16 You are to slay the ram,
  you are to take its blood
  and you are to toss it on the altar, all around.

17 And the ram you are to chop up into carcass-choppings,
  you are to wash its innards and its legs
  and you are to put (them) on its choppings and on its head

18 and are to turn-into-smoke the entire ram, on the altar;
  it is an offering-up for YHWH,
  Soothing Savor,
  a fire-gift for YHWH it is.

ally moves from describing the priestly garb to the ritual through which
the priests are installed in their sacred office. First, sacrifical animals and
bread are brought and prepared; then the priests are systematically
clothed in their sacred vestments. After the first animal is slaughtered, its
blood is dashed against the altar and the innards are burned as an offering;
then the second ram is slain, and its blood is placed on the priests' extremi-

  2 **matza:** See 12:8 and the accompanying note.
  6 **sacred-diadem:** See 28:36 above; the diadem was apparently in the shape
     of a flower, and was a "sign of consecration" (DeVaux 1965).
  9 **to wind caps:** Like small turbans: see the note to 28:40, above.
  14 **removal-of-sin:** Another major concern of the cult: the purity of the
     sanctuary. This is also reflected in the Levitical description of the Day of
     Purgation (Yom Kippur) in Lev. 16.
  18 **Soothing Savor:** Heb. *re'ah niho'ah*. The original signification of this
     concept must have been the common ancient one of feeding the gods, and
     hence the idea of an attractive smell. Already in Gen. 9:21 (after the
     Flood), however, it has been severed from that context, and the smell only
     pleases God and induces him to be more merciful with human beings.

19 And you are to take the second ram
    and Aharon and his sons are to lay their hands on the head of
       the ram.

20 You are to slay the ram,
    you are to take (some) of its blood
    and you are to put (it)
    on the ear lobe of Aharon and on the right ear lobe of Aha-
       ron's sons,
    and on the thumb of their right hands and on the thumb-toe
       of their right feet,
    then you are to toss the blood on the altar, all around.

21 You are to take some of the blood that is on the altar, and
       some of the oil for anointing,
    and you are to toss it on Aharon and on his garments, on his
       sons and on his sons' garments with him,
    that he and his garments may be hallowed, and his sons and
       his sons' garments with him.

22 You are to take the fat from the ram,
    the tail, the fat that covers the innards and what hangs over
       the liver, the two kidneys and the fat that is on them,
    and the right thigh,
    for it is the ram for giving-mandate;

23 and one loaf of bread and one cake of oil-bread and one
       wafer from the basket of *matza* that is in the presence of
       YHWH;

24 you are to place them all
    on the palms of Aharon and on the palms of his sons,
    and you are to hold them high as a high-offering, in the
       presence of YHWH.

25 You are to take them from their hand
    and you are to turn-them-into-smoke on the altar, beside the
       offering-up,
    for a Soothing Savor in the presence of YHWH,
    it is a fire-gift for YHWH.

26 You are to take the breast from the ram of giving-mandate
       that is Aharon's,
    and you are to hold it high as a high-offering, in the presence
       of YHWH,
    that it may be an allotment for you.

27 So you are to hallow the breast for the high-offering, and the
     thigh of the raised-contribution,
   that is held-high, that is raised
   from the ram of giving-mandate,
   from what is Aharon's and from what is his sons'.
28 It is to be Aharon's and his sons',
   a fixed-allocation for the ages, on the part of the Children of
     Israel,
   for it is a raised-contribution,
   and a raised-contribution is it to be on the part of the Chil-
     dren of Israel,
   from their well-being–offering meals,
   their raised-contribution for YHWH.
29 Now the garments of holiness that are Aharon's
   are to belong to his sons after him,
   to anoint them in them and to give-them-mandate in them.
30 For seven days is the one of his sons that acts-as-priest in his
     stead to be clothed in them,
   the one who comes into the Tent of Appointment to attend
     at the Holy-Place.

ties. Blood is sprinkled on the priests' garments; then they hold up the
fat-parts and breast of the ram, and follow by offering it up. Then the
priests eat the cooked flesh of a special ram, the remains of which are to be
burnt. Finally, the altar is purified.

After the regular sacrifice is specified (vv.38–41), the section ends with
a powerful meditation on the purpose of the Tabernacle: "hallow" occurs
three times, and "dwell" twice. In a word: by "meeting" with the Children of Israel at the Tent, God's glory makes tent, altar, priests, and most
important, the people of Israel, holy. Indeed, the root *kaddesh*, "holy,"
occurs numerous times in the chapter, presaging its multiple use in the
next book, Leviticus.

  20 **ear lobe . . . thumb . . . thumb-toe:** These comprise the extremities of
       the body, and thus are a way of including the entire body symbolically.
  24 **high-offering:** The earlier translation of "wave-offering" has been shown
       to be incorrect by Milgrom (1983).
  26 **allotment:** For the priests.
  27 **that is held-high, that is raised:** Heb. *asher hunaf va-asher huram.*

31 And the ram for giving-mandate you are to take
    and are to boil its flesh in the Holy-Place.

32 Aharon and his sons are to eat the flesh of the ram, along
        with the bread that is in the basket,
    at the entrance of the Tent of Appointment.

33 They are to eat them—those who are purged by them,
    to give-them-mandate, to hallow them;
    an outsider is not to eat (them), for they are holiness.

34 Now if there be anything left over of the flesh of giving-
        mandate or of the bread, by morning,
    you are to burn what is left by fire,
    it is not to be eaten, for it is holiness.

35 You are to make (thus) for Aharon and for his sons,
    according to all that I have commanded you,
    for seven days, you are to give-them-mandate.

36 A steer for removing-sin, you are to make-ready for each
        day, concerning the purging,
    that you may remove-sin from the altar, by your purging it,
    and you are to anoint it, to hallow it.

37 For seven days you are to purge the altar, that you may
        hallow it.
    Thus the altar will become
    holiest holiness;
    whoever touches the altar shall become-holy.

38 And this is what you are to make-ready on the altar:
    year-old lambs, two for each day, regularly.

39 The first lamb you are to make-ready for the morning,
    and the second lamb you are to make-ready at twilight.

40 A tenth-measure of fine-meal, mixed with beaten oil, a
        quarter of a *hin*,
    and (as) libation, a quarter of a *hin* of wine—for the first
        lamb.

41 And the second lamb you are to make-ready at twilight,
    like the leading-donation of the morning, and like its liba-
        tion, (that) you make-ready for it,
    for a Soothing Savor,
    a fire-gift for YHWH;

42 a regular offering-up, throughout your generations,

at the entrance to the Tent of Appointment, in the presence
   of YHWH;
for I will appoint-meeting with you there,
to speak to you there.
43 So I will appoint-meeting there
with the Children of Israel,
and it will be hallowed
by my Glory.
44 I will hallow the Tent of Appointment and the altar,
and Aharon and his sons I will hallow,
to be-priests for me.
45 And I will dwell amidst the Children of Israel
and I will be a God for them,
46 that they may know
that I am YHWH their God
who brought them out of the land of Egypt
to dwell, myself, in their midst,
I, YHWH their God.

31 **boil:** This clearly indicates that the food in question is meant for the priests' consumption, since sacrifices were normally completely burned.
33 **purged:** Purified.   **outsider:** Not in the sense of "foreigner," but of "one unauthorized" for the purpose, a layman (Clements 1972).
36 **purging it:** Or "purging in regard to it."
37 **whoever:** Others, "whatever."   **become-holy:** When a person came in contact with holy objects, he became temporarily removed from the every-day, in a state resembling what we, in a sense more negative than the Bible means it, would call contamination (as in radioactivity).
38 **make-ready:** Others, "offer."   **year-old:** That is, newly mature and hence in a state of perfection.
40 **hin:** About a gallon.
41 **leading-donation:** As part of the terminology of sacrifice, the *minha* was to "lead to" God (just as *'ola* bears the sound of "ascend," and *korban* "bring-near") (Buber and Rosenzweig 1936).
46 **that they may know:** This pervasive theme of Exodus finds its true resolution through the Tabernacle texts—not only will the Israelites experience ("know") God through the "wonders" wrought on their behalf in Egypt, but also through their communication with him in ritual.

30:1 You are to make an altar, a smoking-site for smoking-incense,
     of acacia wood are you to make it,
  2 a cubit its length and a cubit its width;
     square is it to be, and two cubits its height,
     its horns from it.
  3 You are to overlay it with pure gold—
     its roof, its walls all around, and its horns,
     and you are to make a rim of gold all around.
  4 And two rings of gold you are to make for it, beneath its rim,
     on its two flanks, you are to make (them) on its two sides,
     that they may be for holders for poles, to carry it by (means
        of) them.
  5 You are to make the poles of acacia wood
     and you are to overlay them with gold.
  6 And you are to put it in front of the curtain that is over the
        coffer of Testimony,
     in front of the purgation-cover that is over the Testimony,
     where I will appoint-meeting with you.
  7 And Aharon is to send-up-in-smoke, fragrant smoking-
        incense on it,
     morning by morning;
     when he polishes the lamps, he is to send-it-up-in-smoke.
  8 And when Aharon sets up the lamps,
     at twilight,
     he is to send-it-up-in-smoke,
     regular smoke-offering in the presence of YHWH, through-
        out your generations.
  9 You are not to offer-up upon it any outsider's smoking-in-
        cense,
     either as offering-up or as leading-donation,
     nor are you to pour out any libation upon it.
 10 Aharon is to do-the-purging upon its horns,
     once a year,
     with the sin-removing blood of purgation;
     once a year
     he is to do-the-purging upon it,
     throughout your generations,
     holiest holiness is it for YHWH.

 11 Now YHWH spoke to Moshe, saying:

12 When you lift up the heads of the Children of Israel, in
      counting them,
    they are to give, each-man, a purgation-payment for his life,
      for YHWH,
    when they count them,
    that there be no plague on them, when they count them.
13 This (is what) they are to give, everyone that goes through
      the counting:
    half a *shekel* of the Holy-Place *shekel*—twenty grains to the
      shekel—
    half a *shekel*, a contribution for YHWH.

The Incense Altar (30:1–10): This altar, which is not mentioned again, is
seen by some as a later interpolation (DeVaux 1965): here it links up with
what has gone before through the theme of purging (purification), in verse
10. For more on the incense itself, see verses 22ff., below.

Census and Ransom (30:11–16): Continuing the theme of purgation, divine
command provides for a ransom to be given to the priests, in order to
remove ("purge away") sin incurred by census-taking.
    The idea that numbering the people could bring down the wrath of God
is portrayed in most striking fashion in II Sam. 24:1–9, where David
usurps God's prerogative in numbering the men for military purposes,
leading to a plague among the people. It seems that a census was viewed as
a dangerous undertaking, perhaps analogous to the taking of photographs
among certain peoples (which is felt to be threatening to one's essence).
One who can number, can control (Gaster 1969).

30:6 **in front of . . .:** Some ancient versions and manuscripts omit this entire
      line as a redundancy.
   7 **fragrances:** Incense.   **when he polishes:** Others, "when he dresses" or
      "trims."
   9 **outsider's smoke:** This prohibition is violated by Aharon's sons in Lev.
      10:1 ("offering outsider's fire"), resulting in their death by "fire from
      before YHWH."
  10 **do-the-purging:** On the day of Yom Kippur, when the ancient sanctuary
      was, as it were, detoxified (of sins).
  12 **lift up the heads:** In idiomatic English we would say "count heads."
      purgation-payment: Others, "ransom."
  13 **shekel:** Literally, a "weight" of silver. Coins as such are not documented
      in the land of Israel until centuries after the events documented in Exodus
      took place. For a full discussion of biblical currency, see Sellers (1962).

14 Everyone that goes through the counting, from the age of
    twenty years and upward,
    is to give the contribution of YHWH.
15 The rich are not to pay-more and the poor are not to pay-less
    than half a *shekel*
    when giving the contribution of YHWH,
    to do-purgation for your lives.
16 You are to take the silver for doing-purgation
    from the Children of Israel
    and are to give it over for the construction-service of the
      Tent of Appointment,
    that it may be for the Children of Israel
    as a remembrance in the presence of YHWH,
    to do-purgation for your lives.

17 Now YHWH spoke to Moshe, saying:
18 You are to make a basin of bronze,
    its pedestal of bronze,
    for washing,
    and you are to put it between the Tent of Appointment and
      the altar;
    you are to put water therein,
19 that Aharon and his sons may wash with it
    their hands and their feet.
20 When they come into the Tent of Appointment
    they are to wash with water
    so that they do not die,
    or when they approach the altar, to be-in-attendance,
    to send up fire-offering in smoke for YHWH,
21 they are to wash their hands and their feet,
    so that they do not die.
    It is to be for them a law for the ages,
    for him and for his sons, throughout their generations.

22 Now YHWH spoke to Moshe, saying:
23 And as for you, take you fragrant-spices, essence,
    streaming-myrrh, five hundred,
    cinnamon-spice, half as much—fifty and two hundred,
    fragrant-cane, fifty and two hundred,

24 and cassia, five hundred
    by the *shekel*-weight of the Holy-Place,
    as well as olive oil, a *hin,*
25 and you are to make (from) it anointing oil of holiness,
    perfume from the perfume-mixture, of perfumer's making;
    anointing oil of holiness is it to be.
26 You are to anoint with it
    the Tent of Appointment
    and the coffer of Testimony
27 and the table and all its implements
    and the lampstand and all its implements
    and the altar for smoke-offerings
28 and the altar for offering-up and all its implements
    and the basin and its pedestal.
29 You are to hallow them
    that they may become holiest holiness,
    whoever touches them is to become-holy.

The Basin (30:17–21): Returning to the familiar stylistic pattern of the Tabernacle account, "You are to make. . . ," we are told of the basin in which the priests washed. Yet this brief aside links up with the motif of protection from death that was encountered earlier (see 28:35).

The Anointing Oil (30:22–33): "Holy" is once again heard as a key word, both in the sense of making something sacred and in the sense of being reserved for special use only. Oil was used in many ancient cultures for positive purposes; elsewhere in the Bible, of course, it played its role in the anointing of kings and prophets, as well as the courteous treatment of guests and after bathing. Oil, then, carried with it connotations of brightness (see Psalm 104:15) and life itself.

14 **twenty years:** The age for military service (and so referring to males).
18 **basin:** Others, "laver." The Hebrew denotes something round.
20 **so that they do not die:** Twice here, underscoring the power of water to do away with ritual impurity.
23 **essence:** Lit., "head." **five hundred:** The measure here is "by the *shekel*-weight," as clarified in the next verse.
25 **perfume . . . perfume-mixture . . . perfumer's:** Heb. *rokah mirkhahat . . . roke'ah.* The verb seems to mean "to mix."
26 **to anoint with it/ the tent . . .:** Oil is thus used to anoint not only people but also objects.

30 And Aharon and his sons you are to anoint,
   you are to hallow them
   to be-priests for me.
31 And to the Children of Israel you are to speak, saying:
   Anointing oil of holiness
   this is to be for me
   throughout your generations.
32 On any (other) human body it is not to be poured out;
   in its (exact) proportion, you are not to make any like it—
   holiness it is,
   holiness shall it remain for you.
33 Any man who mixes perfumes like it
   or who puts any of it on an outsider
   is to be cut off from his kinspeople.

34 Now YHWH said to Moshe:
   Take you fragrant-spices,
   drop-gum, onycha, and galbanum,
   (these) fragrances and clear incense;
   part equalling part are they to be.
35 You are to make (with) it smoking-incense,
   perfume, of perfumer's making,
   salted, pure—holy.
36 You are to beat some of it into fine-powder
   and are to put some of it
   in front of the Testimony
   in the Tent of Appointment,
   where I will appoint-meeting with you;
   holiest holiness is it to be for you.
37 As for the smoking-incense that you make,
   you are not to make any for yourselves in its (exact) propor-
      tion;
   holiness shall it be for you, for YHWH.
38 Any man that makes any like it
   to savor it
   is to be cut off from his kinspeople.

31:1 Now YHWH spoke to Moshe, saying:
   2 See,
     I have called by name

Betzalel son of Uri, son of Hur, of the tribe of Yehuda.
3 I have filled him with the spirit of God
in practical-wisdom, discernment and knowledge
in all kinds of workmanship,
4 to design designs,
to make them in gold, in silver and in bronze,
5 in the carving of stones for setting and in the carving of
wood,
to make them through all kinds of workmanship.
6 And I, here I give (to be) with him
Oholiav son of Ahisamakh, of the tribe of Dan;

The Incense (30:34–38): This particular incense, warns the text, was to be used only for the sanctuary and not for everyday purposes.

The offering-up of incense was a feature common to worship all over the ancient Near East. At least two reasons have been advanced for its use: purification, and a fragrance pleasing to the deity. It is also curious how our text speaks of God's being with the Israelites as a column of cloud and of fire; the incense smoke might also then be reminiscent of this divine manifestation.

Craftsmen (31:1–11): As the Tabernacle account opened with a summary description of what was to be constructed, so it ends, with some names added. The craftsmen for the task, Betzalel and Oholiav, are depicted as "wise" (Heb. *hakham*), that is, skilled; they will make what Moshe has been given to see.

32 **according to its proportion:** That is, according to an exact "recipe."
33 **cut off:** The exact meaning of this is not clarified anywhere, but it seems to indicate the death penalty. It is often mentioned in connection with violations of the cult (see 12:15, for example).
34 **drop-gum . . .:** The identification of some of these substances is debated.
35 **salted:** Salt was employed in sacrifices perhaps originally to ward off demons; it has taken on importance in both worship and folklore (viz., the practice of throwing salt over one's shoulder). Some suggest that salt was used simply to improve the taste of the food, or to absorb the blood.
31:2 **called by name:** Or "chosen/singled out."
3 **spirit of God:** Or "breath of God," the transfer of which to human beings in the Bible results in great strength, leadership qualities, or, especially, prophetic inspiration.
6 **Oholiav:** Trad. English "Oholiab"; the name means "Tent of Father/God," rather appropriate here.

in the mind of all those wise of mind I place wisdom,
that they may make all that I have commanded you:
7 the Tent of Appointment
and the coffer of Testimony
and the purgation-cover that is over it
and all the implements of the Tent
8 and the table and all its implements
and the pure lampstand and all its implements
and the altar for smoke-offering
9 and the altar for offering-up and all its implements
and the basin and its pedestal,
10 and the officiating garments
and the garments of holiness for Aharon the priest and the
    garments of his sons for being-priests
11 and oil for anointing
and fragrant smoke for the holy-offerings—
according to all that I have commanded you, they are to
    make.

12 Now YHWH said to Moshe:
13 And you, speak to the Children of Israel, saying:
However: my Sabbaths you are to keep!
For it is a sign
between me and you, throughout your generations,
to know that I, YHWH, hallow you.
14 You are to keep the Sabbath,
for holiness is it for you,
whoever profanes it is to be put-to-death, yes, death!
For whoever makes work on it—
that person is to be cut off from amongst his kinspeople.
15 Six days is work to be made,
but on the seventh day
(is) Sabbath, Sabbath-Ceasing, holiness for YHWH,
whoever makes work on the Sabbath day is to be put-to-
    death, yes, death.
16 The Children of Israel are to keep the Sabbath,
to make the Sabbath-observance throughout their genera-
    tions
as a covenant for the ages;

17 between me and the Children of Israel
   a sign is it, for the ages,
   for in six days
   YHWH made the heavens and the earth,
   and on the seventh day
   he ceased and paused-for-breath.

18 Now he gave to Moshe
   when he had finished speaking with him on Mount Sinai
   the two tablets of Testimony,
   tablets of stone,
   written by the finger of God.

The Sabbath (31:12–17): *The Tablets* (31:18): As a reminder of the Sabbath's importance amid all the anticipated construction activity, the Israelites are now commanded to observe the holy day. The section is also a prelude to the Golden Calf story, which will be concerned with improper "making"; and "make" appears in a variety of different contexts.

A second prelude draws the initial Tabernacle section to a close. Moshe receives God's word engraved in stone, by God himself; this will presumably be deposited in the "coffer" of which the text spoke in its opening chapter (25). But the section is forward-looking as well, in that the tablets will play a dramatic role in the story immediately following this passage.

10 **officiating:** The Hebrew (*serad*) is not entirely clear, but may be related to *sharet*, "attending" (in the sanctuary).
13 **However:** In contrast to all the previous activity, the Israelites are not to forget about the Sabbath, the "ceasing" from work (so too Rashi). *Akh* may also be taken as a positive term, "above all."
17 **paused-for-breath:** A rather daring anthropomorphism which, by describing God's resting, encourages humans and animals to do the same (see 23:12).
18 **he gave:** God gave. **the finger of God:** Just as in Egypt (8:15), God intervenes in human affairs here as well.

PART V The Covenant Broken and Restored

(32–34)

Without the story that follows, the book of Exodus would be incomplete—or at least hopelessly idealistic and idealized. Thanks to the inclusion of the Golden Calf episode, we recognize the people of Israel so familiar from the bulk of the wilderness narrative—stubborn, untrusting, and utterly unable to comprehend what has just occurred at Sinai (note the parallel between this section and 15:22ff.: after witnessing the awesome displays of God, the people fall prey to typical human anxieties about their own survival). We are also given a classic biblical description of God in this story—that he is demanding but also compassionate.

There is no doubt that the narrative wishes to portray the breaking of the recently made covenant, and also to focus once again on the anxiety about God's presence that pervades the whole book. Some see it as a political polemic, given that a similar story is found in I Kings 12:28ff., about Jeroboam's split from the Solomonic monarchy; according to this theory, the Exodus account is a projection backward of the sin of the Northern Kingdom. Jeroboam, leading a secessionist movement, intended to set up a sanctuary to rival Jerusalem. At the same time, the Exodus story does appear first, and thereby helps to explain why Jeroboam's deed was considered so terrible by later generations.

But surely the Golden Calf story plays such an important role in the present book of Exodus as to sidestep the question of which version came first. It puts into sharp relief the nature of the people, its leader, and its God, and provides some insights into the complex relationships between these parties; it focuses particular aspects of the Tabernacle idea (see above); and it makes clear the difficulties of the emerging faith community.

The story also contributes some welcome dramatic scenes at this point. It is as if the reader has awakened from a dream: major characters, including God himself, reemerge as real personalities, while secondary characters (Aharon and Yehoshua) are fleshed out. Everywhere there are fierce emotions: doubt, anger, panic, pleading for mercy, courage, fear. And, indeed, the entire enterprise of Exodus hangs in the balance, as God wishes only to destroy the faithless people (a rough parallel exists in Genesis 22, where all that has previously been promised to Avraham is threatened). Only after the stark emotions just mentioned have been cathartically absorbed, and the covenant restored, can there be a return to the task at hand—the building of an abode for the divine amid the very human community of Israel. As to the stylistic aspects of the story, we should note the repeated use of the verbs "see" and "know," among others. Their transformation at different points of the story signals a return to these earlier Exodus themes, this time with a new urgency and a new enterprise at stake: the continuity of the fledgling people.

32:1 Now when the people saw that Moshe was shamefully-late in
          coming down from the mountain,
       the people assembled against Aharon
       and said to him:
       Arise, make us a god who will go before us,
       for this Moshe, the man who brought us up from the land of
          Egypt,
       we do not know that has become of him!
   2 Aharon said to them:
       Break off the gold rings that are in the ears of your wives,
          your sons and your daughters,
       and bring (them) to me.
   3 All the people broke off the gold rings that were in their
          ears,
       and brought (them) to Aharon.
   4 He took (them) from their hand,
       fashioned it with a graving-tool,
       and made it into a molten calf.
       Then they said:
       This is your God, O Israel,
       who brought you up from the land of Egypt!
   5 When Aharon saw (this), he built an altar before it,
       and Aharon called out and said:
       Tomorrow is a festival to YHWH!

6 They (arose) early on the morrow,
   offered offerings-up
   and brought well-being-offerings;
   the people sat down to eat and drink
   and proceeded to revel.

The Sin of the Molten Calf (32:1–6): We have spent twelve chapters—a major portion of the book of Exodus—dwelling on the heights of Sinai; we have witnessed revelation, law-giving, the command to build a shelter for the presence of God, and the establishment of a priestly cult. But now, as Moshe prepares to descend from the mountain, we are reminded of the other side of the coin: the real world of human frailty. This has occurred before, at the very same site: in Chapters 19 and 20 we observed a fearfulness on the part of the people toward getting too close to the divine, as a power too awesome to deal with. Now the fear goes the other way, and, with the disappearance of Moshe, the intermediary, turns to despair. The very thing that had been warned against in the Decalogue (and hence, the first of the terms of the covenant)—the making of a "hewn-image/ or any figure/ that is . . . on the earth beneath" (20:4), and bowing down to it (20:5)—takes place here, requested by the people in their hour of need. It is abetted by, of all people, their divine spokesman and priest, Aharon.

Some scholars have sought to soften the sin of the calf by claiming that the Israelites did not view it as an idol but rather merely as a representation of the divine. This does not seem to be borne out by the text, either in the Decalogue or later in the Jeroboam incident, which is often equated with the most heinous crimes (see I Kings 16:26).

32:1 **saw:** Ironically, after all the "seeing" of revelation in Chapters 19–24, what now impresses the people most is Moshe's absence, leading to a need to make a god that can be "seen." **was shamefully-late:** Others, "delayed," but the Hebrew verb (*boshesh*) carries the connotation of "causing-shame/embarrassment." **a god:** Others, "gods"; but there is one calf and one god that it represents. **go before us:** As in 23:23 the meaning is to lead, especially in battle.

2 **break off:** Or simply "remove."

4 **fashioned it with a graving-tool:** Others, "case it in a mold" or even "tied it in a bag" (see Plaut 1981). **calf:** Or young bull, symbol of fertility in Canaan. **this is your God . . .:** Cf. 20:2 above, "I am YHWH your God, who brought you out. . . ."

5 **called out:** Or "proclaimed."

6 **proceeded:** Or the Hebrew *kum* can be understood as "arose," as opposed to "sat down" in the phrase to follow. **revel:** There seems to be a sexual connotation here (as in Gen. 26:8; 39:14, 17) which would support the use of the calf as the divine symbol.

7 YHWH said to Moshe:
Go, down!
for your people
whom you brought up from the land of Egypt
has wrought ruin!
8 They have been quick to turn aside from the way that I
    commanded them,
they have made themselves a molten calf,
they have bowed to it, they have slaughter-offered to it,
and they have said: This is your God, O Israel, who brought
    you up from the land of Egypt!
9 And YHWH said to Moshe:
I see this people—
and here, it is a hard-necked people!
10 So now,
let me be,
that my anger may rage against them
and I may destroy them—
but you I will make into a great nation!
11 Moshe soothed the face of YHWH his God,
he said:
For-what-reason,
 O YHWH,
should your anger rage against your people
whom you brought out of the land of Egypt
with great might,
with a strong hand?
12 For-what-reason
should the Egyptians (be able to) say, yes, say:
With evil intent he brought them out,
to kill them in the mountains,
to destroy them from the face of the soil?
Turn away from your raging anger,
be sorry for the evil (intended) against your people!
13 Recall Avraham, Yitzhak and Yisrael your servants,
to whom you swore by yourself
when you spoke to them:
I will make your seed many
as the stars of the heavens,

Response: God's Anger (32:7–14): Now that the people have committed what amounts to a capital crime, the issue at stake is what the punishment shall be. After informing the unsuspecting Moshe of what has taken place down below, with the words *"your* people [italics mine] . . . has wrought ruin"* (v.7), God indicates his intent to destroy Israel, and to found a new nation beginning with Moshe. However, early Jewish tradition already sensed that something deeper might be happening here. The phrase "let me be" (Heb. *hanikhoti*), it has been observed, suggests that God actually wishes Moshe to argue with him, and this is supported by his acquiescence in record time (v.14). Indeed, the text never says "God's anger raged," reserving that key verb for Moshe (v.19). What we learn from this section is not only God's forgiving nature but something significant about Moshe: faced with a dictator's dream—the cloning of an entire nation from himself—he opts for staunchly defending the very people who have already caused him grief through their rebelling, and who will continually do so in the ensuing wanderings. And he does not even eschew blackmail to attain his goal. His argument in verse 12, that the Egyptians will jeer at this God who liberated a people only to kill them in the wilderness, rings truer in a pagan context than in the Bible. But the next verse reveals Moshe's vision: he knows that his task is to continue the foundation established by the Patriarchs and to assure the continuity that has been imperiled so many times before.

7 **your people:** God not so subtly renounces his kingship of Israel.
   wrought ruin: The verb *shahet* is often used to describe moral decay (see Gen. 6:11–12).
8 **turn aside from the way:** In the Bible, as in many religious systems, the correct mode of behavior is often called "the way" or "path." Here it is probably elliptical for "the way of God." Postbiblical Judaism calls its system of laws *Halakhah*, from the Hebrew *halokh*, "to go/walk."
9 **hard-necked:** Others, "stiff-necked." The usage of "hard" ironically recalls the earlier hard-hearted character, Pharaoh.
11 **soothed:** Lit., "softened."
12 **be sorry:** Others, "repent" or "change your mind." **the evil:** Destruction. The biblical use of "evil" (*ra'*) corresponds more closely to our idea of "ill" as in "ill-fortune"; it includes not only immorality but also disasters that befall people.
13 **recall:** This particular form of the verb *zakhor* (with the preposition *le-*) means "to remember to one's credit" (Childs 1974). **I will make . . .:** Recalling the promise to Avraham and Yitzhak in Gen. 15:5 and 22:17, also 26:4.

and all this land which I have promised,
I will give to your seed,
that they may inherit (it) for the ages!

14 And YHWH let himself be sorry concerning the evil
that he had spoken of doing to his people.

15 Now Moshe faced about to come down from the mountain,
the two tablets of the Testimony in his hand,
tablets written on both their sides,
on this-one, on that-one they were written;

16 and the tablets were God's making,
and the writing was God's writing,
engraved upon the tablets.

17 Now when Yehoshua heard the sound of the people as it
shouted, he said to Moshe:
The sound of war is in the camp!

18 But he said:
Not the sound of the song of prevailing,
not the sound of the song of failing,
sound of choral-song is what I hear!

19 And it was,
when he neared the camp
and saw the calf and the dancing,
Moshe's anger raged,
he threw the tablets from his hands
and smashed them beneath the mountain.

20 He took the calf that they had made,
burned it with fire,
ground it up until it was thin-powder,
strewed it on the surface of the water
and made the Children of Israel drink it.

21 Then Moshe said to Aharon:
What did this people do to you
that you have brought upon it (such) a great sin!

22 Aharon said:
Let not my lord's anger rage!
You yourself know this people, how set-on-evil it is.

23 They said to me: Make us a god who will go before us,
for this Moshe, the man who brought us up from the land of
Egypt,

Response: Moshe's Anger (32:15-29): In a sense, the text backtracks chronologically here, to focus solely on Moshe. The first four verses are prefatory but important. Possibly to set the drama of the scene to follow, Moshe is described as carrying the "tablets of the Testimony," which are dubbed the work of God. Yet another point is being made: the work of God is contrasted with the imperfect work of human beings, the law with its hope versus the idol with its underlying despair.

Sounds of revelry, implied as being worse than sounds of war, reach Moshe, and upon his descent into the Israelite camp he loses control. But smashing the tablets has implications beyond the emotional: it is a legal voiding of the covenant (as in the English "breaking an agreement"). Moshe deals with all concerned in swift succession: the calf is destroyed, Aharon is confronted, and the people are brutally purged.

It is possible that there are historical considerations behind this section. Some see the portrayal of Aharon, who certainly comes across as weak, as part of a strain in the political thinking of a later period. According to this view, the later decline of Aharon's priestly line is reflected in his behavior here. Others see the "mandating" of the Levites (v.29) as a reflection of a later power struggle among the priestly classes in Israel. Childs (1974)

16 **God's making . . . God's writing:** In contrast to the "making" of the Calf.

17 **as it shouted:** Heb. *be-re'o*, possibly a pun on *ve-ra* ("set-on-evil") in verse 22.

18 **song:** Heb. *'anot*, as distinct from *shira* in 15:1. **prevailing . . . failing:** Heb. *gevura . . . halusha*, meaning "victory" and "defeat." **choral-song:** Or "antiphonal (alternating) song." The Hebrew is *'annot* as opposed to *'anot*. But some interpreters view it as identical to the two previous uses, and find something missing here (as in "the sound of ——— is what I hear.").

19 **the calf and the dancing:** Apparently both angered Moshe. **beneath the mountain:** The very same place where the covenant was concluded! (Cassuto 1967).

20 **burned . . . ground . . . strewed . . . made . . . drink:** The first three of these verbs also occur together in a Canaanite (Ugaritic) text, describing the goddess Anat's destruction of the god Mot; our text perhaps plays off that literature (Childs 1974). At any rate, Moshe's action is the equivalent of making the Israelites "eat their words." As has long been noted, this echoes the treatment of the suspected adulteress in Num. 5:11-31; the connection appears intentional, in light of the constant "marriage" imagery used of God and Israel in the Bible (Sarna 1986 discusses the parallels at length).

we do not know what has become of him!

24 So I said to them: Who has gold?
They broke it off and gave it to me,
I threw it into the fire, and out came this calf.

25 Now when Moshe saw the people: that it had gotten-loose,
for Aharon had let-it-loose for whispering among their foes,

26 Moshe took-up-a-stand at the gate of the camp
and said:
Whoever is for YHWH—to me!
And there gathered to him all the Sons of Levi.

27 He said to them:
Thus says YHWH, the God of Israel:
Put every-man his sword on his thigh,
proceed and go back-and-forth from gate to gate in the
camp,
and kill
every-man his brother, every-man his fellow, every-man his
neighbor!

28 The Sons of Levi did according to Moshe's words.
And there fell of the people on that day some three thousand
men.

29 Moshe said:
Be-mandated to YHWH today,
even though it be every-man at the cost of his son, at the cost
of his brother,
to bestow blessing upon you today.

30 It was on the morrow,
Moshe said to the people:
You, you have sinned a great sin!
So now, I will go up to YHWH,
perhaps I may be able to purge away your sin.

31 Moshe returned to YHWH and said:
Ah now,
this people has sinned a great sin,
they have made themselves gods of gold!

32 So now,
if you would only bear with their sin— !
But if not,
pray blot me out of the record that you have written!

33 YHWH said to Moshe:
   Whoever sins against me,
   I blot him (alone) out of my record.
34 So now,
      go,
   lead the people to where I have spoken to you.
   Here, my messenger will go before you,
   but on the day of my calling-to-account,
   I will call-them-to-account for their sin.

finds Aharon's role in the story to be a literary one: he is a foil for Moshe. Aharon is willing to capitulate to the people, seeing them (perhaps realistically) as "set-on-evil" (v.22). Moshe holds fast to his dream of a "kingdom of priests" (19:6) and thus demands of himself a type of leadership that cannot compromise. The Calf story, then, focuses not only on the great crime of idolatry but also on the nature of Moshe as leader. It is the resumption of the biblical portrait of Moshe, which will return again with greatest force throughout the book of Numbers.

After the Purge (32:30–33:6): Although blood has been spilled to punish the guilty, Moshe must still explate Israel's sin. In this vein, he offers to be erased from God's "record" if the people are not forgiven. Then commences God's reply, couched in terms of who will lead the people to the Promised Land. He will not do it himself, as previously (see the glorious image of 13:21–22), but through the agency of a "messenger." He will fulfill his promise to the Patriarchs, but not himself among his "hard-

24 **out came this calf**: Aharon's reply sounds like that of a child who has been caught in the act.
25 **gotten-loose**: The same verb (*paro'a*) was used in 5:4, where Pharaoh complained about the Israelites. **for whispering**: A derisive kind of whispering.
27 **every-man . . .**: the repetition stresses the horror of the situation.
28 **three thousand**: Another stereotyped number (e.g., Samson kills 3,000 Philistines in Judges 16:27).
32 **blot . . . out**: Erase, as in writing. **record**: Heb. *sefer*, earlier (17:14) rendered as "account."
34 **my messenger will go before you**: Apparently restoring the state of affairs promised in 23:20ff. **calling-to-account**: In Gen. 50:24, *pakod* meant "taking account of," that is, remembering the Israelites in their Egyptian bondage.

35 And YHWH plagued the people
    because they made the calf that Aharon made.

33:1 YHWH said to Moshe:
      Go, up from here,
      you and the people that you brought up from the land of
          Egypt,
      to the land of which I swore to Avraham, to Yitzhak and to
          Yaakov, saying:
      I will give it to your seed.
   2 I will send a messenger before you
      and will drive out the Canaanite, the Amorite and the Hittite
          and the Perizzite, the Hivvite and the Yevusite—,
   3 to a land flowing with milk and honey.
      But: I will not go up in your midst,
      for a hard-necked people are you,
      lest I destroy you on the way!
   4 When the people heard this evil word
      they mourned,
      no man put on his ornaments (again).
   5 Now YHWH said to Moshe:
      Say to the Children of Israel:
      You are a hard-necked people—
      if for one moment I were to go up in your midst,
      I would destroy you!
      So now, take down your ornaments from yourselves,
      that I may know what I am to do with you.
   6 So the Children of Israel stripped themselves of their orna-
          ments from Mount Sinai on.

   7 Now Moshe would take the Tent
      and pitch it for himself outside the camp, going-far from the
          camp.
      He called it the Tent of Appointment.
      And it was,
      whoever besought YHWH
      would go out to the Tent of Appointment that was outside
          the camp.
   8 And it was:
      whenever Moshe would go out to the Tent,

all the people would rise,
they would station themselves, each-man, at the entrance to
    his tent,
and would gaze after Moshe
until he had come into the Tent.
9 And it was:
whenever Moshe would come into the Tent
that the column of cloud would come down
and stand at the entrance to the Tent,
and he would speak with Moshe.

necked" people. Their "sin" (the word occurs eight times in verses 30–34)
has destroyed that possibility.

An interesting chord is struck at the end. Israel must strip themselves of
their ornaments, the spoils of battle, as it were, from the Egyptians. Those
ornaments had been used to build the Calf. The final note is ominous: God
is yet to decide "what to do with you," reminiscent perhaps of another
scene with identical wording—2:4, where Moshe's sister had followed the
little-ark downstream, "to know what would be done to him." In both
cases, the people of Israel stand on the brink of disaster, saved only by
divine intervention.

Moshe at the Tent (33:7–11): This brief digression seems to function as
support for Moshe's role, so important in the book as a whole and in this
story in particular. Only one who is accustomed to speaking to God face to
face (see also Deut. 34:17) can effect forgiveness for Israel's crime.

35 **they made . . . Aharon made:** Heb. ambiguous; possibly a scribal error.
    Or the ambiguity may serve to shift the blame from the perpetrator to the
    act itself (Edward Greenstein, personal communication).
33:1 **the people that you brought up:** The use of "you" (Moshe) suggests that
    God still has not fully reaccepted them.
3 **I will not:** Myself, in person, as it were.
6 **stripped themselves:** This feels analogous to having one's battle ribbons
    stripped off, or having one's spoils taken away.
7 **outside the camp:** Already in early Jewish tradition it was pointed out
    that this phrase often has negative connotations (that is, one was sent
    outside the camp because of ritual impurity), and it has been suggested
    that our passage shows Moshe separating himself from the sinning people.
    On the other hand, it is usually the carrier/causer of impurity who goes
    outside!
9 **he:** God.

10 And all the people would see
the column of cloud
standing at the entrance to the Tent,
and all the people would rise,
they would bow down,
each-man at the entrance to his tent.

11 And YHWH would speak to Moshe
face to face,
as a man speaks to his fellow.
Now when he would return to the camp,
his attendant, the lad Yehoshua,
would not depart from within the Tent.

12 Moshe said to YHWH:
See,
you,
you say to me:
Bring this people up!
But you,
you have not let us know
whom you will send with me!
And you,
you said:
I have known you by name,
and you have found favor in my eyes!

13 So now—
if I have, pray, found favor in your eyes,
pray let me know your ways,
that I may (truly) know you,
in order that I may find favor in your eyes:
See,
this nation is indeed your people!

14 He said:
If my presence were to go (with you), would I cause you to
rest-easy?

15 He said to him:
If your presence does not go,
do not bring us up from here!

16 For wherein, after all, is it to be known
that I have found favor in your eyes,

I and your people?
Is it not (precisely) in that you go with us,
and that we are distinct,
I and your people,
from every people that is on the face of the soil?
17 YHWH said to Moshe:
Also this word that you have spoken, I will do,
for you have found favor in my eyes,
and I have known you by name.
18 Then he said:
Pray let me see your Glory!

Moshe's Plea and God's Answer (33:12–34:3): Continuing the dialogue with God from 32:34f., Moshe now pleads that what is necessary is nothing less than the personal assurance that God will lead the people. Six times the verb "know" echoes, along with repetitions of "pray" and "favor"—and so the issue at hand is intimacy and the bonded relationship of covenant. Significantly, also, Moshe refers to Israel three times as "your people," trying to force God to acknowledge them as his own once more. Answering Moshe's request for intimacy, God agrees to let him get close, but with limits, and we are reminded of Sinai once more (see the boundary-setting in 19:12–13, 21ff.). The earlier revelation scene is about to be replayed, in altered form—most notably, without the people themselves present.

11 **face to face:** See Gen. 32:31, where Jacob is amazed at still being alive after an encounter with a manifestation of God. In the ancient world in general, direct contact with the gods is often portrayed as leading to madness or death (see the Greek story of Semele, the mortal mother of the god Dionysus). Cf. verse 20, below. **Yehoshua/ would not depart:** Once again, he appears in a fragmentary way, but importantly, as Moshe's attendant (and so he will be not only a military leader, as in 17:9ff., but also a spritual one).
13 **know:** Intimately. **indeed your people:** And not only Moshe's, as God suggests in verse 1.
16 **that we are distinct:** The text returns to a motif important in the Plague Narrative.
18 **your Glory:** In the Greek story, Semele desires to see Zeus in full battle dress; the Hebrew narrative is understandably more vague.

19 He said:
    I myself will cause all my Goodliness to pass
    in front of your face,
    I will call out the name of YHWH
    before your face:
    that I show-favor to whom I show-favor,
    that I show-mercy to whom I show-mercy.
20 But he said:
    You cannot see my face,
    for no human can see me and live.
21 YHWH said:
    Here is a place
    next to me;
    station yourself on the rock,
22 and it shall be:
    when my Glory passes by,
    I will place you in the cleft of the rock
    and screen you with my hand
    until I have passed by.
23 Then I will remove my hand;
    you shall see my back,
    but my face shall not be seen.
34:1 Then YHWH said to Moshe:
    Hew yourself two tablets of stone
    like the first-ones,
    and I will write on the tablets the words
    that were on the first tablets
    which you smashed.
2 And be ready by the morning:
    go up in the morning to Mount Sinai,
    station yourself for me there, on top of the mountain.
3 No man is to go up with you,
    neither is any man to be seen on all the mountain,
    neither are sheep or oxen to graze in front of this mountain.
4 So he hewed two tablets of stone like the first-ones.
    Moshe (arose) early in the morning
    and went up to Mount Sinai,
    as YHWH had commanded him,
    and he took in his hand the two tablets of stone.
5 YHWH came down in the cloud,

he stationed himself beside him there
and called out the name of YHWH.
6 And YHWH passed before his face
and called out:
YHWH YHWH
God,
showing-mercy, showing-favor,
long-suffering in anger,
abundant in loyalty and faithfulness,
7 keeping loyalty to the thousandth (generation),
bearing iniquity, rebellion and sin,
yet not clearing, clearing (the guilty),
calling-to-account the iniquity of the fathers upon the sons
    and upon sons' sons, to the third and fourth (generation)!
8 Quickly Moshe did-homage, on the ground, bowing low,
9 and said:
Pray if I have found favor in your eyes,
O my Lord,

God Reveals Himself (34:4–9): This passage is another one of the climaxes of the book, of which I spoke in "On the Book of Exodus and Its Structure," above. In contrast to the scenes given in other ancient literatures, where, for instance, the texts speak of a physical brightness too great to bear, or of epic descriptions of the gods, our passage is remarkably brief and devoid of physical description. All that is ventured here is a statement

19 **that I show-favor . . .:** Recalling the earlier answer to Moshe in 4:13. The meaning here is "I choose to whom to reveal myself."
23 **my back:** That is, hiding the actual appearance of God.
34:2 **in the morning:** As at Sinai, there is no question of a night vision/illusion.
6–7 **YHWH YHWH . . .:** These two verses became an important part of later Jewish liturgy, and are known as the "Thirteen Attributes of God." **showing-mercy, showing-favor:** Heb. *rahum ve-hanun.*
7 **third and fourth (generation):** This may mean an entire household, that is, generally the largest number of generations alive at one time (Clements 1972).
8 **Quickly:** This, as perhaps the greatest moment of divine–human intimacy in the Bible, is the one most ripe for forgiveness, and Moshe seizes the opportunity.

pray let my Lord go among us!
Indeed, a hard-necked people is it—
so forgive our iniquity and our sin,
and make-us-your-inheritance!

10 He said:
Here,
I cut a covenant:
before all your people I will do wonders
such as have not been created
in all the earth, among all the nations.
Then shall all the people among whom you are, see
the work of YHWH, how awesome it is,
which I do with you.

11 Be-you-watchful
of what I command you today!
Here, I am driving out before you
the Amorite, the Canaanite, the Hittite, the Perizzite, the
    Hivvite and the Yevusite,—

12 keep-you-watch,
lest you cut a covenant
with the settled-folk of the land against which you are coming,
lest they become a snare among you.

13 Rather:
their altars you are to pull down,
their standing-pillars you are to smash,
their tree-poles you are to cut down.

14 For: You are not to bow down to any other god!
For YHWH—
Jealous-One is his name,
a jealous God is he!

15 —Lest you cut a covenant with the settled-folk of the land:
when they go whoring after their gods
and slaughter-offer to their gods,
they will call to you to eat of their slaughter-offering;

16 should you take of their women (in marriage) for your sons,
their women will go whoring after their gods,
and they will cause your sons to go whoring after their gods.

17 Molten gods you are not to make for yourselves!

18 The Festival of *Matzot* you are to keep;
   for seven days you are to eat *matzot*, as I commanded you,
   at the appointed-time, in the New-Moon of Ripe-Grain,
   for in the New-Moon of Ripe-Grain you went out of Egypt.
19 Every breacher of a womb is mine,
   and every one that your herd drops-as-male, breacher
      among oxen and sheep;
20 the breacher among asses you are to redeem with a sheep,
   and if you do not redeem it, you are to break-its-neck.
   Every firstborn among your sons you are to redeem.

of God's essence, or, more precisely, of his essence for human beings: merciful but just. This image, which had such a great influence on the development of Christianity and Islam as well as Judaism, is of the highest importance in the understanding of the biblical God; it is almost as if the text is saying "This is all that can be known, intimately, of this God, and this is all one needs to know." There is no shape, no natural manifestation (in contrast to the thunder and lightning approach at Sinai—but one should bear in mind what has just happened with the Calf): only words, which describe God's relationship to human beings.

Moshe hastens, at the climactic moment, to plead on behalf of the people. Most curious is the fact that God does not seem to agree to "go in their midst," nor does he ever give in and reinstate Israel with the term "my people" (see v.10). Nevertheless, it appears that the rift between deity and people has been satisfactorily repaired, given what comes next.

The New Covenant (34:10-28): A preamble (vv. 10-16) promises God's continued "wonders" and warns emphatically against Israel's mixing with the Canaanites upon its future possession of the land. Once the actual

10 **Here . . .:** Does God ever really answer Moshe's request to "let my Lord go among us!"? We can only tell by the ending of the entire book, when all seems right again (40:34-38). **Then shall all . . . see:** The Hebrew word order is "Then shall see . . ."
13 **standing-pillars:** These stood near Canaanite altars (Plaut 1981). **tree-poles:** Phallic idols.
14 **jealous:** Cf. 20:5, above.
15 **whoring:** A common biblical metaphor for faithlessness to God.
16 **their women:** They are singled out as the ones enticing the Israelite men into idolatry, perhaps based on the prominence of goodesses and sacred prostitutes in Canaanite worship.
19 **drops-as-male:** Others, "every male."

No one is to be seen in my presence empty-handed.

21 For six days you are to serve,
   but on the seventh day, you are to cease,
   at plowing, at grain-cutting, you are to cease.
22 The Festival-observance of Weeks you are to make for
      yourselves,
   of the first-fruits of the wheat cutting,
   as well as the Festival-observance of Ingathering
   at the turning of the year.
23 At three points in the year
   are all your male-folk to be seen
   in the presence of the Lord, YHWH,
   the God of Israel.
24 For I will dispossess nations before you, and widen your
      territory,
   so that no man will desire your land,
   when you go up to be seen in the presence of YHWH your
      God,
   at three points in the year.

25 You are not to slay with anything fermented my blood offer-
      ing.

   You are not to leave-overnight the festival-offering of
   Passover.

26 The beginning of the first-fruits of your soil you are to bring
      into the house of YHWH your God.

   You are not to boil a kid in the milk of its mother.

27 YHWH said to Moshe:
   Write you down these words,
   for in accordance with these words
   I cut with you a covenant, and with Israel.

28 Now he was there beside YHWH
   for forty days and forty nights;
   bread he did not eat

and water he did not drink,
but he wrote down on the tablets the words of the covenant,
the Ten Words.

legislative content of the passage begins in verse 17, one notes the continuation of the stylistic pattern which began with verse 10: Deuteronomic
language. The laws bespeak an agricultural society, not a nomadic one,
and suggest that the warning against blending with Canaanite society may
be from the perspctive of a later period—an Israel long settled in the land.
Although some scholars see Egypt as the origin of the Calf symbol, it also
has a well-known existence in Canaanite mythology, as a symbol of Baal,
god of fertility. Therefore the connection between our text and that of
Kings may be close indeed, and the Calf story may have had a very
contemporary ring to later audiences.

As is typical of the Calf narrative, our passage concludes, not only with
wider issues—the formal writing-down of the covenant—but also with
Moshe: that he neither ate nor drank during the encounter with God. We
see the story both from its inception and its end concerned with the man
whose task it must be to bring the divine word to the Israelite people.

Moshe Radiant (34:29–35): As if to underscore the point just made, and
like the Tent section in Chapter 33, the Calf account ends with a focus on
Moshe's leadership. Gone is any reference to the molten image; the central
concern is the effect of God's communication upon Moshe. Indeed,
"speak" occurs seven times here, and the formula "the skin of Moshe's
face was radiating" three times. Putting this section at the end of the
narrative leaves the reader with the sense that Moshe's prayer for God's
closeness in Chapter 33 has at last been answered, and that his very body
now bears the sign of divine favor (note the use of the rich symbol of
light). Communication between God and Moshe, with Israel witnessing

21 **serve:** Here perhaps connoting farm work, as in Gen. 2:5, 4:12. See also
Ex. 20:9.
21 **plowing . . . grain-cutting:** For once, the Bible specifies the work that is
not to be done on the Sabbath.
22 **turning of the year:** When the last harvest occurs (September-October),
and hence connected to a solar calendar model.
23 **points:** Lit., "beats."   **Lord:** Cf. the note to 23:17.
24 **no man will desire your land:** Not even desire it, much less take it away.
28 **Ten Words:** These are known in the Bible as such, not as the "Ten
Commandments."

29 Now it was
    when Moshe came down from Mount Sinai
    with the two tablets of Testimony in Moshe's hand,
    when he came down from the mountain
    —(now) Moshe did not know that the skin of his face was
        radiating because of his having-spoken with him,—
30 Aharon and all the Children of Israel saw Moshe:
    and here, the skin of his face was radiating!
    So they were afraid to approach him.
31 Moshe called to them,
    and then Aharon and all those exalted in the community
        came back to him,
    and Moshe spoke to them.
32 Afterward all the Children of Israel approached,
    and he commanded them
    all that YHWH had spoken with him on Mount Sinai.
33 Now when Moshe had finished speaking with them,
    he put a veil upon his face.
    Now whenever Moshe would come into the presence of
        YHWH, to speak with him,
    he would remove the veil, until he had gone out;
34 and whenever he would come out and speak to the children
        of Israel that which he had been commanded,
35 the Children of Israel would see Moshe's face,
    that the skin of Moshe's face was radiating;
    but then Moshe would put back the veil on his face,
    until he came in to speak with him.

and therefore involved again (in contrast to its removal from this activity at
the beginning of Chapter 32), may now proceed again without interruption, and it will now be possible and appropriate to resume construction of
the structure whose purpose it is to embody God's presence in the world of
human beings.

29 **radiating:** Or "radiant." As is well known, Michelangelo created his famous horned status of Moses (in the Roman church of San Pietro in
   Vincoli) on the basis of the Latin translation of the Bible, the Vulgate,
   which rendered the Hebrew *karan* as "horned." There have now been
   found other ancient Near Eastern texts that support this reading, although
   the present context and comparative religion seem also to throw weight to
   "radiating."

PART VI The Building of the Dwelling (35–40)

A̲s if nothing had gone awry, the narrative now returns to describe how the Dwelling was built. This time, as was noted by the sages of the Talmud, the order follows the natural logic of construction (i.e., dwelling, tapestries, covering, boards, sockets, bars, etc., and then the ritual objects), rather than the earlier one of sanctity (i.e., coffer, purgation-cover, table, lampstand, etc., and then the structure itself). The most notable omission is the carrying out of priestly ordination; that is reserved for Leviticus 8, perhaps so as not to interfere with the narrative momentum of the construction process, or else to focus more on the Dwelling itself and its divine resident. The only major interruption in this part is 38:21–31, which fits in with one of the important themes of these chapters: the extent of the Israelites' contribution to the sanctuary.

As there is no need to repeat what was said about each part of the Tabernacle in the commentary to Chapters 25–31, the commentary here will be limited to brief remarks on the differences between the two long Tabernacle sections (Parts IV and VI); here Cassuto (1967) has provided most of the necessary material.

35:1 Now Moshe assembled all the community of the Children of
         Israel
      and said to them:
      These are the words that YHWH has commanded, to do
         them:

   2 For six days is work to be made,
      but on the seventh day
      there is to be for you holiness,
      Sabbath, Sabbath-Ceasing for YHWH;
      whoever makes work on it is to be put-to-death.
   3 You are not to let fire burn throughout all your settlements
      on the Sabbath day.

   4 Now Moshe spoke to all the community of the Children of
         Israel,
      saying:
      This is the matter that YHWH has commanded, saying:
   5 Take, from yourselves, a raised-contribution for YHWH,
      whoever is of willing mind is to bring it,
      YHWH's contribution:
      gold, silver, and bronze,
   6 violet, purple, worm-scarlet, byssus and goats'-hair,
   7 rams' skins dyed-red, dugongs' skins,
      acacia wood,
   8 oil for lighting,
      spices for oil of anointing and for fragant smoking-incense,
   9 onyx stones and stones for setting,
      for the *efod* and for the breastpiece.
  10 And everyone wise of mind among you
      is to come and is to make all that YHWH has commanded:
  11 The Dwelling, its tent and its cover,
      its clasps and its boards,
      its running bars, its columns and its sockets;
  12 the coffer and its poles,
      the purgation-cover and the curtain for the screen;
  13 the table and its poles and all its implements,
      and the Bread of the Presence;
  14 and the lampstand for lighting and its implements and its
         lamps,

and the oil for lighting;
15 and the altar for smoke-offering and its poles,
    and the oil for anointing,
    and the fragrant smoking-incense;
    and the entrance screen for the entrance of the Dwelling;
16 the altar for offering-up and the bronze lattice that (belongs)
        to it, its poles and all its implements;
    the basin and its pedestal;
17 the hangings of the courtyard, its columns and its sockets,
    and the screen for the gate of the courtyard;
18 the pins of the Dwelling and the pins of the courtyard, and
        their cords,
19 the officiating garments for attending at the Holy-Place;
    the garments of holiness for Aharon the priest
    and the garments of his sons for acting-as-priest.

20 So everyone in the community of the Children of Israel
    went out from Moshe's presence,

The Sabbath Restated (35:1–3): Bracketing the Calf Narrative, we return to the regulations concerning the Sabbath, which receive here a different explanation from what was given in 31:12–17. There the stress was on the symbolic nature of the Sabbath day, but in the present context no reason for observance is given. Cassuto (1967) understands this as a clarification of the rules of "making" as the Dwelling is about to be constructed.

The Contribution Restated (35:4–19): The theme returns to that of the opening of the Tabernacle account in Chapter 25, with a list of what was to be brought for the "work of the Dwelling."

Preparations for the Construction (35:20–36:7): The account of what the Israelites brought as contributions for the work, and the description of

35:3 **You are not to let fire burn:** This prohibition perhaps reflects the anthropological use of fire as a transforming force in culture (see Fredman 1983). Since the Shabbat was apparently to be static in nature, or at least transformative of time alone, fire (which by its nature causes chemical changes) could not be employed. **throughout all your settlements:** And not only in the area of building the Dwelling (Cassuto 1967).

21 and then they came, every man whose mind uplifted him,
    and everyone whose spirit made-him-willing brought
        YHWH's contribution
    for the skilled-work on the Tent of Appointment, for all its
        service (of construction), and for the garments of holiness.
22 Then came men and women alike, everyone of willing mind,
        they brought
    brooch and nose-ring and signet-ring and necklace, every
        kind of gold object,
    every man that wished to hold-high a high-offering of gold
        to YHWH;
23 and everyone with whom could be found
    violet, purple, worm-scarlet, byssus and goats'-hair, rams'
        skins dyed-red and dugongs' skins,
    brought it.
24 Everyone that raised a raised-contribution of silver and
        bronze
    brought YHWH's contribution,
    and everyone with whom could be found
    acacia wood for all the work of the service (of construction),
    brought it.
25 And every woman wise of mind,
    with their hands they spun
    and brought their spinning—
    the violet, the purple, the worm-scarlet and the byssus,
26 and every one of the women whose mind uplifted them in
        practical-wisdom
    spun the goats'-hair.
27 And the exalted-ones brought
    the onyx stones and the stones for setting,
    for the *efod* and for the breastpiece,
28 and the fragrant-spice and the oil
    for lighting, for oil of anointing, for fragrant smoking-in-
        cense.
29 Every man and woman
    whose mind made-them-willing to bring (anything) for all
        the workmanship
    that YHWH had commanded (them) to make through
        Moshe, the Children of Israel brought it,
    freewill-offering for YHWH.

30 Now Moshe said to the Children of Israel:
    See,
    YHWH has called by name
    Betzalel son of Uri, son of Hur, of the tribe of Yehuda,
31 he has filled him with the spirit of God
    in practical-wisdom, in discernment and in knowledge,
    and in all kinds of workmanship
32 to design designs,
    to make (them) in gold, in silver and in bronze,
33 in the carving of stones for setting and in the carving of
        wood,
    to make all kinds of designed workmanship,
34 and (the ability) to instruct he has put in his mind,
    he and Oholiav son of Ahisamakh, of the tribe of Dan;
35 he has filled them with wisdom of mind
    to make all kinds of workmanship
    of the carver, the designer and the embroiderer,
    in violet, in purple, in worm-scarlet and in byssus,
    and of the weaver—
    makers of all kinds of workmanship
    and designers of designs.
36:1 So are Betzalel and Oholiav to make,
    and every man wise of mind
    in whom YHWH has put wisdom and discernment,

those who were to carry it out, is long and repetitive. This factor, with the
addition of a refrainlike pattern of key words (e.g., "mind," "willing,"
"service," "work," "wise," "design," "brought"), strongly portrays the
people's enthusiasm for and participation in the sacred task. Verses 3–7
push the narrative to a crescendo, with the people actually bringing much
more than is needed (and may also be a contrast to their briefly stated
surrendering of jewels in the Calf episode, 32:3).

22 **necklace:** This is a conjecture, as the meaning of the Hebrew *kumaz* is
    uncertain.
25 **spun:** The Hebrew verb *tavoh* occurs only here in the Bible.
34 **(the ability) to instruct:** Now that the actual construction is about to take
    place, it is crucial that the head craftsman be not only skilled himself, but
    a master instructor as well.

to know (how) to make all the work for the service of (constructing) the Holy-Place,
for all that YHWH has commanded.
2 So Moshe called
for Betzalel, for Oholiav,
and for all men wise of mind into whose mind YHWH had
put wisdom,
all those whose mind uplifted them to come-near for the
work,
to make it.
3 And they took from Moshe all the contributions
that the Children of Israel had brought for the work of the
service of (constructing) the Holy-Place,
to make it.
Now they brought him further, freewill-offering, morning
after morning;
4 and came, all the wise-ones who were making all the skilled-
worked for the Holy-Place,
man after man, from their skilled-work that they were making,
5 and said to Moshe, saying:
The people are bringing much more
than enough for the service of (doing) the work
that YHWH has commanded, to make it!
6 So Moshe commanded and they had a call go throughout the
camp, saying:
Man and woman—let them not make any further work-
material for the contribution of the Holy-Place!
So the people were restrained from bringing;
7 the work-material was enough for them, for all the work, to
make it, and more.

8 Then made all those wise of mind among the makers of the
work,
the dwelling, of ten tapestries
of twisted byssus, violet, purple and worm-scarlet;
with winged-sphinxes, of designer's making, was it made.
9 The length of each one tapestry, twenty-eight by the cubit,
and the width—four by the cubit,
of each one tapestry,
one measure for all of the tapestries.
10 Then were joined five of the tapestries, each-one to each-one,

and five tapestries were joined, each-one to each-one.

11 Then were made loops of violet
on the edge of the one tapestry, at the end of the one joint;
thus were made in the edge of the end tapestry at the second
joint.

12 Fifty loops were made on the one tapestry,
and fifty loops were made at the end of the tapestry that is at
the second joint,
opposite the loops, this-one to that-one.

13 Then were made fifty clasps of gold
and then were joined the tapestries, this-one to that-one,
with the clasps,
so that the dwelling became one-piece.

14 Then were made the tapestries of goats'-hair for a tent over
the dwelling,
eleven tapestries were they made.

15 The length of each one tapestry (was) thirty by the cubit,
and four cubits, the width of each one tapestry,
one measure for the eleven tapestries.

16 Then were joined five of the tapestries separately
and six of the tapestries separately.

17 Then were made loops, fifty (of them), at the edge of the end
tapestry, at the joint,
and fifty loops were made at the edge of the second joining
tapestry.

18 Then were made clasps of bronze, fifty (of them),
to join the tent together,
to become one-piece.

19 Then was made a covering for the tent, of rams' skins dyed-
red,
and a covering of dugongs' skins, above it.

Dwelling II (36:8-19): Missing here (cf. 26:1-14) is the description of how
the tapestries were to be joined to the boards; the section pertains to the
actual making of the tapestries.

36:10 **each-one to each-one:** In 26:3, the parallel passage, the text reads "each-
one to the other." This is one example of the changes that occur between
Chapters 25-31 and 35-40; the reader should consult the parallel accounts
for the differences in wording.

20 Then were made the boards for the Dwelling,
    of acacia wood, standing-upright;
21 ten cubits the length of the board
    and a cubit and a half the width of each one board,
22 with two pegs for each one board, parallel this-one to that-one,
    thus were made for all the boards of the Dwelling.
23 And then were made the boards for the Dwelling:
    twenty as boardwork on the Negev border, southward,
24 and forty sockets of silver were made beneath twenty of the
      boards,
    two sockets beneath each one board for its two pegs
    and two sockets beneath each other board for its two pegs;
25 and for the second flank of the Dwelling, on the northern
      border, were made twenty as boardwork,
26 with their forty sockets of silver,
    two sockets beneath each one board
    and two sockets beneath each other board.
27 And for the rear of the Dwelling, toward the sea, were made
      six boards,
28 and two boards were made for the corners of the Dwelling,
      at the rear,
29 so that they were of twin-use, (seen) from the lower-end,
    and together formed a whole-piece, toward the top, toward
      the first ring;
    thus were made for the two of them, for the two corners.
30 So there were eight boards with their bases of silver, sixteen
      bases,
    two bases each, two bases beneath each one board.
31 Then were made running-bars of acacia wood,
    five bars for the boards of the Dwelling's one flank
32 and five bars for the boards of the Dwelling's second flank,
    and five bars for the boards of the Dwelling at the rear,
      toward the sea.
33 Then was made the middle running-bar, to run amidst the
      boards,
    from (this) end to (that) end.
34 And the boards were overlaid with gold,
    and their rings were made of gold, as holders for the bars,
    and the bars were overlaid with gold.

35 Then was made the curtain
     of violet, purple, worm-scarlet and twisted byssus;
     of designer's making was it made, with winged-sphinxes.
36 Then were made for it four columns of acacia
     and were overlaid with gold, their hooks of gold,
     and four bases of silver were cast for them.
37 Then was made a screen for the entrance to the Tent
     of violet, purple, worm-scarlet and twisted byssus,
     of embroiderer's making,
38 and their columns, five (of them), and their hooks,
     and their tops and their binders were overlaid with gold—
     and their bases, five, of bronze.

37:1 Then Betzalel made
     the coffer, of acacia wood,
     two cubits and a half its length,
     a cubit and a half its width,
     and a cubit and a half its height.
  2 He overlaid it with pure gold, inside and outside,
     and made for it a rim of gold all around.
  3 He cast for it four rings of gold
     (to be) upon its four feet,
     with two rings on its one flank
     and two rings on its second flank.
  4 He made poles of acacia wood
     and overlaid them with gold,

Boards II (36:20–34): In reference to 26:15–30, the present text has omitted the command to erect the entire strucutre. The passage is limited in a
manner similar to the previous section.

Curtain and Screen II (36:35–38): Again (cf. 26:31–37), only the making
of the objects themselves is described, not their positioning within the
Tabernacle.

Coffer and Purgation-Cover II (37:1–9): Parallel to 25:10–22, this account
specifies Betzalel as the artist, otherwise behaving like the other passages
in this chapter.

5 he brought the poles into the rings on the flanks of the
   coffer, to carry the coffer.

6 He made a purgation-cover of pure gold,
   two cubits and a half its length
   and a cubit and a half its width.

7 He made two winged-sphinxes of gold,
   of hammered-work did he make them,
   at the two ends of the purgation-cover.

8 One sphinx at the end here
   and one sphinx at the end there,
   from the purgation-cover did he make the sphinxes, at its
   two ends.

9 And the sphinxes were spreading (their) wings upward,
   with their wings sheltering the purgation-cover,
   their faces, each toward the other;
   toward the purgation-cover were the sphinxes' faces.

10 He made the table of acacia wood,
   two cubits its length,
   a cubit its width,
   and a cubit and a half its height.

11 He overlaid it with pure gold.
   And he made a rim of gold for it, all around,

12 and made a border for it, a handbreadth all around,
   thus he made a rim of gold for its border, all around.

13 He cast for it four rings of gold
   and put the rings at the four edges, where its four legs (are).

14 Parallel to the border were the rings,
   holders for the poles, to carry the table.

15 He made the poles of acacia wood, and overlaid them with
   gold,
   to carry the table.

16 He made the implements that are on the table:
   its plates and its cups,
   its bowls and jars, from which (libations) are poured,
   of pure gold.

17 He made the lampstand of pure gold,
   of hammered-work did he make the lampstand, its shaft and
   its stem,

its goblets, its knobs and its blossoms were from it;
18 six stems issuing from its sides,
   three lamp-stems on the one side,
   three lamp-stems on the second side:
19 three almond-shaped goblets on the one stem, with knobs
      and blossoms,
   and three almond-shaped goblets on the other stem, with
      knobs and blossoms—
   thus for the six stems that were issuing from the lampstand.
20 And on the lampstand (itself) four almond-shaped goblets,
      with their knobs and their blossoms,
21 a knob beneath two stems, from it,
   a knob beneath two stems, from it,
   and a knob beneath two stems, from it,
   for the six stems that were issuing from it.
22 Their knobs and their stems were from it,
   all of it one-piece of hammered-work, of pure gold.
23 He made its lamps, seven (of them),
   and its tongs and its trays, of pure gold.
24 From an ingot of pure gold did he make it, with all its
      implements.

25 He made the altar for smoking-incense, of acacia wood,
   a cubit its length and a cubit its width,
   squared, and two cubits its height,
   from it were its two horns.
26 He overlaid it with pure gold—

Table II (37:10–16): This corresponds to 25:23–30, with the omission of
the Bread of the Presence.

Lampstand II (37:17–24): The parallel account is 25:31–40, except for
details there regarding its placement in the overall structure.

Incense Altar II (37:25–28): This is a case similar to that of the lampstand
(cf. 30:1–5).

its roof, its walls all around, and its horns,
and he made a rim of gold for it, all around.

27 Two rings of gold did he make for it, beneath its rim,
on its two flanks, on its two sides,
as holders for poles, to carry it by (means of) them.

28 He made the poles of acacia wood,
and overlaid them with gold.

29 And he made the anointing oil of holiness
and the fragrant smoking-incense, pure, of perfumer's making.

38:1 Then he made the altar of offering-up, of acacia wood,
five cubits its length, five cubits its width, square,
and three cubits its height.

2 He made its horns on its four points,
from it were its horns.
He overlaid it with bronze.

3 He made all the implements for the altar,
the pails, the scrapers, the bowls, the forks and the pans;
all its implements, he made of bronze.

4 He made for the altar a lattice, as a netting of bronze is
made,
beneath its ledge, below, (reaching) to its halfway-point.

5 He cast four rings on the four edges of the netting of bronze,
as holders for the poles.

6 He made the poles of acacia wood
and overlaid them with bronze.

7 He brought the poles through the rings on the flanks of the
altar,
to carry it by (means of) them;
hollow, of planks, did he make it.

8 He made the basin of bronze, its pedestal of bronze,
with the mirrors of the array-of-women that were arrayed-
in-waiting at the entrance of the Tent of Appointment.

9 And he made the courtyard:
on the Negev border, southward,

   the hangings of the courtyard, of twisted byssus, a hundred
      by the cubit,
10 with their columns, twenty, their sockets, twenty, of
      bronze,
   the hooks of the columns and their binders, of silver.
11 And on the northern border, a hundred by the cubit,
   their columns, twenty, their sockets, twenty, of bronze,
   the hooks of the columns and their binders, of silver.
12 And on the sea border, hangings, fifty by the cubit,
   their columns, ten, their sockets, ten,
   the hooks of the columns and their binders, of silver.
13 And on the eastern border, toward sunrise, fifty by the
      cubit,
14 (namely:) hangings of fifteen cubits to the shoulder-piece,
   their columns, three, their sockets, three,
15 and for the second shoulder-piece—(over) here and (over)
      there for the gate of the courtyard—
   hangings of fifteen cubits,
   their columns, three, their sockets, three.
16 All the hangings of the courtyard all around, of twisted
      byssus,

Anointing Oil and Incense II (37:29): To round out the description of the
incense altar, the text adds mention of these ingredients (cf. 30:25, 35).

Altar II (38:1–7): Parallel to 27:1–8, the major omission is "to receive its
ashes" (27:3), which does not relate to the actual construction.

Basin and Pedestal II (38:8): Only one line is used to record the making of
the basin; the parallel account in 30:17–21 says much more about its
function. There is a brief allusion in this verse about the "mirrors" which
were the raw material for the basin; Cassuto (1967) sees this as a contemporary citing of what must have been a well-known tradition about the
special contribution of the Israelite women, above and beyond the official
contributions listed in Chapter 35.

Courtyard II (38:9–20): Corresponding to 27:9–19, there are a number of
wording divergencies from the earlier passage, but none of these is particularly significant.

17 and the sockets for the columns, of bronze,
the hooks of the columns and their binders, of silver,
and the overlay for their tops, of silver, they themselves
bound with silver,
all the columns of the courtyard.

18 The screen of the courtyard gate, of embroiderer's making,
of violet, purple, worm-scarlet and twisted byssus,
twenty cubits in length,
their height along the width, five cubits,
corresponding to the hangings of the courtyard,

19 their columns, four, their sockets, four, of bronze,
their hooks, of silver,
and the overlay for their tops and their binders, of silver,

20 and all the pins for the Dwelling and for the courtyard all
around, of bronze.

21 These are the accountings of the Dwelling,
the Dwelling of Testimony,
that were accounted by Moshe
for the service of the Levites,
under Itamar, son of Aharon the priest:

22 So Betzalel son of Uri, son of Hur, of the tribe of Yehuda
had made
all that YHWH had commanded Moshe,

23 and with him, Oholiav son of Ahisamakh, of the tribe of
Dan,
carver, designer, embroiderer in the violet, purple and
worm-scarlet and byssus.

24 All the gold that was made-use-of in the work, in all the
work of (building) the Holy-Place,
all the gold from the high-offering (was)
twenty-nine ingots and seven hundred thirty *shekels*, by the
Holy-Place *shekel*.

25 And the silver accounted for by the community (was) a hundred ingots,
and a thousand and seven hundred and seventy-five *shekels*
by the Holy-Place *shekel*,

26 a *beka*/split-piece per capita, the half of a *shekel* by the Holy-
Place *shekel*,

for every one who went through the counting,
from the age of twenty years and upward,
for the six hundred thousand and three thousand and five
hundred and fifty.

27 There were a hundred ingots of silver for the casting of the
bases of the Holy-Place and of the bases of the curtain,
a hundred bases per hundred ingots, an ingot per base.

28 And the thousand, seven hundred and seventy-five they
made into hooks for the columns,
and overlaid their tops and bound them.

29 And the bronze from the high-offering (was) seventy ingots,
and two thousand and four hundred *shekels*.

30 They made with it the sockets for the entrance of the Tent of
Appointment,
the altar of bronze, the netting of bronze that belonged to it,
all the implements of the altar,

31 the sockets of the courtyard all around and the sockets of the
courtyard gate
and all the pins of the Dwelling and the pins of the courtyard, all around.

Accountings (38:21–31): A new section enters here, continuing to achieve
the effect of impressing the audience. Previously the reader was to be
struck by the Israelites' zeal in piling up contributions for the new sanctuary (36:3–7); now, toward the end of the actual construction work, there is
a full accounting of the considerable material that went into it. The list
follows the standard order of value: gold, silver, and bronze.

38:21   **the accountings:** I.e., the inventory of materials used to construct the
Dwelling.   **Itamar:** Previously mentioned only in the genealogical list of
6:23 and the enumeration in 28:1.

24   **ingots:** Others, "talents." These were of fairly large weight, perhaps 75
pounds.

26   **603,550:** A more specific number than the "about 600,000" mentioned in
12:37, it has been shown by Cassuto (1967) to conform to a patterned
scheme (600,000 + 7,000/2 + 100/2), and hence may be a number designed more for didactic than for reporting purposes.

39:1 Now from the violet and the purple and the worm-scarlet
     they made the officiating garments for attending at the
       Holy-Place
     and they made the garments of holiness that are for Aharon,
     as YHWH had commanded Moshe.

  2 Then was made the *efod*
     of gold, violet, purple, worm-scarlet and twisted byssus.
  3 Then were beat out sheets of gold
     and they were split into threads,
     to make-use-of-them amidst the violet, amidst the purple,
       amidst the worm-scarlet and amidst the twisted byssus,
     (all) of designer's making.
  4 Shoulder-pieces they made for it, (to be) joined together,
     on its two ends joined.
  5 The designed-band of its *efod* that was on it, was from it, of
       like making,
     of gold, violet, purple, worm-scarlet and twisted byssus,
     as YHWH had commanded Moshe.

  6 They made the onyx stones,
     surrounded by braids of gold,
     engraved with seal engravings, with the names of the Chil-
       dren of Israel.
  7 They placed them on the shoulder-pieces of the *efod*,
     as stones of remembrance for the Children of Israel,
     as YHWH had commanded Moshe.

  8 Then was made the breastpiece
     of designer's making, like the making of an *efod*,
     of gold, violet, purple, worm-scarlet and twisted byssus.
  9 Square it was, doubled they made the breastpiece,
     a span its length and a span its width, doubled.
 10 They set-it-full with four rows of stones—
     a row of carnelian, topaz, and sparkling-emerald, the first
       row,
 11 the second row: ruby, sapphire and hard-onyx,
 12 the third row: jacinth, agate, and amethyst,
 13 the fourth row: beryl, onyx and jasper;
     surrounded, braided with gold in their settings.

14 And the stones were with the names of the Children of
    Israel,
    twelve with their names,
    signet engravings, each-one with its name,
    for the twelve tribes.
15 They made, on the breastpiece, laced chains, of rope-making,
    of pure gold:
16 They made two braids of gold and two rings of gold,
    and put the two rings on the two ends of the breastpiece,
17 and put the two ropes of gold on the two rings on the ends of
    the breastpiece,
18 and the two ends of the two ropes they put on the two
    braids,
    and put them on the shoulder-pieces of the *efod*, on its
    forefront.
19 They made two rings of gold,
    and placed them on the two ends of the breastpiece, on its
    edge that is across from the *efod*, inward,
20 and they made two rings of gold and put them on the two
    shoulder-pieces of the *efod*, below, facing frontward, par-
    allel to its joint, above the designed-band of the *efod*.
21 They tied the breastpiece from its rings to the rings of the
    efod, with a thread of violet,
    to be (fixed) on the designed-band of the *efod*,

Garments II (39:1): Although in scribal tradition this verse is connected to
the previous section, it makes sense as the start of a new one, as it concludes with what will now be in one form or another the refrain to the end
of the book: "as YHWH had commanded Moshe" (see also vv.5, 21, 26,
29, 31, 32, 42, 43; then 40:16, 19, 21, 23, 25, 27, 29, and 32).

Efod and Breastpiece II (39:2–21): Corresponding to 28:6–30, the account
of how these garments were constructed conforms to the previous pattern:
their function "for remembrance" and more, so movingly laid out in
Chapter 28, is not mentioned.

  39:3 **to make-use-of them amidst:** Or "to work them into."
     6 **surrounded by braids:** Heb. *meshubbot mishbetzot.*
     8 **an efod:** Some ancient versions read "the *efod.*"

the breastpiece was not to be dislodged from the *efod*,
as YHWH had commanded Moshe.

22 Then was made the tunic of the *efod*
   of weaver's making, all of violet.
23 The head-opening of the tunic (was) in its middle, like the
   opening for armor,
   a seam-edge for its opening, all around—it was not to be
   split.
24 They made, on the skirts of the tunic, pomegranates,
   of violet, purple, worm-scarlet and twisted byssus.
25 They made bells of pure gold
   and they put the bells amidst the pomegranates
   on the skirts of the tunic, all around,
   amidst the pomegranates:
26 bell and pomegranate, bell and pomegranate,
   on the skirts of the tunic, all around,
   for attending,
   as YHWH had commanded Moshe.

27 They made the coat of byssus, of weaver's making,
   for Aharon and for his sons,
28 and the turban of byssus,
   the splendid caps of byssus,
   the breeches of linen, of twisted byssus,
29 and the sash of twisted byssus, violet, purple, and worm-
   scarlet, of embroiderer's making,
   as YHWH had commanded Moshe.

30 They made the plate (for) the sacred-diadem of holiness, of
   pure gold,
   and wrote upon it writing of signet engravings:
   Holiness for YHWH.
31 They put on it a thread of violet, to put on the turban from
   above,
   as YHWH had commanded Moshe.

32 Thus was finished all the service (of construction) for the
   Dwelling, the Tent of Appointment.
   The Children of Israel made (it)

according to all that YHWH had commanded Moshe,
thus they made.

33 And they brought the Dwelling to Moshe:
the tent and all its implements,
its clasps, its beams, its bars and its columns and its bases,

34 the covering of rams' skins dyed-red and the covering of
dugongs' skins,
the curtain for the screen,

35 the coffer of Testimony and its poles
and the purgation-cover,

36 the table, all its implements and the Bread of the Presence,

37 the pure lampstand, its lamps—lamps for arranging, and all
its implements,
and the oil for lighting,

38 the altar of gold,
and anointing oil and the fragant smoking-incense
and the screen for the entrance of the Tent;

39 the altar of bronze and the netting of bronze that belongs to
it, its poles and all its implements,
the basin and its pedestal;

Tunic II (39:22–26): Parallel to 28:31–35, this account leaves out the protective function of the tunic cited in 28:35.

Other Priestly Garments II (39:27–29): The parallel text is 28:39–43. This passage should come after the section on the head-plate, as was the case in the earlier passages; Cassuto (1967) explains the inversion as characteristic of the construction texts—all the weaving is to take place together.

Head-Plate II (39:30–31): Characteristically, the function of the plate is omitted (cf. 28:36–38).

The Completion of the Parts: Bringing Them to Moshe (39:32–43): The listing of all the elements of the Dwelling fittingly closes the account of their construction, with a certain grandeur, and, because of the pace, even a certain excitement. The key term "service (of construction)" occurs three times.

32 **made:** More idiomatically, "did" (similarly in 39:42, 43 and 40:16). See Gen. 6:22, where Noah also follows God's instructions to the letter.

37 **lamps for arranging:** Others, "lamps in due order." **implements:** Others, "fittings."

40 the hangings of the courtyard,
    its columns and its sockets,
    and the screen for the courtyard gate,
    its cords and its pegs
    and all the implements for the service (of constructing) the
        Dwelling, the Tent of Appointment;
41 the officiating garments for attending at the Holy-Place, the
        garments of holiness for Aharon the priest and the gar-
        ments for his sons, to be-priests—
42 according to all that YHWH had commanded Moshe,
    thus had made the Children of Israel,
    all the service (of construction).
43 Now Moshe saw all the work, and here: they had made it
        as YHWH had commanded,
    thus had they made.
    Then Moshe blessed them.

40:1 Now YHWH spoke to Moshe, saying:
   2 On the day of the first New-Moon, on the first (day) of the
        New-Moon,
      you are to erect the Dwelling, the Tent of Appointment.
   3 You are to place there the coffer of Testimony
      and you are to screen the coffer with the curtain.
   4 You are to bring in the table and arrange its arrangement,
      you are to bring in the lampstand and are to set up its lamps,
   5 you are to put the altar of gold (there), for smoking-incense,
        before the coffer of Testimony,
      and you are to place the screen of the entrance for the
        Dwelling,
   6 you are to put the altar for offering-up before the entrance of
        the Dwelling, the Tent of Appointment,
   7 you are to put the basin between the Tent of Appointment
        and the altar,
      and you are to put water therein.
   8 You are to place the courtyard all around, and you are to put
        the screen for the gate of the courtyard (there).
   9 Then you are to take the anointing oil
      and you are to anoint the Dwelling and all that is in it,
        you are (thus) to hallow it and all its implements, that they
            may become holiness;

10 you are to anoint the altar for offering-up and all its imple-
      ments,
    you are (thus) to hallow the altar, that the altar may become
      holiest holiness;
11 you are to anoint the basin and its pedestal,
    you are (thus) to hallow it.

More significant is what has long been noted: the literal parallels between our section and the initial creation story in Genesis (see, for instance, Leibowitz 1976 and Sarna 1986). The phrases "Thus was finished . . ." (v.32), "And Moshe saw all the work: and here, they had
made it" (v.43), and "Then Moshe blessed them" (v.43), echo "Thus
were finished . . ." (Gen. 2:1), "Now God saw all that he had made,/ and
here: it was exceedingly good" (Gen. 1:31), and "God gave the seventh
day his blessing" (Gen. 2:3). At the end of the passage describing the
erection of the Tabernacle, there is an additional parallel: "So Moshe
finished the work" (40:33); cf. Gen. 2:2: "God had finished . . . his
work." The close parallels suggest what we find in the case of many
cultures: human building, especially (but not exclusively) of sanctuaries,
is to be viewed as an act of imitating God. The Israelites, at the close of the
book chronicling their founding as a people, link up with God's scheme in
creating the world. The Dwelling is therefore a reflection of the perfection
of the world and the divine hand that oversees it. Yet neither the people
nor Moshe pronounces the Genesis words "it was (exceedingly) good"
over the sanctuary; that would be human *hubris*.

Final Instructions: Setting Up (40:1–16): Most prominent in God's commands to erect the Tabernacle are two related verbs: "hallow" and
"anoint," each of which occurs in one form or another eight times here. So
the major theme here is not the actual building, but dedication for a
purpose. Included in this section, as it was in Part IV, is the appointment
of Aharon and his sons to "be-priests."

40:2 **the first New-Moon . . . the first (day):** The date is almost a year after
      Israel's departure from Egypt. The completion of the sanctuary takes
      place on the first day of the month (new moon), whereas the exodus had
      occurred on the fifteenth (full moon), also considered a sacred time.

12 You are to bring-near Aharon and his sons to the entrance of
    the Tent of Appointment,
    you are to wash them with water,
13 and you are to clothe Aharon in the garments of holiness;
    you are to anoint him,
    you are (thus) to hallow him, to be-priest to me,
14 and his sons you are to bring-near,
    you are to clothe them in coats,
15 and are to anoint them as you anointed their father, that they
    may be-priests for me;
    that shall become for them—their being-anointed—priest-
    hood for the ages, throughout their generations.
16 Moshe made (it)
    according to all that YHWH had commanded him,
    thus he made.

17 And so it was on the first New-Moon in the second year, on
    the first (day) of the New-Moon,
    the Dwelling was erected.
18 Moshe erected the Dwelling:
    he put up its sockets,
    he placed its boards,
    he put up its bars,
    he erected its columns,
19 he spread out the tent over the Dwelling,
    he placed the cover of the tent over it, above,
    as YHWH had commanded Moshe.

20 He took and put the Testimony in the coffer,
    he placed the poles of the coffer,
    he put the purgation-cover of the coffer, above,
21 he brought the coffer into the Dwelling,
    he placed (there) the curtain of the screen and screened the
    coffer of Testimony,
    as YHWH had commanded Moshe.

22 He put the table in the Tent of Appointment,
    on the flank of the Dwelling, northward, outside the
    curtain,

23 he arranged on it the arrangement of the Bread of the Pres-
    ence, in the presence of YHWH,
  as YHWH had commanded Moshe.

24 He placed the lampstand in the Tent of Appointment,
  opposite the table, on the flank of the Dwelling, southward,
25 he set up the lamps in the presence of YHWH,
  as YHWH had commanded Moshe.

26 He placed the altar of gold in the Tent of Appointment,
    before the curtain,
27 and sent-up-in-smoke on it fragrant smoking-incense,
  as YHWH had commanded Moshe.

28 He placed (there) the screen for the entrance of the
    Dwelling,
29 the altar for offering-up he placed at the entrance of the
    Dwelling, of the Tent of Appointment,
  and offered-up on it the offerings-up and the leading-dona-
    tions,
  as YHWH had commanded Moshe.

30 He placed the basin between the Tent of Appointment and
    the altar,
  and put water therein, for washing,
31 that Moshe and Aharon and his sons might wash from it
    their hands and their feet,

The completion of the sanctuary takes place, appropriately, on the first
day of what was the month of the exodus a year earlier; it is also ten
months after the people reached Sinai. The dedication thus combines the
ideas of sacred space and sacred time.

The Implementation (40:17–33): Meaningfully, the formula "as YHWH
had commanded Moshe" ends each of the seven paragraphs that describe
the erection of the Dwelling.

32 (that) whenever they came into the Tent of Appointment
        and whenever they came-near the altar, they might wash,
    as YHWH had commanded Moshe.

33 He erected the courtyard all around the Dwelling and the
        altar,
    and put up the screen for the courtyard gate.

    So Moshe finished the work.

/34 Now the cloud covered the Tent of Appointment,
    and the Glory of YHWH filled the Dwelling.
 35 Moshe was not able to come into the Tent of Appointment,
        for the cloud took-up-dwelling on it, and the Glory of
            YHWH filled the Dwelling.
 36 Whenever the cloud goes up from the Dwelling,
    the Children of Israel travel on, upon all their travels;
 37 if the cloud does not go up,
    they do not travel on, until such time as it does go up.
 38 For the cloud of YHWH (is) over the Dwelling by day,
    and fire is by night in it,
    before the eyes of all the House of Israel
    upon all their travels.

נשלם ספר ואלה שמות

שבח לאלהי המילדות

The End: God's Glory (40:34–38): The book ends, not with a paean to the
completed structure or its builders, but with a description of how its
purpose was fulfilled. Central is the "cloud," basically synonymous with
God's "Glory," which now dwells among the people of Israel. At the end
of the book of Exodus, which began with a people in servitude to an
earthly god-king, we find a people that has completed one aspect of service
to a divine king, ready to set forth on their journey to a Promised Land in
the company of the king's inextinguishable presence.

APPENDIX

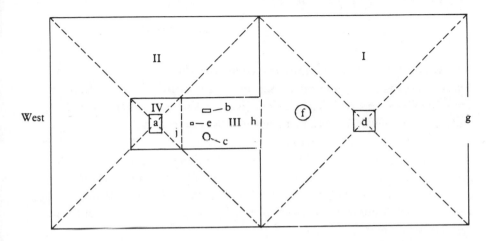

SCHEMATIC FLOOR PLAN OF THE DWELLING

I	Outer Court	a	Coffer	e	Altar for Incense
II	Inner Court	b	Table	f	Basin
III	Holy-Place	c	Lampstand	g	Entrance
IV	Holiest Holy-Place	d	Altar	h	Screen
				j	Curtain

According to the measurements given in Chapters 25–30, the proportions are as follows:

Perfect Squares (1:1) are the Outer Court, the Inner Court, the Holiest Holy-Place, the Altar, and the Altar for Incense.

Perfect Rectangles (2:1) are the Whole Structure, the Holy-Place, and the Table.

The relationship of the whole structure to each court is 2:1, as is that of the Holy-Place to the Holiest Holy-Place.

The relationship of the entrances (Entrance, Screen, and Curtain) is 2:1:1.

The Coffer and the Altar appear to stand at the exact centers of their respective squares. They share proportions different from those above: their length/width/height ratios are 5:3:3 (Coffer) and 5:5:3 (Altar). The departure from the standard 2:1 ratio may be an attempt to draw attention to these two holy objects, which functioned as the spiritual as well as geographical centers of the Israelite encampment in the wilderness.

SUGGESTIONS
FOR FURTHER READING

AS A WORK that is of central importance to both Judaism and Christianity, Exodus has spawned an immense secondary literature. Tradition-minded Jews and Christians will as a matter of course make use of ancient exegetes and their medieval successors to get a fuller understanding of Exodus; much of this material is available in English translation (e.g., through the work of M. M. Kasher listed below, translations of the Midrashim, and of the Church Fathers and Luther). As far as modern commentaries are concerned, here too the amount of material is vast. The reader would be well advised to consult the solid and extensive bibliographies found in Childs (1974) and Sarna (1986).

The list below, which cites only two works not in English, is intended to supplement *Now These Are the Names* in four areas: interpretation of the Exodus text, ancient Near Eastern background, biblical history, and a literary approach to the Bible. It is a rather eclectic list which, it is hoped, will stimulate further interest in specific areas or specific texts. Also included here is material referred to in the Commentary and Notes (cited there by author and date).

Medieval Hebrew Commentaries

Abravanel	Isaac Abravanel, fifteenth-century Spain
Bekhor Shor	Joseph ben Isaac Bekhor Shor, twelfth-century France
Ibn Ezra	Abraham Ibn Ezra, twelfth-century Spain
Kimhi	David Kimhi, twelfth- to thirteenth-century France
Ramban	Moses ben Nahman, thirteenth-century Spain
Rashi	Solomon ben Isaac, eleventh-century France

Modern Works

Abrahams, Israel. "Numbers, Typical and Important." In *Encyclopedia Judaica*, vol. 12. Jerusalem, 1972.

Ackerman, James. "The Literary Context of the Moses Birth Story." In

Literary Interpretations of Biblical Narratives, edited by Kenneth R. R. Gros Louis, James Ackerman, and Thayer S. Warshaw. Nashville, Tenn., 1974.

Albright, William F. "What Were the Cherubim?" In *The Biblical Archaeologist Reader*, no. 1, edited by G. Ernest Wright and David Noel Freedman. New York, 1961.

Alter, Robert. *The Art of Biblical Narrative*. New York, 1981.

Andersen, Francis. *The Hebrew Verbless Clause in the Pentateuch*. Nashville, Tenn., 1970.

————. *The Sentence in Biblical Hebrew*. The Hague, 1974.

Auerbach, Erich. *Mimesis*. New York, 1952.

Bar Efrat, Shimon. *The Art of the Biblical Story* [Hebrew]. Tel Aviv, 1979.

Beck, Harrell F. "Incense." In *The Interpreter's Dictionary of the Bible*, vol. 2. New York, 1962.

Buber, Martin. *Israel and the World*. New York, 1948.

————. *The Prophetic Faith*. New York, 1949.

————. *Moses*. New York, 1958.

————. *On the Bible*. New York, 1968.

————, and Rosenzweig, Franz. *Die Schrift und ihre Verdeutschung* [German]. Berlin, 1936.

Campbell, Joseph. *The Hero with a Thousand Faces*. Princeton, N.J., 1972.

Cassuto, Umberto. *A Commentary on the Book of Exodus*. Jerusalem, 1967.

Childs, Brevard W. *The Book of Exodus: A Critical, Theological Commentary*. Philadelphia, 1974.

Clements, Ronald E. *Exodus* (Catholic Bible Commentary). Cambridge, 1972.

Cohn, Robert L. *The Shape of Sacred Space: Four Biblical Studies*. Chico, Calif. 1981.

Cross, Frank Moore. *Canaanite Myth and Hebrew Epic*. Cambridge, Mass., 1973.

Culley, Robert. *Studies in the Structure of Hebrew Narrative*. Philadelphia, 1967a.

————, ed. "Oral Tradition and Old Testament Studies." *Semeia*, vol. 5 (1976b).

Daiches, David. *Moses: The Man and His Vision*. New York, 1975.

Daube, David. *Studies in Biblical Law*. Cambridge, 1947.

————. "Direct and Indirect Causation in Biblical Law." *Vetus Testamentum*, vol. 11 (1961).

————. *The Exodus Pattern in the Bible.* London, 1963.

DeVaux, Roland. *Ancient Israel: Its Life and Institutions.* New York, 1965.

————. *The Early History of Israel.* Philadelphia, 1978.

Driver, Samuel R. *Exodus. (Cambridge Bible).* Cambridge, 1911.

Exum, J. Cheryl. "You Shall Let Every Daughter Live: A Study of Ex. 1:8–2:10." *Semeia,* vol. 28 (1983).

Fishbane, Michael. "The Sacred Center: The Symbolic Structure of the Bible." In *Texts and Responses: Studies Presented to Nahum N. Glatzer on the Occasion of His Seventieth Birthday by His Students.* Leiden, 1975.

————. *Text and Texture.* New York, 1979.

Fox, Everett. "The Bible Needs to Be Read Aloud." *Response,* vol. 33 (Spring 1977).

————. "The Samson Cycle in an Oral Setting." *Alcheringa: Ethnopoetics,* vol. 4, no. 1 (1978).

————. "A Buber-Rosenzweig Bible in English." *Armsterdamse Cahiers voor exegese in bijbelse Theologie,* vol. 2 (Kampen, Holland, 1980).

————. *In the Beginning.* New York, 1983.

Frankfort, Henri. *Before Philosophy.* New York, 1951.

Fredman, Ruth Gruber. *The Passover Seder.* New York, 1983.

Friedman, Richard Eliot, ed. *The Poet and the Historian: Essays in Literary and Historic Biblical Criticism.* Chico, Calif., 1983.

Gaster, Theodor H. *Passover: Its History and Traditions.* New York, 1949.

————. *Myth, Legend and Custom in the Old Testament:* New York, 1969.

Geller, Stephen A. "The Struggle at the Jabbok: The Uses of Enigma in a Biblical Narrative." *Journal of the Ancient Near Eastern Society of Columbia University,* no. 14 (1982).

Ginsberg, H. L. *The Israelian Heritage.* New York, 1982.

Ginzberg, Louis. *The Legends of the Jews.* Philadelphia, 1937.

Glatzer, Nahum N. *Franz Rosenzweig: His Life and Thought.* New York, 1961.

Greenberg, Moses. "Crimes and Punishments." In *The Interpreter's Dictionary of the Bible,* vol. 1. New York, 1962.

————. *Understanding Exodus.* New York, 1969.

————. "Some Postulates of the Biblical Criminal Law." In *The Jewish Expression,* edited by Judah Goldin. New York, 1970.

————. "Exodus, Book of." In *Encyclopedia Judaica,* vol. 6. Jerusalem, 1972.

Greenstein, Edward L. "The Riddle of Samson." *Prooftexts,* vol 1, no. 3 (September 1981).

————. "Theories of Modern Bible Translation." *Prooftexts*, vol. 8 (1983).

————. "Biblical Law." In *Back to the Sources*, edited by Barry W. Holtz. New York, 1984a.

————. "Medieval Bible Commentaries." In *Back to the Sources*, edited by Barry W. Holtz. New York, 1984b.

————. "Understanding the Sinai Revelation." In *Exodus: A Teacher's Guide*, edited by Ruth Zielenziger. New York, 1984c.

————. "The Torah as She Is Read." *Response*, vol. 14 (Winter 1985a).

————. "Literature, The Old Testament as." In *Harper's Bible Dictionary*, edited by Paul J. Achtmeier. San Francisco. 1985b.

Gunn, David M. *The Story of King David: Genre and Interpretation*. Sheffield, England, 1978.

Haran, Menahem. "The Nature of the 'Ohel Mo'edh' in the Pentateuchal Sources." *Journal of Semitic Studies*, vol. 5 (1960a).

————. "The Use of Incense in Ancient Israelite Ritual." *Vetus Testamentum*, vol. 10 (1960b).

————. *Temples and Temple Service in Ancient Israel*. Winona Lake, Ind., 1985.

Hertz, Joseph H. *The Pentateuch and Haftorahs*. London, 1960.

Hyatt, J. Philip. *Commentary on Exodus*. (New Century Bible). London, 1971.

Isbell, Charles. "The Structure of Exodus 1:1–14." In *Art and Meaning: Rhetoric in Biblical Literature*, edited by David A. Clines, David M. Gunn, and Alan J. Hauser. Sheffield, England, 1982.

Jackson, Bernard S. "The Ceremonial and the Judicial: Biblical Law as Sign and Symbol." *Journal for the Study of the Old Testament*, vol. 30 (October 1981).

Kasher, Menahem M., ed. *Encyclopedia of Biblical Interpretation*, vols. 7–9. New York, 1967–1969.

Keil, Carl, and Delitzsch, Franz. *Commentary on the Old Testament in Ten Volumes*. Vol. 1, *The Pentateuch*. Grand Rapids, Mich., 1968.

Kikawada, Isaac. "Literary Convention of the Primeval History." *Annual of the Japanese Biblical Institute*, no. 1 (1975).

————, and Quinn, Henry. *Before Abraham Was*. Nashville, Tenn., 1985.

Kirk, G. S. *Myth: Its Meaning and Functions in Ancient and Other Cultures*. Berkeley, Calif., 1970.

Knight, Douglas A., and Tucker, Gene, eds. *The Hebrew Bible and Its Modern Interpreters*. Philadelphia, 1985.

Kosmala, Hans. "The 'Bloody Husband'." *Vetus Testamentum,* vol. 12 (1962).

Lauterbach, Jacob Z., ed. *The Mekilta de-Rabbi Ishmael.* Philadelphia, 1976.

Leibowitz, Nehama. *Studies in Shemot I and II.* Jerusalem, 1976.

Levine, Baruch A. *In the Presence of the Lord.* Leiden, 1974.

Licht, Jacob. *Storytelling in the Bible.* Jerusalem, 1978.

Lichtenstein, Murray H. "Biblical Poetry." In *Back to the Sources,* edited by Barry W. Holtz. New York, 1984.

Mendenhall, George. "Covenant Forms in Israelite Tradition." *Biblical Archaeologist,* vol. 17 (1954).

Meyers, Carol. *The Tabernacle Menorah.* ASOR Dissertation Series no. 2. Missoula, Mont., 1976.

Milgrom, Jacob. *Studies in Cultic Theology and Terminology.* Leiden, 1983.

Miller, J. Maxwell. *The Old Testament and the Historian.* Philadelphia, 1976.

Nohrnberg, James. "Moses." In *Images of Man and God: Old Testament Short Stories in Literary Focus,* edited by Burke O. Long. Sheffield, England, 1981.

Orlinsky, Harry M. *Notes on the New Translation of the Torah.* Philadelphia, 1970.

Paul, Shalom. *Studies in the Book of the Covenant in the Light of Biblical and Cuneiform Law.* Leiden, 1970.

Plaut, W. Gunther. *The Torah: A Modern Commentary.* New York, 1981.

Lord Raglan. *The Hero.* New York, 1979.

Rosenberg, Joel. "Biblical Narrative." In *Back to the Sources,* edited by Barry W. Holtz. New York, 1984.

Ryken, Leland. "The Epic of the Exodus." In *Literature of the Bible.* Grand Rapids, Mich., 1974.

Sarna, Nahum M. *Exploring Exodus.* New York, 1986.

Schneidau, Herbert N. *Sacred Discontent: The Bible and Western Tradition.* Berkeley, Calif., 1976.

Scholem, Gershom. *The Messianic Idea in Judaism.* New York, 1972.

Sellers, Ovid P. "Weights and Measures." In *The Interpreter's Dictionary of the Bible,* vol. 4. New York, 1962.

Sonsino, Rifat. *Motive Clauses in Hebrew Law: Biblical Forms and Near Eastern Parallels.* SBL Dissertation Series no. 45. Chico, Calif., 1980.

Sternberg, Meir. *The Poetics of Biblical Narrative.* Bloomington, Ind., 1985.

Talmon, Shemaryahu. "The 'Desert Motif' in the Bible and in Qumran Literature." In *Biblical Motifs: Origins and Transformations*, edited by Alexander Altmann. Cambridge, Mass., 1966.

Tigay, Jeffrey H. "On the Meaning of t(w)tpt." *Journal of Biblical Literature*, vol. 3, no. 101 (September 1982).

Turner, Victor. *The Ritual Process: Structure and Anti-Structure*. Chicago, 1969.

Ullendorff, Edward. *Is Biblical Hebrew a Language?* Wiesbaden, Germany, 1977.

Vansina, Jan. *Oral Tradition: A Study in Historical Methodology*. London, 1965.

Walzer, Michael. *Exodus and Revolution*. New York, 1985.

Weinfeld, Moshe. "Congregation." *Encyclopedia Judaica*, vol. 5. Jerusalem, 1972a.

———. "Covenant." *Encyclopedia Judaica*, vol. 5. Jerusalem, 1972b.

WEEKLY PORTIONS IN JEWISH TRADITION

Genesis

In the beginning	(Bereshit)	1:1
Noah	(Noah)	6:9
Go-you-forth	(Lekh lekha)	12:1
Now YHWH was seen by him	(Va-yera)	18:1
Now Sara's life	(Hayyei Sara)	23:1
Now these are the begettings	(Toledot)	25:19
Yaakov went out	(Va-yetze)	29:10
Now Yaakov sent messengers	(Va-yishlah)	32:4
Yaakov settled	(Va-yeshev)	37:1
Now at the end of two years	(Mikketz)	40:1
Now Yehuda came closer	(Va-yigash)	44:18
And Yaakov lived	(Va-yehi)	47:28

Exodus

Now these are the names	(Shemot)	1:1
I was seen by Avraham	(Va-era)	6:2
Come to Pharaoh!	(Bo)	10:1
Pharaoh had set the people free	(Be-shallah)	13:17
Now Yitro	(Yitro)	18:1
Now these are the judgments	(Mishpatim)	21:1
Take me a raised-contribution	(Teruma)	25:1
Command the Children of Israel	(Tetzave)	27:20
When you lift up the heads	(Ki tissa)	30:11
Now Moshe assembled	(Va-yak'hel)	35:1
These are the accountings	(Pekudei)	38:21